First Edition

THE COMPREHENSIVE PUBLIC RELATIONS READER

Function and Practice

Bob "Pritch" Pritchard, M.A., APR, Fellow PRSA
and Jensen Moore, Ph.D.

*The University of Oklahoma,
Gaylord College of Journalism and Mass Communication*

 cognella® | ACADEMIC PUBLISHING

Bassim Hamadch, CEO and Publisher

Kassie Graves, Director of Acquisitions and Sales

Jamie Giganti, Senior Managing Editor

Miguel Macias , Senior Graphic Designer

Angela Schultz , Senior Field Acquisitions Editor

Michelle Piehl , Project Editor

Alisa Munoz, Licensing Coordinator

Abbey Hastings, Associate Production Editor

ISBN: 978-1-5165-8071-6 (pbk)/978-1-5165-0872-3 (br)

CONTENTS

SECTION

FOUNDATIONS OF PUBLIC RELATIONS

1

Every introduction to a subject should begin at the beginning. In this section of our exploration of public relations, we'll start by looking at what public relations is and how it came to be, starting from the earliest beginnings of civilization to today's digital age and globalization.

Ethics and the law are critical components of the successful practice of public relations. Many textbooks cover these areas toward the end of the course, but we feel they set the foundation for everything that follows, so we'll explore what you *can* do versus what you *should* do. Law can keep us within the bounds of a minimum ethical standard, but we want to move beyond that to begin to inculcate a true commitment to the ethical practice of public relations by looking at professional guidelines and the Public Relations Society of America (PRSA) Code of Ethics, as well as the typical causes of and solutions to our ethical dilemmas. We'll wrap up that discussion by discussing the ethical decision-making process.

Looking at what influences how public relations professionals communicate will allow us to explore the communication models and theories that form our foundational understanding of communication processes. Basic motivational theory, understanding how ideas are adopted, and knowing the barriers to communication are key to the communication process. We also need to know how various approaches to communication can impact our success, so we'll look at the spectrum of techniques, from propaganda to persuasion and influence theories. Media theories can help us understand how the media set agendas and frame information. We also need to know what other limitations to consider.

In the final chapter of this section, we'll look at what it takes to get a seat at the decision-making table and the importance of business literacy to public relations. Starting with understanding that public relations is a management function, we'll look at the aspects of leadership and teamwork in helping us find our place in the organization. Matching public relations goals and objectives to the vision, mission, and values of the organization is critical to our success. The roles a public relations practitioner plays in the organization are also important, and we'll explore various ways to ensure we're more than order takers, instead arriving at our desired destination as counselors and advisers to top management.

WHAT IS PUBLIC RELATIONS, AND HOW DID IT BEGIN?

Reading 1.1:
"Public Relations
Defined"
By Joseph Harasta

The definition of public relations has been debated for nearly as long as the profession has existed. Therefore, it's appropriate to begin our study of public relations by developing a common understanding of the practice. To that end, this chapter contains a reading from scholar and teacher Joseph Harasta entitled "Public Relations Defined."

We will follow with an exploration of the expectations and challenges that exist in public relations, along with the social significance of the profession. We'll also differentiate our field from advertising, marketing, journalism, strategic communication, and integrated marketing communications so you can understand where public relations stands alone and where it fits with these various other professions.

But it's also important to trace the development of public relations over time, so apart from this reading, we'll explore the history of the field from its ancient beginnings, including the significance of the Rosetta Stone and the use of public relations by Julies Caesar and the church.

We'll look at how public relations contributed to colonial America (1584–1776), particularly in promoting settlement of the New World and its part in our struggle for independence.

Public relations started to come into its own during our expansion westward (1800–1897). Land speculators and the railroads used public relations techniques to promote this expansion. This was also the age of industrialization, with its concerns over business practices. Large corporations such as Mutual Life Insurance and the Westinghouse Corporation further defined the profession. And it was during this period that the term "public relations" was coined.

The early 1900s saw the age of press agentry and public information (1900–1916). This was known as the "seedbed" era, when P.T. Barnum, Ivy Lee, and President Teddy Roosevelt advanced our understanding of public relations and the use of various publicity and public information techniques. *Press agentry* uses one-way communication, and is often not based on research. While also using a one-way communication approach, *public information* uses research and is more journalistic in form.

The two world wars saw the development of *two-way asymmetrical* communications. This form used scientific persuasion and encouraged limited feedback from the audience. In 1917–1918, George Creel adopted a style of communicating about the First World War that eschewed vilifying the enemy and focused instead on patriotism and the contributions people needed to make to the war effort. The "Booming Twenties" (particularly between 1919 and 1929) saw the rise and contributions of the great names in public relations, including Edward Bernays, Doris Fleischman, and Arthur Page. Public relations advanced greatly during the Roosevelt Era and World War II (1930–1945). President Franklin Roosevelt was a master at communications, with his "fireside chats," and Louis Howe and Elmer Davis made great contributions to our understanding of the field.

The postwar era (1946–1964) birthed the Public Relations Society of America (PRSA), the preeminent global association for public relations professionals. Pioneers in public relations education and scholarship Scott Cutlip and Allen Center helped elevate the profession to the board of directors level, giving the field an opportunity to have a seat at the decision-making table. Inez Kaiser, educator, public relations expert, and entrepreneur, broke both the gender and race barriers as the first African American woman to run a public relations company with national clients.

Scholar and philosopher Marshall McLuhan gave us one of the cornerstones of media theory during the period of protest and empowerment (1965–1985), coining the phrases "the medium is the message" (McLuhan 1964a) and the "global village" (McLuhan 1962). Of note, he also predicted the internet thirty years before it became a reality (Stewart 2000).

The godmother of the Public Relations Student Society of America, Betsy Plank, blazed an amazing sixty-three-year career in public relations. She is also called the "First Lady of Public Relations" because that career was filled with many firsts, including being the first woman to head a company department and the first female president of PRSA (Plank Center 2016). Her commitment to education and students is legendary; she helped create PRSSA in 1967 and the Champions for PRSSA in 1981.

We'll close our study of the rich history of public relations with an exploration of the Digital Age and globalization (1986–present). Fundamental to this era is the *two-way symmetrical* model of public relations where the goal is mutual understanding between and organization and its publics, with a focus on relationship building.

Four modes of PR:
1. Press Agentry
2. Public Info
3. two-way asymmetrical
4. two-way symmetrical

"PUBLIC RELATIONS DEFINED"

By Joseph Harasta

Given the tremendous responsibility and persuasive nature of public relations, it is important to understand its two basic functions: communicating and counseling[1].

The first of these two functions, communicating, is rather straightforward. Every organization needs consistent, correct, and complete communication between itself and its many stakeholders. Because public relations deals primarily with understanding relationships much more than with its two other strategic communication siblings—marketing and advertising—it makes sense that the public relations practitioners within an organization should be the ones responsible for developing and sustaining these means of communication. After all, no one within an organization knows the day-to-day relationships between the organization and its stakeholders or publics more than the public relations practitioner. The public relations functions within an organization can and do directly impact the organization's ability to succeed because successful and long-term relationships depend so highly on communication. The second function, which is no less important, equally influences organizational success, but is less well known than communication.

Counseling may at first seem unlikely as one of the two major functions of public relations. However, once you realize that as an organization's management acts so too does the public's opinions of it, you can then see this function's importance. Generally, the public relations practitioner within an organization is not going to be the company's leader—such as the president or CEO. However, because the president or CEO's decisions obviously influence the organization's actions, it is important that those actions be in the best interests of its key stakeholders. Often company leaders focus on revenues and the financial stability of their company. However, sometimes the relationships a company maintains can take a back seat to the money it makes. Often, company presidents and CEOs do not see the direct connection between financial success and relationship success—until there is a crisis. But, the day-to-day functions of any successful organization must include not only the financial decisions of the company, but also its relationship decisions. The clearest example is the relationship between a company and its consumers.

Obviously, a commercial enterprise needs customers to buy its products or services, but it is not just the product that influences consumer behavior, but also the company's brand or image. It is the public relations practitioner's job to safeguard the image or brand. For example, in 2010 the BP oilrig disaster in the Gulf of Mexico created a direct counseling-to-financial-success connection—namely, when BP President Tony Hayward made statements in the media, it affected his company's image quite negatively. As if the actual incident weren't bad enough, Hayward's comments that he wanted the incident resolved as quickly as possible, saying, "I just want my life back," struck many people as callous and insensitive—especially to the millions of people who make their living from the waters of the Gulf of Mexico and who were directly affected by his company's actions[2]. Protests, media condemnation, and even boycotts followed. In this example, Hayward would have been well advised to choose his words carefully (communication) and listen to his public relations team's advice (counseling). It is always important to strategize internally as to what an organization should do and say and then spread that information to the outside world. Often, however, organizational leadership will make hasty comments, say too much, or just say the wrong things—usually attributable to poor public relations counseling. When this happens, the problems and fallout from it become the public relations department's problem to fix. Therefore it is always best to proactively counsel management on its decisions in terms of how they can influence those stakeholder relationships that took so long to develop. Being a voice in the boardroom is critical to not only public relations success, but also overall organizational success. To gain this voice, it is important to understand the distinction between managers and leaders.

MANAGERS VERSUS LEADERS

Managers are generally task oriented. They are concerned with the "How to" and "Must do" elements of singular tasks. Heavy on persuasive threats, they get their employees to work, but never really inspire them to succeed. You can think of these people as those who say comments like, "That's the way we have always done it" or "That's not the way things are done here." On the other hand, leaders are much more goal oriented: Heavy on inspiration and producing convincing messages that allow their employees to feel empowered and want to succeed for the organization's good. These individuals develop camaraderie and buy-in from their employees. These people ask such questions as, "What do you [employees] think we should do?" and "What can we do to make this work?" Note the use of the word "we." Leaders empower employees to want to work—not because their paychecks depend on it, but because they see value and worth in their work. For the public relations practitioner, developing this sense of leadership versus management feel within an organization is crucial, and it begins at the top through motivated and empowering public relations counseling.

That is not to say this is easy. Tight deadlines, financial pressures, and busy schedules make the process often easier said than done. However, one element will always gain the attention of top organization leadership—money. For public relations, there are two types of bottom lines: the financial and the relational[3]. Getting leadership to understand and appreciate the second as much as they do the first is the best way to move a company's public relations initiatives from the basement to the "C" suite where the CEO, COO, and other executives make important decisions. Once leadership understands the connection between positive relationships and positive revenues, the sooner they will be on board with public relations suggestions and decisions. Another aspect is explaining the progress of public relations initiatives.

Generally, organizational leaders are interested in outcomes most. Because, by their very nature, public relations efforts are not always clear-cut in their outcomes in terms of figures and dollars, public relations is not always taken as seriously by leadership as it should be. For example, a company spends $1 million on a six-month advertising campaign. At its end, the success or failure, or outcome of the campaign is clear—did sales increase during the six months to make the investment worthwhile? Known as return on investment (ROI)[4], these types of outcomes allow for evidence of success or failure of a campaign. However, public relations does not always work this way. Getting someone to like your company's brand does not immediately reflect financial success, which is the type of success that many organizational leaders care about most. Strong, long-term relationships take time to develop. While it is obvious to most people that when people start disliking and criticizing a company, usually via word-of-mouth, that the success of an organization will start to decline is not always accepted by management.

Convincing company leadership of it is usually difficult, especially when they care mainly about the immediate returns on their investments. However, public relations professionals have developed a means of illustrating their departments' worth to organizational leadership. Known as Benchmarking[5], public relations initiatives can be measured and their outcomes illustrated to leadership.

THE VALUE OF PUBLIC RELATIONS

Benchmarking in a public relations sense entails measuring the organization's reputation at the beginning, throughout, and at the conclusion of a public relations initiative. It is a way to show that a company's reputation improved and how this improvement resulted in tangible benefits such as greater exposure and sales. For example, consider a small start-up restaurant in your town. It needs exposure to increase notoriety of it—after all, if no one knows about it, no one can patronize it. However, the restaurant does not have a lot of disposable money to create advertisements and air them on local television stations or print them in the local newspapers. This is where public relations efforts can show their worth. By hosting events like a "locals' night out" or sponsoring an area sports team, the restaurant begins the build notoriety and attracts attention. These initiatives are less expensive than traditional advertising, but when implemented well, they can garner just as many benefits. Remember the local television station and newspaper that the restaurant's owners wished they could afford advertising for? Well, informing the area's media of the locals' night out or the sponsorship deal can attract them to air and publish stories on it. The restaurant gains exposure, illustrates its goodwill to the community, and does it in a way that's more credible and trustworthy than through traditional, expensive advertising. Generally, people will believe a message from a journalistic source like the local television news or newspaper more than the same message in a paid advertisement. After all, everyone expects an advertisement to focus on the positives of the restaurant, but the local media does not have a stake in the restaurant, so it is more likely to be believed by the public. These types of third-party endorsements are critically important to showing public relation's values to those who may not understand it. More people find out about the restaurant, more people patronize it, they spread news of it to their friends, coworkers, and family via word-of-mouth, and the restaurant starts making money—all for the investment of a special event and maybe a sponsorship of the town's little league team, as well as a little public relations work. That is not a bad return on investment (ROI) and shows how the public relations efforts paid off to the restaurant's owners via benchmarking. At the opening of the restaurant, notoriety and revenue was nil, three months later, for example, people found out about it through those local stories, and revenue increased. This method illustrates public relation's worthiness to the financial as well as the relational bottom lines.

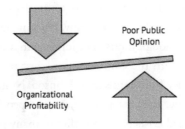

The preceding illustration presents a hypothetical, yet accurate, picture of public relations affecting opinion and in turn financial success. However, a real-life case illustrates this phenomenon on a much larger scale, and it is the preeminent public relations case study—one that set the standard when it comes to showing that public relations is essential to organizational success—both reputational and financial.

THE TYLENOL CASE[6]

In late September of 1982, a 12-year-old girl, Mary Kellerman, died in a suburb outside of Chicago after ingesting Extra-Strength Tylenol laced with cyanide. Shortly after her death, Adam Janus as well as his brother Stanley Janus and Stanley's wife, Theresa, also died from taking Extra-Strength Tylenol, all from the same bottle, all from cyanide poisonings—10,000 times the amount needed to kill a human. Like Mary's, their deaths also occurred in a suburb of Chicago. Three others would also soon die—all linked by their use of Extra-Strength Tylenol, and all from the Chicago area. Investigators quickly urged Chicago residents to avoid the medicine through broadcast messages on the news as well as police loudspeakers patrolling the Chicago suburbs.

Authorities realized that because the medicine came from different manufacturing facilities, and the fact that only select bottles of Extra-Strength Tylenol were affected, the likelihood of tampering in the factory was unlikely. Both local and federal investigators felt that the introduction of cyanide to Extra-Strength Tylenol must have occurred after the pills left Johnson & Johnson's factory, the maker of the pain medicine. Over 700 phone calls flooded Chicago area hospitals with people reporting symptoms of poisoning after taking Tylenol. Because of the very nature of the incidents, news of it quickly spread across the country. Soon, a few isolated cases from outside Chicago became the most reported news nationwide, even garnering international coverage. Because the incidents included a product that most Americans took and had in their homes coupled with quick deaths of the seven victims, fear quickly took hold over the nation. As with many cases such as these, this fear was

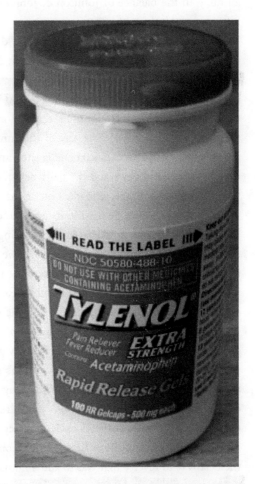

FIGURE 1.1. Tylenol bottle with safety cap

exacerbated by numerous, unrelated copycat crimes. Reports of deaths linked to Extra-Strength Tylenol came from states far and wide, which only validated the fears of many. It was no longer a lunatic outside of Chicago who may be responsible, but now it seemed as though Johnson & Johnson may be at fault. It was later determined that these copycat crimes had nothing to do with the Chicago cases—just people taking advantage of the situation to hide their own murders or extort money from Johnson & Johnson. Nonetheless, the reports of these cases did affect Americans' fears about the medicine. The perception that a few people in a region were dying from taking tainted Tylenol could now be a widespread crisis became reality to many people who were vowing never to take the drug again.

Needless to say, the impact this scare had on Johnson & Johnson's image, and in turn, its financial success, was huge. At that time, Tylenol was the number-one pain reliever in the United States. The medicine revolutionized the pharmaceutical industry; up until its introduction, just about the only non-prescription pain drug was aspirin. Tylenol was so important to Johnson & Johnson's bottom lines that it represented 35 percent of the company's billion-dollar revenues. The company had invested so heavily in and depended so greatly on its success, that the permanent removal of the drug from the market and public fear of it might have ended Johnson & Johnson's great success. Billions of dollars, millions of consumers, and thousands of employees all hung in the balance of Johnson & Johnson's public relations response to the crisis—and its lessons would influence the industry forever.

Because information about the cyanide deaths around Chicago and the copycat murders elsewhere were coming from the mainstream media, Johnson & Johnson's public relations team knew it needed to post company responses and plans where the public got its information—the media itself. Remember the development of public opinion really begins with the organization developing its plans and actions. Even though the event was out of the control of Johnson & Johnson, the response and reaction to it was in its control. In 1982, Americans got their news, or "knowledge" as part of the Innovation Diffusion Process, through the mainstream news media. Long before the Internet, social media sites, and pundit shows on 24-hour cable news channels existed, the local evening and world news and the daily newspapers were the only choices for up-to-date information. Knowing this, Johnson & Johnson embarked on an information campaign in these media to clarify misconceptions, alleviate fears, and encourage trust in its brand and its products. Moreover, because many Americans were fearful of Johnson & Johnson's products and demanding recalls to protect people, the company realized that a voluntary recall in the Chicago area would illustrate the company's commitment to its consumers' safety over its financial bottom line. This action further reinforced the positive image the company needed at this time while also showing its responsibility to safeguarding the public. Recalls cost millions of dollars, but Johnson & Johnson knew that the severity of the situation warranted this drastic measure.

Up until this crisis, Johnson & Johnson was a company known for its health and wellness products and generally a company few people really knew anything about other than its products—if you needed bandages, you bought Band-Aids, Johnson & Johnson's name for them, but you did not need to know much more about the company—just that its products had always been around was enough for most Americans. However, once the crisis took hold, Johnson & Johnson's public relations team counseled company president James Burke to appear on television as well as offer interviews to reporters. The company's public relations department knew that fear is the absence of confidence. In this case, people no longer felt confident in Johnson & Johnson's products, and the best way to reverse that was to add a human face to the company. By appearing on national news shows like *60 Minutes*, which had been the bane of many companies, James Burke offered fearful consumers a trusting face to go along with its statements of commitment and reassurance. Part of the success of this campaign was the knowledge that to many people, seeing is believing. This would be a crucial ingredient to Johnson & Johnson's additional public relations efforts.

Because the television media were reporting so greatly on the Tylenol scare, Johnson & Johnson decided to use it as a resource. No broadcast company in the world can send reporters to every story—they rely on public relations professionals to supply some of this information too. If the evening news was going to broadcast interviews and images from pharmacies and customers, then Johnson & Johnson would send its own side of the story. Probably few other responses to the Tylenol poisonings were as successful as Johnson & Johnson's development of video new releases (VNRs) and video news conference (VNCs). These videos were produced by Johnson & Johnson and included statements from key organizational spokespersons like James Burke and images of the company's manufacturing facilities and processes. The video was given to news organizations for their use to edit and include in their nightly broadcasts. Video of consumers stating their fears and anxieties over Tylenol were replaced with images of millions of bottles of Tylenol speeding through Johnson & Johnson's factories, which clearly illustrated the impossibility of someone taking a bottle off the completely mechanized machines, poison it, and then place it back in the assembly line destined for consumers. By seeing the level of mechanization and speed of manufacturing and packaging, Americans began to realize that Johnson & Johnson could not be at fault, and that it really was the work of an outside criminal bent on adding cyanide to bottles of Tylenol after they had already left the factories. Public opinion was starting to shift in Johnson & Johnson's favor. However, even though national poll numbers were showing the public's belief in the company, Johnson & Johnson was not clear of financial ruin.

National poll numbers showed that 87 percent of Americans supported Johnson & Johnson and felt that the company was not at fault for the tampering and deaths. However, 61 percent still would not purchase Tylenol. Clearly, Johnson & Johnson's public relations efforts had won the battle over public opinion, but to the company's leadership, the war was far from won. In addition to the media-centered public relations efforts, Johnson & Johnson also embarked on a personal communications campaign whereby consumers could use toll-free hotline to ask questions and received up-to-date information—remember websites were at least ten years away. In addition, the company decided that if fear was the result of a lack of confidence and trust in the product and not in the company as the poll numbers indicated, then the product itself must change.

Up until the poisonings, medication like Tylenol was generally packaged in only a bottle placed in a box. There was no reason to make the packaging tamper resistant because no one had ever really tampered with medicine before. However, after the Tylenol case, Johnson & Johnson introduced the first modern tamper-resistant package. Its triple-seal bottle became the industry standard and reassured consumers of the product's purity. Also, Johnson & Johnson changed the form of Tylenol. First introduced as a capsule, Johnson & Johnson later offered Tylenol as a tablet. The capsule could be taken apart, its contents emptied and replaced with something else, and reshaped to look as though it was not tampered with. A tablet would be nearly impossible to take apart and reform. Moreover, if a tablet gets wet, it turns to mush—something you may have experienced if you have ever taken aspirin without water. By replacing capsules with tablets, introducing the triple-seal package, and reversing public opinion via the media, Johnson & Johnson was able to do what many at the time thought was impossible. By February of 1983, the company had regained 95 percent of its pre-Tylenol-crisis revenues for the product. Such an astounding reversal of such a monumental crisis had never been seen before, and it was the first time that sound public relations efforts were credited for this success[7]. This case clearly showed public relations' worth for a company that was on the brink, and in many ways, introduced public relations as a valuable asset in the corporate boardroom.

An interesting side note to this case is that Johnson & Johnson suffered a very similar repeat incident just four years later. Company officials shook their heads at how this could be happening all over again. However, Johnson & Johnson learned its lesson from the 1982 case so well that the duration and severity of the 1986 incidents did not affect the company as greatly—an example of why case studies are so important and useful for public relations practitioners.

In addition to its groundbreaking effect on the field of public relations as far as its now being appreciated by management and needed for crisis recovery, the Tylenol case also provided several case lessons that are as valuable today as they were over 30 years ago. The following have become universal lessons from the Tylenol incident, and they are still used as the principles of effective crisis management.

1 **Social Responsibility Works.** Social responsibility is the idea that an organization or company does what is ethical, moral, and legal not solely for the organization's benefit, for all of society's benefit. Johnson & Johnson was not legally required to spend millions retooling its factories and manufacturing processes when it introduced the triple seal and replaced capsules with tablets. Johnson & Johnson knew that this decision was its responsibility rather than a mandate from a government agency. However, it cannot be underestimated the positives that social responsibility offers organizations using these tactics. No one can deny that they are mutually beneficial for the company and society; however, mutual benefit is also one of the hallmarks of any good relationship and a mainstay of sound public relations.

2 **Good Reputations Can Save.** Johnson & Johnson began nearly 100 years before the Tylenol scare. It was a trusted company whose products became ubiquitous to the American medicine cabinet. The company's products were used by millions of Americans in 1982, but more importantly, their parents and grandparents before them had used Johnson & Johnson products. Americans grew up with Johnson & Johnson's products—everything from its baby shampoo to cutting-edge pain relievers. This trust enabled the company to recover and respond more quickly than a company with no established brand identity, which illustrates why successful brands should be cherished. People trusted the company and its products for generations, and when the company asked for even more trust during a frightening time, people were willing to give Johnson & Johnson the benefit of the doubt.

3 **Consumers Trust When the Company Commits.** Similar to social responsibility, commitment is something that must be proven. Johnson & Johnson needed to issue an immediate statement; however, all of the statements and promises in the world won't go far without action. Akin to "seeing is believing," "actions speak louder than words" best describes this third lesson. Making promises to protect consumers is great, but if those promises are not kept, whatever trust and goodwill an organization had will quickly go away. Promises are integral to any solid relationship. Johnson & Johnson made good on its promises to protect and safeguard its customers even if it cost the company millions—their safety was more important than the monetary bottom line. However, this measure would of course later affect Johnson & Johnson's economic bottom line as well—a clear illustration of the power of a company's current reputation on its financial future.

4 **Victimized Companies Recover Better.** Johnson & Johnson had their positive reputation and brand quality set in most Americans' minds. The company demonstrated its commitment to its consumers in many ways—from recalls to repackaging. This, combined with official reports from respected agencies like the FBI, helped shape public opinion in favor of Johnson & Johnson. The company, which had been a part of American culture for so long had built a brand of honesty, sincerity, and quality for decades. When a madman in Chicago decided to murder people by tampering with Johnson & Johnson's flagship product, people became disgusted and enraged that such a thing could happen to their trusted company. It was not just the seven innocent people who died from taking poisoned Tylenol who were the victims, but the company that manufactured the product as well. The building and maintenance of Johnson & Johnson's positive image and reputation enabled it to recover its trust more easily than a company without a positive brand. The development and maintenance of positive image is directly the responsibility of the public relations department.

5   **Public Relations Helps the Financial Bottom Line.** This case provides many public relations lessons that have stood and will stand the test of time even in the face of advancing technology. But its greatest impact on the field of public relations was that it finally illustrated that sound, supported, and socially responsible public relations will impact a company's financial bottom line, just as much as advertising and marketing. Before the Tylenol incident, public relations was confused with other strategic communication fields, such as marketing; maligned as inherently deceptive in its practices; and the domain of manipulators and spin doctors. This case, however, brought the field newfound and enduring respect across multiple industries, and it is one of the main reasons the field has flourished since.

No one has ever been convicted of the 1982 Tylenol murders. Theories and allegations have surrounded the case over the decades. The primary suspect, James Lewis, was arrested for mailing a ransom note to Johnson & Johnson stating that the murders would cease if the company paid him[8]. Johnson & Johnson did offer a $100,000 reward, but all Lewis received was 13 years in federal prison for extortion—not the murders. Investigators have never closed the case, and it is hoped that new DNA analysis technology may shed new light on this case. Ironically, Lewis released a novel entitled, *POISON!*, which he claims is totally fictional and has nothing to do with the 1982 Tylenol poisonings.

A final aspect to the Tylenol case is four major lessons it provided public relations practitioners. As you'll see later, case study lessons are tremendously helpful for public relations professionals—they help guide actions and set up the fundamentals of public relations practice—ones that are seen in case after case.

1   **Immediate Action Leads to Long-term Results.** Historically, the longer an organization waits to address a situation or crisis, the more severe the damage from it will be to the company's two bottom lines: reputational and financial. More so today because of the 24-hours news cycle than in 1982, the speed of an organization's actions and reactions to issues and problems is paramount to public relations crisis management. The speed of public relations efforts is often as important as the actual effort—timing is everything, but it can sometimes be a balancing act to determine the most appropriate plan. Because news moves so quickly today and nearly anyone can access information anywhere and at any time, organizational responses to issues are also expected to be immediate. However, that can also sometimes be quite problematic to real-world public relations. In 1982, Johnson & Johnson understood the severity of the incidents it faced near Chicago. Because of the life-and-death situation, the company immediately began working with authorities who determined the poisonings, at the early stages, were centered near Chicago. Johnson & Johnson issued a recall of Chicago-area Tylenol, issued statements of concern and remorse to the victims' families, and detailed how the company was working with investigators—all openly and candidly. Most companies up until that time were hesitant to take responsibility for something like a product tampering, but Johnson & Johnson understood that accepting responsibility was not the same as accepting blame. Johnson & Johnson did nothing wrong; however, it was still its product that was linked to the seven deaths. Additionally, issuing recalls are not only expensive, but to some, connote that the organization knows it is at fault and was ordered to recall their product. Johnson & Johnson willingly recalled their product and made this point known. Moreover, the company continuously updated a worried nation as information became known. When the company did not know the answers to the public's questions, it acknowledged that it did not know, but would keep working to find out and keep people in the loop. However, the risk to making immediate statements and addressing issues is that it might call attention to the problem—more attention and focus than would be if the company did not address it so openly.

On the other hand, the greatest threat to waiting to see if a problem will pass and not making statements is that if the problem does not blow over and becomes a major crisis, to the public, the company looks irresponsible and unconcerned. Generally, the decision to address a situation and the level of concern is dictated by the nature of the incident. For Johnson & Johnson, the seven deaths linked to its product warranted immediate and widespread reaction. A less severe situation may not need such a level of attention—that is the balancing act where case study analyses can help public relations practitioners make these important, yet tricky decisions.

2   **Sound Research Is Integral to the Public Relations Decision-Making Process.** As mentioned in lesson one, case studies provide clues and suggestions for public relations practitioners. Johnson & Johnson's 1986 Tylenol scare was not as severe as the 1982 incident because the company learned what worked and what did not and applied it to the second poisonings. These types of lessons come from case study research and analyses. By seeing what organizations and individuals do in certain situations, public relations practitioners can make more informed decisions about how to react to issues or problems. No two cases are ever identical; however, by looking at opinion polls, responses, and actions in different cases, public relations practitioners arm themselves with information to make the best decision for their situation. Throughout the 1982 Tylenol case, Johnson & Johnson continuously monitored national opinion poll numbers to determine which of their responses were resonating best with the public. If poll numbers showed that more people approved of Johnson & Johnson's brand image following airings of video news releases showing the production lines of Tylenol, then more visual evidence like it was developed and disseminated to media outlets. If poll data showed that a corporate response statement was not improving the public's view of the company, a more personal message was written to replace it. Johnson & Johnson learned what worked and what did not as the crisis unfolded. Without sound research, public relations decision-making can best be described throwing darts at dartboard while blindfolded. You may hit your target if you are lucky, but chances are you will miss the target and need a lot of darts to even hit the board. Good research and sound data analyses allow public relations practitioners to home in on the bull's-eye and hit the target with fewer darts—research equals efficient and effective public relations. It is the hallmark of all successful public relations initiatives.

3   **Continuous Communication Furthers Trust and Confidence.** Communication is the foundation on which all good interpersonal relations are built—the same goes for public relations. Johnson & Johnson kept the public involved and informed as the Tylenol scare unfolded. Without this communication, people are likely to believe anything. Rumor mills start turning, misperceptions become reality, and trust and confidence quickly erode. Few elements influence public opinion more than communication from an organization. With it, the public is informed and feels confident about the organization because the information the public is getting is coming from the organization—not a second-hand source. Moreover, today everyone expects this level of communication. In 1982, Johnson & Johnson went out on a limb and decided the open, honest, and thorough communication would be the hallmark of its crisis-management strategy. For the most part, this level of transparency had not been seen from a large corporation before, and once the public got it, it offered a refreshing level of trust and confidence—just the ingredients needed to help replace their fears with trust. Since then, the public has grown to expect communication like this. In addition to this expectation, organizational reticence leaves the public to their own devices to seek and believe what they see and hear. Losing control of a situation is devastating to public relations efforts, and communication is a major part of that control. Sources of information no longer become important to the public as long as they can obtain information and news. The Hurricane Sandy example illustrates this when the public began accepting and believing fabricated stories and manipulated photos. Public relations practitioners must counsel their organizations to remain open and honest, as well as active in their communications—during good times, but especially during bad times.

4   **Evaluate Your Successes and Failures to Learn for Next Time.** Testing the success, failure, and in-betweens from public relations initiatives is key to long-term organizational growth and its lessons. Success and failure in life teaches many lessons for people, and it can do the same for organizations.

Johnson & Johnson found convincing people that the company should be trusted worked, but that still did not equate to persuading them to buy Tylenol. The company's public relations team realized that additional steps would be necessary to restore the financial security of the organization. The video news releases, interviews with company leaders, and active communication only went so far. The company also needed to invest heavily in retooling its facilities and revamping its manufacturing process to ultimately persuade Americans to purchase Tylenol. Evaluation inherently goes hand-in-hand with research. Research provides direction during a campaign or crisis, but evaluation shows what worked and what did not in the long-term, big-picture sense. From these lessons, the public relations practitioner knows what to eliminate in the future, what to emphasize, and what to rework in his or her efforts. Too often, evaluation is not taken as seriously as it should be. Organizations often see results in success or failure—without much regard as to how and why they succeeded or failed. Additionally, real-world public relations results are usually not so cut and dry—generally even the most successful campaign can be improved and the worst failing can provide opportunities. Without evaluation, these two major improvements are usually overlooked, underappreciated, or completely ignored. Successful organizations and strong public relations efforts look back at what they have done to determine their plans for the future.

This case also provides the aspiring public relations practitioner the opportunity to understand another key principle to public relations practice: the difference between the court of law and the court of public opinion. Because public relations is focused on positively influencing public opinion, understanding the challenges, and difference between rather clear-cut rules (court of law) and the fickle nature of public opinion enables practitioners to more fully see the phenomenon of public opinion.

The table below illustrates the two courts that arrive at judgments about people and events—one rationally, the other capriciously[9]. The purpose of this analysis is to show how difficult and unfair public relations work can be. Because public relations deals with the court of public opinion most, the table provides another glimpse into the challenges that practitioners face when trying to influence and maintain a positive image and brand with an often irrational public.

COURT OF LAW	COURT OF PUBLIC OPINION
1. Driven by facts. The defense and prosecution in a courtroom present their cases using evidence to sway the judge or jury to favor their argument. The process is based on logic and the idea that people are generally sensible and rational if given the facts to make a decision.	**1. Driven by a variety of elements.** Anything and everything is admissible as evidence in the court of public opinion. Here, facts can sometimes get in the way of a good story. There is often little in the way of rational decisions because they are driven by emotion and personal beliefs.
2. Based on rules. Courtroom procedures are enforced and must be followed by those presenting their cases. There are also penalties for breaking those rules, which helps to keep the proceedings running smoothly and evenly for everyone involved.	**2. No rules.** Anything goes in the court of public opinion. Because of this, there can be no enforcement of a "right" or "wrong." So-called rules of society are the closest thing, but those change frequently and are generally not officially punishable.
3. Deliberate consideration of evidence. Those making judgments as to the guilt or innocence of someone must think unbiased and clear thoughts to determine an outcome.	**3. Capricious and arbitrary.** Emotions and reactionary thoughts create unpredictable outcomes. Weighing the pros and cons of a case means little.
4. Characters are constant. The judge, prosecution, defense, and jury all have the established responsibilities and duties in the court of law.	**4. Characters change.** Opinion leaders such as politicians and celebrities come and go, and with them go their influence and power. They are replaced with new leaders whose influence could be the exact opposite of the first.
5. Someone is in charge. With set rules come authorities with the capacity to enforce protocols and fairness.	**5. No one is in charge.** No single individual necessarily has influence or dominance over anyone else. Authority is capricious at best, and any power that someone has can quickly go away.

6. Some items are inadmissible. With rules, penalties, and people with authority to enforce them comes guidelines about what can be used to influence others and what cannot.	**6. Everything's admissible.** Nothing is off the table. Anything, no matter if it is true or not, can be used to sway people's opinions.
7. Clear procedures and structure. Everyone has a turn to present their evidence logically and rationally with equality and fairness.	**7. No order or structure.** Anything and everything can happen at any time. There are no rights or guides to make the "proceedings" fair. Often, it is he who talks loudest who gets heard, not he who talks most rationally and correctly.
8. Uniformity. Generally, all homicide cases follow the same process; all burglary, the same. The due process of the law ensures that each person will receive a fair and equal trial.	**8. Unevenness.** No two cases in the court of public opinion are the same procedurally. Times change, people's priorities change, and technology advances—all of these aspects affect how a case is "tried" in the court of public opinion.

As you can see, the court of law is much more straightforward and simpler in terms of persuading others that a "client" is innocent. For Johnson & Johnson, it had to present its case to the world to show its innocence regarding the poisoning case. The company had to contend with rumors, copycat crimes, media sensationalism, and limited access to the public when defending itself. More recent cases provide another example of how these two courts differ. In one of the most infamous cases, the 1993 O. J. Simpson case, when the court of law exonerated him of murder, yet most of the public condemned him as guilty[10]. The 2011 murder trial of Casey Anthony also reflects the difference between the court of public opinion and the court of law. Upon Anthony's not-guilty verdict, thousands of Americans showed their disgust at it through demonstrations and vigils, which clearly showed their belief that Anthony was guilty[11]. The court of law makes determinations based on evidence and predictable procedure. The court of public opinion is influenced by speculation, evidence that may not be true, and the influence of the media and opinion leaders. Accordingly, winning cases in the court of public opinion is much more difficult and can often be more frustrating for the public relations practitioner than for the lawyer.

PUBLIC RELATIONS RESPONSIBILITIES

The responsibilities for the public relations practitioner can be overwhelming; however, by now you can see the primary duties that branch off the two major functions of public relations—counseling and communicating—to win public opinion. The following list includes the sub-duties most common in the public relations practice.

1 **Researching.** As you have seen, good research is integral to sound public relations work. There is, however, an important difference between good research and average or just bad research. Good research is focused, appropriate, and well planned to meet specific objectives and gain detailed data. Sound research answers the question, "Where are we, and how can we get where we want to go?"

2 **Advising.** Similar to counseling, public relations professionals must advise their organization's leaders on which steps to take and consider how their decisions might affect the public's opinion of the organization and its brand. Advising also goes to all levels of the organization—remember that one of the most valuable assets any organization can possess is good employees. Public relations is just as much a part of internal operations as it is with the organization's external image. Good advisement answers the question, "Where can we go?"

3 **Strategic Thinking.** Research, analysis, and mindshare, or the use of the collective knowledge of people, all play a role in strategic thinking[12]. Without strategies based on sensible, logical, and realistic knowledge, public relations efforts are on track to fail. Taking into account a situation's past and present

through detailed investigation enables public relations practitioners to sensibly plot and plan their organization's future. Strategic thinking answers the question, "What will get us there?"

4   **Strategic Planning.** Branching out from strategic thinking comes strategic planning, writing the map that will be used to guide the organization and further its image and brand in the future. The planning responsibility entails setting goals, objectives, strategies, tactics, as well as the means to evaluate them all. It is the culmination of research that answers the question, "How will we get there?"

5   **Communication Planning.** Communication planning moves public relations work from behind the scenes within the organization to revealing the plan to the public. Action items such as events, news releases, and sponsorship programs are all examples of the public side of communication planning. The tactics from strategic planning, now communicated openly, answer the question, "Are we getting there?"

6   **Evaluation.** The last of the major responsibilities of public relations looks to the past to judge successes and missteps on the way to achieving organizational goals. What worked, what did not, and what we can learn from them for next time encompass evaluation. The major question that evaluation helps answer is, "Did we get there?"

BIBLIOGRAPHY

1. Tesser, A. (1988). *Toward a self-evaluation maintenance model of social behavior*. In Berkowitz, L. advances in experimental social psychology. New York: Academic Press.

2. Grunig, James E; Hunt, Todd (1984). *Managing public relations* (6th ed.), Orlando, FL: Harcourt Brace Jovanovich.

3. Phillips, David (2006). Towards relationship management: Public relations at the core of organizational development. *Journal of Communication Management, 10*(2).

4. Michel, W., Shoda, Y., & Smith, R. E. (2004). *Introduction to personality: Toward an integration*. New York: John Wiley.

5. Young, Gregory G. (1978). *Your personality and how to live with it*. New York: Atheneum/SMI.

6. Oldham, John M. & Morris, Lois B. (1995). The new personality self-portrait: Why you think, work, love and act the way you do. New York: Bantam.

7. Bennett, P. D. (1995). The American Marketing Association dictionary of terms. New York: McGraw-Hill.

8. Grunig, James E. and Hunt, Todd. (1984). *Managing public relations 6e*. Orlando, FL: Harcourt Brace Jovanovich.

9. Neumeier, M. (2004). *The dictionary of brand*. New York: AIGA Center for Brand Experience.

10. Standard & Poor's (2005). *The Standard & Poor's 500 guide*. McGraw-Hill Professional: New York.

11. New York Times. (1985). Topics: Cars and colas coke jokes. *New York Times*. Retrieved from: http://www.nytimes.com/1985/10/23/opinion/topics-cars-and-colas-coke-jokes.html

12. Oliver, Thomas. (1986). *The real Coke, the real story*, London: Penguin.

13. Donsbach, Wolfgang. (2008). *The international encyclopedia of communication*. Malden, MA: Wiley-Blackwell.

14. Cialdini, R. B., Borden, R. J., Thorne, A., Walker, M. R., Freeman, S., & Sloan, L. R. (1976). Basking in reflected glory: Three (football) field studies. *Journal of Personality and Social Psychology*, 34, 366–375.

15. The Coca-Cola Company. (2012). The real story of New Coke. Retrieved from http://www.coca-colacompany.com/history/the-real-story-of-new-coke

16. Bernays, E. (2011). *Crystallizing public opinion (Reprint edition)*. New York: IG Publishing.

17. Katz & Lazarsfeld (1955). Personal influence. New York: Free Press.

18. Staubhaar, LaRose, Davenport (2009). *Media now*. Belmont, CA: Wadsworth Cengage Learning.

19. Harasta, J. (2014). Jersey strong, right?: A communications analysis of New Jersey's post-Hurricane Sandy tourism recovery. *Case Studies in Strategic Communication*, 3.

20. Lovett, Mitchell; Peres, Renana; Shachar, Ron. (2012). On brands and word-of-mouth. *Journal of Marketing Research 50*(4): 427–444.

21. Yankelovich, Daniel; David Meer. (2006). Rediscovering market segmentation. *Harvard Business Review*, 1–11.

22. Rogers, Everett M. (1962). *Diffusion of innovations*. Glencoe, Ontario: Glencoe/McGraw-Hill: Free Press.

23. Strategic Business Insights. (n.d.). About VALS. Retrieved from http://www.strategicbusinessinsights.com/vals/about.shtml

24. Cantril, H. (1965). *The pattern of human concerns*. New Brunswick, NJ: Rutgers University Press.

25. Public Relations Society of America. (2012). What is public relations: PRSA's widely accepted definition. Retrieved from http://www.prsa.org/AboutPRSA/PublicRelationsDefined/#.VAYiG0u4mFI

26. McClam, E., & Weber, H. R. (2010, June 11). BP's failure made worse by PR mistakes. NBC News. Retrieved from http://www.nbcnews.com/id/37647218/ns/business-world_business/t/bps-failures-made-worse-pr-mistakes/#.VAYkOUu4mFI

27. Norman, Wayne; Chris MacDonald (2004). Getting to the bottom of 'Triple bottom line.' *Business Ethics Quarterly 14*(2): 243–262.

28. Farris, Paul W., Neil T. Bendle, Phillip E. Pfeifer, & David J. Reibstein (2010). *Marketing metrics: The definitive guide to measuring marketing performance*. Upper Saddle River, New Jersey: Pearson Education, Inc.

29. Farris, P. W., Neil T., Bendle, P. E., Pfeifer, & Reibstein, D. J. (2010). *Marketing metrics: The definitive guide to measuring marketing performance*. Upper Saddle River, New Jersey: Pearson Education, Inc.

30. Bell, R. (n.d.) The Tylenol terrorist. Crime Library. Retrieved from http://www.crimelibrary.com/terrorists_spies/terrorists/tylenol_murders/index.html

31. Stansberry & Smith. (2008). *Public relations practice: Managerial cases and problems, 7th ed*. Upper Saddle River, NJ: Pearson.

32. CNN. (2009, Feb 5). Law enforcement to review Tylenol murders. CNN. Retrieved from http://www.cnn.com/2009/CRIME/02/04/tylenol.murders/index.html

33. JM Moses (1995). Legal spin control: Ethics and advocacy in the court of public opinion. *Columbia Law Review*.

34. USA Today. (1997, Feb. 5) Racial factor tilts the scales of public opinion. *USA Today*. Retrieved from http://usatoday30.usatoday.com/news/index/nns212.htm

35. Flock, E. (2011, July 6). Casey Anthony verdict shocks media: attorneys black "talking heads." *Washington Post*, Retrieved from http://www.washingtonpost.com/blogs/blogpost/post/casey-anthony-not-guilty-verdict-shocks-media-attorneys-blast-talking-heads/2011/07/05/gHQAHhIXzH_blog.html

36. Litwin, L. (2003). *The public relation's practitioner's playbook: A synergized approach to effective two-way communication*. Dubuque: IA: Kendall-Hunt.

37. Marston, J. (1963). *The nature of public relations*. New York: McGraw-Hill.

38. Kunhardt, Philip B., Jr.; Kunhardt, Philip B., III; Kunhardt, Peter W. (1995). *P.T. Barnum: America's Greatest Showman*. New York: Alfred A. Knopf.

39. Harrison, S. & Moloney, K. (2004). Comparing two public relations pioneers: American Ivy Lee and British John Elliot. *Public Relations Review*, 30: 205–215.

40. New York Times. (1995, March 10). Edward Bernays, 'Father of public relations' and leader in opinion making dies at 103. *New York Times*. Retrieved from http://www.nytimes.com/books/98/08/16/specials/bernays-obit.html

41. Sweeney, Michael S. (2001). *Secrets of Victory: The Office of Censorship and the American Press and Radio in World War II*. Chapel Hill, N.C.: University of North Carolina Press.

42. Bernays, Edward L.; Cutler, H.W. (1955). *The Engineering of Consent*. Norman, OK: University of Oklahoma Press.

43. Bernays, E. (1928). *Propaganda*. Brooklyn, NY: IG Publishing.

44. Grunig, J. E. (1984). *Managing public relations*. Independence, KY: Cengage Learning.

45. Mohr, Betty. (1994). The Pepsi Challenge: Managing a crisis. *Prepared Foods*. Retrieved from: http://www.highbeam.com/doc/1G1-15312359.html

46. Stansberry & Smith. (2008). *Public relations practice: Managerial cases and problems, 7th ed*. Upper Saddle River, NJ: Pearson.

47. Federal Trade Commission. (n.d.). Statutes enforced or administered by the commission. ftc.gov. Retrieved from: http://www.ftc.gov/enforcement/statutes

48. United States Supreme Court. (March 9, 1964). *New York Times v. Sullivan*, (376 U.S. 254). Retrieved from: http://www.bc.edu/bc_org/avp/cas/comm/free_speech/nytvsullivan.html

49. Maslow, A. H. (1943). A theory of human motivation. *Psychological Review 50*(4) 370–96.

50. Pierce, W. D., Cameron, J., Banko, K. M., So, S. (2003). Positive effects of rewards and performance standards on intrinsic motivation. *The Psychology Record*. pp. 561–579.

51. Fair III, E. M., Silvestri, L. (1992). Effects of rewards, competition and outcome on intrinsic motivation. *Journal of Instructional Psychology*. 3–9.

52. Dunham, R. B. (1977). Relationships of perceived job design characteristics to job ability requirements and job value. *Journal of Applied Psychology*. 760–763.

53. Cotton, J. L., Vollrath D. A., Froggatt K. L., Lengnick-Hall M. L., & Jennings, K. R. (1988). Employee participation: Diverse forms and different outcomes. *Academy of Management Review, 13*:8–22.

54. Pew Research. (2013). Climate change and financial instability seen as top global threats. Pew Research Center. Retrieved from: http://www.pewglobal.org/2013/06/24/climate-change-and-financial-instability-seen-as-top-global-threats/

55. Boykoff, M. & Boykoff, J. (July 2004). Balance as bias: global warming and the US prestige press. *Global Environmental Change Part A 14*(2): 125–136.

56. Lippman, W. (1922). *Public opinion*. San Diego: CA. Harcourt, Brace, and Co.

57. Shoemaker, Pamela J. & Vos, Tim P. (2009). *Gatekeeping Theory*. New York: Routledge.

58. The Associated Press. *The Associated Press Stylebook 2014* (Associated Press Stylebook and Briefing on Media Law). New York: Associated Press.

59. Rahim, M., Antonioni, D., & Psenicka, C. (2001). A structural equations model of leader power, subordinates' styles of handling conflict, and job performance. *International Journal Of Conflict Management, 12*(3):191.

60. Fearn-Banks. K. (2011). *Crisis communications*. New York: Routledge.

61. Emblemetric. (n.d.). Procter & Gamble's new logo: By the numbers. Eblemetric. Retrieved from: http://www.emblemetric.com/2013/05/06/procter-gambles-new-logo-by-the-numbers/

62. Taylor, M. & Kent, M. L. (2010). Anticipatory socialization in the use of social media in public relations: A content analysis of PRSA's Tactics. *Public Relations Review, 36*(3):207–214.

63. Goumans, F. (2014, Jan. 3). Friday five: Social media tips for 2014. PRSAY. Retrieved from: http://prsay.prsa.org/index.php/2014/01/03/friday-five-social-media-tips-for-2014/

64. Barash, David (2002). *Peace and conflict*. Thousand Oaks, CA: Sage Publications.

65. Bowman, S. and Willis, C. (2003). We media: How audiences are shaping the future of news and information. *The Media Center at the American Press Institute*.

66. Steenberg, T., & Avery, J. (2010, Feb. 4). Marketing analysis toolkit: Situation analysis. *Harvard Business Review*. Retrieved from http://hbr.org/product/marketing-analysis-toolkit-situation-analysis/an/ 510079-PDF-ENG

67. Kabel, M. (2006, July 18). "Wal-Mart, critics slam each other on web." *The Washington Post*.

68. Norman, Al (2004). The Case Against Wal-Mart. *Raphel Marketing*, 7.

69. Zook, M., & Graham, M. (2006). Wal-Mart nation: Mapping the reach of a retail colossus. *In Brunn, S. D. Wal-Mart World: The World's Biggest Corporation in the Global Economy*. New York: Routledge. 15–25.

70. Hodal, K., Kelly, C., Lawrence, F. (2014, June 10). Revealed: Asian slave labour producing prawns for supermarkets in US, UK. *The Guardian*.

71. Nations Restaurant News. (2012, Nov. 12). Top 100 Chains: U.S. Sales *Nations Restaurant News*.

72. International Business Times. (2008, May 22). McDonald's Holds down Dollar Meal, Making Menu Healthier. *International Business Times*

73. Armstrong. M (1996). *Management processes and functions*. London: CIPD.

74. Bhasin, K. (2011, Aug. 30). 12 McDonald's menu items that failed spectacularly. *Business Insider*. Retrieved from: http://www.businessinsider.com/failed-mcdonalds-items-2011-8?op=1

75. Pew Research Group. (2013). Social networking use. Pew Research Group. Retrieved from: http://www.pewresearch.org/data-trend/media-and-technology/social-networking-use/

76. Techopedia. (n.d.). SoLoMo. Retrieved from: http://www.techopedia.com/definition/28492/solomo

77. Coombs, W. Timothy (2012). Parameters for crisis communication in "The Handbook of Crisis Communication" Eds. W. Timothy Coombs & Sherry J. Holladay, West Sussex, UK: Blackwell Publishing Ltd.

78. Basso, J. & Randall, H. (2012). The writer's toolbox: A comprehensive guide for public relations and business communication. Dubuque: IA: Kendhall-Hunt.

79. Revkin, A. C. (2006, May 22). 'An Inconvenient Truth': Al Gore's fight against global warming. *New York Times*. Retrieved from: http://www.nytimes.com/2006/05/22/movies/22gore.html?_r=0

80. McLuhan, M., Powers. B. R. (2012). The global village: Transformations in world life and media in the 21st Century. Oxford, UK: Oxford University Press.

81. Vocus. (2014). Vocus releases "The state media 2014 report." Vocus. Retrieved from: http://www.vocus.com/about-us/press-release/vocus-releases-the-state-of-the-media-2014-report/

82. Journal of Integrated Marketing Communications. (n.d.). What is IMC? Northwestern University. Retrieved from: http://jimc.medill.northwestern.edu/what-is-imc/

2

WHAT YOU CAN DO VERSUS WHAT YOU SHOULD DO

Public Relations Law and Ethics

Reading 1.2: "Public Relations of Character" By Dick Martin and Donald K. Wright

Many works on public relations, including textbooks, put the discussion of law and ethics toward the back of the book. We feel it important enough to begin our introduction to the profession with such a discussion.

As authors Dick Martin and Dr. Don Wright note in the reading for this chapter, "the law outlines the minimal requirements of the truth," which is a critical part of ethical public relations (Martin and Knight 2015, p. 58). To that end, we'll explore a number of legal requirements and their implications for public relations, including laws on *copyright, trademark,* and *intellectual property.* We'll also discuss the rules governing *fair use* and employee and corporate speech. Because public relations writing is public, we need to understand what constitutes *defamation*, which now includes *libel* and *slander* as umbrella terms used by the courts.

Finally, we'll need to understand the various regulations placed on the work of the public relations profession by government agencies such as the Federal Trade Commission and the Securities and Exchange Commission.

Most of our time will be spent, however, in the world of ethics. Working from a common definition, we'll look at and discuss professional guidelines and concepts such as the public interest, honesty and integrity, accuracy and truth, fair dealings, safeguarding confidences, and conflicts of interest. We'll also explore Codes of Ethics, which are essential tools for the ethical practice of public relations.

Most of the time, we don't set out to do wrong or be unethical. Most of our issues are created by the ethical dilemmas we face in our day-to-day lives. We'll take the opportunity to look at and solve case studies and situations that can present these dilemmas.

This exploration will include the concept of ethical advocacy—how we can ethically advocate for our organization while serving the public interest. As we are often called the "conscience of the organization," we'll look at the various aspects of the ethical decision-making process and complete this unit with an exploration of the public relations professional and the accrediting process.

"PUBLIC RELATIONS OF CHARACTER"

By Dick Martin and Donald K. Wright

There is a good chance, were Aristotle alive today, he would be energetically engaged in trying to sort out where "the good" lay in the relatively new inventions of mass media, consumer markets, and public relations.

But why would we want to consult someone who slept in his clothes, would not know what to do with a newspaper let alone a computer, and never even saw a flush toilet? If ethics has forward motion, Aristotle gave it much of its initial propulsion, and progress made since builds on his thinking. In fact, some contemporary thinkers have suggested we could do worse than to return to the Aristotelian ideal in the conduct of our modern lives. Aristotle certainly did not have the last word on the ethical practice of public relations. But it is a good place to start.

So we start where Aristotle did—with the belief that the "goodness" of any endeavor is measured in terms of excellence in attaining purpose. How closely did Ellsworth, Lee, Bernays, and Page adhere to the qualities, or virtues, necessary to achieve their purpose? What are those virtues? And what was their purpose anyway?

It is worth noting here that Arthur Page seemed to have a different purpose than the other three.[1] In fact, he made it pretty clear in his "job interview" that he was not interested in a "publicity job." From the start, he considered his new position a general management position focused on helping the company fulfill its obligations to society, as well as to its customers. With the acquiescence of his boss and his board of directors, that is precisely what he did over his 20-year career.

Ellsworth, Lee, and Bernays, however, shared a common purpose. In part, it was ostensibly to inform the public about a business (respectively the phone company, coal mine owners, and an assortment of consumer brands). In some cases, it was also to persuade the public to take a particular action (eat bacon) or to believe a certain idea (telephone competition is unnecessary; the coal mine owners are treating their employees fairly; the president of Guatemala is a Communist). … For now, we will assume these public relations pioneers had pure intentions; that is, their goal was to help the public make better decisions.

Aristotle would have approved of that purpose. He far preferred to be governed by many farmers, shepherds, and potters acting in the common interest (the "polity") than to be ruled by any number of people acting in their own interest. The key, though, is that the *polity* has to be well informed in order to recognize the common interest.[2]

VIRTUE

Having stipulated pure purpose, we turn to the qualities (virtues) Aristotle would expect to see in excellent communications. Plato enumerated four cardinal virtues—**prudence, justice, temperance**, and **courage**. Aristotle, a supremely practical man, recognized that different spheres of life might require other virtues and added as many as eight to Plato's list, including **patience, friendliness**, and **truthfulness**.

That last virtue is arguably essential in any ethical communication or relationship. Telling the truth is the very first of the so-called Page Principles, drawn from Arthur W. Page's speeches and memos by the association of senior communications officers that bears his name.[3] And not surprisingly, considering its source, it is immediately followed by "prove it with action."

But what does it mean to tell the truth? Ivy Lee suggested that the concept is entirely subjective. One man's truth is another man's opinion. Facts have little objective reality; they depend entirely on interpretation. Lee might have advised his clients to tell the truth, but from that point forward, they were on their own. His hands were off the wheel.

We should emphasize here that truth is not the only virtue on which the ethics of public relations depend, but it is a good place to start because it is deceptively hard to pin down.

THE NATURE OF TRUTH

Philosophers have been arguing about the nature of truth for millennia, about as long as they have been debating the existence of reality. Perhaps, the nonphilosophers among us can agree on a provisional definition: *truth is conformity to facts or reality*, what is termed "**veracity**." But ethicist Kirk Hanson points out that, in practice, even that straightforward notion lies on a continuum with a notoriously slippery slope.[4]

Just below actual truth—conformance to reality—is a closely related concept: *disclosed truth*. Public relations people do not have to say everything they know to be truthful. Some facts are confidential; some are irrelevant; some might even be misleading if their context were misunderstood. For example, in planning layoffs, every organization is asked to prepare multiple options. Releasing all that raw information would not tell anyone anything truly useful and could lead people to the wrong conclusions. Other times, it could be needlessly damaging. When AT&T's data networks suffered a daylong outage in 1998, the company quickly traced the problem to a technician who installed some faulty software. The *New York Post* wanted his name. But what purpose would releasing it have served? Management was responsible for providing the software, training technicians, and ensuring the procedures they followed were fail-safe. Fingering the technician would have been irresponsible.

But disclosed truth can also be so self-servingly selective as to be misleading. The late novelist-essayist Alan Harrington once compared public relations to flower-arranging. "Public-relations specialists make flower arrangements of the facts," he said, "placing them so that the wilted and less attractive petals are hidden by sturdy blooms."[5] This amounts to a well-worn technique called "spinning," which we will discuss more fully shortly.

Then there are *plausible interpretations* of facts. We say the glass is half full; you say it's half empty. Technically, we are both right. We are not arguing about how much water is in the glass, just what it means. Statistics are particularly useful in buttressing one interpretation or the other. But some believe the manipulation of numbers is a whole category of lying all to itself. Mark Twain famously said, "There are three kinds of lies: lies, damned lies, and statistics."[6]

It is said that "figures do not lie, but liars"—and some public relations people—"figure." In the right hands, numbers and graphs can be manipulated to support almost any interpretation of data. For example, we can easily establish with mathematical certainty that the average human being has one testicle and one breast. A full exposition of lying with statistics is beyond this book's intent (and its authors' capabilities). But thankfully scholars have jumped into the breach with books of their own. Among the best is a 60-year-old classic, *How to Lie with Statistics* by mathematician Darrell Huff (1954/1993). He is the guy who came up with the original "gee-whiz graph," exaggerating small differences by setting a chart's baseline to a value greater than zero (1993 pp. 62–67). The PRSA and the United Kingdom's Chartered Institute for Public Relations have partnered with their respective country's leading associations of professional statisticians and data analysts to publish best practice guides for using statistics in communications.[7] For more on this from a public relations perspective, see Michaelson and Stacks (2014).

Incorrect interpretations follow. For example, we know for a fact that a McDonald's Big Mac has about half the cholesterol as a three-piece serving of KFC fried chicken (75 mg versus 145 mg). Conveniently ignoring the fact that it has almost 50 percent more calories (550 versus 320), and a third more fat (29 grams versus 19 grams), we promote its lower cholesterol and claim it is better for your heart than KFC fried chicken.

Or maybe we promote our client's vodka as "gluten-free." In fact, all vodka is gluten-free, despite its earlier life as a mash of barley, wheat, or rye. But we suspect that because we have highlighted it on the bottle, some celiac victims and food purists will assume it makes a difference. The Kremlin's public relations guy in Berlin, Germany, would call all this "the tendentious presentation of facts" which is really a way of lying about lying.[8]

And then, of course, there are *outright lies*. Public relations people know they are not supposed to lie. But in a 2010 survey, while only 12 percent admitted to disseminating false information themselves, nearly three-quarters (73 percent) said they believed public relations people lie in the course of their work.[9] The survey also suggests public relations practitioners have a flexible notion of lying. Just 29 percent considered withholding information morally equivalent to lying. And three quarters said public relations people have no obligation to communicate information that may damage their clients.

TRUTH AND THE LAW

Some ethicists suggest we turn to the law for guidance in defining the minimal contours and limits of truthful speech. On that score, it is worth noting that the practice of public relations is one of four jobs specifically protected by the U.S. Constitution. (The others are the clergy, journalists, and lobbyists.)

It is right there in the first amendment—"Congress shall make no law … abridging the freedom of speech." The founding fathers had individuals in mind when they banned "abridging" free speech. And since corporations are not mentioned in the Constitution, the full range of their rights has never been entirely clear, but they have always been thought to have some of the rights individuals enjoy, such as the right to due process and the right to enter contracts. And, of course, the courts have long recognized reasonable limits on individuals' free speech. It is not lawful, for example, to yell "Fire!" in a crowded theater.

Beginning in the 1970s, the Supreme Court began applying first amendment rights to corporations in a series of decisions.[10] The Court held that companies engage in two kinds of speech, each with its own set of rules and regulations, though this has become a murky area of the law for reasons we will soon discuss.

- "Commercial speech" is motivated by profit and proposes a commercial transaction.
- "Corporate speech," by contrast, deals with social or political issues and seeks to affect policy or strengthen relationships.

COMMERCIAL SPEECH

The Supreme Court allows regulation of commercial speech if there is a substantial government interest at stake, such as protecting the public from harm, and the regulation is narrowly tailored to that purpose. So laws designed to protect the public from misleading claims are constitutional. You cannot say you are discounting your product 50 percent if you are selling it at the same old price. Of course, the law leaves plenty of room for what it terms "puffery," which is widely perceived as merely an expression of the seller's opinion and usually discounted as such by any prospective customers. Whether you drink Coke or not, you know there is no way to prove it is the world's most refreshing soft drink. That is puffery and gets a free pass. Similarly, Wonder Bread can claim to build strong bodies 12 ways because it adds 12 vitamins to the dough. The rest is puffery. On the other hand, Gaines Burgers dog food once claimed it provides all the milk protein a dog needs. The Federal Trade Commission (FTC) deemed that claim *deceptive* because dogs do not need milk protein, and it is misleading to suggest they do.

Linda Goldstein, a lawyer specializing in communications law, warns that many public relations campaigns face "heightened regulatory scrutiny" from the FTC, which wants to ensure that marketers disclose any "material connection" between themselves and anyone who endorses their products.[11] "Recently, the FTC's view of what constitutes an endorsement and what constitutes a material connection has become so restrictive," she warns, "that even the most benign social media campaigns could be implicated."

Goldstein cautions that encouraging customers to blog, Tweet, or post photos of a client's products could trigger the agency's endorsement guidelines if some kind of incentive is involved. Even offering a prize for the best post could cross the line. It is all explained in 21-page guidelines.[12] But that has not stopped companies like Lord & Taylor from paying fashion bloggers to post photos of themselves in one of the retailer's new dresses. The dresses promptly sold out and, as this was being written, the retailer had not heard from the FTC. But the bloggers were on the receiving end of so much criticism, they added retroactive "#sponsored" hashtags to their posts and the retailer itself promised to act more ethically in the future, though they termed it a "process improvement."[13]

The FTC is just one of many agencies that regulate commercial speech, depending on its nature. For example, the Federal Drug Administration regulates pharmaceutical advertising to protect public safety. The Securities and Exchange Commission regulates financial communications, for example barring companies from selectively disclosing material information to favored investors.

Public relations people also have to be careful that their passion for representing their client or promoting their client's product does not deteriorate into *fraud*. Under common law, fraud is misrepresentation of a material fact with the intent to deceive. It can be saying something that is not true or failing to disclose something that is important. A *material fact* is one that a reasonable person would depend on in making a decision. And acting with reckless disregard of the consequences can constitute intent. The person being deceived only has to show they had reason to rely on the false information and doing so resulted in injury. And you cannot use "the client made me do it" as a defense. If you help a client commit fraud, you can be found just as guilty. That is why agencies typically indemnify clients for suits arising out of the creative materials they produce, such as photo releases, while they ask clients to indemnify them for claims arising from the information they provide the agency, such as product and service claims.

CORPORATE SPEECH

By comparison, *corporate speech* was once thought to have greater protection than commercial speech. Because it deals with public policy issues, it was thought to constitute opinion that contributes to the free flow of information and less vulnerable to claims of being false or misleading. But in 2003, the Supreme Court let stand a lower court decision that seemed to erase the distinction between corporate and commercial speech.

The case had to do with a series of news releases Nike issued to rebut accusations its sneakers were made in Asian sweatshops. An activist named Mark Kasky sued Nike for false advertising. Nike responded that its views on a public issue were entitled to First Amendment protection. The local court agreed and dismissed the case, but the California Supreme Court overturned the ruling, saying Nike's news releases were subject to false advertising laws. The United States Supreme Court initially agreed to review the case, but ultimately sent the case back to the trial court without issuing a ruling. The parties then settled out of court, leaving many people wondering if the distinction between commercial and corporate speech was still valid. On the other hand, according to a recent Harvard Law School study, "nearly half of First Amendment legal challenges now benefit business corporations and trade groups, rather than other organizations or individuals" (Coates, 2015, February 27). For example, in the 2010 Citizens United case, the Supreme Court seemed to expand corporate speech when it upheld a company's right to run ads advocating a position on public policy or social issues, including political candidates.[14] It was a controversial decision that is still being debated.

But there are even more immediate legal concerns for public relations people in the exercise of corporate or commercial speech. Defamation is the legal term for harming someone's reputation by spreading false information about them. In print, it's called libel; in speech, it's slander. But whatever you call it, it is trouble. In some states, it is a criminal offense. The criteria for defamation are quite complicated, differ by jurisdiction, and apply a little differently to public personalities. But as a general rule, it is always wise to make sure the expression of an opinion is labeled as such and backed up with supporting facts.

Included in the right to privacy … is the "right to publicity." Although the specifics can vary from state to state, this generally concerns the appropriation of a person's name or likeness for commercial purposes. Originally, it was designed to protect people's privacy, but these days it is also considered a property right. If there is money to be made from someone's likeness, that person has the right to control it. In fact, the right of publicity has even been extended to identifiable buildings and animals.

It is also illegal (and unethical) to use other people's creative work without getting their permission. The sheer profusion of easily clicked, copied, and pasted images on the Internet makes them seem like free goods. They are not. Someone expended lots of calories and maybe even money in their creation. To claim any of it as your own is lying. The law does allow "fair use" of copyrighted material, but as attorney Kerry Gorgone put it, "You don't get to discuss 'fair use' until you've been sued, and lawsuits are expensive."[15]

Finally, public relations people can break the law—not to mention act incredibly unethically—by padding their expense accounts or filing false billable hours. That is called lying and when it leads to the receipt of unearned compensation it is another form of stealing. The former head of FleishmanHillard's operations in Los Angeles was sentenced to federal prison for overbilling the Los Angeles Department of Water and Power for the agency's services. He had perfectly logical reasons for the way he billed the water department, but all it got him was 42 months in jail.

TRUTH AND PUBLIC RELATIONS

If the law defines the minimal requirements of the truth, where does that leave us in the practice of public relations? Aristotle's notion of purpose suggests a provisional definition. Veracity—or conformance to reality—hinges on the use to which a given set of facts will be put:

> In public relations, telling the truth means giving people substantially all the information a reasonable person needs to make an intelligent, voluntary decision, whether buying a company's products, investing in it, working for it, welcoming it into their community, or supporting it in some other way.

That does not mean public relations practitioners need to give people *all* sides of an issue, including what opponents or competitors allege. It is fair to assume that in the free market of products and ideas, others will have an opportunity to present their side. But telling the truth does mean you can withhold material information or engage in misdirection so people ignore other points of view. If your product has side effects or the kind of flaw that might change someone's mind about it, telling the truth requires you to reveal them. Telling the truth also means doing our very best to confirm the accuracy of the information we share. And if we discover we gave people bad information—or if they draw erroneous conclusions from what we said—we do not ignore it or cover it up. We correct it and set people straight. To do otherwise is to lie.

[C]onsider what it means in a practical situation faced by the public relations people at Kraft Foods.

MINI-CASE

Kraft makes a popular baking chocolate. Sometime in 2013, many home bakers noticed the packages on grocery shelves had suddenly shrunk—from eight ounces to four. But apparently in some stores, the price stayed the same. That raised the eyebrows of the *New York Times'* "Haggler" columnist, who quickly fired an e-mail to the Kraft public relations department, asking what gives.

One can only imagine what goes through your mind when an e-mail from someone identifying himself as the "Haggler" from the *New York Times* lands in your inbox, but Kraft's spokeswoman was happy (and we suspect, relieved) to tell him the price should have gone down. "The suggested retail price for the four-ounce package is $2.89," she e-mailed back, "while the suggested retail price for the old eight-ounce package was $3.89."

Perhaps, suspecting $2.89 is not half of $3.89, the Haggler dug out his calculator and crunched the numbers discovering the price per ounce actually went *up* by 47 percent. Back he went to e-mail: "Isn't this just a price increase in semi-clever disguise?" he asked. Here's what Kraft's spokeswoman said:

> Our consumers have told us that they prefer this size over the larger size because the majority of our Baker's recipes call for four ounces or less. The easy-break bar makes it faster to melt and easier to break apart. And they can buy only what they need for a recipe, so the product is fresher.

Fair enough, the *Times*'s intrepid columnist said, but why did the price go up? After a pause, Kraft replied:

Our packaging change for Baker's Chocolate was driven by consumer research. Our consumers have told us that they prefer this size over the larger size because the majority of our Baker's recipes call for four ounces or less.

"Ooo-kay," the by-now exasperated reporter persisted, "I think you said that already, but did your consumers tell you to raise the price?" Finally, after an even longer pause, Kraft's wily spokesperson said:

> Our new four-ounce size of Baker's Chocolate is competitively priced with other brands.

What the *Times'* columnist wrote at this point is worth reprinting.

> The reality is that for many items, production costs have been rising. Given these circumstances, a price increase is perfectly understandable and arguably inevitable. What's odd is that few manufacturers, it seems, ever level with consumers about what might be valid reasons for higher prices.[16]

Kraft's spokeswoman answered the question she wished had been asked—why did you change the size of the package—rather than the one actually posed—why did the price go up? Her answer did not have to ignore the company's perspective. Indeed, the Haggler wondered why so many companies fail to level about it.

MEDIA TRAINING

No wonder some journalists believe media relations is really just a con game. Consider what one writer for the *Columbia Journalism Review* had to say about media training: "Media training teaches people all the fancy steps they need to answer the questions they want to answer, not those of an inquisitive reporter. The result: in too many cases, instead of shedding light, interviews cloud public discourse."[17]

Indeed, most media training seems to have been inspired by a quip Henry Kissinger reputedly once made at the beginning of a news conference—"Does anyone have any questions for my answers?" It teaches spokespeople to formulate a message that serves their purpose and then to "bridge" to it no matter what they are asked. That is undoubtedly what the Baker's chocolate spokesperson was trying to do, however unskillfully.

Ethical media training helps spokespeople communicate more clearly and in ways that contribute to public discussion. One of us wrote a short book entitled *The Executive's Guide to Handling a Press Interview* early in his career. The very first tip in the book was "always tell the truth." But that advice was not prompted by any real concern for ethics; it was based on the near certainty that few lies survive close inspection or the erosion of time. Eventually, the truth comes out. And once reporters catch you lying—or even hiding the truth—they will never trust you again (Martin, 1997).

On rereading our short guide to dealing with the media, we were gratified (and relieved) to discover it primarily emphasized techniques for getting a point across, (e.g., taking the public's point of view, avoiding jargon, dealing with interruptions, and side-stepping traps like repeating loaded words). But it did not deal with the bane of modern-day communications—*spinning*—because back when our little opus was published, the word had not yet entered the lexicon. We wish it never had.

SPINNING AND FRAMING

"Spinning" is emphasizing (or deemphasizing) facts to produce a more favorable response from the spinner's point of view. It makes bad facts look good and good facts look better. The *Oxford English Dictionary* dates its usage from the mid-1970s, around the time our brief tome came out and in the politically charged wake of the Watergate scandal. Spin probably derives from the practice of hitting a ball so it twists in a particular direction and, appropriately enough, it was first applied to politicians.[18] But as the media paid more attention to business news, it was quickly applied to company spokespeople as well. Public relations people became known as "Spin Doctors." Unfortunately, spinning facts so only their best side shows not only skates on the edge of lying, it is psychologically dangerous. If you shade the truth often enough, you can lose track of it entirely.

Spinning, however, is not the same as a closely related concept—*framing*. Framing is all about defining the context within which communication will take place (Goffman, 1974). Every thought we have and every word we express is framed in some way. Framing or context is what gives words meaning. Some truths can only be seen when they appear within the proper frame. On the other hand, spinning is usually intended to conceal truth, to direct attention away from it.

Framing can tilt discussion in a certain direction. For example, calling "estate taxes" "death taxes" takes the issue out of the realm of accounting and invites the question, "Why should I pay taxes for dying?" While that frames the issue in a particular way, it is not inherently misleading. It is simply defining the issue in favorable terms to those who would like to eliminate the tax. However, like any rhetorical device, framing can be manipulative. This is especially obvious when someone frames issues differently depending on the audience being addressed. For example, Republican pollster and word-maven Frank Luntz published talking points on immigration that carried two different sets of message for candidates, depending on the audience being addressed.

"While Americans are most concerned about the economic impact of illegal immigration, crime is a close second," he told them. "Particularly in border and industrial states with heavy illegal populations, the perception of illegal immigration and increased fear of crime are closely related." The message for general audiences then should be: "Stopping illegal immigrants at the border means less crime." But when addressing Hispanic audiences, he warned, "Hispanic Americans reject the assertion that illegal immigration fosters a general culture of lawlessness." So when addressing them "Talk about 'the system' as the problem." Point out that if the immigration system worked better—if the border were more secure and the documentation process faster—people would be more likely to obey the laws.[19]

Whether such advice amounts to cynical spinning or contextual framing is open to debate. Certainly, in today's world of 24/7 media, few politicians think what they say to one group will never reach the ears of others. But that does not mean they will not slant their remarks to their audience's preconceived beliefs and interests, emphasizing different messages accordingly. *The difference between ethical framing and unethical spinning lies in one's intention, whether it is to reveal or hide the truth.*

SECRETS

The flip side of telling the truth is keeping confidences—not only those of clients or employers, which should be obvious, but also those of the media and stakeholders. Tipping a favored reporter about a story another journalist is pursuing may be a way to curry favor, but it is a form of theft that harms the reporter whose scoop you have helped steal and corrupts the free functioning of the media, which is a public good.

On the other hand, keeping secrets can lead to ethical problems of their own. Obviously, no ethical practitioner would hide wrongdoing. But public relations should have a bias toward open and trusting communications with all stakeholders. Practitioners should press clients to carefully weigh the tradeoffs between protecting sensitive data and giving stakeholders the information they legitimately need to make informed decisions. Often, the people most in the dark about an organization's practices and performance are its own employees. But ethicist Sissela Bok (1989) has described how organizational secrecy can inhibit its employees' judgment. Secrecy "shuts out criticism and feedback," she wrote, "leading people to become mired down in stereotyped, unexamined, often erroneous beliefs and ways of thinking" (p. 25). The same principle applies in the larger community within which public relations practitioners seek to create meaning.

PUBLIC RELATIONS CHARACTER

Alasdaire Macintyre (1998) suggests entering a "practice" such as public relations carries obligations that go beyond truth-telling. "To enter into a practice is to enter into a relationship not only with its contemporary practitioners," he writes, "but also with those who have preceded us in the practice, particularly those whose achievements extended the reach of the practice to the present point" (p. 194). This suggests that character or virtue manifests in two ways—in the internal quality of the activity we are practicing (what he called its "internal good" or "goods of excellence") and in whatever external impact it has (its "external good" or "goods of effectiveness" (Kelvin, 1998, p. 55)).

From the perspective of internal good or excellence, ethical public relations is *not* simply a matter of following a set of rules. It also means figuring out what kind of practitioner we want to be and developing the lifelong habits to support it. It means having the courage to stretch our capabilities to their limits, the honesty to recognize our limitations, and the humility to learn from those with greater experience. It means working to improve the overall practice of public relations as an end in itself, not simply as a means to some other goal such as greater personal stature or renown.

From the perspective of the practice's internal excellence, truthfulness would certainly be at the top of any public relations practitioner's list of essential virtues. But others are also important. Ethicist Robert Solomon compiled his own list of business virtues:

> There are a great many virtues that are relevant to business life ... Just for a start, we have honesty, loyalty, sincerity, courage, reliability, trustworthiness, benevolence, sensitivity, helpfulness, cooperativeness, civility, decency, modesty, openness, cheerfulness, amiability, tolerance, reasonableness, tactfulness, wittiness, gracefulness, liveliness, magnanimity, persistence, prudence, resourcefulness, warmth, and hospitality (1992 pp. 317–339).

From that list of 28 virtues, which is far from exhaustive, we can select three in addition that, in our experience, have particular application to the practice of public relations:

> **Honesty**—Honesty is an uncompromising and consistent commitment to truthfulness in word and action. It is the path to winning the trust of clients and, ultimately, of the publics they serve and on whom they depend.

> **Courage**—Public relations people are often in the position of speaking truth to power, telling them uncomfortable facts they may not want to hear. That requires self-confidence and the courage to be the bearer of bad news or the asker of tough questions.

> **Persistence**—Neither of us has ever been asked to lie in our professional life. We were never asked to hide or disguise the truth. But simply *finding* the truth was often a challenge. In a large company, information is scattered across organizations, people hoard it and dole it out as it suits their purposes, often with their own unique interpretation. It is especially difficult to distinguish what is true from what is speculative or simply wishful thinking in the heat of a crisis. Discovering the truth requires stubborn tenacity.

A public relations counselor's job is to dig out the facts of a situation, assess their meaning, and communicate them responsibly to relevant stakeholders. A data dump is not responsible communications, nor is abdicating their interpretation to others. Effective counselors try to understand the facts from their stakeholders' points of view so they can give them all the information they need to act intelligently and prudently.

That is not as easy as it sounds. Roger Bolton knows firsthand, having practiced public relations at the most senior levels in government and at companies such as IBM and Aetna, before becoming president of the Arthur W. Page Society. "It's hard work," he wrote,

> because self-delusion can easily convince an enterprise of things that aren't really fully, objectively true, and rooting out the natural bias takes both diligence and an ability to see the world through the objective eyes of others. It also takes guts to stand up for the truth against the natural instincts of an organization to let the little lies or omissions put it in a better light than it deserves.[20]

Now ask yourself, how well did Barnum, Ellsworth, Lee, and Bernays do by these standards in the situations described earlier?

SUMMARY

From what we have learned, the ethical quality of public relations practice should be measured against standards of excellence and effectiveness, aligned in the common purpose of contributing to people's happiness or human flourishing. If Barnum, Ellsworth, Lee, and Bernays succeeded in persuading people to do or believe something that was harmful to them, it couldn't be ethical no matter how clever or effective their technique.

We have seen that truthfulness is a fundamental virtue in the practice of public relations. But it is also a nuanced quality. Barnum's happy hokum skirted the edges of truthfulness but everyone was usually in on the gag. In fact, his hyperbole was part of the entertainment and arguably contributed to people's enjoyment. Few people felt cheated even when they discovered his "Feejee Mermaid" was literally stitched together. Ellsworth, on the other hand, stepped over the bounds of truthfulness when he used advertising dollars to convince editors to run his "news stories." The stories themselves may have been truthful, but their presence in the news columns was a sham, suggesting editors considered them worthy of readers' attention. Ivy Lee's concept of the truth as whatever his client believed is just as misleading. Truth is conformance to reality, not to someone's self-interested conception of it. And Bernays' efforts to convince women to smoke may have started as a harmless stunt, but it was ultimately detrimental to their health, which Bernays himself regretfully concluded late in his life.

In public relations, telling the truth means ensuring the veracity of the information you share (i.e., it substantially conforms to all the facts the public reasonably needs to make an intelligent, voluntary decision). Truth, so defined, is the bedrock of ethical public relations. And, as it happens, that also requires practitioners to develop virtues such as courage and persistence because ensuring the veracity of such facts is seldom easy.

[...]

NOTES

1 Other than the 1956 interviews for Columbia University's oral history project cited here, Page did not write a memoir. What we know of his approach to public relations must be inferred from his many speeches which are archived at Penn State College of Communications' Arthur W. Page Center: http://comm.psu.edu/page-center/resources/other-resources/page-speeches.

2 For more on Aristotle's views on the most practical political regime, see *Book IV of Politics*, which is available online at http://classics.mit.edu/Aristotle/politics.html.

3 The Arthur W. Page Society is an association of chief communications officers of leading corporations, the CEOs of the world's largest public relations agencies, and leading academics from the nation's top business and communications schools. The seven Page Principles are tell the truth, prove it with action, listen to the customer, manage for tomorrow, conduct public relations as if the whole company depended on it, realize a company's true character is expressed by its people, and remain calm, patient, and good-humored. Page himself didn't write these principles; they were drawn and inferred from his speeches, memos, and example by the Society's founders. See http://www.awpagesociety.com/about/the-page-principles/.

4 The "continuum of truth" is based on a presentation Kirk Hanson made to the annual meeting of the Arthur Page Society, in September 2003. Hanson is executive director of the Markula Center for Applied Ethics at Santa Clara University.

5 Quoted by Auletta, K. (2007, February 12). The Fixer, *New Yorker*. http://www.newyorker.com/magazine/2007/02/12/the-fixer

6 Twain attributed the remark to British Prime Minister Benjamin Disraeli in "Chapters From My Autobiography" which appeared in the *North American Review* literary journal on September 7, 1906, p. 471. http://www.gutenberg.org/files/19987/19987-h/19987-h.htm. The original source has never been found in Mr Disraeli's papers, however, and it is likely Twain wrote it himself.

7 The PRSA's guidelines are available online at http://www.prsa.org/Intelligence/BusinessCase/Documents/StatisticsBestPracticesGuide.pdf. Accessed September 5, 2015. The Chartered Institute of Public Relations' guidelines are at https://www.mrs.org.uk/pdf/CIPR%20MRS%20RSS%20Guidelines%20for%20using%20statistics%20in%20communications%20CIPR.pdf. Accessed September 5, 2015.

8 The Kremlin's man in Berlin explained his country's propaganda in these terms to Troianovski, A. (2014, August 21). Russia ramps up information war in Europe. *Wall Street Journal*. http://online.wsj.com/articles/russia-ramps-up-information-war-in-europe-1408675046. Accessed July 22, 2015.

9 *PR Week* commissioned the survey. See Sudhaman, A. (2010, February 3). PR professionals believe 'spin' is entrenched in industry, survey shows. *PR Week*. http://www.prweek.com/article/981450/pr-professionals-believe-spin-entrenched-industry-survey-shows. Accessed July 22, 2015.

10 The most important of these decisions were *Virginia State Pharmacy Board v. Virginia Citizens Consumer Council* (1976), *First National Bank of Boston v. Bellotti* (1978), and *Central Hudson Gas & Electric Corp. v. Public Service Commission* (1980).

11 Goldstein, L. (2015, December 31). Top 3 legal issues facing marketers in 2015. *Wall Street Journal*. http://mobile.blogs. wsj.com/cmo/2014/12/31/outside-voices-top-3-legal-issues-facing-marketers-in-2015/. Accessed July 22, 2015.

12 The FTC guidelines, ".com Disclosures," were issued in March 2013 and are available online at https://www.ftc.gov/ sites/default/files/attachments/press-releases/ftc-staff-revises-online-advertising-disclosure-guidelines/130312 dotcomdisclosures.pdf. Accessed July 22, 2015.

13 Beck, M. (2015, April 3). Did Lord & Taylor's Instagram influencer campaign cross the line? *Marketing Land*. http:// marketingland.com/did-lord-taylors-instagram-influencer-campaign-cross-the-line-123961. Accessed July 22, 2015.

14 *Citizens United v. Federal Election Commission*, No. 08-205, 558 U.S. 310. (2010, January 21). http://www.supremecourt. gov/Search.aspx?FileName=/docketfiles/08-205.htm. Accessed September 9, 2015.

15 Gorgone, K. (2015, June 4). The new guide to minimizing legal risks in social media marketing. *BusinessGrow.com*. http://www.businessesgrow.com/2015/06/04/legal-risks-in-social-media-marketing/. Accessed July 22, 2015.

16 Segal, D. (2013, June 22). The Haggler: Halving the portion, but not the price. *New York Times*. http://www.nytimes. com/2013/06/23/your-money/halving-the-portion-but-not-the-price.html?module=Search&mabReward= relbias%3Ar%2C%7B%221%22%3A%22RI%3A8%22%7D. Accessed July 22, 2015.

17 Lieberman, T. (2004, January/February). Answer the &%$#* question. *Columbia Journalism Review*.

18 For an interesting discussion of the etymology of "spin," see the Oxford Word Blog at http://blog.oxforddictionaries. com/2011/09/a-journey-through-spin/

19 Luntz's advice is in a 25-page advisory issued by his firm and published on the liberal-leaning web sire, the Daily Kos. These quotes appear on page 22–24. See: Luntz, Maslansky Strategic Research. (2005, October). Respect for law & economic fairness: Illegal immigration prevention. http://images.dailykos.com/images/user/3/Luntz_frames_immigration.pdf. Accessed July 22, 2015.

20 Bolton expressed this view in the Page Society Blog, PageTurner on February 17, 2015. See "Tell the truth,". http:// www.awpagesociety.com/2015/02/tell-the-truth-021/. Accessed July 22, 2015.

3

WHAT INFLUENCES HOW PUBLIC RELATIONS PROFESSIONALS COMMUNICATE

Communication Models and Theories

Reading 1.3:
"Theories of Mass Communication"
By Daniel Walsch

Most of the scholarly body of knowledge about how public relations professionals can communicate effectively comes from other disciplines. It is then tested and molded to fit the particular circumstances of public relations.

Our reading for this chapter takes us through some of the bedrock theories and models that help us understand how we need to communicate in order to be effective in that effort. But we'll need to take a deeper dive to help us understand how to sustain the effects of our communication.

Beginning with Maslow's Hierarchy of Needs, we'll begin to understand human motivation at its basic level. It's necessary for us to explore *propaganda* and propaganda devices, as this can be, if we're careful and ethical in our efforts, a fruitful area for the public relations practitioner. Equally important and somewhat related are theories of persuasion and influence. *Persuasion* is especially important to the public relations professional as we are expected to change negative public opinions, develop positive opinions, and maintain favorable opinions. We will discuss the six principles of persuasion: liking, reciprocity, consensus/social proof, consistency, authority, and scarcity. We will also discuss the limits of persuasion including: competing messages, lack of message penetration, self-perception, and self-selection.

Understanding the diffusion of ideas, the public opinion process, and how opinion leaders impact our communication efforts is important. Knowing something about the barriers to communication can help us avoid those barriers or at least lessen their impact. It's also important for us to understand the limitations of theories and models.

Finally, we'll discuss several media theories, including *agenda setting* and *framing*. Taken together, this unit will help us build a solid foundation for our communications efforts.

"THEORIES OF MASS COMMUNICATION"

By Daniel Walsch

Looking at these various periods in U.S. history, it is interesting how scholars assessed them from a communication perspective. For instance, I could not identify many major communication theories focusing on the aspect of communication exchange between publics. Instead, scholars seemed more intent on examining the level of success of the communication effort. What happens that leads one public to sway another? What are the mechanics of such a process? Following are examples of leading communication theories that, collectively, contribute to greater understanding of this act, yet with limitations. The limitations of the theories are found in not taking a closer look at the possibility of extended engagement or interaction occurring as a result of a communication act. For instance, is the primary purpose of communication to generate a tangible result, or is it found in the connection or exchange between two entities? While the scholars certainly acknowledge the exchange between publics, their focus seemed to be more on the result of that interaction. Communication for the sake of communication is a concept that has been given low priority.

MAGIC BULLET THEORY

World events in the 1930s served as an inspiration for the creation of this theory. Looking back, perhaps it was no coincidence that the rise of fascism occurred at a time when radio—a technological advancement in communication—was so popular. This famous "noise box" was a main source of entertainment and information for many Americans and for families throughout the world. The magic bullet theory emerged out of an awareness that the media are a powerful tool or vehicle for reaching a massive audience. Theorists took this a step further by suggesting the medium of radio was also highly influential. Judging by the success of the Nazi movement toward getting hundreds of thousands of people to accept, in particular, fascism, it was believed that media and media alone was the key way to sway large numbers of people.

The magic bullet theory was also known as the "hypodermic needle theory" because it represented a clear effort on the part of users of the media to inject specific information into their publics (Croteau & Hoynes, 1997). Without question, radio, and the media in general, were great ways to reach many people at once. Other theorists, however, quickly pointed out that to accept the magic bullet theory was to accept the notion that the public is highly vulnerable to powerful messages coming from the media (Davis & Baron, 1952). It also suggested a sizeable element of passivism among the public. By this, I mean the magic bullet theory implied the general public is akin to a giant lump of soft clay that can be reshaped and controlled by people and/or entities with strong and convincing messages. Thus, this theory showcased the power of one-way communication designed to persuade the public. This was a rather negative assessment of the public at large. Perhaps, at least in part, because of that unflatteringly depiction, mass communication theorists came to embrace the notion that people themselves play a greater role in communication than was first surmised (Katz, 1957).

I agree the masses are not necessarily the malleable lump that the magic bullet theory suggests. This is not to say we cannot and do not find examples of this even in today's world, though perhaps not on the level we saw in the 1930s when the magic bullet theory was introduced. Specifically, I am looking at the internal communication of large corporations as an instance. The Roche Corporation, headquartered in South Africa, is an international entity focusing on developing medicines and diagnostics that has taken steps in recent years to enhance the communication abilities of its leadership. In 2002 Roche, with offices and clientele throughout the world, implemented a set of core corporate principles in which its values and missions were outlined to minimize any misunderstandings among all employees regarding the company's strategies and direction (Huber & Boyle, 2005).

Roche created leadership teams to not only better engage employees in the implementation of the corporate strategies but also to ensure deeper compliance. This comprehensive internal strategy included employee newsletters, departmental meetings, and continuous briefing sessions for employees. Collectively, they provided the Roche Corporation with greater buy-in from its many employees toward the organization's financial stability and betterment. Thus, the magic bullet theory is found in the internal efforts of the Roche Corporation in that the entity's executives represent the media vehicle that serves as the primary source of information and even motivation for the masses that, in this case, are the Roche employees. This example of the magic bullet theory represents one-way communication. At Roche Corporation, management practiced a top-down style of communication. In this case, the magic bullet theory was successful as it helped sway employees to more actively support management's efforts.

TWO-STEP THEORY

Building on the magic bullet theory, creation of the two-step theory seems almost inevitable. Introduced in the 1940s, it formally brought into the discussion the role and heavy influence of opinion leaders in the public conversation. People of societal weight and not just the media, theorists said, helped determine what issues of the day were important as well as how they should be assessed, handled, or acted upon (Toroldahl, V. C. 2001). More specifically, social scientists introduced the concept that mass media actually influenced the opinion leaders of the day who, in turn, held greater sway over the views and actions of the masses. Yes, the theorists said, the media were still extremely powerful, but so, too, were opinion leaders (Baran, 2003). As a result of their perceived values, perceived competence, and level of visibility or notoriety, certain individuals were deemed to be opinion leaders (Katz, 1957). These opinion leaders, it should be noted, were not necessarily famous people such as politicians, religious leaders, or movie stars. Instead, more often than not they could be and were well-known neighbors, relatives, friends, or coworkers (Katz & Lazarsfeld, 1955). In this sense, the media were a junior partner in the mix of swaying public opinion.

A variation of this theory was the "n-step theory," which still focused on the influence of opinion leaders. The difference was that figures of influence varied. For instance, someone might turn to a film critic to decide what movie to see over the weekend but then tap into the expertise of their local car mechanic for guidance on what car to purchase.

Inevitably, however, theorists and social scientists began poking holes in the two-step theory though not nearly as much as they did with its predecessor, the magic bullet theory. While acknowledging the power of social influencing, critics found the two-step theory to be a bit fuzzy in explaining the actual flow of communication (Staubhaar, LaRose & Davenport, 2009). The magic bullet theory was pretty direct in comparison: media to public. But regarding this two-step theory, opinion leaders became part of the mix. Did they trigger the initial message or merely receive it from the media and then pass it along to the general public? Scholars had mixed responses to this. Some gave greater weight to the influence of opinion leaders than did others. Either way, scholars viewed effective communication as the result of powerful one-way communication efforts. The more a communication effort was able to persuade its intended publics, the more effective scholars viewed it to be. Thus, while opinion leaders were seen as playing a bigger role in this mix, scholars continued to view communication as a one-way effort.

Yes, the two-step theory was the next step in the evolution of how communication was portrayed and interrupted. It was a bit more complex than the more direct magic bullet theory. At the same time, however, the two theories are not all that different. Each contends communication is a one-way endeavor: a sender puts forth a message and receiver receives it. With the enhanced role of the opinion leader, however, the two-step theory suggests people are not necessarily the passive or powerless creatures that were initially portrayed in the magic bullet theory (Lowery & Defleur, 1995). In fact, turning to opinion leaders as another source of information suggests a level of proactiveness and engagement on the part of the public.

DIFFUSION THEORY

This theory represents a natural progression from the magic bullet theory and the two-step theory. The former emphasized the heavy influence of the media while the latter suggested it was people—specifically opinion leaders—who had more influence on the general public when it came to the spreading of ideas and suggesting actions. The diffusion theory incorporates the thrust of each into one. It identifies the media as a primary source of information while acknowledging it is people that possess and wield the most influence over their peers (Guth & Marsh, 2009). Interpersonal communication is a key here, people sharing their experiences with others. With this interpretation, it suggests that everyone, not just those who are famous or fictional characters made popular via such medium as television and the movies, can be and often are the real opinion leaders (Lowery & DeFeur, 1995). For instance, I am sure all of us can relate to this when we think of the influence our parents have had on us over our growing years and perhaps even into our adulthood. And then there are friends and coworkers who may recommend books for us to read, vacation spots to visit, or restaurants to sample. This, then, suggests that influence some may wield over others is often situational. While the auto mechanic may guide my actions on what to do about my car, this same person in all likelihood will have little, if any, sway over me in terms in where I should go to get a good haircut.

Most of us, however, only take advice from those we find credible. When my car is acting up, I tend to trust the auto mechanic when he or she explains what I should do about it. Because of their perceived expertise, I find them credible. But the credibility I grant them is the result of more than just giving it to them based on their job or title or the fact they may be dressed in a manner that I happen to equate with being a mechanic. There is also the matter of listening to them talk about cars and, as best I can, assessing whether they seem to have an impressive base of knowledge. How well they do and how openly I keep my mind ultimately determine my decision to place the welfare of my car in their hands. This speaks to the importance of listening, an act that enhances interactions in both personal and professional settings (Brunner, 2008). On a personal level, it enhances the bond between people while helping them develop a deeper understanding of each other. On a professional level, it can put organizations in front of emerging issues and allow for more proactive responses (Plati, 2005).

The concept of diffusion reinforces the notion of people influencing people. Viewed as a process by which an innovation is communicated through specific channels among members of a social system (Rogers, 1995), its very workings are contingent on the interaction of individuals in which people share information. Taking this a step further, Rogers identified five stages of innovations—decisions that people follow as a result of the initial sharing of information. The five stages: knowledge or acknowledged awareness of what has been shared with them; attitude toward what has been shared with them; actual adoption of what has been shared with them; implementation in some form of what they have learned; and confirmation or evaluating the results of their implementation. These steps illustrate the reality that communication in terms of connections with others is continuous though not necessarily always in a straight line. Our interactions with others are many, vary in length and intensity, represent emotional or intellectual investment, and are smooth or rough. Together, they comprise our own social existence (Rogers & Escudero, 2004).

Another of the significant elements of this theory is that it revisits the role of the media. Is the media's primary purpose to influence or to merely inform? Such an important question is as timely today as it was when this theory was introduced, particularly in this time of niche journalism when reporters are being given greater license to inject their own interpretations or opinions on issues of the day rather than just presenting facts objectively. One would be hard-pressed to tune into any news program on cable television, for instance, and find current event topics reported without heavy doses of bias. Also, even with media outlets that strive to present objective reporting, they include opinion pieces and editorials in their overall presentations. Newspapers are an obvious example. Thus, even in the media we see traces of internal conflict when it comes to communication. Looking at newspapers again, one only has to visit the op-ed page of many newspapers to see a range of opinions expressed on various current event issues. Given that, is their purpose to inform, persuade, or do both?

This question regarding media brings to mind a similar one that continues to be discussed by scholars of public relations: Is the primary purpose of public relations to persuade or is it to establish partnerships? This difference is effectively represented in two models set forth more than twenty-five years ago by James Grunig and Todd Hunt (1984). They labeled the two models two-way asymmetrical and two-way symmetrical. The two-way asymmetrical model represents a form of public relations designed to influence thought and/or behavior. The creators of the model described it as a selfish form of public relations as it does not lend itself to dispute or conflict resolution (Grunig & Hunt, 1994). The two-way asymmetrical model is more apt to be followed when organizations are designing strategic ways to raise their profits, increase membership, or enhance their image or reputation (Smith, 2009). The two-way symmetrical model, however, does focus on conflict resolution. It speaks to attempts by communicators to create a mutual understanding between publics (Okay & Okay, 2008). An example of this might be found in strategies that bring together two publics such as senior citizens and young adults to collaborate on behalf of an issue that affects them both. Interestingly, surveys among public relations practitioners have shown this model to be highly popular (Ibid). All four of the Grunig-Hunt models and others will be dissected in greater detail throughout this text. In terms of the magic bullet, two-step, and diffusion theories, it is important to note, collectively, that they represent efforts to provide greater understanding of the workings of communication. They also illustrate a lack of acknowledgement that there is more to communication than putting forth information or calls for action. Specifically, what about feedback? What about responses to the releasing of information or cries for action? On a more fundamental level, how does a simple conversation between two people fit in with the various communication theories cited above? Presently, that question is not addressed.

Thus, journalism and public relations—for years considered to be not unlike the Hatfields and McCoys in that the very existence of one always seemed to be at cross-purposes with the other—both trigger intriguing debates as to their fundamental purposes. For journalism: Does it exist to inform or persuade? For public relations: Does it exist to create partnerships or persuade? History suggests the answer to both is "yes." The two do have multiple purposes. The question, particularly as of late, is how good of a job is each doing at distinguishing between their primary purposes.

AGENDA-SETTING HYPOTHESIS

Much like the magic bullet theory, this hypothesis is very simple. It also speaks to the heavy role of the media. Simply put, this hypothesis suggests the mass media does not tell people what to think, but rather what to think about (Mccombs, 2004). In many ways, this notion remains as viable today as it did when it was introduced in the early 1970s. Numerous books on this topic, in fact, have been written. One of the topic's leading authors and critics on the national media is Robert McChesney. Communication scholars decry what he views as an unhealthy amount of control by media conglomerates over what information or news is passed along to the general public (2004). Such a perspective gives insight into why so many public relations professionals, pioneered by Bernays and carried on to the present day, work so hard at pitching stories to the media. If they are successful in placing a story in the electronic or print media on behalf of their client, for example, then they have made the entity they represent part of the public's agenda. Even with the rise of social media, placing stories with the media remains a top priority among any professional communicator's litany of strategic goals.

As efforts to place stories in the media have intensified over the years, the concept of framing has become part of the public lexicon. This speaks to the matter of not just making a client part of the media's agenda or daily storyboard, but controlling or framing the specific way a client is portrayed (Nelson, Clawson & Oxley, 1997). Given this current reality, it is ironic in the way it tends to make journalists and public relations practitioners collaborators in what is passed along to the public. Granted, the public relations pros may be silent or junior partners, but just the same their fingerprints are part of the mix.

But the agenda-setting hypothesis does not just apply to the traditional external role played by the media. It can be found as well within organizations, particularly when it is management that oversees virtually all forms of internal communication, including newsletters, web pages, meetings, publications, and e-mails. Those tools of internal communication, as they pertain to employees or organizational members, are as traditional as tools of external communication, including newspapers, radio stations, television, even social media, are to members of the general public. If those internal tools of communication are controlled by management, then it is management that plays a heavy hand in determining what the workers will read and/or hear about. In other words, management controls the agenda.

Nearly one hundred years ago, Taylor wrote that two fundamental purposes of internal public relations, as controlled by management, are efficiency and control (1911). The mechanics of such internal communication efforts is one way: top-to-bottom. Such an agenda serves as a way of engineering unchallenged compliance with managerial decisions (Kennan & Hazleton, 2005). It also places the workers in a position of being totally reliant on whatever information management decides to share with them.

Not surprisingly, this so-called style of internal communication has been challenged over the years. Criticisms of it also apply to the agenda-setting hypothesis itself. One of the first and perhaps still the reigning champ of criticisms was advanced by Mayo, founder of the human relations theory. Mayo said organizations are never more efficient than when group relationships are created and allowed to prosper (1933). Further, for groups to do well, their interactions must possess a free flow of information (two-way communication). Following Mayo's assessment, Barnard said management and workers must enjoy an interactive framework in which they jointly create the organizational fabric and operative functions (1938). Thus, regarding internal communication, there needs to exist horizontal flow mixed with the more traditional vertical.

Finally, to drive this point home on a more contemporary note, researchers have identified several key characteristics that an organization's internal communication component (public relations office) must possess in order to be most effective and to provide most benefit to the organization itself. They are: senior communicators must be an active part of the organization's strategic management team; senior communicators must be part of the strategic management process; senior communications team must be generously comprised of both men and women; and the senior communications team must be allowed to operate with some level of independence from both management and the workers (Botan & Hazleton, 2006).

The three mass communication theories—magic bullet, two-step, and diffusion—and the agenda-setting hypothesis represent a fairly steady progression in perspectives on how communication works. Collectively, they solidify the notion that communication is an action-reaction endeavor. The portrait painted by the magic bullet theory, for instance, depicts the influence of the media on the masses. The two-step theory inserts opinion leaders into the mix. It suggests it is largely the mass media's leaders or the most influential figures of the day who serve as the primary receiver of the information and/or messages that media emit and who thereby end up influencing the public the most in how they transmit it. The diffusion theory takes the basic premise of the two-step theory and inserts another set of opinion leaders into the mix. These additional influential parties are non-famous folks who are elevated to levels of influence because of their expertise or credibility in any given situation. A beautician who advises customers on how they should wear their hair would be an everyday example of this. Finally, the agenda-setting hypothesis speaks to the notion that information to which the public is exposed is fairly tightly controlled. In these four communication theories and hypothesis then, the only real feedback touched upon is found in the actions of the public on the receiving end of the communicated messages or information. Is its response one of compliance or rejection? Interestingly, but unfortunately, none of the theories or the hypothesis put forth goes beyond a possible response or reaction from the public other than those two options. It seems the creators of these theories only saw communication as an act of being heard. Scholars seemed to suggest the most important aspect of the communication act is the sending of the message and that the most important player is the sender. Not nearly as much weight was given to how well or clearly the message was or is received or the actual response or feedback triggered by the message's receiver.

SHANNON-WEAVER MODEL OF COMMUNICATION

These theories and the public relations models we have addressed speak to the spreading of information to masses of people along with their sources of influence. But what about the actual mechanics or logistics of communication? Putting aside such elements as emotion and targeting messages, there is the physical act itself. One person speaks and another person listens. What could be simpler than that? Taken from that one-dimension perspective, it is difficult to cite anything more direct. Of course, reality tells us something quite different. Interactions or acts of communication are rarely as simple as they might appear. Think of any errand any of us might run. All we have to do is drive to the local dry cleaner's, pick up our shirts, and come home. That, too, is straightforward. But it becomes potentially more complex when one factors in such variables as contending with other drivers, making sure you have enough gas in your car, making sure you have money in your wallet to pay for the shirts, and dealing with other customers at the dry cleaner's itself. The result is something seemingly simple, yet is actually multidimensional.

One of the better-known clichés is "speak when spoken to." (How many times have parents said that to their children?) People, as we know, also speak when they feel they have something to say or simply want to be heard.

While the objective of being heard is all right as far as it goes, it only represents one piece of the best kind of communication: circular dialogue. By that, I mean the maintenance of an open line or channel of communication between two entities in which as a matter of routine neither side monopolizes their exchange. In the communication spectrum, not only should senders of a message and receivers be equal participants, but they should also be constantly exchanging roles. To illustrate, I refer to two scientists—Claude Shannon and Warren Weaver—who in 1948 attempted to explain the logistics of a simple attempt at communication (Shannon & Weaver, 1963). The Shannon-Weaver model represents one of the earliest acknowledgements that for communication to be truly effective, then a response component must be present. In other words, the existence of two-way communication must be present. Another unique aspect of their communication model is that while it is simple in structure, it also highlights the complexity of any communication exchange and the potential impediments to its success. Their model continues to be as relevant today as it was back then. As articulated by Shannon and Weaver, the communication exchange, not surprisingly, begins with a sender. Ultimately, that entity's message is received by a receiver (who else?). Again, could anything be more straightforward than that? But where the model's complexity kicks in is in the journey of the message from sender to receiver and what happens to the message after the receiver receives it.

At the time Shannon and Weaver devised their communication model, they were affiliated with the Bell Telephone Company. Thus, the basis for their model was the mechanics of a telephone conversation. Working from that scenario, the message begins with an initiative from the sender. This entity conjures up something they want to impart to another. But knowing what to say and knowing how to say it is not the same thing. Consequently, the sender is faced with the dilemma of figuring out how best to articulate their message. Shannon and Weaver called this step encoding. Once that is done, however, there is still no guarantee the message will successfully make its way to the person or entity to whom it is intended. Any possible roadblock or hurdle is referred to as noise. In the case of a telephone conversation, noise could range from a busy signal to no one being on the other end of the line to static or outside interference. The emergence of noise does not automatically mean the sent message has been compromised. It can be, of course, but it can also simply represent the emergence of conflicting sound or other messages that make it more difficult for the receiver to either receive or understand it. As a teacher, for example, I experience noise all the time. Standing in front of a class full of students, it is not uncommon to see a number of them checking their iPhones for messages or even sending e-mails to friends via their laptops. As much as technology enhances the classroom experience for both instructor and student, it also presents an occupational hazard as well. But I digress.

At this point in the communication effort as outlined by Shannon and Weaver, the onus of the process shifts toward the sender. Much as the sender needed to make a two-prong decision—deciding upon the message and how best to articulate it—the receiver needs to physically hear the message as well as understand it. The understanding or deciphering step is referred to as decoding. So, the elements of the Shannon-Weaver model include receiver, encoding, possible noise, decoding, and sender. But it does not end there. There is now the matter of the receiver's response. However the receiver responds, even if with a simple "thank you" or by abruptly hanging up, the sequence of the communication process is reversed. Receiver becomes sender and vice versa. The reversal of roles and back and forth of the exchange continues for the duration of the conversation.

The Shannon-Weaver model is important in any detailed discussion of communication because it is out of this verbalization of a communication exchange between two individuals, publics, or organizations from which the elements of the many communication models and/or theories put forth by scholars and practitioners before and after 1948 can be traced. One obvious spin-off is the S-E-M-D-R approach (Seitel, 1984). This model outlines the main participants or players in the communication process: sender, encoding, message, decoding, and receiver. It echoes the elements put forth by Shannon and Weaver. Another is R-P-C-E (Guth & Marsh, 2009). The main steps here are research, planning, communication, and evaluation. This particular approach represents a slight variation of S-E-M-D-R in that it stresses the importance of communicators gaining a sense of history before launching any outreach effort and assessing the success of what they have attempted. Both approaches are taught in many introductory public relations classes throughout the country.

I will be alluding to the Shannon-Weaver model throughout this book and applying it to real world challenges. Additionally, in doing so, I will attempt to incorporate the reality of our internal conflicts into our plethora of communication deliberations. It has been more than sixty years since Shannon and Weaver introduced their communication model. Like a good song, it maintains a timeless viability. My concern today, however, is that basic elements within the model are being sidetracked or ignored. Specifically, I am referring to the steps of encoding, noise, and decoding. Are people taking the necessary time to try and communicate in a way that is understandable? If so, what is the state of noise or interference as compared with pre-Shannon-Weaver? How well are we trying to create messages that are understandable and/or relevant to our intended publics? How well are we as a people understanding or even trying to understand what messages are being sent to us? My premise is we are declining in each of these areas. As a result, we are not communicating as effectively as we should or need to. The mechanics of communication are beginning to erode or, at the very worst, not being followed. Between encoding and decoding, a growing imbalance is occuring in which more people, in their attempts to be heard, are focusing their energies more on determining how best to send messages than they are to receive them. My response is to not only share my concern with others but attempt to provide insight into the complexity of our communication efforts as a way of helping all of us recharge our communication batteries.

It is important to give a nod to another model of communication that was presented at the same time as what Shannon-Weaver put forth. This one is similar, yet with an important twist. It takes into account the results of an interaction between the message sender and the message receiver. Created by Harold Lasswell, a leading political scientist in the first two-thirds of the twentieth century, the steps of this model are as follows: sender-message-channel-receiver-effect (1948). While Lasswell's observation gives a nod to Shannon and Weaver, he also seems to acknowledge the diffusion theory and Rogers' five steps in innovative decisions triggered by receiving and sharing information. Lasswell said effective communication included a surveillance of the environment by the participating parties, a correlation of components within society, and a cultural transmission between generations. Thus, both drive home the importance of what results from an interaction between two people or entities.

REFERENCES

Baran, S. 2003. *Theories of mass communication*. New York: McGraw-Hill.

Barnard, C. 1938. *The functions of the executive*. Cambridge, MA: Harvard University Press.

Botan, C. H. & Hazleton, V. 2006. *Public Relations Theory II*. Mahway, NJ: Lawrence Erlbaum Associates Inc.

Brunner, B. R. 2008. Listening, communication & trust: Practitioners' perspectives of business/organizational relationships. *The International Journal of Listening 22*, 73–82.

Croteau, D. & Hoynes, W. 1997. *Industries and audiences: Media/society*. London: Pine Forge Press.

Davis, D. K. & Baron, S. J. 1952. *Mass communication and everyday life: A perspective on theories and effects*. Belmont: Wadsworth Publishing.

Grunig, J. E. & Hunt, T. 1984. *Managing public relations*. New York: Holt, Rinehart & Winston.

Grunig, J. E. & Hunt, T. 1994. *Public relations techniques*. Fort Worth, TX: Harcourt Brace College.

Guth, D. W. & Marsh, C. 2009. *Public relations: A values-driven approach*. New York: Pearson.

Huber, J. & Boyle, P. 2005. Roche's holistic approach to leadership communication: Clarifying communication roles and responsibilities for leaders. *Strategic Communication Management* October/November, vol. 9 (6), 18–21.

Katz, E. & Lazarsfeld, P. 1955. *Personal influence*. New York: The Free Press.

Katz, E. 1957. The two-step flow of communication: An up-to-date report on a hypothesis. *Public Opinion Quarterly 21*, (1), 61–78.

Kennan, W. R. & Hazleton, V. 2005. Internal public relations, social capital, and the role of effective organizational communication (311–340). In C. H. Botan & V. Hazleton, eds., *Public Relations Theory II*. New York: Lawrence Erlbaum Associates.

Lasswell, H. D. 1948. The structure and function of communication in society. In L. Bryson, ed., *The communication of ideas*. New York: Harper & Company.

Lowry, S. A. & DeFleur, M. L. 1995. *Milestones in mass communication research*. White Plains, NY: Longman Publishers.

Mayo, E. 1933. *The human problems of an industrial civilization*. New York: Macmillan.

McChesney, R. W. 2004. *The Problem of the Media: U.S. Communication Politics in the 21st Century*. New York: Monthly Review Press.

Mccombs, M. 2004. *Setting the agenda: The mass media and public opinion*. Malden, MA: Blackwell Publishing Inc.

Nelson, T., Clawson, R. & Oxley, Z. 1997. Media framing of a civil liberties conflict and its effect on television. *American Political Science Review 91* (3), 567–583.

Okay, Ayemir & Okay, Alya 2008. The Place of Theory in Public Relations Practice. *Public Relations: From Theory to Practice*, Tricia L. Hansen-Horn and Bonita Dostel Neff, eds. Boston: Allyn & Bacon.

Plati, C. 2005. Listen. *Social Policy 35*, 49–50

Rogers, E. M. 1995. *Diffusion of Innovations*. 4th ed. New York: Free Press.

Rogers, L. E. & Escudero, V. 2004. *Relational Communication: An Interactional Perspective to the Study of Process and Form*. London: Lawrence Erlbaum Associates.

Seitel, F. P. 1984. *The practice of public relations*. 2nd ed. Columbus, OH: Charles E. Merrill Publishing Co.

Smith, R. D. 2009. *Strategic planning for public relations*. New York: Routledge.

Straubhaar, J., LaRose, R., & Davenport, L. 2009. *Media now*. Belmont, CA: Wadsworth Cengage Learning.

Taylor, F. W. 1911. *The principles of scientific management*. New York: Harper Brothers.

Toroldahl, V. C. 2001. Two-step flow of communication model. *Public Opinion Quarterly 30* (4), 609–623.

Weaver, W. & Shannon, C. 1963. *The mathematical theory of communication*. University of Illinois Press.

4

A SEAT AT THE TABLE

The Importance of Business Literacy in Public Relations

Today, more than ever, public relations professions need to understand the business of business. This includes understanding how to interpret basic business tools such as a profit and loss statement. But it also includes understanding, at a deeper level, where and how public relations as a management function fits within an organization.

We start our exploration of this very important part of the profession with a reading from Dr. Shannon Bowen, who takes us into a deeper understanding of why organizations need public relations and the various specialized roles of the practice.

With this foundational knowledge of public relations as a management function, we'll proceed to explore important concepts of leadership and teamwork, two of the most important concepts and skills for the continuing success of public relations professionals. We'll also delve into the need to understand the organization's mission, vision, and values and how any public relations effort must tie directly to all three. This will lead us to a discussion of the role of public relations in shaping organizational policies.

An important discussion will be had on the various roles a public relations practitioner can and will play within the organization. The duties and responsibilities of the public relations professional change depending on whether he or she is a communication technician, a communication facilitator, or a problem-solving facilitator. Sometimes we fill the role of expert prescriber, so it's important for us to understand both the concept and role. We often find ourselves managing change. And each of these roles operates within a framework of mutual benefit.

Public relations scholars have long explored pathways to influence within an organization's decision-making body and process. To that end, we will discuss the concept of power within an organization, starting with Porter's "Five Forces" model (Porter 1979). While this was originally intended to assist businesses in building strategies to obtain or maintain market position, we can nonetheless take some lessons applicable to organizational influence, which we'll discuss in detail.

Similarly, business scholar Dr. Sydney Finkelstein discusses four dimensions of power: structural, ownership, expert, and prestige (Finkelstein 1992). As the power of top managers remains a key role in strategic decision making, we need to understand where we can accrue influence and best fit into the power relationships within an organization.

Directly related to this concept of power is the role of the *dominant coalition* within an organization. "The dominant coalition is the social network of individuals having the greatest influence on the selection of an organization's goals and strategies" (Finkelstein 1992, p. 506), and this is perhaps the best and most accessible path to a seat at the decision-making table.

"PUBLIC RELATIONS AS A MANAGEMENT FUNCTION"

By Shannon Bowen

In this chapter, we will expound on this management function, explaining why companies need public relations and how the public relations function is comprised of specialized roles.

FUNCTIONS OF MANAGEMENT

Organizations usually have several management functions to help them operate at their maximum capacity: research and development, finance, legal, human resources, marketing, and operations. Each of these functions is focused on its own contribution to the success of the organization. Public relations' unique function is to help the organization develop and maintain relationships with all of its key publics and stakeholders by effectively communicating with these groups. Communication is key in maintaining a satisfactory, long-term, trusting relationships with publics and stakeholders.

As described earlier, public relations provides the greatest value to an organization when it is used *strategically*. But what does this really mean? Think of it this way: In an effective organization, all the major functions are linked together by a common set of strategies that tie in to an overall vision of the future and an underlying set of values. Perhaps a computer company has as its vision, "To become the low cost provider of computing power to the developing world." From this vision, senior management develops a set of strategies that address areas like sourcing, the manufacturing footprint, marketing, design, human resource development, and product distribution. When all the elements are in sync, the company grows in a steady, profitable manner.

An important component of this set of strategies is a *communication* strategy. For example, it will be critical that all employees in the organization understand that strategy and their role in executing it. Many business failures are ultimately attributable to the confusion caused by poor communication. How many times have you received poor customer service from an employee in a restaurant or retail outlet? In all likelihood, the organization that employed this worker intended for him or her to deliver good service to you. But somewhere along the line the communication flow broke down. Perhaps the employee's direct supervisor or the store manager was not an effective communicator. Whatever the cause, the end result is a dissatisfied customer and diminished loyalty to the relationship.

In addition to reaching employees, a successful organization must also communicate effectively with its customers, its suppliers, and if it is a public company, its shareholders. For each key public, a set of messages must be developed as well as a plan to reach the public in the most efficient way. If the company is targeting young people with its message, a high-impact article in the *Wall Street Journal* is going to completely miss the mark for this strategic public. If instead the public is high net-worth investors, a clever YouTube video may also not be the right answer.

Although public relations has a unique and important function within organizations, it is often practiced differently depending on the role the top communicator plays within the organization, as we discuss next.

PUBLIC RELATIONS ROLES

In general, public relations professionals can be communication managers who organize and integrate communication activities, or they can be communication technicians who primarily write and construct messages. Research in this area led to the identification of four specific roles: the technician role and three types of communication managers.

Most practitioners begin their careers as **communication technicians.** This role requires executing strategies with the communication tactics of news releases, employee newsletters, position papers, media placements, Web site content, speeches, blogs, and social media messaging. Practitioners in this role are usually not involved in defining problems and developing solutions, but base their tactics on the technical skill of writing. The **expert prescriber** is similar to the role a doctor performs with a patient: He or she is an authority on a particular industry, problem, or type of public relations and is given the primary responsibility to handle this function as a consultant or with little input or participation by other senior management. The **communication facilitator** is a boundary spanner who listens to and brokers information between the organization and its key publics. According to Cutlip, Center, and Broom, the goal of this role is "to provide both management and publics the information they need for making decisions of mutual interest."[1] The **problem-solving facilitator** collaborates with other managers to define and solve problems. This role requires that the professional is a part of the dominant coalition of the organization and has access to other senior managers. The problem-solving facilitator helps other managers think through organizational problems using a public relations perspective.

Research on these four roles found that the communication technician role was distinct from the other three roles and that the latter three roles were highly correlated.[2] In other words, an expert prescriber was also likely to fulfill the role of the communication facilitator and the problem-solving facilitator. To resolve the lack of mutual exclusiveness in the latter three roles, they were combined into one role: **communication manager.** The dichotomy between the communication technician and the communication manager more accurately explained the responsibilities of public relations practitioners within organizations.

Research indicates that practitioners in a predominantly technician role spend the majority of their time writing, producing, and placing communication messages.[3] Typically, those in this role are creative and talented with language and images. Their capacity to create and produce messages with powerful imagery and evocative language is very important to the execution of public relations tactics. However, technicians rarely have a seat at the management table and do not have a voice in the strategy of the organization. Once the strategy is decided, the technician is brought in to execute the deliverables (or tactics) in the strategy.

The communication manager is involved in the strategic thinking of an organization and must be able to conduct research and measurement and share data that informs better decisions for managing relationships with key publics. The communications manager thinks strategically, which means he or she will be focused on the efforts of the organization that contribute to the mutually beneficial relationships that help an organization achieve its bottom-line goals. These efforts are not limited to communication strategies, but include monitoring an organization's external environment, scanning for issues that might impact the organization, and helping an organization adapt to the needs of its stakeholders.

A study on excellence in the practice of public relations found that one of the major predictors of excellence was whether the role of the top public relations executive was a manager role or a technician role.[4] Those in the management role were much more likely to have a positive impact on the organization's public relations practice. In order for corporate communication to function strategically, the executive in charge of the function must have a place at the decision-making table.

THE C-SUITE

Virtually all organizations are run by a senior leadership team that is responsible for setting strategy and carrying out the organization's vision. Although publicly traded companies, as well as nonprofit organizations, may be governed ultimately by a board of directors, this board looks to the chief executive and his or her senior team to operate the company on a day-to-day basis.

The key functions in an organization include finance, headed by a chief financial officer (CFO); legal, which reports to the General Counsel; human resources, led by a chief personnel officer (CPO); information services, reporting to the chief information officer (CIO); marketing, often led by a chief marketing officer (CMO); and communication, which reports to the chief communications officer (CCO). These functional areas serve the operations of the company, which in some cases report to a president or chief operating officer. In many cases the CEO also is president/COO (chief operating officer) of the organization.

Although organizational structures vary from company to company, these basic functional areas are usually present in the senior team. In some cases, the communication function is subordinated under another area, such as marketing, legal, or human resources. When this is the case, it becomes more difficult for the senior communications leader to play a meaningful role in the strategic decision-making process. The communication function brings to the senior team a different perspective from these other areas. The legal function is focused primarily on compliance with the law; marketing is focused primarily on the company's competitive position with the customer; human resources (HR) is focused almost exclusively on employee compensation and development issues. In other words, communication is the only function with eyes on *all* the publics inside and outside of the organization, and should be included in strategic decision making.

ROLE OF COMMUNICATION IN DECISION MAKING

One of the common denominators for officers in the C-suite is the imperative to make good decisions that affect their ability to positively contribute to the goals of the organization. The ability to make good decisions often defines a valuable manager. To make good decisions, managers need good information. By definition, good information helps reduce uncertainty in making a decision. Rarely is a decision made with utter certainty, but managers need enough information to have confidence that their decisions will result in positive consequences. This information is provided as data regarding these various functions: product testing, market research, legal precedents, and financial statements. Since public relations' role is to help the organization develop and maintain good relationships, it must provide data or information about how the organization can achieve this. This is how strategic public relations earns its seat at the executive table.

The communication function looks at all the stakeholders in the organization and uses a variety of tools and tactics to enhance relationships with these publics. At its best, the communication function uses research and monitoring methods to keep a finger on the pulse of internal and external perceptions of the organization. It uses a variety of communication channels to enhance the organization's reputation. And most importantly it provides strategic counsel to the organization's leaders to help the team make better decisions.

Some have suggested that the communication function serves or should serve as the *corporate conscience*. They contend that communication leaders have a uniquely objective perspective that allows them to weigh the sometimes conflicting needs of different publics and to help the organization make more balanced decisions. Although there is much truth to this perspective, we add that the conscience of the organization, its moral obligation to do the right thing, is one that is shared by all who lead it, including the CEO, the board, and the senior management team.

As the top communication professional, the CCO has an important responsibility to ensure that all key stakeholders are given due consideration when critical decisions are made. In that regard, the CCO acts as the voice for many who are not in the room when choices are made. He or she must keep in mind the minority shareholders, overlooked employee segments, nongovernmental organizations, special interest groups, elected officials, community leaders, and others who may be affected by the decision and who have influential roles in their respective areas.

By providing this overarching perspective, the CCO does much more than deliver tactical communication products. This strategic counsel is what CEOs and other leaders are increasingly seeking in all members of the senior team. By delivering it, the CCO enhances the value of the function and ensures ongoing participation in charting the future course for the company.

STRATEGY AND PROFIT MOTIVATION

Public relations as a profession is often thought of as nothing more than a simple set of tactics. Far too often those in the profession are portrayed in the media and in popular culture as a group of empty-headed party planners or deceptive flacks willing to say anything to get publicity for their clients. The tools of the trade—news releases, press conferences, media events, employee newsletters—are considered as discrete tactics that rarely if ever are driven by an underlying strategy.

This, like other stereotypes, is simply not supported by fact. As practiced by most large organizations and agencies, public relations is an integral part of overall strategy. Communication programs are developed based on extensive research to address specific business objectives with stated outcomes, target audiences, and key messages. The results of these efforts can be measured, both qualitatively and quantitatively.

Think of it this way: When an organization develops a strategic plan, it usually does so with a relatively small number of key executives. These leaders look at the company's strengths, organization, challenging issues, and potential problems that could arise. They consider the organization's financial position, its growth prospects, its competitive position, and the changing landscape in which it operates.

When they have considered all of these factors, they map out a strategy that will build on the company's current strengths, address its relative areas of weakness, take advantage of opportunities, and prepare for looming threats. They may decide, for example, to be the low-cost provider in their industry segment. Or they may decide to take advantage of their expertise in new product development, or to exploit their superior distribution network.

At some point, the strategy must be executed by a much larger, geographically dispersed network of employees. This is where the communication strategy becomes crucial. If a company has a long track record of fighting with its employees over issues like pay, benefits, union representation, child care programs, or workplace safety, it will be much more difficult to call upon them to launch a new initiative aimed at improving customer service.

In large measure, an important role of the communication function team is to help balance the needs of all publics—employees, investors, customers, communities—as the organization makes key decisions. For example, assume that a company is facing financial difficulties due to declining market share in one part of the United States. They are faced with the decision of closing a regional plant since that level of manufacturing capacity is no longer needed. In the past, they simply might have turned to the public relations executive and said, "We're closing the Milwaukee plant. Try to put a good face on it." An organization that views the communication function as a strategic partner instead would say,

> We've got too much manufacturing capacity; operations is recommending that we close Milwaukee. We'd like you to take a look at the impact this will have with our employees, customers, and the community there and help us measure this as we examine the alternatives. There may be another choice that won't be as painful to the organization.

Balancing the needs of publics is just one facet of the impact public relations can have on achieving organizational goals. It obviously depends on the organization, but in almost every case, effective communication programs help drive strategy from conception to delivery. Successful internal communication programs can improve the ability of supervisors to motivate employees and build pride in the organization. Creative external communication programs can improve customer relationships, build brand recognition, encourage investor interest in a publicly traded company, and increase the effectiveness of traditional advertising and marketing efforts. Community outreach programs can help local residents appreciate the impact of a company on the surrounding area in which it operates. The impact of well-conceived strategic communication programs can be profound, and many companies have already benefitted by recognizing this importance and building upon the strengths public relations brings to the table.

In 2007, the Arthur W. Page Society, a membership organization of chief communications officers at the largest corporations, agency CEOs, and leading academics, produced a white paper called *The Authentic Enterprise*.[5] The report examined the evolving role of the senior communications executive in 21st-century business. According to this report, the role of the CCO is much broader than it was even a few years ago. The CCO of today and tomorrow must assert leadership in the following:

- Defining and instilling company values
- Building and managing multistakeholder relationships
- Enabling the enterprise with "new media" skills and tools
- Building and managing trust[6]

The communication executive does not own these responsibilities alone. They are shared with other members of the leadership team. But the communication executive can and should take a lead role in ensuring that these responsibilities are fulfilled by the organization.

BUSINESS ACUMEN

Having a seat at the decision-making table is not a right, it is a privilege. Think of it this way: If you were planning an extended trip to Mexico, you would probably want to brush up on your Spanish before embarking. You could probably get by without speaking Spanish, but you would be far more effective and much better accepted by the locals if you at least made an attempt to speak their native language.

It is not so different at the management table. There the participants are speaking the language of business. They are talking about margin performance and market capitalization and earnings growth. They are discussing business strategy and market share and competitive position. If you are not conversant in this terminology and the thinking behind it, you are at a distinct disadvantage as a team member.

The Page Society surveyed chief executive officers at large multinational corporations to determine how these CEOs viewed the role of the chief communications officer in a successful executive team. According to results reported in the *Authentic Enterprise* white paper, the most important attribute of an ideal CCO or communications manager was detailed knowledge of the business.

> This is far and away the most critical quality for a top communications executive. All CEOs believe that their businesses are large and complex entities, and that their companies cannot be communicated well if their top communications executives do not intimately understand them.[7]

Why does this understanding matter to CEOs and other members of the C-suite? In order to build persuasive communication programs that advance the objectives of the organization, the communication team, especially those who lead it, must first understand these objectives. They must also understand the context in which the organization is pursuing the objectives—both the business context and in external forces.

It is extremely important to build credibility with the publics you are trying to reach. When a spokesperson for an organization cannot convey anything beyond what is contained in carefully scripted talking points, the recipient of the information loses trust and confidence in the individual. Many reporters are reluctant to speak to a media relations professional if they believe that individual does not really understand the organization or the industry in which it operates. Communication professionals who have a thorough understanding of business, government, community issues, and the specific organization they serve are simply more valuable contributors to the overall effort.

Gaining knowledge about an organization and its business objectives does not mean gaining the expertise needed to be CFO, General Counsel, or head of accounting. There are some fundamental areas that are important to understand, general principles that will help communications professionals speak more credibly and work as more valued team members.

For example, publicly traded, for-profit companies all operate within a set of guidelines, standard benchmarks, and mileposts that help their publics gain insight about their financial health, prospects for growth, and competitive position. These measures can provide a quick snapshot of an organization's health in the same way that temperature, pulse rate, and blood pressure readings can give a physician a measure of a patient's well-being.

MAINTAINING CORE COMPETENCIES

How does one gain much of the knowledge referenced earlier in addition to staying current with rapid changes? In some cases it makes sense to do so by pursuing additional educational opportunities. A number of courses are offered, for example, that teach basic finance for nonfinancial managers. Some communication professionals return to school to pursue a Master of Business Administration (MBA) or executive Master of Arts (MA).

Even without taking these steps, we can learn a great deal by simply following the business media, especially the *Wall Street Journal*; the major business magazines such as *Business Week*, *Fortune*, and *Forbes*; and broadcast media such as *CNBC* or *Fox Business*. The Internet also provides an endless source of information about individual companies and issues that affect all types of organizations and industries.

In the end, conversations with colleagues can provide incredible educational opportunities. The ability to listen, to ask insightful questions and to learn from others enables the communication professional to gain ample knowledge of the workings of business in general and a single company or organization more specifically. This knowledge, combined with an understanding of the industry and the ability to utilize communication expertise, provides a valuable combination of specialized abilities that can be used to benefit the entire organization.

CHAPTER SUMMARY

Research on best practices of public relations sponsored by the International Association of Business Communicators suggests that excellent public relations occurs when the senior communications officer is part of the dominant coalition and has a presence in the C-suite.[8] When the public relations function is relegated to a communication technician role, it is not fulfilling its unique management function.

As mentioned previously, this status must be earned. Public relations professionals gain that access by providing essential information and counsel necessary for making important decisions. When these communication professionals have the advanced knowledge of strategic public relations, including research and evaluation, and demonstrate business acumen, they should be a part of that management team. [...]

NOTES

1 Cutlip, Center, and Broom (2006).

2 Dozier and Broom (1995), pp. 3–26.

3 Broom and Dozier (1986), pp. 37–56.

4 Grunig, J. E. (1992).

5 The Authentic Enterprise (2007).

6 The Authentic Enterprise (2007), pp. 29–30.

7 The Authentic Enterprise (2007), p. 44.

8 Bowen et al. (2006).

REFERENCES

Bowen, S. A., Heath, R. L., Lee, J., Painter, G., Agraz, F. J., McKie, D., et al. (2006). The business of truth: A guide to ethical communication. San Francisco, CA: International Association of Business Communicators.

Broom, G. M., & Dozier, D. M. (1986). Advancement for public relations role models. *Public Relations Review, 12,* 37–56.

Cutlip, S., Center, A., & Broom, G. (2006). *Effective Public Relations* (9th ed.). Upper Saddle, NJ: Pearson Prentice Hall.

Dozier, D. A., & Broom, G. M. (1995). Evolution of the manager role in public relations practice. *Journal of Public Relations Research, 7,* 3–26.

Grunig, J. E. (Ed.). (1992). *Excellence in public relations and communication management.* Hillsdale, NJ: Lawrence Erlbaum Associates.

SECTION

CAREERS IN PUBLIC RELATIONS

The five chapters that comprise this section are all aimed at helping you understand the broad functional areas of public relations as well as what you need to do to prepare yourself for an internship and/or entry-level position.

Chapter 5 introduces all the things you need to consider as you prepare for your public relations career, starting with the range of work available to you and moving on to the various organizational roles you can and will play, and how much they are likely to pay. Personal qualifications and attitudes are discussed, as are the tools you'll need to master to find that internship or job.

Chapter 6 begins our tour of the functional areas of public relations with a discussion of the corporate, agency, and nonprofit worlds. It includes the various competencies expected of young professionals entering the business world.

In Chapter 7, we expand our exploration of public relations into the fast-growing health care and life science arena. We also look at your opportunities in education.

Government and public affairs, covered in Chapter 8, are not areas typically explored by young professionals as they prepare to enter the work force. We'll look here at the basic roles and responsibilities of public relations practitioners at the federal, state, and local levels of government. We'll look at lobbying, and we'll wrap up with an exploration of corporate public affairs and the role of public relations in election campaigns.

The final chapter in this section, Chapter 9, introduces you to the world of sports, entertainment, and travel and tourism public relations. A very popular area for many students, we'll take an in-depth look at sports and entertainment, including the *cult of celebrity* and how to get publicity for celebrities. We'll finish by exploring the increasingly popular world of travel and tourism, including the complete spectrum of responsibilities, from stimulating the public's interest in visiting a place to ensuring visitor safety.

5 PREPARING FOR PUBLIC RELATIONS JOBS

Reading 2.1: "Tools for Successful Job Searching" By Victor A. Bloomfield and Esam E. El-Fakahany

At the end of the day, we want to take all the knowledge, skills, and abilities acquired during the tenure of our postsecondary education and turn it into a job. While public relations continues to be a growing profession, the competition for the top jobs is still fairly significant.

While the reading for this chapter is aimed specifically at those seeking an academic career, it nonetheless provides great tools you can use in your internship and job search. We'll also discuss the range of work available to you with a public relations degree, along with the personal qualifications and attitudes required of those in the field.

We'll also explore organizational roles, salaries, and your value to the organization to help you begin the internship or job search with a realistic road map in hand. We'll talk about the value of internships as well as how to get the most out of those work experiences.

Personal branding is of the utmost importance in successful public relations careers, so we will discuss ways to edge out the competition and use your brand to your advantage. This will involve getting to know who you are as a future professional, what your passions are, and what you want other public relations professionals to know about you. Our discussions will include tips and tricks for creating great resumes, cover letters, business cards, and portfolios. We'll also talk about the importance of references and how to go about securing them.

We'll wrap this chapter up with a discussion of the growth of the profession, with a focus on the most recent trends so you'll better understand the landscape of the job market.

"TOOLS FOR SUCCESSFUL JOB SEARCHING"

By Victor A. Bloomfield and Esam E. El-Fakahany

CURRICULUM VITAE, RÉSUMÉ, AND COVER LETTER

Often there is confusion regarding the contents of a curriculum vitae and a résumé. Your curriculum vitae, literally a "journey of life," should contain a summary of your past and present educational and professional activities, starting from college graduation. There is no page limit. Most job openings in academia and research organizations require a vitae. A résumé, on the other hand, is a very brief document (usually a couple of pages) that succinctly states your career objectives and qualifications. This format is often required by industry. However, larger companies often ask for a full curriculum vitae. The cover letter that accompanies your curriculum vitae or résumé should highlight why you are applying for a particular job and why you believe you are a good fit for it.

CURRICULUM VITAE

While there is no set format for a curriculum vitae, the following elements should be included:

- Name, address for correspondence, contact phone numbers, e-mail address
- Education history: degrees and conferral dates, names of granting institutions, dissertation title, and name of advisor
- Postdoctoral training (if applicable): dates, name of advisor and institution, area of research
- Work experience, including teaching and research
- Current research interests and future plans
- Summary of research techniques and methods with which you have experience

- Grants and fellowships: type of funding (e.g., individual fellowship, research grant, contract), funding source, project title, your role (trainee, principal investigator, consultant, etc.), amount, and dates
- Honors and awards
- Membership in professional societies
- Professional service: participation on committees in and outside of your institution, leadership experience, consulting activities, editorial services (e.g., reviewing research manuscripts for a journal)
- Invited research presentations: dates, titles, and names of inviting institutions
- Publications: original-research papers, book chapters, and invited review articles; include full titles, authors' names as they appear in the publication, and complete citations
- Published conference abstracts: title, authors' names, dates and place of conference, and name of the conference or hosting organization

It is OK to include papers accepted for publication or under review. You can also mention important papers that are in their final stages of preparation, but no more than one or two, especially if you have only a few papers already published or in press. Listing one published paper and five in preparation strongly suggests procrastination and poor time management. For each such paper you do include, state the planned submission date and the name of the target journal.

Do not include the following information in your vitae:

- Age or date of birth
- Ethnicity, place of birth, nationality (unless the job advertisement specifies that only U.S. nationals or permanent residents are qualified)
- Social security number
- Political and religious preference
- Marital status or sexual orientation
- Hobbies

If you are applying for an academic job that emphasizes teaching you should include a detailed description of your teaching experience. We suggest you address the following points and provide necessary documentation when applicable.

- Subjects you have taught or are prepared to teach
- Courses or workshops you attended to enhance your teaching skills
- Experience with classroom diversity
- Technology teaching skills
- Sample syllabus, course assignments, and student assessments
- Student evaluation of your teaching

You may also be asked to submit a statement of your teaching philosophy, and some search committees may request a course syllabus with sample lesson plans. Submit these materials as an addendum to your vitae.

The following online resources provide guidelines, examples, and templates of curricula vitae:

- Department of Psychology, Hanover College, http://psych.hanover.edu/handbook/vita2.html
- About: Job Searching, http://jobsearch.about.com/od/cvsamples/

RÉSUMÉ

A résumé is structured to indicate briefly how your experience matches the requirements of a specific job. Thus, you should prioritize your skills and experiences to parallel the specific set of skills required. A résumé usually starts with your contact information. Use your home address if you do not want others to know you are applying for jobs and where you are applying. Describe your educational background, starting with undergraduate education. List names and locations of institutions, the types and dates of degrees obtained, and the names of your advisors (where applicable). List honors and awards, including educational and research fellowships. Include professional societies in which you are a member.

Chronologically summarize your training and employment history, including names of employers/trainers, dates, and addresses and phone numbers of contacts. Some recommend adding a very brief summary of your accomplishments in each place of employment or training. Alternatively, you can list individual skills followed by associated work or training experiences: for example, "Experience in molecular dynamics; applied computer-assisted modeling to determine the conformation of the thyroid hormone receptor" or "Drug design and synthesis; applied computational chemistry to design and synthesize polymers with potentially exceptional adhesive properties." Be informative yet succinct. Finally, list your publications and presentations at scientific conventions. Use guidelines similar to those discussed above in relation to writing a curriculum vitae. You could either include a list of references and contact information, or state that references are available upon request. For a diverse collection of résumés and templates, see http://jobsearch.about.com/od/sampleresumes/.

COVER LETTER

Employers usually require that you include a cover letter with your curriculum vitae or résumé when applying for a job. You should structure your cover letter to convey two main messages. First, why you are interested in this particular job and this particular employer. Second, what training and experience distinguishes you from other applicants. Don't reiterate everything that's stated in your vitae or résumé. Just summarize the highlights, using the position description as a guide to what's most important. A cover letter also gives you the opportunity to talk about your attitude in working with others, approach to problem solving, and future plans and aspirations.

Nowadays it is common to ask job hunters to submit their application materials online. This speeds up communication, cuts down cost, and saves a few trees. It would be wise to convert your documents to PDF, to avoid inadvertent changes in text and formatting. Formatting your application for multiple employers also makes it easy for you to apply for more job opportunities. Be careful, however. Make certain you are sending the right application material to a given employer. A quick click of the mouse on the wrong file attachment could be embarrassing. Also, follow up with a hard copy if your application includes material that requires special representation (e.g., glossy color illustrations).

OTHER DOCUMENTATION

If you are applying for an academic position you might be asked to submit a summary of your future research directions, teaching philosophy, or both. A teaching philosophy is a self-reflective statement of how you approach various aspects of teaching, both in terms of planning and execution. It is important to carefully connect your beliefs about effective teaching and the specific strategies you have used or plan to use to implement them. Address your thoughts and plans regarding all types of teaching you might be required to do at a given setting: small and large classes, labs, and so on. A University of Minnesota Web site on teacher training suggests several questions, some of which are paraphrased here, that you might ask yourself as you develop your teaching philosophy (http://www1.umn.edu/ohr/teachlearn/tutorials/philosophy/prompts.html):

- What do you think constitutes "good teaching" (i.e., teaching that promotes learning)?
- How does what you believe about good teaching enhance, resonate with or flow from the basic content, theory, and skills required for learning in your discipline?
- What does good teaching look like in practice?
- How would your students describe your teaching?
- How do you assess student learning?
- How do you assess your teaching effectiveness?
- How have you modified your teaching in response to student feedback? How do you put your philosophy of teaching into practice?
- What metaphor would best describe your teaching?

THE JOB INTERVIEW

A job interview is in some ways like a blind date. Its main purpose is to let your prospective employers know more about you than the contents of your vitae. You should also use the opportunity to learn more about the employer and the job. Ideally, the interview should have a significant positive impact on your final ranking as a job candidate. You have a vital proactive role in making this happen. A wise strategy is to prepare for the interview with the attitude that you might not be the top candidate going in. You must ensure that the process leaves your interviewers utterly impressed and fully aware of your unique strengths and skills. While it is always wise to recap the highlights of what is already stated in your vitae, your main goal is to add something more. Use the interview to convince the employer that you are even better than what your vitae or résumé says.

DO YOUR HOMEWORK

Much preparation is required to ensure a successful interview. You will need time to gather information and to practice, so start early.

You should collect information about both the department in which you hope to be hired and the organization of which it is a part. Learn about its research, lead scientists, and products, if any. With the advent of the Internet, this information is only a couple of mouse clicks away. There are also online resources that compare academic institutions and industrial firms. For example, the National Science Foundation provides information on academic institutions' level of research funding, number of graduate students and postdocs and their distribution by discipline, and sources of financial support (http://www.nsf.gov/statistics/). Ask your research advisor and other faculty what they know about the department and organization where you are interviewing. Past employees or trainees of the organization may provide reliable inside information, but bear in mind that some past employees may hold grudges against their former employer.

Collect similar information about other departments within the organization that could impact your job. Inquire about the possibility of meeting with key individuals in these departments during the interview. Give some thought before the interview to how you might collaborate with these individuals and how they might benefit from your expertise.

Familiarize yourself with the job responsibilities prior to the interview. Talk with people in your network who have similar positions in other organizations. Be as specific as possible in your information gathering, both in terms of the types of duties involved and the expected time distribution among them. Be aware that this distribution varies from one organization to another depending on its type, mission, size, history, and culture. You will certainly learn more during the interview, but you absolutely need to go in primed with initial knowledge.

Tabulate the anticipated job duties, then list ways in which you are qualified to perform each of them. More importantly, think of the special talents, education, and training that you believe will make you superior to others in performing each task. You must be ready to answer the central, albeit commonly unspoken, question "Why should we hire you?"

THE INITIAL PHONE INTERVIEW

Many employers start the process of candidate selection with a phone conversation. This might be a brief informal chat or a formal interview lasting up to an hour. In either case the phone interview serves to prescreen candidates for interest, professionalism, and personality. Some questions are usually crafted to find out if you are genuinely interested in this particular job. Others aim at assessing your general attitude, work ethic, and personality traits. This is your point of entry; come prepared. One obvious disadvantage of phone interviews is that you cannot observe the interviewer's body language, which in person would give you an indication of when to elaborate on a point or clarify an ambiguous answer. A video link, which is sometimes used, solves this problem. In both telephone and on-site interviews, interviewers are prohibited by EEOC regulations from asking any questions related to marital or parental status or sexual, political, or religious orientation. At the end of the phone interview you will normally be asked if you have questions about the job or the employer. Good questions reflect good preparation and candid interest rather than ignorance.

ANTICIPATING INTERVIEW QUESTIONS

Many books on interviewing skills contain lists of questions you should anticipate during a job interview. Some recommend memorizing canned answers. We do not endorse this strategy. A given question could be asked in many different ways, and in endless combinations with other questions. Pulling together an informative and coherent answer from bits and pieces of memorized information is difficult, if not impossible, especially given the stress of the situation.

On the other hand, it would be a grave mistake not to be aware of the general types of questions asked during job interviews, or not to contemplate general strategies for addressing them. This preparation will provide you with the right frame of mind to help you navigate from one question to the next with ease.

There are five general categories of job interview questions we believe you should anticipate. You cannot expect that these questions will be asked in any particular order or that the interviewers will exhaust one category before moving on to the next. The actual scenario will depend on the flow of the conversation and your answers to previous questions.

- What brought you here? What led you to pursue this particular job opportunity? Are you specifically interested in us or are you window-shopping?
- What transferable skills do you have? Why would hiring you be good for our organization? How do your skills and knowledge mesh with and complement existing expertise? How productive will you be, and how would your presence enhance productivity of the group as a whole?

- What are your personal traits and values? Would you get along with others? Would you lead, follow, or be in the way?
- Why should you be selected over others who have made it to the interview stage, particularly if you all look about equal based on your résumés/vitae?
- Are you affordable?

For the most part, these questions target information that is only partly evident from your vitae. The experiences documented there are important. The job interview is just as important. Do your best to complete the picture during the interview and leave your interviewers wowed. Sometimes you need to be clever and steer the conversation to adequately cover these issues.

Here are some general strategies for addressing the five types of interview question.

WHY DO YOU WANT TO WORK FOR OUR ORGANIZATION?

Employers naturally feel more positive about a candidate who has a clear reason for applying to their organization or organizations like theirs. On the one hand, they do not expect you to target only one place for employment. On the other hand, they will not be impressed to hear that you applied, somewhat randomly, to "a bunch of places."

Specifically summarize the information you have gathered that attracts you to this particular organization. Try to touch on as many of these attributes of the organization as are applicable:

- National/international reputation (in research, teaching, innovation, etc.) or high ranking (research funding, quality of graduate program). Cite specific rankings if you clearly remember this information.
- Reputation as an excellent work environment (without necessarily dropping names, explain how you have arrived at this conclusion).
- Core facilities (expensive equipment, well-equipped libraries, up-to-date teaching facilities). Impress them with your awareness of specifics (e.g., a linear particle accelerator, a unique telescope).

Your knowledge of the organization will have a strong positive psychological impact. In essence, it will make your interviewers feel they are talking to someone they could relate to as a colleague, and you will collect the dividends of your careful preparation.

WHY WOULD HIRING YOU BE GOOD FOR THE ORGANIZATION?

This question will almost always be asked, albeit indirectly. The best strategy in responding is to relate your specific skills and experiences to the job responsibilities and characteristics of the hiring organization. Summarize what you know about the job duties and how your educational and training background would enable you to excel in fulfilling them. State how you plan to prioritize and juggle all responsibilities and which ones you think you will enjoy the most. Also mention what you know about the skills and experiences of the current members of the hiring department and what makes your experience complementary. Show the interviewers how well your qualifications fit the future goals of the organization.

WHAT KIND OR A PERSON ARE YOU?

It is unlikely that you will be asked directly if you have certain negative personal traits, since the "right" answer would be obvious in every case. It would also be inappropriate for you to start listing your personal strengths unless you were specifically asked to do so. A clever way to indirectly deliver this important message is to include examples throughout the interview of how you handled a tough problem or dealt with a problem coworker. Let your interviewers draw their own conclusions about your attitude and personal values.

The following are personal traits and values you would like to convey—but only if you believe you have them.

- Self-motivation and enthusiasm about your work and career
- Creativity and resourcefulness
- A collaborative attitude and the ability to work well with others
- Respect for others and for diversity
- Maturity and responsibility
- Confidence but not arrogance
- Leadership
- Honesty and integrity

WHY SHOULD WE HIRE YOU RATHER THAN ONE OF THE OTHERS ON THE SHORT LIST?

Again, this question will likely be asked in an indirect manner. The question serves more than one purpose:

- To hear again why you consider yourself a good fit for the hiring organization.
- To test for a healthy balance of confidence and realism in self-assessment.
- To test for arrogance.

CAN WE AFFORD YOU?

This question translates: Could we win both the financial and the intellectual competition with other institutions or organizations interested in you? It is human nature to be highly motivated in pursuing a target only if it is deemed reachable. Most questions of this nature develop after the interviewers have decided that you are either the candidate of choice or the first runner-up. You might be asked informally in your first interview, however, if you are also considering other jobs. The most opportune time to ask you this question is during informal conversations over dinner. You are not obligated to answer this question. However, it would be advantageous and potentially profitable for you to let it be known in general terms whether you are considering other organizations and how far you are in the job-hunting process on the other fronts. You would also be wise to mention your general approach and the criteria you plan to use in making a decision. If it is the case, let the interviewers know that their organization stands a fair chance in winning you over, and why. Also indicate, as specifically as possible, how the interview has enhanced your interest in this particular opportunity. We advise you, however, to gracefully evade questions regarding salary expectations. The first interview is definitely the wrong venue for exchanging this type of information. According to Richard Bolles, author of *What Color Is Your Parachute?*, it is too early to talk money when the interview is still at the "who are you?" or "we like you" stages. Wait for the "we must have you" stage. It is too late, however, if you put off salary negotiations to the stage of "we got you."

Some interview questions might strike you as conniving and intended to catch you off guard and extract personal secrets. Other questions might seem open-ended or aimless and confusing. Do not become nervous or paranoid. Bear in mind that those who are interviewing you, if they come from the scientific or technical side of the organization, may not have been trained in professional interview strategies. An obvious exception is the case of interviewers from personnel/human resources departments. (Top industries also train their scientists in interviewing strategies.) Do your best to understand the aim of the question and do not hesitate to ask for clarification, since the vagueness of the question might not be as obvious to the interviewer as it is to you.

It is psychologically comforting to recognize that your interviewers are usually as nervous as you are during the interview. Experience, however, has taught them to hide their anxiety. One source of their worry is the possibility of losing you to another organization. They are also under significant stress as they are trying to find out as much about you as possible in order to make the right hiring decision. You are not on trial during an interview. Rather, you are supposed to be interviewing them as much as they are interviewing you.

MEETING WITH THE SEARCH COMMITTEE

You only have one chance to make a first, and hopefully positive, impression. Dress professionally. Do not use excessive makeup or cologne. Be on time. Treat everybody you deal with before or during the interview with courtesy. Never underestimate the impact of comments made off the cuff by office staff regarding the way you handled yourself. Offer a firm but not painful handshake. Maintain good eye contact but avoid gazing into anyone's eyes. Give everybody around the table their fair share of personal attention. Do not slouch or fidget in your seat. Do not speak too softly or too loudly. Do not mumble. Maintain a two-way conversation. Provide short but thoughtful answers to questions. The rule of thumb is that your answer to each question should not exceed a couple of minutes. Otherwise, you might notice some glazed eyes and infectious yawns around the table. If you feel that you need more time to elaborate on an important point, you can always stop at the two-minute mark and ask if they would like you to elaborate further. Sustain self-confidence but avoid arrogance. Do not talk negatively about people you have worked with, even if prompted. Maintain a sense of humor, without appearing to be a clown. Get your interviewers involved in the conversation. Ask if your points of view and plans fit with theirs and the culture of their organization. This approach has many advantages. First, it will indicate that you are a team player who cares about the opinion of others. Second, it will keep the atmosphere of the interview stimulating. Third, it will tell you if you are on the right track in answering questions. Fourth, it will give your audience an opportunity to ask for more elaboration on statements that could be misinterpreted. Fifth, and most importantly, it will indicate your interest in gathering information about their organization, which will be interpreted as genuine interest in this specific job opportunity.

Politely take the lead if you sense an uncomfortable silence. Give the lead back when your interviewers become more interactive. This requires finesse; you do not want to appear rude or controlling. Learn the art of polite interruption. Use body language to indicate when you are ready to provide an answer to a lengthy, seemingly endless, question. You cannot afford to let time run out without getting your fair share of time to sell yourself. Use your peripheral vision to read people's faces and body language throughout the interview. It will readily tell you how well you are doing. Nods are encouraging; rolling eyes are not. Yawns are a terrible sign of boredom. Take immediate corrective action to get things back on track. Listen carefully to what each person says. This will not only help you address questions appropriately, but will also tell you a lot about where your interviewers are coming from, their priorities, and the culture of the institution.

Toward the end of the interview you will undoubtedly be asked what questions you have for the committee. This is an opportunity not only to gather information you need to make an informed decision if offered the job, but also to serve many other purposes:

- The nature of your questions would reflect on your maturity and depth of thoughts.
- The main theme of questions you choose to ask, and their order, would indicate your priorities. For example, asking more than once about collegiality in the department/organization will clearly indicate that you value respect for others and team spirit.
- If you relate your questions to specific knowledge you have gathered about the hiring organization, you will leave a positive impression as someone who is there because of keen and serious interest in the position.

During this important segment of the interview, your questions must not be mostly about what the hiring organization has to offer you. Rather, you should ask questions related to the following points:

- Expectations. Questions in this area indicate that you are a responsible person who would like to know the specifics of what you are getting into. If you have not already done so, briefly comment on how you see yourself fitting into these roles.
- Roles and responsibilities of different members of the team and the hierarchy of the overall organization.
- Future goals of the organization and plans to get there. This points to your vision and potential leadership. Comment briefly on how your expertise and enthusiasm would be helpful in accomplishing the mission.
- Employee career development programs. Elaborate on your future goals and additional skills you would like to acquire to get there. This will strongly suggest that you value self-improvement and will likely not become stagnant and technologically outdated.

Again, do not inquire about salary or start-up funds. You are still in a very vulnerable position. Leave these questions for the time when the hiring authorities are certain that they want you. Only then do you have negotiating power. In fact, your interviewers, who are likely senior members of the hiring department, might be people you should avoid discussing salary with at all cost. In many instances, a salary offer for a junior but sought-after person is not too far from that of senior members of the group, due to changes in market value of new hires over the years.

REFERENCES AND RESOURCES

Bolles, Richard N. Updated annually. *What Color Is Your Parachute? A Practical Manual for Job-Hunters and Career-Changers.* Berkeley, CA: Ten Speed Press.

Burroughs Wellcome Fund and Howard Hughes Medical Institute. 2004. *Making the Right Moves: A Practical Guide to Scientific Management for Postdocs and New Faculty.* Research Triangle Park, NC: Burroughs Wellcome Fund; Chevy Chase, MD: Howard Hughes Medical Institute.

Chandlers, C. Ray, Lorne M. Wolfe, and Daniel E. L. Promislow. 2007. *The Chicago Guide to Landing a Job in Academic Biology.* Chicago: University of Chicago Press.

Robbins-Roth, Cynthia, ed. 1998. *Alternative Careers in Science: Leaving the Ivory Tower.* San Diego: Academic Press.

CHAPTER

6

FINDING YOUR FIT IN PUBLIC RELATIONS

Reading 2.2:
"Ethics, Leadership and Counseling Roles, and Moral Analysis"
By Shannon Bowen

In this chapter, we'll look at public relations from a functional perspective and take a look at critical competencies. Through the reading presented by Dr. Shannon Bowen, we'll start by taking a deeper dive into ethics and its role in organizational leadership, the role of public relations in decision making, and what constitutes moral analysis.

From there, we'll delve into the work of corporate public relations. We'll look at our role in managing the corporate reputation and relationships with the media, customers, employees, and investors. Further, we'll look at the role we play in marketing communications, and we'll explore other issues and responsibilities.

Then we'll turn our attention to the agency world, with its different pace, roles, and responsibilities. The structure of an agency is very different from the other functional areas of public relations, and it's important to know where you fit in at every step of your career should you take this professional path.

Many students who have hearts for causes find themselves in the nonprofit arena. As we look at the range of work available in this functional area of public relations, we'll focus on the two overarching responsibilities of the nonprofit public relations professional: fundraising and volunteering.

We'll round this chapter out with an in-depth exploration of the competencies expected of the public relations professional, regardless of functional area. We will almost always have responsibility for media relations and media management, internal communication, community relations, and other forms of external communications. We're also expected to be trusted counsel, consensus builder, and negotiator. We live and die based on our credibility, so we must know the proficiencies expected of us in each area.

"ETHICS, LEADERSHIP AND COUNSELING ROLES, AND MORAL ANALYSIS"

By Shannon Bowen

Beginning in the late 1990s and early 2000s, the role of ethics in business took on new meaning. Part of this was driven by business excesses that provoked the U.S. Congress to introduce and pass the Sarbanes-Oxley Act, an act in part driven by business' failure to conduct its business ethically. Public relations professionals have argued for years that ethical business practice is the key to establishing and maintaining relationships with key publics—whether they be stockholders or stakeholders. Ethical considerations in the practice of public relations have been on the forefront of public relations education for years, but because public relations practitioners had seats at the management table, they were not always taken seriously. This chapter introduces and examines ethics and its role in organizational leadership, the public relations professional's role in decision making, and what constitutes moral analysis.

ETHICS

Questions of how to guide behavior and differentiate between right and wrong have intrigued mankind for thousands of years. From the ancient philosophy of Plato and Aristotle to the Enlightenment of Hume, Kant, Mill, and the theoretical approach of Jesus, Buddha, Confucius, Mohammad, and Aquinas, to modern-day philosophy, we explore the questions of right versus wrong, good versus evil, light versus darkness. Singer averred, "Ethics is about how we ought to live."[1] Given Singer's simple definition of ethics, public relations ethics is about how we *ought* to communicate. Much goes on behind that communication for the public relations professional. Issues managers must identify potential problems, research must be conducted, and both problems and potential solutions must be defined in an ethical manner. Therefore, **ethics** can be defined for public relations as *how we ought to decide, manage, and communicate.*

ETHICS AND TRUST

Communication is *not* the ultimate goal of public relations. Our goal is building *relationships* through the use of ethical communication, listening, and strategic alliances, while collaboratively incorporating the ideas of others into organizational policy. We try to build both the means and fluency to create dialogue with our publics. If the purpose of public relations is to build relationships with publics, trust is an essential part of any ongoing relationship. Whether those publics are inside the organization, such as employees, management, administrative workers, or outside the organization, such as suppliers, distributors, retailers, consumers, communities, and governments, ethics is the linchpin that holds together relationships.

To understand the importance of ethics in relationships, imagine the following scenario. If you purchased a product from a company that advertises that it is the highest quality, you might feel exploited were you to find out that the organization sold the product knowing it was manufactured with defective components. Chances are, you would not want to have a long-term relationship with that organization, meaning that you would not become a repeat purchaser of their product. Through this simple example it becomes apparent that the ethics of an organization have a nebulous yet certain impact upon relationships with publics.

ETHICAL CULTURE

Ethics intersects with all levels of an organization. From the assembly line to middle management, ethics must play a role in decision making in order for an organization to be the most successful that it can possibly be. To be certain, much of the responsibility for ethics rests at the top of the organization, because without a vision and leadership from the top instilling the importance of ethics and the values of the organization, ethical behavior tends not to flourish. In other words, *public relations should act as the ethical conscience of the organization* by including the views of publics in decision making, but everyone in the organization must value ethics, most importantly the leaders of an organization.

This multipronged ethics function is what ethicists call "institutionalizing corporate conscience."[2] The ethics function must be a part not only of public relations but also of the corporate culture. This section will show you how to identify values, instill ethical values throughout the organization's culture, and consider and resolve ethical dilemmas.

SYSTEMS THEORY RATIONALE FOR ETHICS

Many entry and midlevel public relations professionals often wonder how they got into the territory of philosophy and ethical decision making. Allow us to explain the answer in terms of systems theory and you will soon understand why a working knowledge of moral philosophy is an absolute must for the public relations manager.

As a specialized field, public relations is in danger of being myopic or atomized. Laszlo explained that such specialized knowledge can form a barrier to entry and result in isolation, meaning that reality is viewed in fragments rather than holistically.[3] The contrasting view is **systems theory**, similar to biological systems or ecological systems, such as the body being comprised of a circulatory system, a nervous system, a digestive system, and so on. This organic view of systems was applied to society by the philosopher Luhmann to explain society as comprised of interdependent but somewhat autonomous social systems comprising the larger whole.[4] In organizational terms, an organization is a system comprised of smaller subsystems. Public relations is the function that communicates both among the subsystems of an organization and with its external environment, comprised of consumers and

1   Management (coordinates and directs all other activities)

2   Disposal (marketing and sales)

3   Production (manufacturing)

4   Adaptation (research and development)

5   Maintenance (physical surroundings)

An open system is interdependent with its environment; the environment supplies many necessities of production, including labor, and the information necessary to adjust to market trends and manage the organization effectively. Closed systems are rare, as most organizations have varying degrees of interdependence with their environments, and thus, varying degrees of openness.

FIGURE 6.1. The organizational subsystems within systems theory.

other publics. In systems theory terms, the **environment** is anything outside of the conceptual "boundary" of the organization. Those inside the boundary of the organization normally have a financial relationship with it; those in the environment can come and go across the boundary of the organization as consultants, for example, or they can exist wholly within the environment. Information freely crosses this boundary both as inputs to the organization when research is conducted, and output from the organization when it communicates with external publics.

In systems theory terms, public relations is a part of the management subsystem (see Figure 6.1). Similar to a nervous system, management is the brain of the organization and communication is used to coordinate its activities. The other subfunctions in a typical organization are occupied with their own areas of expertise, yet public relations must interact with them both in collecting data, identifying potential issues or problems, socializing new employees, and building organizational culture. These activities require an enormous amount of communication, listening, collaborative problem solving, and management skill. Public relations managers enact this internal communication function both across organizational subsystems, from management in a top-down fashion, and back to management when reporting on the internal state of affairs. Essentially, public relations acts as a communication conduit that facilitates the smooth internal operations of an organization.

Boundary Spanning and Counseling on Ethics

Public relations practitioners also span the boundary of an organization in maintaining relationships with publics in the external environment. When they cross this boundary in order to collect data, either formally or informally, they are known as "boundary spanners." Public relations managers scan the environment looking for messages of concern, and changing trends, thereby identifying problems with their publics within their industry. This process of monitoring the environment for potential issues of concern is called **environmental scanning**.[5]

By acting as boundary spanners, maintaining relationships with publics outside the organization, and collecting information from outside the organization through environmental scanning, the public relations function is perfectly situated to advise on ethical matters. Understanding the values of publics with whom the organization has relationships is enormously valuable because their ethical values can be represented in management decision making by the public relations manager. She or he is already familiar with the strategic publics in the environment of the organization, their desires, priorities, and issues with the organization. The relationships the public relations managers seek to build and maintain are a source of valuable input and information during ethical decision making because those publics can be consulted on issues important to them. The public relations manager is tasked with representing those views in top management decision-making sessions. No other organizational function is better suited to understand the needs and values of external publics than is the communication function. The legal department, no doubt, is well versed in understanding government and regulatory publics, but will have little knowledge of the values of publics extending beyond the legislative arena. Likewise, the marketing function will be knowledgeable about the values of consumers, but will have little knowledge of the values of the communities surrounding manufacturing sites. Only public relations fills this knowledge gap in terms of systems theory. By understanding and incorporating the values of publics, more ethically inclusive, diverse, pluralistic decisions can be made. These decisions result in a greater harmony between the organization and publics over time, fewer lawsuits, fewer disgruntled publics, fewer boycotts, and can prevent an expensive loss of reputation.

Ethics Counseling: Pros and Cons

One caveat to using a systems perspective to justify why public relations should act as an ethical counsel to senior management is that few public relations practitioners have actually studied ethics in a rigorous manner. Those who have studied ethics are likely to be more senior-level professionals, reporting to the top of their organization (normally the chief executive officer [CEO]), earning an above average salary, and the majority are male. This finding does not mean that younger, entry or mid-level and female professionals have less ethical reasoning ability, only that they have fewer chances in which to advise their organizations on ethical choices. Ethics study and training are encouraged as a way to remedy this problem; we will delve into moral deliberation shortly.

Is Public Relations in the Dominant Coalition?

A caveat of using public relations as an ethics counsel is that the public relations manager must have a seat at the senior management table in order to advise on these matters. The worldwide International Association of Business Communicators (IABC) study discussed later found that 30% of public relations professionals report directly to the CEO, 35% report one level below the CEO or have a dotted line (indirect) reporting relationship to the CEO. That finding is good news because it means that about 65% of public relations professionals worldwide have access to their CEOs and say they advise at least occasionally on ethical matters. However, the remaining 35% of public relations professionals reported no access to their senior management, meaning that they are not at the table when important ethical decisions are made, nor can they advise or give input on these decisions. Professionals oftentimes have little influence on policy, and the ethical decisions they must face are smaller in magnitude, often dealing with only technical aspects of the public relations function. For those, ethics study is often needed in order to advance their ascent into management.

PUBLIC RELATIONS: ETHICAL CONSCIENCE ADVISER

Should public relations advise on ethics? The public relations practitioners in a worldwide study reported the highest levels of agreement to these statements: "Ethical considerations are a vital part of executive decision-making" (mean 4.61 of 5.0 maximum) and "public relations practitioners should advise management on ethical matters" (mean 4.12 of 5.0 maximum).[6]

Clearly, there is agreement in the industry that management must consider ethics and that the role of ethical counsel falls on the shoulders of the public relations manager. Managers of communication need to consider two ethical roles and learn the basis of ethics to foster their ability to enact each. These two distinct ethical roles were first identified by the IABC *Business of Truth* study and also have been found in subsequent research.[7] The first role is managing the values inside the organization, including conducting ethics training. The second role is helping to analyze and deliberate ethical decisions alongside top management incorporating the knowledge of publics gained through boundary spanning. We will study each role thoroughly to prepare you for the many ethical challenges to be managed as a professional communicator.

Ethics Role 1: Organizational Values—The "Chicken Versus Egg" Dilemma

All organizations have a certain personality that scholars call organizational culture, and that culture also has values or values certain concepts above others.[8] Even a lack of concrete values *is* a value of sorts. Will organizations, particularly profit-seeking businesses, take a citizenship role in society? Or will they use society to achieve their own ends? These types of questions can help you discern the values of organizations. Looking specifically at an organization, you can assess the values it holds by reading mission statements,[9] policy documents,[10] codes of conduct, and ethics statements;[11] examining the statements of leaders[12] and its statements toward publics[13] and communities;[14] and the use of the organization's Web site as a dialogue building tool or simply as an advertisement.[15]

The reason we referred to a chicken and egg dilemma is because it is very difficult to determine whether ethical individuals drive ethical behavior or organizational culture drives ethical behavior, and which one comes first. Is it possible to turn an organization that holds little regard for ethics into an ethically exemplary one? Can ethics thrive in an organization in which the CEO cares little for such pursuits? What if the CEO exemplifies ethical leadership but takes over a historically unethical organization? Public relations is inextricably involved in questions such as these because it is responsible for communicating with internal publics, for helping to create and drive an enduring mission of the organization, and for helping foster an organizational culture that is responsible and includes the views of publics outside the organization.

The answer to the chicken and egg dilemma certainly varies according to organization and industry. However, ethicists generally hold that an organizational culture valuing ethics is more important than individuals.[16] Even the most ethically conscientious employee could not have prevented the bankruptcy of Enron.[17] One study exploring the chicken and egg dilemma concluded that an ethical organizational culture must be in place to foster and reward ethical decision making, lest an ethical individual making commendable decisions will not be encouraged or rewarded for doing so and thus cannot change the organizational culture toward the ethical.[18] In fact, organizations supportive of ethical decision making incorporate ethical debate and deliberation as a highly valued activity in their organizational culture.[19]

In order to act on this knowledge, the public relations function is responsible for helping to learn the values of the organization through conducting internal research and to refine and encourage the laudable values. Building an organizational culture focused on ethics takes much time and effort and a consistent commitment to communicate about not only the importance of organizational values but also the crucial role and decision making of ethical analyses. Contrary to what some managers believe, ethical decisions are not "easy" but come into play when many valid and competing views are present.[20] Building an organizational culture in which ethical debate is encouraged comes from delineating the organization's values, then reiterating those values consistently so that all employees know them, thereby encouraging the application of discussion of those values. Requiring ethics training at all levels of the organization is also necessary, as is insisting that leaders "walk the talk" to acting ethically and modeling ethical behavior.[21] They should evaluate employees based on their identification of ethical issues or conflicts, and reward ethical behavior. Ethics training is normally conducted by the public relations function or an internal relations specialist from the public relations department. It can take many forms, from online training to in-person retreats, to workbook modules, or discussion of case studies. The essential component of acting as a values manager for your organization is in identifying what the organization holds as a value and working to keep that concept central in all decisions throughout the organization.

For example, Johnson & Johnson's (J&J) well-publicized credo values the patients who use their products first, as their primary public. Therefore, patient-centered decisions dominate the decision-making framework when ethics are discussed at J&J. We can contrast that with an organization who values the bottom line above all other pursuits, a company who values innovation, one who values responsibility, or one who values respect. Different values of importance in the decision-making framework will result in a different organizational culture.

Through the communication outlets of internal relations such as employee Web sites, intranet, magazines, newspapers, blogs, and other communication channels, the public relations function can work to both understand the current values of internal publics and to instill the desired ethical values into the organizational culture. Ethical training programs could be used to educate employees of all levels on the values and ethical decision-making paradigm of the organization. It is important to have clarity and a vision of ethical values that is reinforced at all levels of the organization. Consistency, clarity, repetition, and a reward system in place for ethical decision making often speed the rate at which internal publics adapt to and adopt the values of the organization.[22]

Ethics Role 2: Ethical Counselor to Management

A second approach to ethics that public relations managers can take in an organization is to advise or counsel senior management on ethical decisions. The public relations counselor is perfectly situated in an organization to know the values of publics, and can help to incorporate those views of publics into strategic decisions and planning. She or he can discuss these issues with the CEO and advise him or her on how ethical decisions would impact the reputation of the organization.

Ethical decision-making paradigms and analyses are not usually necessary if there is a clear right and wrong in the situation. Ethical paradigms for moral analyses are helpful when there are two or more conflicting arguments of merit. If there are many "right" points of view then it is time to use an ethical decision-making paradigm to decide which decision alternative is most congruent with the values of the organization. The issues management team meetings can include the views of publics when the public relations professional is present to represent them in these meetings. Additionally, the public relations manager can use ethical decision-making frameworks to analyze the situation from multiple perspectives, and to advise the CEO and executive management on the morally desirable course of action.

Advising the CEO on ethics requires a number of qualifications on the part of the public relations manager. Training in ethics or moral philosophy is essential for ethical analysis, and that training can be academic or professional in nature. It is a must that the public relations manager understand the basics of moral reasoning in order to conduct thorough analyses and advise the CEO on ethics. The analysis of competing and valid decisions is a difficult, exceedingly complex pursuit. Having a public relations manager devoted to conducting these intensive analyses is sometimes the only way that a CEO can hear a countervailing point of view, as these executives are often surrounded by "yes men" who provide no critical analysis in the decision at hand. To prevent the sort of group think that often occurs in these situations, it is vital that the public relations executive be as objective as possible in the analyses of ethical decisions. Providing an objective ethical analysis to the CEO is one way that public relations adds value to the effectiveness of the organization.

NOTES

1 Singer (1994), p. 3.

2 Goodpaster (2007).

3 Laszlo (1996).

4 Luhmann (1984).

5 Stoffels (1994).

6 Bowen, Heath, Lee, Painter, Agraz, McKie, et al. (2006).

7 See Bowen, Heath, Lee, Painter, Agraz, McKie, et al. (2006); Bowen (2008), pp. 271–296.

8 Goodpaster (2007); Sims and Brinkman (2003), pp. 243–256.

9 Bowen and Broom (2005).

10 Seeger (1997).

11 Murphy (1998).

12 Kidder (2005).

13 Curtin and Boynton (2001).

14 Leeper (1996), pp. 163–179.

15 Bowen (2009b, August 7).

16 Sims (1994).

17 Sims and Brinkman (2003), pp. 243–256.

18 Bowen (2000).

19 Bowen (2004b), pp. 311–324.

20 Bowen (2002), pp. 270–283; Goldberg (1993).

21 Parks (1993).

22 Goodpaster (2007).

23 Bowen (2006), pp. 330–352.

REFERENCES

Baron, M. W. (1995). *Kantian ethics almost without apology*. Ithaca, NY: Cornell University Press.

Bowen, S. A. (2000). *Is ethical public relations ingrained in organizational culture or is it the domain of individual practitioners?* Paper presented at the meeting of the Public Relations Society of America Educators Academy, Communication Sciences Division, Miami, Florida.

Bowen, S. A. (2002). Elite executives in issues management: The role of ethical paradigms in decision making. *Journal of Public Affairs, 2,* 270–283.

Bowen, S. A. (2004b). Organizational factors encouraging ethical decision making: An exploration into the case of an exemplar. *Journal of Business Ethics, 52,* 311–324.

Bowen, S. A. (2006). Autonomy in communication: Inclusion in strategic management and ethical decision-making, a comparative case analysis. *Journal of Communication Management, 10,* 330–352.

Bowen, S. A. (2008). A state of neglect: Public relations as "corporate conscience" or ethics counsel. *Journal of Public Relations Research, 20*, 271–296.

Bowen, S. A. (2009b, August 7). *Applied ethics and stakeholder management on corporate websites.* Paper presented at the meeting of the Association for Education in Journalism and Mass Communication, Boston, MA.

Bowen, S. A. (2009c). What communication professionals tell us regarding dominant coalition access and gaining membership. *Journal of Applied Communication Research, 37*, 427–452.

Bowen, S. A., & Broom, G. M. (2005). Internal relations and employee communication. In S. M. Cutlip, A. H. Center & G. M. Broom (Eds.), *Effective public relations* (Chapter 9). Upper Saddle River, NJ: Pearson Prentice Hall.

Bowen, S. A., Heath, R. L., Lee, J., Painter, G., Agraz, F. J., McKie, D., et al. (2006). *The business of truth: A guide to ethical communication.* San Francisco, CA: International Association of Business Communicators.

Christians, C. G. (2008). Between the summits: Media ethics theory, education and literature. In J. M. Kittross (Ed.), *An ethics trajectory: Visions of media past, present and yet to come* (pp. 29–53). Urbana, IL: University of Illinois/the Institute of Communications Research.

Cooper, T. W. (2009). *The quintessential Christians: Judging his books by their covers and leitmotifs.* Paper presented at the Association for Education in Journalism and Mass Communication, Boston. Council of Public Relations Firms (2009). Resources section. Retrieved February 6, 2010, from http://www.prfirms.org

Curtin, P. A., & Boynton, L. A. (2001). Ethics in public relations: Theory and practice. In R. L. Heath (Ed.), *Handbook of public relations* (pp. 411–422). Thousand Oaks, CA: Sage.

De George, R. T. (2006). *Business ethics* (6th ed.). Upper Saddle River, NJ: Pearson Prentice Hall.

Elliott, D. (2007). Getting Mill right. *Journal of Mass Media Ethics, 22*, 100–112.

Goodpaster, K. E. (2007). *Conscience and corporate culture.* Malden, MA: Blackwell.

Kant, I. (1963). *Lectures on ethics* (L. Infield, Trans.). Indianapolis, IN: Hackett.

Kidder, R. M. (2005). *Moral courage: Taking action when your values are put to the test.* New York: HarperCollins.

Laszlo, E. (1996). *The systems view of the world: A holistic vision for our time.* Cresskill, NJ: Hampton Press.

Leeper, K. A. (1996). Public relations ethics and communitarianism: A preliminary investigation. *Public Relations Review, 22*, 163–179.

Luhmann, N. (1984). *Social systems* (J. Bednarz & D. Baecker, Trans.). Stanford, CA: Stanford University Press.

Martinson, D. L. (1994). Enlightened self-interest fails as an ethical baseline in public relations. *Journal of Mass Media Ethics, 9*, 100–108.

Murphy, P. E. (1998). *Eighty exemplary ethics statements.* Notre Dame, IN: University of Notre Dame Press.

Parks, S. D. (1993). Professional ethics, moral courage, and the limits of personal virtue. In B. Darling-Smith (Ed.), *Can virtue be taught?* Notre Dame, IN: University of Notre Dame Press.

Paton, H. J. (1967). *The categorical imperative: A study in Kant's moral philosophy.* New York: Harper & Row.

Ross, W. D. (2002). *The right and the good.* Oxford: Clarendon Press.

Seeger, M. W. (1997). *Ethics and organizational communication.* Cresskill, NJ: Hampton Press.

Sims, R. R. (1994). *Ethics and organizational decision making: A call for renewal.* Westport, CT: Quorum.

Sims, R. R., & Brinkman, J. (2003). Enron ethics (or, culture matters more than codes). *Journal of Business Ethics, 45*, 243–256.

Singer, P. (1994). Introduction. *In Ethics* (pp. 3–13). Oxford: Oxford University Press.

Stoffels, J. D. (1994). *Strategic issues management: A comprehensive guide to environmental scanning.* Milwaukee, WI: Pergamon.

Wright, D. K. (1985). Can age predict the moral values of public relations practitioners? *Public Relations Review, 11*, 51–60.

CHAPTER

EXAMINING TOP CAREERS IN PUBLIC RELATIONS

Health Care & Life Sciences and Education

Reading 2.3:
"Health as
Profit: Public
Relations in Health
Communication"
By Jeffrey
Springston and
Ruth Lariscy

In the last chapter, we looked at the "big three" functional areas of public relations: corporate, agency, and nonprofit. Along with that, we explored the basic competencies expected of today's professional.

But one of the fastest-growing areas of public relations is in health care and life sciences. We'll look at the range of work available in this area, particularly in hospitals and their marketing communications arms. As the authors of this chapter's reading explain, there is a strong need for a "broadly based, issues-oriented public relations strategic function."

We'll explore other lesser-known public relations career fields. Associations need professional communicators, as do social service organizations and advocacy groups.

The final area we'll explore in this chapter is education. Colleges and universities have very sophisticated communications departments. Most school districts have at least one professional communicator on staff. Many elementary and secondary schools also employ public relations practitioners. The challenges at all three levels are in some ways similar to those in the other functional areas, but each has its unique challenges, as you'll see through our discussion.

"HEALTH AS PROFIT: PUBLIC RELATIONS IN HEALTH COMMUNICATION"

By Jeffrey Springston and Ruth Lariscy

Public relations is a powerful force in society and an essential component of our economy. This is particularly evident in the $400,000 billion plus health care industry where most medical services—from physician care to hospital stays, to pharmaceutical sales and health insurance—function in a highly competitive environment. In the wide breadth of for-profit health organizations—HMOs, hospitals, nursing homes, pharmaceutical companies, medical clinics, and health-science research centers to name a few—strong need exists for the broadly based, issues-oriented public relations strategic function. While public relations is vital to both for-profit and not-for-profit health care organizations, this [article] focuses on the role of advocacy messages and campaigns in the for-profit sector of health communication.

DEFINING AND DISTINGUISHING

Before examining the role of for-profit health care public relations, it is important to first clarify terms. Much understandable confusion exists regarding how public relations, marketing, and advertising are similar and how they differ. These terms are often referred to synonymously, and indeed there are many situations in which they overlap, especially in the for-profit sector. However, there are important fundamental differences between the three functions.

Under ideal circumstances, both public relations and marketing are part of an organization's strategic management. Both functions deal with messages and media, public opinion, and segmentation of audiences or "publics." A primary distinction between marketing and public relations, however, is in how publics come to exist. In marketing, publics are typically targeted and sought in order to achieve the goal of selling the organization's products, services, or point of view. In public relations, creation of a public is issue driven; publics often come into existence whether an organization wants them to or not. Public relations scholars generally view the population as a collection of individuals whose inclusion in a particular public is driven by a common interest, need, or concern (e.g., Seitel, 1993; Wilcox, Ault, Agee, & Cameron, 2000).

There are certainly instances and environments, notably the for-profit sector, where public relations and marketing functions are highly complementary. Given marketing's focus on selling the organization, it is clearly associated with customer service, product development, distribution, packaging, pricing, and retailing. Effective public relations, in part, allows the marketing function to accomplish its objectives by providing an environment that is free of conflict, discord, and antagonism. Public relations focuses on developing productive relationships with a wide variety of groups including the community, elected officials, government regulators, employees, investors, and the media. It is important to note that these groups may be, but most often are not, consumers who would be targets for the organization's marketing objectives. Rather, public relations manages relationships with important groups (publics) who have the ability to impact the organization through public opinion often ultimately resulting in regulation.

A second important distinction between the two functions is philosophical. Hutton (2001) noted that there is a different mind-set between the two functions. The marketing mind-set tends to be more aggressive, competitive, hyperbolic, and focused on selling. The public relations mind-set tends to be more conciliatory and concerned with fostering mutual understanding and cordial relations with important publics (audiences). Philosophically, the public relations mind-set seeks to not only adjust public attitudes and behavior to the benefit of the organization, but also to facilitate change in the organization to benefit the public. The exception to this conciliatory posture is when an organization is under what it considers unwarranted attacks by an outside group(s). Not all groups are interested in negotiating a mutually beneficial position. In such cases, an organization's public relations efforts will aggressively fight for its position.

Whereas these are important differences between public relations and marketing, the two functions share many of the same tools, which contributes to the confusion surrounding their functions. For example, the campaign steps are essentially the same. They include:

- Researching the situation to determine opportunities or threats
- Analyzing and segmenting publics
- Establishing campaign goals and objectives
- Developing message strategies and tactics
- Selecting channels of communication
- Implementing, maintaining, and evaluating the campaign

Another specific tool used by both marketing and public relations is advertising. Advertising is the purchase of media space or time to promote a product, service, or viewpoint. Unlike publicity, which refers to third-party media coverage such as news stories about a company and its products or services, advertising content and presentation are directly controlled by the sponsoring organization. Whereas marketing is more likely to use advertising to achieve its goals, and public relations is more likely to seek publicity to achieve its aims, this is not always the case. For example, when a pharmaceutical company uses advertising to promote the sales of a particular drug, it is clearly a marketing effort. On the other hand, when that same company produces advertising that touts its philanthropic efforts in a community, it is a public relations effort.

In order to maximize benefit, marketing, public relations, and advertising need to work in concert with one another. As Heath (1994) and others pointed out, an organization needs to speak with one "voice." This [article] focuses on public relations theory and practice rather than marketing, though areas where the two should integrate are addressed.

USES OF PUBLIC RELATIONS IN HEALTH COMMUNICATION

Health issues and the financial burden of health care remain of paramount interest and importance to an exceedingly high percentage of Americans. Compared to many other issues, including elections of public officials, health overshadows even those that may receive more time and attention from media news and information reports. As a result of this heightened interest, for-profit health organizations have considerable stake in the manner health issues are presented and discussed. Public relations is at the center of this critically important presentation and discussion of health issues via the media.

Some public relations practices have an established place in health organizations, most notably hospitals. Brochures, newsletters and health fairs are standard productions for hospital public relations departments. The 1990s saw dramatic new challenges facing health care businesses and practices; arguably, health care became *the* issue of the 1990s, driven by two increasingly critical problems: cost and access that necessitated introduction of both increased and innovative public relations strategies to meet them (Cutlip, Center, & Broom 2000).

Public relations activities in for-profit health practices and organizations may be classified according to their goals and may include the following: (1) protect corporate image and build brand and name equity for the corporate client; (2) create a positive public opinion climate for health issues, products, and companies in order to win regulatory and legislative approvals; (3) reduce costs and save time for health care providers and payers by reducing managed care pay outs and by educating and training consumers regarding preventive health practices, symptoms, and treatment options; and (4) assist the marketing function by increasing sales for prescription and over-the-counter drugs and by attracting patients to a particular health care provider, facility, or company. There are numerous examples that illustrate each category.

PROTECT CORPORATE IMAGE AND BUILD BRAND EQUITY

There are several traditional ways through which corporations build equity in their name and protect and enhance their corporate image. Whereas the following is not an exhaustive list, each of the examples illustrates opportunities for the organization to receive positive news coverage.

Change in Corporate Structure. Whether there is a corporate merger, buyout, or simpler reorganization, such business issues provide opportunity to enhance corporate image. One such example is the purchase of San Diego-based S. D. Dura Pharmaceuticals in 2000 for $1.8 billion by the Irish drugmaking giant Elan Corporation (*San Diego Union Tribune*, 2000). The purchase provided numerous chances for Elan to publicize the economic benefits that will accrue to San Diego County as a result of the purchase, as well as the enhanced ability to market new pharmaceuticals resulting from the combination of resources. While it is difficult to measure the value of such publicity, the use of positively framed news stories to build brand equity and enhance image is a widely practiced public relations technique.

Introduction of New Technique or Product. Association of a corporate name with a life-saving technique or product is another invaluable method for image enhancement and equity development. One Chicago-based clinic is often cited in news stories as a leader in a technique, called preimplantation genetics diagnosis, that is increasingly being used to detect genetic diseases and prevent them prior to in vitro fertilization (*Chicago Sun Times*, 2000). Recurring use of the name of the clinic in stories about the procedure helps build strong brand identity. Similarly, when a corporation is linked with a prestigious research institution to introduce its product, a halo effect may embrace both the corporation and the research institution. Such is the case in the release of a new cancer treatment, by the Moffitt Cancer Center in Tampa and Yale University (*St. Petersburg Times*, 2000). Association of the treatment center with research is a positive element of image enhancement for health care facilities.

Establishment of the Corporate Brand as a Credible Information Source on Industry Issues. Placement of highly competent individuals from an organization as expert sources in news stories is a long-practiced technique of corporate image building. Thus, Phizer Inc. is one beneficiary of the release of a World Health Organization (WHO) report that predicts that by the year 2020 up to 40% of all deaths will be related to cardiovascular diseases (BusinessWorld, 2000). How? Consider this news story lead: "People should be more conscious of their heart nowadays. Clinical studies show that cases of cardiovascular disease (CVD) continue to increase, said pharmaceutical firm Phizer Inc." While the article text subsequently explains that the study was conducted by the Cardiology Division of the WHO Health Department, Phizer is repeatedly cited as the spokesperson.

Of equally positive benefit is when a corporation becomes an information source for consumers on how consumers can maximize benefits from the corporation's products and services. A classic example of this is found in this story, from a London newspaper, that explains how consumers can lower their health insurance costs (Why Only the Best Is Good Enough, 2000). The sources for this information are the health insurance providers themselves. They are positively framed as providers of useful information for consumers—in this case, they are advising customers how to save money on the product they sell.

Repair and Restore Industry Image. Finally, the managed care industry itself is struggling with a public backlash against HMOs and is relying heavily on public relations to improve its beleaguered image (Miller, 2000). A group of 22 of the largest managed-care companies in the United States formed the Coalition for Affordable Quality Healthcare in early 2000 to mount a massive public relations campaign on behalf of the entire industry (*USA Today*, 2000). The Coalition has spent over $9 million on television ads designed to improve the image of managed care health providers. Such efforts, Although designed to improve the overall industry image, powerfully reflect on the individual corporate images of the sponsors and enhance brand equity for all participating organizations.

CREATE POSITIVE PUBLIC OPINION CLIMATE TO WIN REGULATORY AND LEGISLATIVE APPROVALS

The image of the managed care industry is a critical component driving health reform legislation across the nation (Easterbrook, 2000). According to the National Conference of State Legislatures, medical issues dominated legislative agendas in 1999, with 1,400 health care bills passed in state capitals; more than 1,600 hundred such bills were under consideration during the first quarter of 2000 alone (Cohen, 2000). At the national level, private industry lobbying has largely assumed leadership of health care reform, placing industry corporate reputation management at the center of the national health care debate (Pear, 2000). At both state and federal levels, legislators are debating initiatives that would place heavier regulation on managed care and make it easier for patients and doctors to take legal action against managed health care plans.

Public relations ammunition was deployed during the summer 1999, when the Senate was battling over managed care reform (*Politics & Polity*, 1999). The American Medical Association ran a full-page ad in *USA Today* that asked "Criminals all have rights. Why don't patients?" Text in the ad elaborated: "any legislation should give physicians the final say when it comes to deciding what's medically necessary ... give patients the right to a fair and timely appeal of denials and hold health plans and insurance companies accountable for their actions" (*USA Today*, 1999). The AMA ran other ads in specific states urging readers to contact their representatives and urge them to vote for "patients' rights" (*Philadelphia Inquirer*, 1999). Such campaigns have become common since the success of the "Harry and Louise" ads that helped defeat the 1994 Clinton health reforms (*Politics & Polity*, 1999).

Individual health care plans also report increasing their public relations efforts with several key publics in order to enhance legislative approvals and prevent unwanted regulatory acts. United HealthCare produces statistical reports showing its program's results, including patient recovery times, and publicizes these outcomes to patients, doctors, and media; Humana developed an Internet campaign that promotes success stories of patients and corporate goals; Blue Cross/Blue Shield of Florida enlisted support of patients and doctors to publicize positive aspects of their services to legislators, patients, and providers (*Politics & Polity*, 1999).

REDUCE COSTS AND SAVE TIME

When for-profit health organizations become an active voice in educating potential consumers about symptoms of illnesses and how consumers can both recognize and initially treat certain health conditions, the organizations become an important information source that benefits three groups: consumers, health care providers, and themselves. Consumers benefit by being informed—that aspirin may help reduce the severity of heart attack, for example. Health care providers benefit by saving time and reducing costs—the more consumers know on their own, the less time health professionals spend educating them; the more consumers know to self-medicate to lessen the severity of a condition, the more economical the treatment of the individual can be. And the corporations benefit by increasing sales of their products, by enhancing their own credibility as they are seen as a valuable source of health information, and thus assisting development of image enhancement and development of greater brand equity.

Numerous examples abound. Information on how to quit smoking is provided in advertising and news stories about nicotine-substitute products. Symptoms of osteoporosis are documented in advertisements for treatment drugs. And recognition of sometimes obscure conditions—like glucose intolerance—may be distributed by the publisher of a cookbook that contains exclusively gluten-free recipes (Tips Help Diagnose, Treat Celiac Disease, 2000). Symptoms of osteoarthritis are widely discussed in news reports about the possibility that a gelatin drink might reduce arthritis pain (Gelatin Drink May Reduce Arthritis Pain, 2000). Knox NutraJoint is manufactured by Nabisco, which commissioned the study. The more a for-profit health organization— be it a producer or service provider—can assist in the education of consumers, the greater the benefits for all parties.

ASSIST THE MARKETING FUNCTION: PROMOTION OF SALES AND SERVICE

Prescription Drugs. While much advertising is designed to introduce new prescription drugs to consumers, press releases that accomplish the same purpose are increasingly important. Unlike advertisements, which are constrained by time (in broadcast) and length (in print), press releases allow for development; patients can read or listen in depth about how to recognize symptoms of a particular condition, about the benefits of a new drug treatment, or about the long-terms consequences of a discovery.

When SmithKline Beecham achieved a breakthrough in developing an antimalaria vaccine, for example, the news value of the story was tremendous. "Malaria, 'Mother of Fevers,' Disease: It Kills Millions Annually. But Promising Results Last Year Have Raised Scientists' Hopes for Finding A Vaccine," is a typical headline reflecting the importance of both the drug and what its development foretells (*Los Angeles Times*, 2000). For years, SmithKline Beecham had regarded its efforts as "an act of charity," given the low interest in what was regarded as a third world disease. But when a link was established between the malaria vaccine and a potential AIDS vaccine, strong interest was rejuvenated, resulting in the breakthrough that has catapulted SmithKline into the media spotlight.

Supplements, Nutriceuticals, and Over-the-Counter (OTC) Drugs. The last decade of the 20th century witnessed dramatic growth in interest in nonprescription remedies, preventive supplements, and alternative medical practices. Although there is no specific count of the number of public relations agencies that manage OTC health product clients, there are ample indications that both the number of firms doing such product-related public relations and the number of health-based clients for agencies already possessing consumer health industry clients are increasing. Since passage of the Dietary Supplement Health and Education Act in 1994, which eased restrictions on dietary supplements and allows manufacturers to make broader health benefits claims, an explosion in the newly created "nutriceutical" and "cosmeceutical" markets occurred (Krantz & Bjerklie, 1997). Nutriceuticals, the blending of nutrients and pharmaceuticals, and cosmeceuticals, the blending of cosmetics and pharmaceuticals, are becoming a major force in the marketplace. The American Pharmaceutical Association estimates that over 80% of pharmacies sell these products, and multibillion-dollar corporations like Monsanto, Dupont, and Procter & Gamble are spending major resources to discover new ways to enhance the health benefits of foods and supplements (Zeisel, 1999).

The popularity of health discussions has proved a bonanza for publicists placing spokespeople for their products and companies on television and radio talk shows, like Oprah Winfrey, and for successfully pitching program segments for infotainment programs, like 20/20. Many of these nontraditional products and practices have been introduced and publicized through effective publicity from public relations. News releases in print, segments on national television news broadcast shows, and talk show appearances by advocates have all been utilized by OTC proponents who advance that, among other things, consumers should be in control of their own treatment plans.

The keys to gaining long-term success in any public relations and marketing campaign are to be completely truthful and to not oversell the product. The OTC/nutriceutical market is no exception. In addition, research by the International Food Information Council demonstrates that consumers perceive health claims on a label to be propaganda from the company, whereas media publicity and nutritional labeling are more believable (Wellner, 1998). Research conducted by reputable scientists is particularly credible, such as the study confirming that glucosamine is an effective treatment for osteoarthritis (Reginster et al., 2001). Many other studies such as those sponsored by the National Institutes of Health investigating the role foods and extracts play in reducing cancer, heart disease, osteoporosis and a variety of other diseases will further fuel the interest in these products (Nelson, 1999).

Physicians. Public relations has become increasingly important to physicians as they seek improved bargaining positions for managed care contracting (*Healthcare PR and Marketing News,* 2000). Whether a press release announces a new piece of advanced technology their practice is using, cites a physician-expert for information on a particular medical condition, or emphasizes a patient human-interest angle in a story, when physicians appear in such positive news stories they enhance their personal reputations and thus their bargaining power.

Physician Web sites are used to promote practices (MCIC Releases 'Health Care and the Internet, 2000). In addition to the kinds of traditional information for releases just mentioned, Web sites are well-suited for publicizing medical research in which the physician is involved; using graphics to illustrate medical procedures employed in the physician's practice; and providing interactive opportunities for patients' questions and comments. There is some evidence that public relations services for physicians will increase in importance as primary care physicians (PCPs) are asked to assume greater responsibilities for their patient populations, particularly by shifting focus from treating sickness to preventing it and promoting health (Tselikis, 1999).

Managed care plans also utilize public relations to market themselves to consumers (Managed Care Efforts That Resonate with Consumers, 2000). Many HMOs regularly practice positioning, for example, connecting with consumers regarding a wide array of issues, before the consumer is a patient needing care. Such communication involves letting members know of pending legislation that may change how their health care is delivered; may keep them informed of any mergers, closures, or reductions in services that may affect them; and may keep them current on what they need to know to manage their own health care, like when there are periods of open enrollment and how to manage a planned health care issue like childbirth.

The Washington, DC-based American Association of Health Plans (AAHP), an association representing health plans, reports spending more than $2 million on public relations efforts in 1999–2000 to enhance the image of managed care generally. Their efforts go beyond launching television and print ads and include conducting press tours and organizing debates on federal and state mandates that would impact managed care firms (Volz, 2000). Another coalition of health care agencies, the Washington, DC-based Health Care Leadership Council, developed a public relations campaign, "Reality 98," to produce a flood of faxes to media whenever a politician or candidate made a misstatement about the managed care industry. There are a number of promising theories that have been applied to public relations but have not been widely applied in health communication. This [article] discusses several of these models and theories.

THEORY AND MODELS

Theory allows health communicators to identify key audiences and understand influences that promote knowledge and mold attitudes and behavior. As Lapinski and Witte (1998) pointed out, an essential element of any effective health communication campaign is that it be guided by theory. These authors argued that theories must be applied that emphasize the interactive nature of communication, are practical and feasible, allow application to unique audiences, and avoid focusing on the individual to the exclusion of social and environmental factors.

PROTECT CORPORATE IMAGE AND BUILD BRAND EQUITY

Druckmiller (1993) argued that a corporate brand is a company's reputation, and this brand reflects the character of the leaders in the organization and their relationship with all stakeholders to the company. He further contended that corporate reputation carries a heavier load than product brands, necessitating continual attention. Any organization can experience threats and crisis events that endanger the reputation, profitability, and, in extreme cases, survival of the organization. The best way to minimize the damage of a crisis is to avoid one in the first place. To accomplish crisis avoidance, an organization must conduct an ongoing program of issues management, which includes scanning the environment, researching potential issues discovered from the scanning process, urging organizational change when necessary, and developing communication strategies focused on preventing the crisis. Although issues management can be successful in warding off many potential problems, crises can and often do engulf even the most vigilant organizations. Therefore, all health care organizations should have a crisis management plan in place in case such an event transpires.

Message Action Plans. Werner (1990) developed a practical crisis system he termed a message action plan or MAP. He argued that a well-planned MAP can overcome many of the inevitable problems that occur during times of crises that can hinder effective communication to the organization's key publics. These problems include emotion, confusion, confidentiality issues, and stress. The key elements of a MAP are knowing key publics with which to regularly communicate; what message elements must be present; what communication techniques are to be used; who is responsible for various duties (e.g., spokespersons, data gathering); how messages and activities should be timed; and how postcrisis evaluations, of both the MAP's effectiveness and conditions that led to the crisis, should be conducted.

Model of Crisis Types. Handling the logistics of a MAP can be worked out well in advance of any crisis. Specific strategies and message components often cannot be anticipated but must be carefully tailored to each unique situation. It is here where public relations models and theories can prove useful to the organizational crisis team. The first step is to identify what type of crisis has occurred. Coombs (1995) developed a two-by-two matrix of crisis types by distinguishing between intentional and unintentional crises and internal versus external ones:

- Accidents (unintentional and internal): Example: A Florida surgeon amputates the wrong limb (Palosky, 1995).
- Transgressions (intentional and internal): Example: An Arkansas-based nursing home company is accused of defrauding the government for millions of Medicare dollars (Malone, 2000).
- Faux pas (unintentional and external): Example: A health clinic being supplied with RotaShield (a diarrhea vaccine before it was pulled off the market in 1999) is linked to some deaths and severe illnesses (Harris, 1999).
- Terrorism (intentional and external): Example: A product like Johnson and Johnson's Tylenol is the target of criminal tampering (O'Connor, 1994).

ATTRIBUTION THEORY AND THE MODEL OF IMAGE RESTORATION STRATEGIES

Coombs (1995) developed a model of image restoration that can guide crisis communicators' responses. The model integrates five basic response strategies derived from the work of Allen and Caillouet (1994) and Benoit (1997): denial, distance, ingratiation, mortification, and suffering. Denial is when an organization denies that there is a crisis. Distancing is when an organization admits there is a crisis but deflects all blame for the crisis toward some external cause. Ingratiation assumes one of three forms: transcendence, bolstering, or praising others.

1   Transcendence is where an organization tries to place the crisis in a larger, more desirable context. For example, a drug company under fire for using animal testing could argue that while such testing may be distasteful, the larger good of finding effective treatments for humans is worth the cost.

2   Bolstering is when an organization reminds the public of the existing positive aspects of the company. For example, a health care company might admit to a serious error, but point out its otherwise strong record and steady contributions to the community.

3   Praising others is used to win approval from the target of the praise. An example would be a managed care organization praising the "fair and professional conduct" of federal investigators during an audit of business practices that were triggered by allegations of fraudulent Medicare billing.

Mortification strategies can also assume one of three forms: remediation, repentance, and rectification. Remediation occurs when the organization agrees to provide some form of compensation to help victims. For example, when a botched surgery occurs, the hospital could agree to pay for all subsequent medical bills for the aggrieved party. Repentance is when an organization offers an unqualified apology for its misdeeds. Rectification involves taking action to prevent a recurrence of the crisis event, such as instituting a review board to survey existing procedures and make necessary changes.

The final strategy is suffering. This refers to a situation in which an organization in crisis points out that it, too, is suffering. Take for example a health clinic that unwittingly administers a vaccine that makes people sick, including patients and some members of its own staff. Clinic spokespersons could point out that their own people are suffering as are other members of the community.

Attribution theory forms the foundation of the model of image restoration strategies by explaining the relationships between crisis situations and appropriate crisis response strategies. The theory holds that judgments toward an organization will be harsher if the perceived cause of a crisis is internal rather than external, and if it is a regular occurrence. Coombs and Holladay (1996) developed a model of four crisis types by combining the dimensions of intentionality and locus of crisis origin. The model includes: accidents (internal and unintentional), transgressions (internal and intentional), faux pas (external and unintentional), and terrorism (external and intentional). As would be expected, the researchers found that individuals were much more forgiving in crisis situations caused by faux pas or terrorism. However, companies must still handle the situation with great care. Whereas individuals may not condemn an organization for an externally caused crisis, they will judge how the crisis is handled.

Crises that originate internally pose the greatest potential problems for an organization. Transgressions are the least forgivable actions. The appropriate response is mortification, including repentance, rectification, and if appropriate, remediation for any parties harmed in the incident. The best response after a transgression is quick and full disclosure. Mitchell (1986) stated that the first 24 hours are the most crucial in forming public opinion about the crisis. Druckmiller (1993) reinforced this, adding that the company should provide essential facts as soon as it is available, that corporate leadership should be visible and approachable, and that communication channels must be selected in a way that information is dispersed quickly and accurately.

Accidents are one of the most likely events a health care organization may encounter. Coombs (1995) argued that organizations must first determine whether major or minor damage has occurred (a subjective judgment), whether any victims are involved, and whether the company has a good or poor performance history. Obviously, crises that involve major damage are the most problematic. Mortification and ingratiation are recommended during these types of events. Situations involving minor damage require distancing and ingratiation; those situations where crisis evidence is false should use denial and clarification.

The managed care industry in particular was besieged by crises in the 1990s. Once held up as the solution to runaway medical costs, managed care organizations are now commonly pilloried by consumers, media, and politicians. A major reason is the perception that what drives the industry is profit over health. The industry image problem is particularly problematic because it is seen as a calculated transgression of long duration. Media coverage is rife with cases of patients or their families complaining about denial of treatment, unnecessary red tape, and slow payments on approved claims. The fact that physicians and other health providers often join in the criticism is particularly damaging to the industry because doctors and nurses are among the most trusted professionals. It is wise for corporations to remember the thoughts of Arthur Paige, the first corporate public relations professional who stated that corporations only exist with approval of the public (Cutlip, 1997).

CREATE A POSITIVE PUBLIC OPINION CLIMATE IN ORDER TO WIN REGULATORY AND LEGISLATIVE APPROVALS

Winning favorable regulation and legislation are among the most important activities health care public relations accomplishes. Without successful public relations efforts, a company's ability to sell a product or service may be severely limited or completely denied. This type of health care public relations often involves arguing the company's position, frequently against opposing organization's arguments. Theories and models of particular utility help the organization clearly identify and track key organizations and publics. This enables an organization to accurately target messages and account for the impact other publics and organizations have on the legislative and regulatory environments.

Situational Identification of Publics Theory. In the attempt to promote a positive climate of public opinion, the health care company must first clearly identify specific publics of concern to the health care organization. A public relations effort is likely to have limited effectiveness if demographics are the sole criteria for identifying important segments of a population. Although knowledge of demographic classification can be very useful (as is discussed later), demographic groups are rarely homogenous in terms of attitudes, knowledge, and opinions. One theory that holds promise for effective health public relations is the situational identification of publics theory (Grunig & Hunt, 1984). This theory offers a mechanism for classifying individuals in relation to their levels of awareness and concern about a particular issue. Situational theory posits that a public's perceptions of an issue or situation can be used to predict the extent to which members of that public will seek out and use information, or how much a public will passively process information they happen to encounter about that particular issue.

Three independent variables are used to make these predictions: problem recognition, constraint recognition, and level of involvement. As the title indicates, problem recognition refers to the extent to which a person is aware of an issue or situation. Constraint recognition refers to the degree to which a person perceives significant constraints or impediments to his or her ability to do anything about an issue. Involvement level refers to the degree to which a person perceives she or he is directly affected by the issue or situation. Grunig (1989) contended that communication behavior can be either active or passive. Active communication involves higher levels of information seeking and deeper information processing. Passive communication is typified by little or no information seeking and processing.

Different combinations of the three independent variables yield numerous possible types of publics. Grunig and Hunt (1984) acknowledged that some combinations are more likely to occur than others. The three most common public types are: active, aware, and latent. An active public is a highly involved group, characterized by high recognition of an issue and perception of few constraints to taking action. An aware public possesses high issue recognition but also perceives significant obstacles to action. These individuals can be either high or low in involvement. A latent public is low in problem recognition, high in constraint recognition, and can perceive either high or low involvement.

Situational theory has the potential of great use to for-profit health care organizations, particularly with regard to promoting positive public opinion climate to achieve favorable legislation and regulation. If a company can distinguish different types of publics, it can create messages that respond to that public's unique characteristics. In a study of a gubernatorial race Hamilton (1992) found that situational theory accurately predicted different levels of communication activity about the election. Whereas this particular study was not health related, the principle applies nonetheless. In the case of promoting favorable health care legislation, situational theory may be invaluable. Time and money can be saved when organizations can identify and reach active publics, the people most likely to take actions, like calling or writing a congressional member, mobilizing others to the cause, or voting for/against a ballot issue.

Situational theory could help other facets of a company's public relations effort as well. For example, messages could be constructed for an aware public that acknowledge perceived obstacles and present viable solutions to overcome those obstacles in order to help sell a product, service, or idea. As an illustration, assume that a company that produces an over-the-counter health supplement to treat depression conducts research identifying a large aware public. This public understands the seriousness of this condition but perceives a number of important obstacles to seeking treatment, including social stigma to seeking professional psychiatric care, concern about the expense associated with seeing a physician, and worry about consuming manufactured chemical antidepressants. Armed with this knowledge, the company could effectively design messages that promote use of its St. John's Wort herbal extract as a private, inexpensive, "natural" way to combat depression.

Public Relations Field Dynamics. In a recently published [article], Springston and Keyton (2001) describe a scenario in which drug maker Eli Lilly Corporation encountered a major threat to its image and its profitability. In the late 1980s, Prozac, one of Eli Lilly's most profitable drugs, came under attack from a group called the Citizens Commission on Human Rights, later discovered to be a nonprofit group established by the Church of Scientology. The church is known for its stance against using drugs for the treatment of psychiatric illness. This group was able to garner so much media attention about the alleged dangers of the drug that it was able to pressure the FDA to temporarily withdraw approval of the drug. Eventually, the American Medical Association and the American Psychological Association spoke out in support of Prozac and Eli Lilly, thus helping to redeem the image of the company and the drug. Prozac was allowed back on the market. This case typifies the reality that organizations can and usually do operate in complex, multipublic environments. While Eli Lilly and the Church of Scientology were the direct antagonists in this particular case, a variety of other actors in the field were salient. In order to effectively manage the public relations environment, Eli Lilly needed to deal with each of these publics in a unique manner.

In spite of the importance of accounting for the entire interaction field, most public relations models only pay lip service to multipublic environments (Leichty & Springston, 1993). Group communication theory offers promise as an approach that recognizes that such environments are both complex and fluid. One such model, Public Relations Field Dynamics (PRFD), is adapted from the study of small group communication and derived from Bales and Cohen's (1979) System for the Multiple Level Observation of Groups (Springston, 1997a, b; Springston & Keyton, 2001; Springston, Keyton, Leichty, & Metzger, 1992).

Springston (1997b) adapted the group system to macrolevel applications vital to public relations. The dimensions in the PRFD system reflect low-influence versus high-influence capability; self-orientation versus community orientation; and friendly versus unfriendly relationships. These three dimensions are essential to the study of public relations. The influence dimension helps determine which groups will be most attentive and involved in a public relations situation. This variable is similar to the involvement variable in situational theory. If, for example, a group perceives an organization to have a large influence on it, the group will likely be more attentive to that organization than it will be to organizations with low perceived influence. Knowledge of how influential a public sees itself to be in relation to the organization provides insight into how likely that public is to exhibit active behavior, helping practitioners determine communication strategy.

The community versus self-dimension reflects perceptions of how motivated an organization is to achieve either an integrative or distributive outcome in a given situation. This ties directly into perceptions of trust. Companies that are perceived to be more interested in the bottom line at the expense of the community have serious public image problems, as many managed care organizations have discovered. Members of the media are often particularly skeptical of an organization's community orientation. In general, the more an organization can demonstrate to the media and other publics that it has a genuine community orientation the more successful the organization is in negotiating its "brand" or position.

Finally, perceptions of friendly versus unfriendly behavior are relevant at all levels of interaction. This dimension taps fundamental notions of friend or foe. PRFD allows organizations to identify allies, antagonists, and potential mediators. Combined, the three dimensions provide a powerful framework to map the entire field or public relations environment. The system is graphically displayed, placing the friendly-unfriendly dimension on the horizontal axis and the community versus self on the vertical axis. The influence dimension is represented by circle size—the more perceived influence, the larger the circle. Figure 7.1 displays three hypothetical actors in a relational field.

REDUCE COSTS AND SAVE TIME

Theory can save time and money in a variety of ways. For example, theory can help identify those individuals most interested in a particular health product or service, eliminating the time and cost that might otherwise be spent on a broader communication campaign. Theory can also assist the health public relations practitioner in determining the most appropriate channel or channels through which to reach members of the target public. Additionally, theory can guide the development of messages in order to increase the likelihood that individuals will engage in preventive behaviors that can save time and money for patients, providers, and payers.

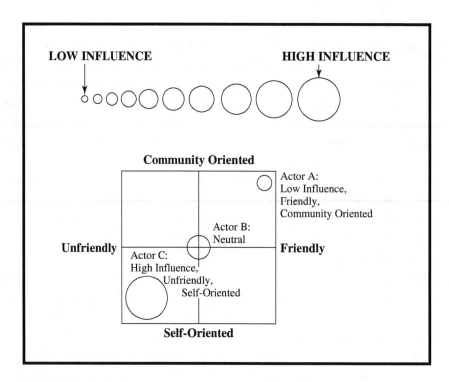

FIGURE 7.1 Field diagrams of the perceived relational landscape.

A number of theories have been used effectively in health communication campaigns, and use of these theories has been widely published (e.g., Jackson & Duffy, 1998; Du Pre, 2000). These include microlevel theories such as the health belief model (Rosenstock, 1974), the theory of reasoned action (Ajzen & Fishbein, 1980), social cognitive theory (Bandura, 1986), the transtheoretical model (Prochaska & DiClemente, 1983), the extended parallel process model (Witte, 1992), and narrative theory (Fisher, 1987); and macrolevel theories such as cultivation theory (Gerbner, Gross, Morgan, & Signorielli, 1994) and diffusion of innovation theory (Rogers & Shoemaker, 1971).

Kaiser Permanente's efforts during the 2000–2001 flu season provide a good example of how important elements of theory were incorporated in a communication campaign to urge Kaiser's at-risk patients to get flu shots and to educate its patients about ways to avoid catching the flu before they were vaccinated. Influenza outbreaks can be very expensive for health care organizations. The cost of a flu vaccine is less than $30 per patient, whereas flu treatment can cost thousands of dollars per severe case. The 2000–2001 flu season threatened to be more costly than usual because the vaccine was in short supply in October and November. This placed a strong onus on communication campaign designers to both educate and influence patients to get vaccinated and also to engage in ways of avoiding the flu until they could get the shot.

Kaiser mounted an aggressive campaign that incorporated key elements of several previously mentioned theories. Diffusion of innovation theory, for example, was demonstrated by Kaiser's use of multiple communication channels to encourage individuals to relay information to friends and family. Kaiser also enlisted the help of highly respected physicians as spokespeople. It was clear that Kaiser understood both the role of opinion leaders and the process of information dissemination through a combination of mediated and interpersonal channels. The company's efforts also reflected an understanding of risk theories such as the extended parallel process model. For example, in publicity Kaiser was able to generate about the issue, Director of Prevention Dr. Ned Calonge outlined the potential severity of the disease and emphasized the susceptibility at-risk patients face with the flu. He also conveyed information that was intended to bolster self-and-response efficacy. In addition to stressing the effectiveness of the vaccine's preventive power, Calonge and other physicians discussed practical ways in which an individual could avoid coming into contact with the flu virus. Dr. Calonge also discussed easy ways to boost the immune system to fight off any contact (Melani, 2000). Overall, this communication campaign demonstrated the practicality of incorporating theory to save both time and money.

ASSIST THE MARKETING FUNCTION: PROMOTION OF SALES AND SERVICE

There is a wealth of classic persuasion and motivation theories to draw from when designing messages to promote product sales. In addition to many of the theories already mentioned in this [article] are those that focus on source credibility (e.g., Petty & Cacioppo, 1986), selective exposure (e.g., McGuire, 1985), and cognitive and affective growth and stability theories (e.g., Festinger, 1957; Levinson, 1978; Leventhal, Meyer, & Nerenz, 1980). These theories all provide useful guidance about how to design messages. The utility of any persuasive theory will depend on the context and purpose of the message, however, one key consideration is whether an organization is trying to sell a product or a service.

There is some debate about the applicability of strategies developed to promote products when used for promoting services (Abernethy & Butler, 1992). This is particularly important since much of the health care industry is service oriented. A number of marketing and advertising studies have focused on the intangible nature of service and how promotion efforts need different strategies (e.g., Grove, Pickett, & Laband, 1995; Stafford & Day, 1995). Service quality is an issue receiving particular focus with the growth of the service economy (Clow, Tripp, & Kenny, 1996).

Parasuraman, Zeithaml, and Berry (1988, 1991) developed a taxonomy that may serve as a useful guide for promoting health services. SERVQUAL categorizes service along five dimensions: reliability, responsiveness, assurance, empathy, and tangibles. Reliability is the organization's ability to provide the promised service(s) dependably. Responsiveness represents the organization's willingness to provide prompt and helpful service. Assurance defines the organization's ability to engender trust and confidence among consumers. This is related to how knowledgeable and courteous an organization's service providers are perceived to be. Empathy refers to the degree to which service is perceived to be individualized and caring. Finally, tangibles is the category that includes professional appearance of personnel, equipment, and physical facilities.

An example of a public relations effort that follows the five dimensions articulated in the SERVQUAL model is the Children's Hospital of Boston (2001) Web site. Reliability and responsiveness are compellingly conveyed through links that walk prospective patients and families through the experiences they will have when receiving treatment in the hospital. The site provides specific detail on a wide variety of subjects including inpatient stay, outpatient visits, medical records, activities for patients, and housing accommodations. Tangibles are reinforced by many images of children with professional-looking caregivers in attractive settings. Finally, the following passage from the site illustrates the tone of assurance and empathy conveyed:

> Colorful images painted along hallways and on windows … a clown's antics … a little red wagon on an inpatient floor … emblems of childhood that remind young people that they are children first and patients second. The importance of Children's Hospital as an institution exclusively dedicated to and designed for its young patients is played out every day when a new pediatric procedure succeeds, or a child smiles in wonder. A pediatric hospital is a serious environment, where childhood illness and disease are faced daily. Yet at Children's, our world of color and play reinforces to caregivers, families, and patients themselves the joy of childhood. (Children's Hospital of Boston, 2001)

IMPLICATIONS FOR THE FUTURE

It is very likely that the rapidly changing health care environment of the 1990s will continue well into the 21st century. A myriad of forces, including escalating costs, shortages of skilled health professionals, advances in medical and communication technology, and changing demographics, will demand new and innovative public relations approaches in for-profit health care. Public relations will become ever more important to the corporate bottom line by advancing positions that protect the organization from threats and unfavorable legislation, promote public wellness and preventive health practices, and assist marketing efforts to sell products and services to various publics and other health care organizations. Future research must focus on greater understanding of the most effective and appropriate public relations strategies for protecting corporate image and building brand equity versus influencing the regulatory and legislative public.

While not discussed at length in this [article], the Internet and other forms of interactive new technology offer tremendous opportunities to forward the health care industry's public relations mission. The Internet will allow for-profit health care organizations to reach specific niche and geographically distant audiences in a way never before possible. Future research should examine under what conditions interactive computer technology effectively replaces person-to-person communication or other forms of mediated communication in public relations efforts. Additionally, the potential of many theories (such as situational theory [Grunig & Hunt, 1984]) are greatest when messages can be individually tailored to a person's beliefs and attitudes. The Internet enables corporations to design completely different messages for active, aware, and latent publics. This is because the technology is highly interactive and individual's beliefs, concerns, and desires can be assessed and responses can be delivered, sometimes instantly. Because of the data-gathering capacity of the Internet, it will be possible for scholars and corporations to continually test and fine-tune the usefulness of different theories. New media technology also holds the promise of cost-effective corporate communication with publics by reducing the need for expensive printed materials and person-to-person contact.

Although the promise of the new media is great, these technologies also create concerns. Future public relations practice and research needs to fully explore such ethical concerns as patients' privacy and care versus costs and what this might mean for health public relations. Future research should also focus on the integration of theories not previously considered in the domain of public relations. Testing combinations of different complementary theories should be conducted to discover the most effective ways in which to achieve organizational goals of increased health and increased profits.

Public relations must also evolve in step with the changing face of health care. Heatherington, Ekachai, and Parkinson (2001) argued that the changing nature of the health care industry demands that public relations personnel continually educate themselves on health care management principles, focus on quality improvements, and seek ways to facilitate productive alliances among former competitors. We concur. Without a thorough understanding of the business of health care and how it is changing, public relations practitioners will not be effective at managing issues before they become major problems. Time and resources must be allotted for continuing education of both public relations managers and technicians. Additionally, public relations needs to be part of the decision-making team at the top of the organization. It is imperative that organizational decision makers be fully informed about the beliefs and propensities of the organization's internal and external publics.

Such understanding is key in order to succeed in continually improving the quality of health products and services. Public relations will be crucial for top management to enlist the support and cooperation among staff needed to successfully initiate quality improvement programs. Models such as SERVQUAL can provide guidance for managers and subordinates to work cooperatively in designing new quality initiatives that respond to the different dimensions of service. As Heath (1994) pointed out, direct contact with an organization's employees often forms the most important and enduring images people have of an organization. It is vital that employees understand the larger picture and their role within that picture.

As health care continues to become an increasingly intertwined network of products and services, public relations will be needed to facilitate ways in which former competitors can work together. As the costs of equipment and facilities go up and difficulty in finding enough qualified personnel increases, competition between competing organizations in a community makes less economic sense. Organizations will need to build strengths in specialized areas and facilitate patient access to other alliance organizations when necessary. Public relations will be key to creating an environment of trust and cooperation between organizations, not to mention the crucial role of working with key publics in order to educate them about the nature of these organizational alliances. Models such as public relations field dynamics can aid health care corporations by mapping the perceptions other organizations and publics have about the corporation. Such mapping can help identify friends, foes, and potential mediators and facilitate the design of communication campaigns strategies and tactics.

Finally, higher education must be responsive to the continually changing needs of the health care industry. Just as the industry is becoming more complex, so must colleges and universities become more complex in order to effectively advance research and prepare students to join the health care industry. During recent years, some colleges and universities have begun to form ties between such diverse schools as business, communication, journalism, medicine, nursing, pharmacy, psychology, and social work. This needs to continue. Such interdisciplinary links will be critical in order to advance research and to fully prepare students, regardless of what position they assume in the industry.

REFERENCES

Abernathy, A. M., & Butler, D. D. (1992). Advertising information: Services versus products. *Journal of Retailing, 68*(4), 398–419.

Ajzen, I., & Fishbein, L. (1980). *Understanding attitudes and predicting behavior.* Englewood Cliffs, NJ: Prentice-Hall.

Allen, M. W., & Caillouet, R. H. (1994). Legitimate endeavors: Impression management strategies used by an organization in crisis. *Communication Monographs, 61,* 44–62.

Bales, R. F., & Cohen, S. P. (1979). SYMLOG: System for the multiple level observation of groups. New York: The Free Press.

Bandura, A. (1986). *Social foundation of thought and action: A social cognitive approach.* Englewood Cliffs, NJ: Prentice-Hall.

Benoit, W. L. (1997). Image repair discourse and crisis communication. *Public Relations Review, 23*(2), 177–186.

BusinessWorld, Philippines. (2000, September 29). Retrieved October 1, 2000, from Lexis-Nexis on line database.

Chicago Sun Times. (2000, September 27). News section, p. 10. Retrieved October 1, 2000, from Lexis-Nexis online database.

Children's Hospital of Boston. (2001, January 20). Retrieved January 20, 2001, from http://www.childrenshospital.org/ services/.

Clow, K. E., Tripp, C., & Kenny, J. T. (1996). The importance of service quality determinants in advertising a professional service: An exploratory study. *Journal of Services Marketing, 10*(2), 129–151.

Cohen, S. L. (2000, May 2). Do nothing Congress risks our health. *USA Today,* p. 27a.

Coombs, W. T. (1995). Choosing the right words: The development guidelines for the selection of the "appropriate" crisis-response strategies. *Management Communication Quarterly, 8*(4), 447–476.

Coombs, W. T., & Holladay, S. J. (1996). Communication and attributions in a crisis: An experimental study in crisis communication. *Journal of Public Relations Research, 8*(4), 279–295.

Cutlip, S. (1997). *Public relations history: From 17th to the 20th century: The antecedents.* Hillsdale, NJ: Lawrence Erlbaum Associates.

Cutlip, S., Center, A. H., & Broom, M. N. (2000). *Effective public relations.* Upper Saddle River, NJ: Prentice Hall.

Druckmiller, B. (1993). Crises provide insights on image: Preparations necessary to protect goodwill when times turn bad. *Business Marketing, 40*(8), 40.

Du Pre, A. (2000). *Communicating about health: Current issues and perspectives.* Mountain View, CA: Mayfield Publishing.

Easterbrook, G. (2000, March 20). Managing fine: How to love your HMO. *New Republic, 222*(12), 21–25.

Festinger, L. A. (1957). *A theory of cognitive dissonance.* Evanston, IL: Row Peterson.

Fisher, W. R. (1987). *Human communication as narration: Toward a philosophy of reason, value, and action.* Columbia: University of South Carolina Press.

Gelatin Drink May Reduce Arthritis Pain. (2000, September 25). *USA Today,* p. 9d.

Gerbner, G., Gross, L., Morgan, M., & Signorielli, N. (1994). Growing up with television: The cultivation perspective. In J. Bryant & D. Zillmann (Eds.), *Media effects: Advances in theory and research* (pp. 17–41). Hillsdale, NJ: Lawrence Erlbaum Associates.

Grove, S. J., Pickett, G. M., & Laband, D. N. (1995). An empirical examination of factual information among service advertisements. *Service Industries Journal, 15*(2), 216–233.

Grunig, J. E. (1989). Publics, audience, and market segments: Segmentation principles for campaigns. In C. T. Salmond (Ed.), *Information campaigns: Balancing social values and social change* (pp. 199– 228). Newbury Park, CA: Sage.

Grunig, J. E., & Hunt, T. (1984). *Managing public relations.* New York: Holt, Rinehart & Winston. Hamilton, P. K. (1992). Grunig's situational theory: A replication, application, and extension. *Journal of Public Relations Research, 4*(3), 123–150.

Harris, G. (1999, October 18). After vaccine's recall, regulators look for holes in the safety net. *Wall Street Journal,* p. 1b.

Healthcare PR and Marketing News. (2000, May 11). News section, p. 9. Retrieved July 9, 2000, from Lexis-Nexis online database.

Heath, R. L. (1994). *Management of corporate communication: From interpersonal contacts to external affairs.* Hillsdale, NJ: Lawrence Erlbaum Associates.

Heatherington, L. T., Ekachai, D., & Parkinson, M. G. (2001). Public relations in the health care industry. In R. L. Heath (Ed.), *Handbook of public relations* (pp. 571–578). Thousand Oaks, CA: Sage.

Hutton, J. G. (2001). Defining the relationship between public relations and marketing: Public relation's most important challenge. In R. L. Heath (Ed.), *Handbook of public relations* (pp. 205–214). Thousand Oaks, CA: Sage.

Jackson, L. D., & Duffy, B. K. (1998). *Health communication research: A guide to developments and directions.* Westport, CT: Greenwood Press.

Krantz, M., & Bjerke, D. (1997, May 12). The self-medication generation. *Time, 149*(19), p. 72.

Lapinski, M. K., & Witte, K. (1998). Health communication campaigns. In L. D. Jackson & B. K. Duffy (Eds.), *Health communication research: A guide to developments and directions* (pp. 139–162). Westport, CT: Greenwood Press.

Leichty, G., & Springston, J. K. (1993). Reconsidering public relations models. *Public Relations Review, 19,* 327–339.

Leventhal, H., Meyer, D., & Nerenz, D. (1980). The common sense representation of illness danger. In S. Rachman (Ed.), *Medical psychology.* New York: Pergamon.

Levinson, D. (1978). *Seasons of a man's life.* New York: Knopf.

Los Angeles Times. (2000, August 21). Health section, p. 5.

Malone, J. (2000, September 3). Nursing homes go hat-in-hand to capital. *The Atlanta Journal and Constitution,* p. P7.

Managed Care Efforts That Resonate with Consumers. (2000, April 27). *Healthcare PR & Marketing News.* Retrieved October 1, 2000, from Lexis-Nexis online database.

McGuire, W. J. (1985). Attitudes and attitude change. In G. Lindzey & E. Aronson (Eds.), *Handbook of social psychology* (3rd ed.). New York: Random House.

MCIC Releases "Health Care and the Internet: Current Trends in Online Information Gathering." (2000, June 7). *PR Newswire.* Retrieved July 18, 2000, from Lexis-Nexis online database.

Melani, D. (2000, October 31). While you wait … what to do until you get your flu shot. *Denver Rocky Mountain News,* Lifestyles section, p. 3d.

Miller, A. (2000, January 16). Aetna US healthcare: Growing pains. *Atlanta Journal Constitution,* p. 1h.

Mitchell, T. (1986). Coping with a corporate crisis. *Canadian Business Review, 13*(3), 17–20.

Nelson, N. J. (1999). Purple carrots, margarine laced with wood pulp? Nutraceuticals move into the supermaket. *Journal of the National Cancer Institute, 91*(9), 755–758.

O'Connor, P. J. (1994, February 25). Report of Tylenol tampering probed in Bedford Park. *Chicago Sun-Times*, p. 23a.

Palosky, C. S. (1995, November 8, final edition). Surgeon fights penalty. *The Tampa Tribune*, Sec. Flor-ida/Metro, p. 6.

Parasuraman, A., Zeithaml, V. A., & Berry, L. L. (1988). SERVQUAL: A multiple-item scale for measuring consumer perceptions of service quality. *Journal of Retailing, 64*(1), 12–37.

Parasuraman, A., Zeithaml, V. A., & Berry, L. L. (1991). Refinement and reassessment of the SERVQUAL scale. *Journal of Retailing, 67*(4), 420–450.

Pear, R. (2000, June 23). In a test case on HMO's patients both win and lose. *New York Times*, p. 12a.

Petty, R., & Cacioppo, J. (1986). *Communication and persuasion: Central and peripheral routes to attitude change.* New York: Springer-Verlag.

Philadelphia Inquirer. (1999, July 8). Retrieved July 18, 2000, from Lexis-Nexis online database.

Politics & Polity. (1999, July 8). Retrieved September 3, 2000, from Lexis-Nexis online database.

Prochaska, J. O., & DiClemente, L. L. (1983). Stages and processes of self-change of smoking: Toward an integrative model of change. *Journal of Consulting and Clinical Psychology, 51,* 390–395.

Reginster, J. Y., Deroisy, R., Rovati, L. C., Lee, R. L., Lejeune, E., Bruyere, O., Giacovelli, G., Henrotin, Y., Dacre, J. E., & Gossett, C. (2001, January 27). Long-term effects of glucosamine sulphate on osteoarthritis progression: A randomised, placebo-controlled clinical trial. *The Lancet, 357*(9252), 54–66.

Rogers, E. M., & Shoemaker, F. F. (1971). *Communication of innovations: A cross-cultural approach* (2nd ed.). New York: Free Press.

Rosenstock, I. M. (1974). Historical origins of the health belief model. *Health Education Monographs, 2,* 328–335.

St. Petersburg Times. Cancer Treatment Shows Promise. (2000, September 28). *St. Petersburg Times*, p. 3b.

San Diego Union Tribune. (2000, September 12). News section, p. A-1.

Seitel, F. P. (1993). *The practice of public relations* (5th ed.). New York: Macmillan.

Springston, J. K. (1997a). Application of public relations theory to breast cancer screening: A worksite study. In J. Biberman & A. Alkhafaji (Eds.), *Business research yearbook: Global business perspectives* (pp. 762–766). Slippery Rock, AR: International Academy of Business Disciplines.

Springston, J. K. (1997b). Assessing the group field. In J. Biberman & A. Alkhafaji (Eds.), *Business research yearbook: Global business perspectives* (pp. 767–771). Slippery Rock, AR: International Academy of Business Disciplines.

Springston, J. K., & Keyton, J. (2001). Public relations field dynamics. In R. L. Heath (Ed.), *Handbook of public relations* (pp. 115–126). Thousand Oaks, CA: Sage.

Springston, J. K., Keyton, J., Leichty, G. B., & Metzger, J. (1992). Field dynamics and public relations theory: Toward the management of multiple publics. *Journal of Public Relations Research, 4*(2), 81–100.

Stafford, M. R., & Day, E. (1995). Retail service advertising: The effects of appeal, medium, and service. *Journal of Advertising, 24*(1), 57–71.

Tips Help Diagnose, Treat Celiac Disease. (2000, September 27). *The Seattle Times*, p. 3g.

Tselikis, P. (1999). Are physicians in step with a new kind of care? *Business & Health, 17*(6), 46–50.

USA Today. (1999, July 8). Retrieved July 17, 2000, from Lexis-Nexis online database.

USA Today. (2000, July 21). News section, p. 18a. Retrieved August 12, 2000, from Lexis-Nexis online database.

Volz, D. (2000). The state of managed care. Marketing Health Services, p. 31. Retrieved September 5, 2000, from Lexis-Nexis online database.

Wellner, A. S. (1998). Eat, drink, and be healed. *American Demographics, 20*(3), 55–60.

Werner, L. (1990, August). When crisis strikes use a message action plan. *Public Relations Journal, 8,* 30–35.

Why only the best is good enough. (2000, September 23). *The London Times,* Features section. Retrieved September 26, 2000, from Lexis-Nexis online database.

Wilcox, D. L., Ault, P. H., Agee, W. K., & Cameron, G. T. (2000). *Public relations: Strategies and tactics.* New York: Longman.

Witte, K. (1992). Putting the fear back in fear appeals: The extended parallel process model. *Communication Monographs, 59*(4), 329–349.

Zeisel, S. H. (1999). Regulation of "nutraceuticals." *Science, 285*(5435), 1853–1854.

EXAMINING TOP CAREERS IN PUBLIC RELATIONS

Government and Public Affairs

Reading 2.4: "Government Relations" By Ed Ingle

This chapter covers two very important functional areas of public relations: government and public affairs.

On the one side of this coin is communication made on behalf of the government. Here, professional communicators are responsible for explaining government actions, regulations, and legislation to the public and for running campaigns. Public relations professionals exist at all levels of government: federal, state, and local. The largest group of public relations professionals resides within the Department of Defense (DOD), as the DOD and all of the uniformed services have extensive operations to ensure the taxpayer is receiving timely and accurate news about where their tax dollars are going.

The focus of the reading for this chapter is the other side of the coin. Most large organizations have communication efforts they plan and execute to help the government understand their needs and desires. For instance, most corporations have a specialized branch of their communications effort aimed at helping federal, state, and local politicians understand the implications of potential and existing legislation and regulation on their industry and organization.

Many organizations also hire lobbyists, who provide them with a more focused advocacy effort for the organization's policy positions in the hope of influencing legislation, regulation, or other government action.

The final area we'll explore in this chapter is the role of public relations in election campaigns. Many of the innovative techniques, tactics, and tools that have translated into mainstream public relations, particularly in digital and social media, are born from the efforts of communication professionals to influence the public to vote for their candidates.

"GOVERNMENT RELATIONS"

By Ed Ingle

Man is by nature a political animal.
— Aristotle

YOU SNOOZE, YOU LOSE

In March 1990, the Energy and Commerce Committee of the U.S. House of Representatives was holding a late night, closed-door session on proposed clean air legislation. Chairman John Dingell of Michigan—the longest-serving member of Congress in history—was presiding over the powerful committee.

It was near midnight and the negotiations had bogged down over a key issue—how to cost-effectively reduce emissions from power plants to address acid rain pollution in the Northeast. In particular, the discussion focused on how to divvy up the new emission allowances or "credits" among the nation's largest coal-burning utilities, primarily located in the Midwest. The proposed legislation capped emissions by allocating a fixed number of credits to the largest emitting plants. Each credit represented one ton of emissions. The more credits a utility received, the more it could legally pollute. As a result, the credits became a very valuable commodity.

On this particular evening, scores of utility lobbyists and their "hired guns" (i.e., lobbying consultants and lawyers) were huddled outside the closed-door session in the foyer of the Rayburn building. Every hour or so, members and committee staff would emerge from the hearing room only to be swarmed by the lobbyists hoping to make a last-minute case for more "credits" and to hear the latest results of the negotiations.

Bob Schule, former White House legislative aide to President Jimmy Carter and then partner in the Washington lobbying firm, Wexler, Reynolds, Fuller, Harrison and Schule,[1] was on hand with his colleague, Ed Ingle, then a twenty-nine-year-old associate and former program analyst at the Office of Management and Budget in the Reagan White House. Ingle had been with the Wexler firm for less than a year and was getting valuable on-the-job training on the lobbying trade. Schule and Ingle were representing Ohio Edison, a large Midwestern utility.[2] They were joined by Bob McWhorter, senior vice president of Ohio Edison, and Bob Giese, another lobbying consultant to Ohio Edison.

Some time after midnight, a corporate lobbyist from another large Midwestern utility, who had been sitting on the gray marble floor in the corner of the foyer, slumped over in exhaustion from the long day. His deep sleep caught the attention of many of those nearby—when suddenly Giese shouted out, "Quick, grab that guy's credits!" The foyer erupted with laughter and the startled corporate lobbyist was jarred from his sleep.

The life-long lesson for Ingle that night on Capitol Hill was this: only those companies who are present and engaged in the policy-making process in Washington will reap the benefits of their efforts. Those not present—or not paying attention—will pay the price of not having a sound corporate government relations function. In other words, "you snooze, you lose."

WHAT IS GOVERNMENT RELATIONS?

Few professions can point to the U.S. Constitution as the basis for their existence. Many are surprised to find that the lobbying profession is one of the few. In fact, you need only look as far as the First Amendment to see the eight words that serve as the basis for this vocation:

> Congress shall make no law respecting an establishment of religion, or prohibiting the
> free exercise thereof; or abridging the freedom of speech, or of the press, or the right of
> the people peaceably to assemble, and to *petition the Government for a redress of grievances*.[3]

Lobbying can take a variety of forms. Meeting with a member of Congress, a congressional staffer, or an executive branch official to influence public policy is a direct form of lobbying. Phone or written communications (e.g., via letter, e-mail, or fax) to these same decision makers are also regarded as direct lobbying.

However, lobbying can also be deployed indirectly. A "grassroots" campaign that encourages constituents of a given congressional district or state to write a letter, send an e-mail, post a message via social media, or make a phone call to a member of Congress or Senator can be an effective form of indirect lobbying.

Providing strategic counsel on political and policy matters to corporate executives is not lobbying, nor is managing the company's political action committee, but both can be important parts of an overall government relations function. Government relations is sometimes referred to as government affairs, and more broadly, public affairs. Regardless of the label, government relations is an important function within a corporation, and lobbying is at the heart of this function.

The lobby of the historic Willard Hotel on Pennsylvania Avenue in Washington, DC, is thought to be where the term "lobbyist" was first coined in the 1870s during President Ulysses Grant's administration. After a long day in the Oval Office, President Grant would frequently escape the pressures of the presidency with a brandy and a cigar in the Willard lobby, where he was approached by people seeking his ear on a given issue. Grant called these people "lobbyists."[4] The term subsequently became associated with individuals who seek out legislators in the lobby or hallway outside of a legislative chamber or meeting place.

Lobbyists can work for a corporation, trade association, law firm, lobbying consulting firm, interest group, or other organization. A lobbyist—particularly a corporate lobbyist—is sometimes referred to as a Washington representative or "Washington Rep" in lobbying parlance. Almost every business or political interest is represented by one or more lobbyists in our nation's capital—interests as varied as agriculture, transportation, energy, education, technology, healthcare, women's rights, abortion rights, gun owners, labor, snack food, florists, and pest management.

The first lobbying law was enacted by Congress in 1946, and required the registration of lobbyists, their employers, and their expenses. In 1995, Congress passed the Lobbying Disclosure Act (LDA), which expanded the definition of a lobbyist and greatly tightened reporting requirements. The LDA defines a lobbyist as any individual who is employed by an organization (or retained by a client) for services that include more than one lobbying contact, and who spends at least 20 percent of his or her time engaged in lobbying activities.[5]

Under the 1995 LDA, lobbyists and/or an organization were required to file semiannual reports disclosing the specific issues they work on, any interests by foreign agencies or businesses in their lobbying activities, and estimates of their lobbying expenses.

In the wake of the Jack Abramoff lobbying scandal of 2005–6, the lobbying profession came under even greater scrutiny. In 2007, Congress passed the Honest Leadership and Open Government Act (HLOGA), which substantially amended parts of the 1995 LDA. HLOGA further increased reporting requirements of lobbying activities and tightened restrictions on gifts and travel of Members of Congress and staff. For example, the frequency of lobbying activity and expense reporting was increased from seminannual to quarterly. And for the first time, HLOGA required registered lobbyists to disclose political contributions on a semiannual basis.

The role of lobbyists was also a popular topic during the 2008 Presidential campaign as evidenced by candidates like then-Senator Barack Obama, who promised

Few professions can point to the U.S. Constitution as the basis for their existence.

Lobbying: The practice of advocating one's policy position to government officials with the hope of influencing legislation, regulation, or other government action.

Government relations: A broader term that includes all forms of lobbying and non-lobbying activities that have the ultimate goal of influencing public policy.

to limit lobbyists' influence if elected. On his second day in office in January 2009, President Obama signed an Executive Order entitled, "Ethics Commitments by Executive Branch Personnel." The Executive Order placed additional gift restrictions on Presidential appointees, banned registered lobbyists from holding positions within the Executive Branch, and banned those who leave the Administration from lobbying the Executive Branch during the remainder of his presidency.

In March 2009, President Obama also issued a memorandum to federal agencies, laying out restrictions on lobbyist communications related to items funded by the $787 billion economic stimulus legislation (American Recovery and Reinvestment Act) signed into law in February 2009.[6]

Despite the additional scrutiny on federal lobbying in recent years, the lobbying industry in Washington, DC is as big as ever. Total lobbying expenditures in 2012 were $3.3 billion—nearly double the amount reported in 2002 according to the Center for Responsive Politics. Although lobbying expenditures rose sharply from 2002 to 2008, reported expenditures have remained flat since 2008—probably more a function of the economy and corporate belt-tightening than added scrutiny.

However, new scrutiny and restrictions on lobbyists have resulted in fewer registrations since 2008. The number of lobbyist registrations has fallen from a high of 14,842 in 2007 to 12,411 in 2012, the lowest level since 2002. Some corporate, trade association, and union employees and executives, who might have otherwise registered in past years in an abundance of caution, are now choosing not to register to avoid the new restrictions and "lobbyist" label.

The top ten corporate lobbying spenders are shown in Table 8.1.

CASE FOR A CENTRALIZED GOVERNMENT RELATIONS FUNCTION

Similar to the case for a centralized media relations function, … it is critical for an organization to speak with one voice on all government relations matters.

It is not uncommon for corporate executives to know a number of state and federal policymakers. In fact, these relationships can be quite beneficial to the company and generally should be encouraged. The company's government relations operation should inventory the relationships of its executives and midlevel managers, and seek to nurture them where possible. However, there is the potential for tremendous risk to the company's policy objectives if the communications with these political contacts are not closely monitored and coordinated by a central function.

Table 8.1 Top Ten Corporate Lobbying Spenders (2012)

1	General Electric Co.	$21,120,000
2	Google Inc.	$18,220,000
3	Northrop Grumman Corp.	$17,540,000
4	AT&T	$17,460,000
5	Boeing Co.	$15,640,000
6	Southern Company	$15,580,000
7	Lockheed Martin	$15,347,350
8	Verizon Communications Inc.	$15,220,000
9	Comcast Corp.	$14,750,000
10	Royal Dutch Shell	$14,480,000

Source: Center for Responsive Politics

At any given time, an organization or company may have numerous policy issues before Congress and the executive branch. Some of these issues may fall under the jurisdiction of the same congressional committees or executive branch officials. For instance, a large U.S. company with interests in trade policy may find itself working closely with the House Ways and Means Committee on a trade agreement before Congress. Meanwhile, the company's tax department may have an important tax issue before the same committee. If two parts of a company are talking to the same committee without coordinating through its government relations office, both policy objectives could suffer. Worse, the company risks being perceived by the committee as unorganized and unreliable, which may jeopardize the company's objectives on future policy matters.

Even very savvy and capable corporate executives and managers should not assume that they can navigate the rocky shoals of politics and policy formulation. What may seem a simple social media posting, phone call, letter, e-mail, or conversation at a social gathering with a government official should not be taken lightly. Government officials may be looking for an endorsement of their idea, legislative proposal, or policy initiative that could contradict other policy objectives of the company or alienate other industry allies.

It is worth noting that some organizations may question the need for a government relations function altogether. But companies like Microsoft have learned that a "Washington presence" is critical to its overall business, and that it pays to engage in the policy and political debate and to have experienced government relations professionals looking out for the company's welfare. Bottom line: a company or organization should integrate government relations into its business plan and ensure that its efforts are coordinated and strategic.

ORGANIZING THE GOVERNMENT RELATIONS FUNCTION

Government relations can reside within a number of broader functions within a corporation, including:

- Legal
- Communication or public relations
- Corporate affairs
- A business unit

The location of a government relations function is driven by a number of factors, such as how a company is regulated or potentially regulated by the federal government and the enforcement exposure of a company by regulatory agencies (e.g., Federal

It is critical for an organization to speak with one voice on all government relations matters.

Companies like Microsoft have learned that a "Washington presence" is critical to its overall business.

Trade Commission, Environmental Protection Agency, Federal Communications Commission, or Food and Drug Administration). Oftentimes, a company that has heavy regulatory or enforcement exposure will locate government relations within the corporate legal department. However, in response to this same regulatory and enforcement exposure—and the likelihood of resulting communication challenges—it also is not uncommon for the government relations function to be located within the communication department.

In some companies, the government relations function falls under the corporate affairs (or public affairs) department. Corporate affairs can serve as a general catch-all for a number of functions, including government relations, communication, and community affairs. Government relations can also reside under a particular business unit of a corporation, especially in companies where that business unit may have its own unique exposure to regulatory and/or enforcement activity.

Regardless where the government relations office resides, it is imperative that there be close coordination with the communication function, both proactively on the company's policy objectives, and reactively to unexpected circumstances as they arise.

The configuration of government relations offices within an organization also varies, and is often dictated by the types of issues a company faces, the size of the operation, and the management style of the head of government relations and the needs of his or her superiors. A corporate government relations function typically covers federal, state, and local affairs. Increasingly, larger companies with overseas operations and/or customers are adding international affairs coverage to their government relations functions. Most medium to large companies will have a government affairs office in Washington, DC, which will house the federal affairs operations, but may also include the state and international affairs functions. (State and international government affairs are covered later in this chapter.) Smaller companies will maintain a government affairs function at their corporate headquarters, which could include as few as one or two people.

A Washington government affairs office for a Fortune 100 company, for example, may include five to ten employees (although a few offices may have as many as twenty to forty employees if the company is heavily regulated or has diverse subsidiaries). The office will usually be led by a vice president, senior vice president, or managing director, who will report to the general counsel or top senior government affairs, communication, or corporate affairs executive back at headquarters. A VP or director of legislative affairs may oversee the office's lobbying activities on the Hill, and a VP or director of regulatory affairs may oversee executive branch lobbying.

Within these offices, you likely will find a combination of political and issue-specific lobbyists. For example, each lobbyist may manage a certain portfolio of issues that he or she will lobby on Capitol Hill and/or in the executive branch. Some offices may divide its lobbying portfolio by the two sides of the Hill and the executive branch; for example, a House lobbyist, Senate lobbyist, and executive branch lobbyist. Some may have a lobbyist for each political quadrant on the Hill, for example, a House Republican, House Democrat, Senate Republican, and Senate Democrat.

Regardless where the government relations office resides, it is imperative that there be close coordination with the communication function.

UNDERSTANDING THE KEY AUDIENCES

For any government relations office in Washington, there are two distinct audiences: Congress and the executive branch. Although they both consist of critical policymakers, these audiences could not be more different in many respects. Congress comprises Senators and House members elected every six or two years, respectively, whose number one goal generally is to get reelected.

The president, the White House, and the political appointees within the cabinet agencies also care about broad public sentiment, reelections (albeit limited to two four-year terms), and the congressional elections which dictate whether a president's party might control the House or Senate. However, they are less moved by the individual voter. As such, the dynamic of how they are lobbied is quite different. For example, one hundred individual voters writing letters to the Department of Health and Human Services about a Medicare provision will not demonstrably change how the HHS secretary will think about that issue. On the other hand, one hundred voters from the district back home writing to a congressman—particularly one who serves on the Ways and Means Health Subcommittee—may indeed have an impact on how that member views the issue and advocates for it in the Congress and with the administration.

Further, political appointees within the executive branch are a mere fraction of the overall federal workforce. While political appointees admittedly occupy the most senior positions within the administration, there are only about 3,000 of them across the federal government among the millions of federal employees. A senior federal career employee is naturally interested in helping the president accomplish his agenda. But a career employee cares less about politics and more about implementing the laws Congress passes via regulation and administering the federal programs under his or her jurisdiction. Lastly, each agency is different, and how you approach a given agency or various officials within an agency should be tailored accordingly.

Capitol Hill is also made up of a wide variety of important audiences. There are one hundred Senators, four hundred thirty-five House Members, and over 15,000 congressional staff—all of whom are associated with various committees, leadership offices, caucuses, and working groups. A successful government relations function will advance its public policy interests by building and nurturing relationships with these key audiences:

- *House and Senate leadership.* It is important to know the members and their staffs who serve in leadership positions in both bodies and on both sides of the aisle. The leadership sets the agenda for each legislative body, and determines which issues get considered and how they ultimately get resolved.
- *House and Senate committees.* Most policy priorities of a company will likely fall under the jurisdiction of a handful of committees. These committees are responsible for holding hearings, drafting legislation, making modifications, reporting legislation out of committee to the full House or Senate, and reconciling the

For any government relations office in Washington, there are two distinct audiences: Congress and the executive branch.

At the end of the day, the elected officials most inclined to come to a company's aid when it needs help are the members of its home state delegation.

differences in House–Senate conference committees. It is imperative that a company cultivate relationships and build allies with members and staff on these committees—both in the majority and minority.

- *Congressional caucuses.* There is a congressional caucus or working group on a myriad of policy issues, such as: intellectual property, agriculture, property rights, the Internet, Vietnam vets, wine, human rights, oil and gas, biotechnology, adoption, and China. These ad hoc groups are made up of members of Congress who have a personal, professional, or district-related interest with these issues. Members of these groups make great targets for building relationships around issues that are important to your company.
- *Home State Senators and Representatives.* At the end of the day, the elected officials most inclined to come to a company's aid when it needs help are the members of its home state delegation. A company with a big presence in a given state or district has one thing going for it: jobs. If a company does nothing else in Washington, it must make sure it keeps its own home district Congressman and its two Senators up to date on issues of importance, and cultivate them as champions for the company.
- *Congressional staff.* The congressional staff who support the 535 House and Senate members are a very important part of the legislative process and should be central to any government relations strategy. This includes the personal staff in each legislator's office, as well as the committee staff. The committee staff (e.g., counsel) and personal issue-specific staff (e.g., legislative assistant) help draft the bills and brief and advise the members. Time and care should be spent in working closely with congressional staff, understanding their value to the process, respecting their relationship and influence with the members, and by all means, not end-running them or blind-siding them along the way.

SETTING THE COMPANY'S GOVERNMENT RELATIONS AGENDA

How a company sets its government relations agenda differs from company to company depending on the issues, the corporate structure, and the various personalities involved. Nevertheless, there are common elements for successful agenda setting that should be taken into consideration.

A company's government affairs agenda should be the result of a healthy collaboration between the government relations function, senior management, and affected business units.

Government affairs agenda setting should not be totally top-down nor should it be only bottom-up. For example, an agenda set solely by the government relations office, without input from senior management and the business units, may be out of step with the company's most important business objectives. Conversely, an agenda set solely by senior management and/or the business units, without input from the government relations office, may not take in to consideration the realities of the current

CASE STUDY: REPUTATION AND INTEGRITY—A BRYCE HARLOW PROFILE

One of Washington's most highly regarded corporate lobbyists was Bryce Harlow. During his forty-year career, Bryce Harlow served as a legislative aide to the House Armed Services Committee, senior legislative advisor to presidents Eisenhower and Nixon, and head of the first Washington government affairs office for Procter & Gamble from 1961 to 1978. In the foreword of the biography entitled *Bryce Harlow, Mr. Integrity*, Dr. Henry Kissinger wrote that Harlow "single-handedly created the entire modern advocacy industry."[7]

In June of 1981, about 250 of Bryce Harlow's friends and business colleagues gathered for a dinner in his honor. It was an event to mark not only his exceptional public and private service, but also his special contributions to the profession of corporate representation in Washington. The funds raised from the dinner became seed money for the Bryce Harlow Foundation, which was incorporated in 1982 as a non-profit organization. The foundation seeks to recognize and inspire gifted leaders, in both public and private sectors, who foster high ethical standards with regard to advocacy, and to "enhance the quality of professional advocacy and increase the understanding of its essential role in the development of sound public policy."

The Bryce Harlow Foundation has continued its annual awards dinners, and the proceeds help fund educational seminars on advocacy and ethics, as well as scholarships for graduate level students interested in pursuing careers in government relations.

Then-Vice President Dick Cheney was the keynote speaker at the 2005 foundation awards dinner in Washington. In his remarks, the vice president commented on the man for whom the dinner was named: "Bryce passed away in 1987, but the foundation has carried on his legacy of service, integrity and patriotism in a way that would no doubt please him." The Vice President continued, "Every day in the West Wing, I work in the office that was once Bryce Harlow's office, and he is someone I think of often. For those of you who didn't get to meet Bryce, you should know that he wasn't a famous or a physically imposing man. He used to say that it's easy to keep a low profile when you're only 5 foot 4; but when it came to knowledge about this city and the understanding of the legislative process and personal integrity and wisdom, Bryce Harlow was a man of incredible stature."[8]

Harlow's own words, published by the foundation in 1984 regarding corporate representation in Washington, ring just as true today:

> Corporate representation is sometimes dangerous, often frustrating, and always time-consuming and difficult. It calls for an unceasing effort to educate and motivate current and potential allies—and to discourage and befuddle foes. It requires the coordination of personal visits, telephone calls, and letters from top management; the flexing of political muscle in the home districts of particularly recalcitrant members of Congress; the fine-tuning of press relations and advertising; and, throughout, a dogged determination to prevail. That may sound tedious and vexing and grim. But for the right person, corporate representation can also be fascinating, challenging, immensely satisfying, and—on balance, most of the time—fun.[9]

public policy and political climate in Washington. As such, a company's government affairs agenda should be the result of a healthy collaboration between the government relations function, senior management, and affected business units.

The government relations office should drive and coordinate the agenda-setting exercise given its understanding of the public policy process. The agenda should be consistent with the overall business and communication objectives of the company and should be updated annually or as changing conditions may dictate. It should take into consideration the business cycle, key lines of business, and related policy and political issues.

The government affairs agenda must also be realistic. Moving an important legislative agenda item from a draft proposal to a bill and on to final enactment can take several years in most cases. It is better to focus attention and limited resources on a realistic number of policy objectives, rather than a long list of items that will never be realized. Once set, it is the charge of the government relations office to implement the agenda. This necessarily involves developing strategy, drafting briefing materials, talking points, and conducting and/or managing the lobbying activities.

SUCCESS AND EXPECTATIONS MANAGEMENT

One of the most difficult tasks of a corporate government relations function is managing expectations within the company. Many times, success in policy and political terms to a senior executive is very different from success to a government relations office.

Politics by its very nature is the practice of the art of compromise. And in compromise, the final result almost always ends up somewhere in the middle. No one side gets everything it wants. So where politics is involved, success is not achieving the perfect, but obtaining a legislative, regulatory, or public policy result that is as close to the company's objectives as possible.

Success from issue to issue may also vary considerably. Success many times is minimizing the damage of harmful legislation that is destined to pass. After the Enron and WorldCom scandals of 2001 and 2002, Congress sought to pass tough corporate governance legislation (Sarbanes-Oxley) and nothing short of an act of God was going to stop it. Therefore, success for a company during that debate was minimizing the damage of a regulatory overreach against a political backdrop that was clearly on the side of the public and not corporate interests.

On the other hand, obtaining a provision that expands the federal R&D tax credit to reduce the corporate tax burden for companies that invest heavily in research is undeniable success. But is it still success if the expanded tax credit is only approved for one year, despite the company's support for at least a three-year approval? If you are appropriately managing expectations, you bet it is. The benefits of a tax credit for one year are better than no credit at all, and the company can fight the good fight again next year to seek the tax credit's continuation.

ROLE OF THIRD-PARTY ADVOCACY

Third-party advocacy has become an increasingly important tool for a company's overall government relations strategy. Medium and large companies should not only have a robust government relations operation, but they should also supplement their direct lobbying efforts through the effective use of third-party advocates. Third parties can include trade associations, coalitions, think tanks, and other interest groups which share the company's policy goals.

- *Trade associations.* Trade associations are formal organizations that generally represent companies from the same industry or "trade." Most companies are members of one or more trade associations that have a presence in Washington, DC. Trade associations can play a vital role in a lobbying campaign by speaking with one voice on a given issue—representing numerous companies and a large, combined employee base. A company could belong to an association as large and diverse as the National Association of Manufacturers (NAM), while also belonging to more trade-specific associations such as the Business Software Alliance (an association of software companies).

  Trade associations can supplement lobbying activities on an issue that is already being lobbied by individual companies, and they can also effectively serve as the sole lobbying voice in situations where companies may not wish to publicly lobby an issue. Nevertheless, a trade association cannot substitute for a company's own government relations function. On any given policy issue, a company may have unique positions on certain provisions that warrant the need for the company to lobby Congress and the executive branch in its own voice. This is a critical point that bears amplifying. Trade associations are vitally important and play a key role in a company's overall government relations function. However, companies should not rely totally on trade associations in Washington to meet their policy objectives.

- *Coalitions.* Unlike trade associations, coalitions are typically more ad hoc, are established around a certain policy issue, and usually cut across multiple industries. Whereas some coalitions are created under a more formal, long-term arrangement, most coalitions are set up as temporary, informal organizations that exist only for the purpose of achieving specific policy objectives—for example, passage of immigration reform legislation, healthcare reform, corporate tax reform, energy security legislation, and so forth.

  Member companies, and in some cases trade associations, finance coalition efforts. Those companies who pay more typically have more say over the day-to-day direction and priorities of the coalition. The funding may pay for full-time

A trade association cannot substitute for a company's own government relations function.

staff and/or outside government affairs consultants to manage the coalition. The coalition allows disparate companies and organizations to come together around a single cause to combine their voices for greater impact with Congress and the executive branch.

- *Think tanks.* Companies seeking to find other voices to support their views on a given policy issue may consider think tanks. A think tank is a collection of academic and government scholars, which may bring a particular political or philosophical bent to its writings and publications; for example, conservative, liberal, libertarian, or somewhere in between. They add credibility and a degree of objectivity to a debate. There are scores of think tanks in Washington. Smaller think tanks may focus on a narrow set of issues, such as defense policy, international affairs, or economic policy. Larger thinks tanks—such as the Brookings Institution, the American Enterprise Institute, and the Center for American Progress—support scholars who cover a wide range of issues. For example, if a particular scholar has written on the issue of energy security, a group of oil companies or its trade association may seek to cosponsor an energy-related symposium with the scholar/ think tank to coincide with consideration of energy legislation before Congress.

- *Grassroots advocacy.* One of the most effective tools in a company's government relations tool box can be the use of third-party "grassroots" advocacy. Grassroots advocacy is an indirect form of lobbying in which constituents of a given congressional district or state are encouraged to write a letter, send an e-mail, post a social media message, or make a phone call to a member of Congress or Senator. "Grasstops" advocacy occurs when influential community leaders (e.g., local or state officials, business owners, and heads of local organizations) are targeted to communicate their feelings on an issue to their respective members of Congress, Senators, or executive branch officials.

Companies, trade associations, and coalitions are also increasingly turning to social media tools to augment their grassroots campaigns. For example, many large companies now host their own public policy blogs. Micro-blog sites (e.g., Twitter) and social networking sites (e.g., Facebook) are also being utilized to generate support or opposition to various legislative proposals aimed at influencing the White House and/or Congress. Ironically, the private sector is merely taking a page from President Obama's successful 2008 and 2012 campaigns, which so effectively demonstrated the grassroots power of these new social media tools.

Corporate America was not the first to use grassroots advocacy. In fact, it was the extensive use of grassroots activities by various interest groups, such as environmental organizations, senior citizens, small business, and human rights that led companies to recognize grassroots advocacy as not only an effective tool but a necessary one. The sheer numbers of lobbying contacts made possible by a successful grassroots campaign demonstrate to lawmakers that an issue is important to their constituents and worthy of consideration.

One final note, whether through third-parties or direct advocacy, the smart use of technology is key to any successful corporate government relations effort.

Companies, trade associations, and coalitions are also increasingly turning to social media tools to augment their grassroots campaigns.

Digital strategies (e.g., including social media and data analytics) are central to how today's top political campaigns run and how the Executive Branch and the Congress governs, so it is critical that companies fully embrace these tools in their own public affairs programs.

ROLE OF THE LOBBYING CONSULTANT

A company's communication department routinely hires outside public relations consultants to supplement its work. Likewise, many companies will enlist external lobbying consultants to enhance its government relations activities and to expand its reach in Washington. In recent years, corporate America has been hiring outside lobbyists at a record clip based on a number of factors. First, companies increasingly view Washington as a more active player in their daily affairs. This is a product of the massive financial bailout and the economic stimulus legislation of 2008 and 2009, and a Democratic White House eager to address major reform efforts in healthcare, energy, climate change, taxation, and corporate governance.

Second, the number of lobbying consultants has increased given the declining cost of entry into the profession as a result of new communications technologies. In 1995, a successful lobbyist needed a downtown office, expensive office equipment and an assistant to type memos, answer the phone, and fax materials. Today, that same lobbyist can thrive with a virtual office via a handheld communications device or "smart phone" to screen calls, receive/send e-mails, use social media, view attachments, and surf the Internet—whether he or she is in the office, in a restaurant, in the car, or on the steps of the Capitol.

Third, during the same period, U.S. corporations have been under pressure to tighten their own payrolls given the challenging economic climate. It is no wonder that our nation's corporations have turned to a greater use of outside lobbying consultants to help them engage in Washington and take advantage of the opportunities. Since 1998, the top 20 lobbying firms combined (in terms of lobbying fees reported), brought in nearly $4 billion (see Table 8.2).

Who are these outside lobbying consultants? Some are former Senators, House members, and executive branch officials. Others are former congressional staff, White House staff, and agency staff. They may have their own one- or two-person consulting shops, or they may be part of a larger lobbying firm or law firm. Some law firms have a separate lobbying arm, composed of lawyers and non-lawyers, who handle the government relations work on behalf of clients. Other law firms have partners and associates, who may register as lobbyists and spend part of their time on government relations activities.

Lobbying firms focus exclusively on government relations services, such as: direct lobbying, strategic counseling, coalition building, grassroots activities, and government-related communication. These firms comprise lawyers, non-lawyers, and policy experts, most of whom have worked for Congress or the executive branch, or both.

Companies increasingly view Washington as a more active player in their daily affairs.

Table 8.2 Top 20 Lobbying Firms (in terms of fees reported from 1998 to mid-2013)

1	Patton Boggs LLP	$496,107,000
2	Akin Gump Strauss Hauer & Feld LLP	$400,045,000
3	Cassidy & Associates	$363,962,100
4	Van Scoyoc Associates	$312,958,000
5	Williams & Jensen	$226,334,000
6	Ernst & Young	$192,076,737
7	Holland & Knight	$179,989,544
8	Quinn Gillespie & Associates (now QGA)	$162,388,500
9	Brownstein, Hyatt, Farber	$159,325,000
10	Hogan & Hartson	$154,633,907
11	Podesta Group	$143,550,000
12	Barbour, Griffith & Rogers (now BGR Group)	$136,820,000
13	Greenberg Traurig	$136,308,249
14	Ogilvy Government Relations	$131,160,000
15	Alcalde & Fay	$129,810,660
16	Carmen Group	$123,975,000
17	Dutko Worldwide	$119,836,766
18	PMA Group	$115,930,578
19	Ferguson Group	$114,527,291
20	Wexler & Walker	$110,625,000

Source: Center for Responsive Politics

Lobbying consultants help a company's overall government relations function in several important ways:

- *Intelligence gathering*. In Washington, as in Brussels and other capitals, information is power. The quicker you have a piece of information, the sooner you can act upon it, and your likelihood of success increases. Good consultants can greatly extend a company's "eyes and ears" capability to either help thwart bad policy or ferret out opportunities that would have otherwise gone unnoticed.
- *Strategic counsel*. There is frankly no substitute for hands-on experience when it comes to government relations. Outside consultants can clearly add depth and breadth to the company's thinking on addressing policy and political challenges and should be utilized early in a company's strategic process.
- *Direct lobbying*. Outside lobbying consultants can increase a company's "boots on the ground" capability where the tactical lobbying of members and/or staff is needed. Most important, outside consultants will invariably bring with them additional relationships with members of Congress, staff, and executive branch officials which can be leveraged on behalf of the company.
- *Communication*. Some government relations consultants can also effectively supplement a company's communication function in an effort to influence

Outside consultants can clearly add depth and breadth to the company's thinking on addressing policy and political challenges and should be utilized early in a company's strategic process.

government officials on a given policy issue—both in Washington and in home district media outlets. Consultants can help with message development, drafting press releases, advertorials, op-eds, blogging, social media strategy, and arranging for media interviews.

A company's government affairs agenda, its priority issues, and the size of its consultant budget will obviously dictate how many outside consultants it may need. It is essential that the company's internal government relations function keep the consultants current on priority issues and engaged regularly—both strategically and tactically. The company should also conduct thorough, annual reviews of its consultants to determine whether the current consultants still map well to the priority issues and are still adding value.

Finally, a company should not only ensure that it follows the letter of the law and the rules that govern lobbying activities, but it should also insist that its outside consultants do the same.

ROLE OF POLITICAL CONTRIBUTIONS

Like it or not, it costs a lot of money to run a House or Senate campaign. Costs are driven by television and radio advertising buys, telemarketing, direct mail, staffing expenses, and political and media consultants. Campaign costs for a U.S. House seat in a contested race can easily exceed $1 million. Costs for running a U.S. Senate campaign can exceed $20 million. Short of major reform in the current political campaign system, these costs will continue to escalate.

Consequently, companies must decide how and whether to participate in the political contribution process. Since federal law prohibits corporate donations to candidates, the only legal option for a company is to establish a political action committee (PAC). Some companies question the need for a PAC, which is money raised through personal, voluntary donations from employees of a company or organization. However, many companies with a Washington presence today either have a PAC or are seriously considering it—particularly in light of the campaign finance law, the Bipartisan Campaign Reform Act (BCRA) of 2002.

BCRA's most notable achievement was ending the prior practice of corporate (and labor organization) contributions or "soft money" going to national party committees, such as the Republican National Committee, the Democratic National Committee, and the party campaign committees for the House and the Senate. Prior to BCRA, organizations and individuals could give large, unlimited soft money donations (e.g., $100,000 or $250,000) to these national party committees as long as the funds were not used to influence federal elections. However, concerns grew as the lines began to blur between the funding of "issue ads" from soft money and the ads' impact on federal political races. Under BCRA, no corporate or labor dollars can be given to these national committees (and individuals must comply with dollar limits). BCRA did preserve "hard money" contributions—personal and PAC donations going to federal candidates—which are subject to strict contribution limits.

A common misperception is that companies with PACs are able to "buy votes" of members of Congress through their donations. When you consider that donations from the largest corporate PACs are limited to $5,000 per election (i.e., primary election or general election), it is hard to believe that a Congressman, whose campaign will likely cost more than $1 million, will change his vote based on a $5,000 donation. And when you consider a Senate campaign that may cost $5 million, $10 million, or even $30 million, a $5,000 donation is clearly not a consequential amount. It is frankly this very reason why Congress and the Federal Election Commission continue to hold PACs out as a meaningful and effective way for individuals, companies, and interest groups to participate in the political process without fear of undue influence.

So if a company cannot expect its PAC to change a member of Congress' vote, then why have one at all? In today's political environment, where the costs of campaigns are so significant, a PAC demonstrates to a Senator or

A PAC demonstrates to a Senator or Congressman that the company respects the political process.

Congressman that the company respects the political process and realizes that it costs money to get reelected. A contribution will not change his or her vote, but it typically will give a company the opportunity to be heard on a priority issue. Most important, a PAC allows a company to support candidates who support its issues and interests.

With that said, a PAC is not a substitute for personal political contributions by corporate executives. In addition to supporting the PAC, executives should be willing to show support for key federal and state elected officials, particularly those who represent the district or state where the company is located and/or has significant facilities.

One should not confuse the use of a traditional PAC discussed above with the advent of so-called Super PACs. Super PACs, which are officially known as "independent expenditure-only committees," rose to prominence in the 2012 election cycle as a result of the 2010 *Citizens United* Supreme Court decision. That decision helped pave the way for corporations, non-profits, unions and individuals to contribute unlimited amounts of money to independent expenditure committees (which can run candidate-specific ads), as long as there is no direct coordination with a candidate's campaign or political party.[10]

Super PACs are regulated by the FEC and donations are publicly reported. As such, most corporations during the 2012 campaign chose not to contribute to Super PACs given the publicity around such contributions and potential for reputational risk. Super PACs played a major role in the 2012 Presidential elections, financed primarily by wealthy individuals on both the right and the left. These independent committees are likely to play an even bigger role in future election cycles, and corporations should continue to tread carefully in this area, while focusing attention on traditional PACs and individual contribution strategies.

STATE AND INTERNATIONAL GOVERNMENT RELATIONS

This chapter has focused primarily on how a corporation might approach the federal government relations function. Large companies are increasingly deploying state and international government affairs operations as part of their overall government relations activities. Many of the components covered in this chapter are also applicable to state and international government relations. However, it is important to note some unique aspects and the need for coordination across all activities.

STATE GOVERNMENT RELATIONS

A presence in the state capital of a company's headquarters is an essential part of the overall government affairs function. State governments oversee a number of areas critical to most companies, such as education, transportation, communications, electricity, and tax issues. Local governments also play an important role on many of these issues. As such, corporate state and local government affairs representation is needed to oversee this function. Other professionals also may be situated around the country in state capitals, where the company may have a large employee base and/or a customer base. These representatives are there to monitor legislative activity that may impact the company and lobby state legislators, the governor's office, and agencies.

In light of increasing gridlock in Washington, many corporations are ramping up state government affairs activities. Companies are working with Governors and state legislators on policies and proposals, which seek to provide regulatory relief or business climate improvements in the absence of (or as the result of) federal legislation. State leaders are anxious to not only keep the jobs they have in their states, but find ways to attract new jobs from other states or overseas. Consequently, corporations are devoting more attention at the state level around tax, energy, and health care issues. Companies are also playing a more active role in engaging Governors and other state leaders on education issues that address skills needed for today's workforce.

Relationships developed with state and local officials can also pay dividends when an official decides to run for federal office. For example, it is common for a city mayor, state legislator, state attorney general, or governor to later run for Congress. As such, coordination between the state and federal teams is important—in terms of relationship building, political giving, grassroots advocacy, and legislative activity that may give rise to federal legislation.

INTERNATIONAL GOVERNMENT RELATIONS

Many large companies have begun expanding their government affairs reach outside of the U.S. in foreign capitals such as Brussels (EU), Tokyo, Beijing, and Moscow. In the last decade, the rise in global competition has brought with it both increasing opportunities for U.S. companies and increasing regulatory action by foreign governments. Some American-based trade associations have staff and presence overseas and can provide some assistance to member companies. Yet, a company that relies heavily on trade, foreign suppliers and markets, or personnel needs its own team of in-country government affairs professionals to engage in the policy and political process and build relationships with key officials. As in the United States, in-country government affairs consultants can also be retained to help supplement a company's own internal team by adding depth and breadth in response to changing conditions and shifts in a country's political leadership.

Each country and government is unique, requiring a tailored approach. Once again, close coordination between the United States and the international government affairs teams is critical. Policies that start in the United States may spread to foreign capitals or vice versa and must be closely monitored. And, in cases where foreign governments are taking U.S. companies to task through regulation and enforcement, U.S. government

Many large companies have begun expanding their government affairs reach outside of the U.S. in foreign capitals such as Brussels (EU), Tokyo, Beijing, and Moscow.

officials—and the pressures they can potentially bring via communications with their foreign counterparts—may serve to positively impact the outcome of these issues.

EXPERT PERSPECTIVES: AN INTERVIEW WITH KARAN BHATIA, VICE PRESIDENT FOR GLOBAL GOVERNMENT AFFAIRS AND POLICY, GENERAL ELECTRIC COMPANY

As head of GE's international law and policy group and a former international affairs expert with the U.S. Government, Karan Bhatia is regarded as one of the world's top international government relations specialists. In an interview from his Washington, DC office, Mr. Bhatia discussed GE's approach to global government relations.

Ingle: What is your role within the company?

Bhatia: I oversee GE's relations with governments outside of the United States. My team works with foreign governments on public policy issues that we consider important to the company's ability to operate effectively around the world. I also oversee our government relations activities with the U.S. Government on international and trade-related matters, including the Departments of State, Commerce and Treasury, the U.S. Trade Representative's office, and the White House's National Security Council.

Ingle: Who do you report to and how is your organization structured?

Bhatia: I report to the company's General Counsel and Senior Vice President, who reports to the CEO. We have a team of about eighty government relations professionals spread across twenty-five capitals around the globe, including Washington. We represent the company on cross-cutting international policy issues, such as trade, market access, environment, and technology and innovation, as well as sector-specific issues like energy, health care or transportation policy.

Ingle: Explain GE's approach to international government relations.

Bhatia: We have a very constructive approach to government relations. That is, we seek to build "trusted relationships" with governments around the world—to serve as a resource for policymakers, to help them assess the business consequences of policy change, to share practical experiences from other jurisdictions, and to brainstorm quietly about possible policy innovations. We remain in regular dialogue with policymakers, utilize various advocacy tools such as studies and white papers, and work with third parties, NGOs (non-government organizations), think tanks, and civil society groups as needed. We make it a point to work with governments at all levels—from the senior-most levels to the career ranks—matching them to the appropriate level of GE executive or representative.

Where possible, we try to employ country nationals to help manage our government affairs activities in the various capitals. We do not rely heavily on outside consultants in our international relations work; we feel it is usually more effective to speak directly to foreign government officials.

Ingle: GE is such a huge global company with over 300,000 employees worldwide. How do you coordinate your activities with other parts of the company?

Bhatia: It's a challenge. First and foremost, we coordinate very closely with our U.S. government relations colleagues in Washington, DC, given the natural synergies and shared objectives between our groups. Second, we work closely with GE's numerous business units to make sure our corporate-level and business-level activities are in sync. Third, we work closely with other functional departments within the company such as our corporate communications colleagues—collaborating on public affairs strategies, speeches, Congressional testimony, press statements, etc. In terms of coordination within my own organization, I am in weekly contact with each of our regional government relations leaders, and I also host a monthly global call with all regional government relations teams. We are also making increased use of online tools—issue trackers, internal web portals and online working groups.

Ingle: What are some of your biggest challenges?

Bhatia: Our constant challenge is to find a way to successfully make the leap to being a truly global company. We cannot escape the fact that we are an American-headquartered company—nor do we want to. We are what we are, and we are proud of that. However, our ultimate goal is to also be seen as a local company in any given country where we do business—a company that is a local employer and invests locally in the community.

American companies have been honing their federal government relations skills in Washington, DC for decades, but we are still only in the early stages of international government relations as a profession. And like in the U.S., the role of foreign governments and their impact on how we do business around the world is increasing—so we have our work cut out for us.

ETHICS IN LOBBYING

It takes twenty years to build a reputation and five minutes to ruin it.

– Warren Buffett

Adherence to sound ethical principles is vital to the lobbying profession, despite public perception to the contrary. The vast majority of registered lobbyists are decent and principled, and they realize that the fastest way to sink one's career is to cross the ethical line and, in doing so, implicate a government official. Just as the fate of Enron's executives serves as a reminder for all corporate executives as to the importance of strong ethical behavior, Jack Abramoff does the same for lobbyists.

The following is an excerpt from the "Code of Ethics" of the Association of Government Relations Professionals (AGRP). Established in 1979 as a non-profit organization, AGRP is the national professional association dedicated exclusively to lobbying. AGRP's mission is to enhance the development of professionalism, competence, and high ethical standards for advocates in the public policy arena.

CODE OF ETHICS OF THE ASSOCIATION OF GOVERNMENT RELATIONS PROFESSIONALS

Article I—Honesty and Integrity

A lobbyist should conduct lobbying activities with honesty and integrity.

Article II—Compliance with Applicable Laws, Regulations, and Rules

A lobbyist should seek to comply fully with all laws, regulations, and rules applicable to the lobbyist.

Article III—Professionalism

A lobbyist should conduct lobbying activities in a fair and professional manner.

Article IV—Conflicts of Interest

A lobbyist should not continue or undertake representations that may create conflicts of interest without the informed consent of the client or potential client involved.

Article V—Due Diligence and Best Efforts

A lobbyist should vigorously and diligently advance and advocate the client's or employer's interests.

Article VI—Compensation and Engagement Terms

A lobbyist who is retained by a client should have a written agreement with the client regarding the terms and conditions for the lobbyist's services, including the amount of and basis for compensation.

Article VII—Confidentiality

A lobbyist should maintain appropriate confidentiality of client or employer information.

Article VIII—Public Education

A lobbyist should seek to ensure better public understanding and appreciation of the nature, legitimacy, and necessity of lobbying in our democratic governmental process. This includes the First Amendment right to "petition the government for a redress of grievances."

Article IX—Duty to Government Institutions

In addition to fulfilling duties and responsibilities to the client or employer, a lobbyist should exhibit proper respect for the governmental institutions before which the lobbyist represents and advocates clients' interests.[11]

GOVERNMENT RELATIONS BEST PRACTICES

The following are eleven best practices that a corporate government relations professional should seek to employ to ensure the most favorable business and reputational outcomes:

1 *Shoot straight.* First and foremost, always tell the truth in all of your lobbying communication, oral and written. Nothing sinks your credibility faster than appearing to play fast and loose with the facts.

2 *Be consistent.* Do not tell one congressional office one thing and another office something else. By all means, you should customize your message to take into account your different audiences (e.g., a member

of the Finance Committee versus a member of the Foreign Relations Committee). However, make sure the underlying facts of your advocacy stay consistent. Members and staff—on both sides of the aisle—routinely talk to one another and compare notes.

3   *Know your issues.* Do your homework before you meet with a government official. Have a clear outline of the key points you want to make, and be prepared to give your thirty-minute pitch in ten minutes if the member or staff starts the meeting late or has to leave the meeting early, which is quite common. Anticipate questions ahead of time, but never shoot from the hip on an answer if you are not sure of the facts. You should not hesitate to say, "I don't know, but I'll get back to you with the answer." Also familiarize yourself with the opposition's arguments and be prepared to address them.

4   *Know your audience.* As part of doing your homework, you want to know before you lobby a Congressman on an education issue that he was a former teacher (or his spouse is a teacher). Likewise, you want to know before you meet with a Senator on a tax issue that she pushed through a state tax measure (e.g., Internet tax), while in a previous capacity, that conflicts with your company's position.

5   *Know your "ask."* A government official will want to know why you are meeting with her and what you are "asking" her to do. For example, to a House staff person you might say, "We would like the Congresswoman to consider voting for H.R. 4545 when it comes up for a vote next week in the House." Keep your "asks" to a minimum, and make sure they are realistic. If you have several "asks" of a member or executive branch official, be prepared to prioritize them.

6   *Know your environment.* Beyond knowing your issue and your audience, you need to be aware of the broader political and policy environment at the time of your meeting. For example, your government relations strategy may call for the introduction of a bill by a friendly member of Congress the last week before the recess. You need to know that the Congressman during that same week might be preoccupied with fighting a base closure commission to keep a military base open in his home district, and your strategy should be modified accordingly.

7   *Offer solutions.* There is nothing that irritates a government official more than a lobbyist who complains about an issue, but proposes no solution to the problem. Be prepared to offer up an alternative that ideally helps the member accomplish her policy objective, while minimizing or eliminating any detrimental consequences to your company.

8   *Listen.* Effectively making your pitch is only half of the equation for a successful meeting. The other half is listening effectively. Listen carefully to what the lawmaker or official is saying. For instance, "We will take a look at your issue" is very different from, "I think we can work with you on this issue." Also, listen carefully to their questions and comments and make sure you are being responsive to their exact questions or concerns.

9   *Be adaptive.* The policy and political environment in Washington is fluid. Conditions can change without notice as a result of unfolding events that might have a direct or indirect effect on your issues. A new presidential initiative on healthcare announced in a State of the Union speech could undercut your own proposal that you had been lobbying on the Hill. In response, you will need to be able to regroup quickly and modify your strategy to reflect these changing conditions.

10 *Believe your own rhetoric.* Your lobbying strategy must be based on a sound policy argument. The world's greatest political maneuvers and strategies will not carry the day for a policy argument that does not hold water. Government officials will see through a hollow argument, particularly if you do not sound convinced yourself and are not enthusiastic about your message.

Make it a priority to know the laws, regulations, and rules that affect you as a lobbyist—and live by them.

11 *Play by the rules (and then some).* Make it a priority to know the laws, regulations, and rules that affect you as a lobbyist—and live by them. Routinely consult an outside ethics, election law, or political legal counsel. And even if you are meeting the letter of the law, and if something does not feel right, do not do it. Always ask yourself: "Would I feel comfortable with my actions being reported on the front page of the *Washington Post, The New York Times* or my hometown newspaper?"

RESOURCES FOR FURTHER STUDY

Publications

Andres, Gary, *Lobbying Reconsidered: Politics Under the Influence*, New York: Prentice Hall 2008.

Baran, Jan Witold, *The Election Law Primer for Corporations*, Chicago: American Bar Association, 2008.

Luneburg, William V., *The Lobbying Manual: A Complete Guide to Federal Lobbying Law and Practice*, Chicago: American Bar Association, 2009.

Thurber, James A., *Rivals for Power: Presidential-Congressional Relations*, Lanham, MA: Rowman & Littlefield, 2013.

Websites

The Center for Responsive Politics, http://www.opensecrets.org.

Library of Congress, Thomas, http://thomas.loc.gov.

Real Clear Politics, http://www.realclearpolitics.com.

The United States House of Representatives, http://www.house.gov/.

The United States Senate, http://www.senate.gov/.

The White House, http://www.white house.gov.

QUESTIONS FOR FURTHER DISCUSSION

1 How significant is it to the practice of lobbying that the First Amendment expressly includes the right "to petition the government for a redress of grievances"?

2 What is the optimal relationship, if any, between the government relations and public relations functions?

3 Given the role of money in political campaigns, how important is it for a company to have a Political Action Committee (PAC) to make contributions to candidates?

4 With lobbying ethics coming under closer scrutiny, how can a company lobby effectively while preserving a reputation for integrity?

5 How important is coalition building in influencing government decision makers?

6 How has technology changed the way both individuals and corporations participate in the public policy-making process?

NOTES

1 The lobbying firm formerly known as Wexler, Reynolds, Fuller, Harrison and Schule, founded in 1981, is now known as Wexler & Walker Public Policy Associates.

2 Ohio Edison is now part of the First Energy Corporation.

3 United States Constitution, First Amendment.

4 Website of Intercontinental Willard Hotel, http://www.washington.intercontinental.com.

5 United States House of Representatives, Office of the Clerk, http://lobbyingdisclosure.house.gov.

6 The White House, http://www.whitehouse.gov/the_press_office/Memorandum-for-the-Heads-of-Executive-Departments-and-Agencies-3-20-09/.

7 Bob Burke and Ralph Thompson, *Bryce Harlow, Mr. Integrity*, Oklahoma Heritage Association, 2000, Foreword by Dr. Henry Kissinger, p. 14.

8 Speech by Vice President Dick Cheney, given at Bryce Harlow Awards Dinner on March 16, 2005, in Washington, D.C., http://www.bryceharlow.org.

9 Bryce Harlow, "Corporate Representation," published by the Bryce Harlow Foundation, Washington, D.C., 1984, http://www.bryceharlow.org.

10 The Center for Public Integrity, http://www.publicintegrity.org.

11 "Code of Ethics," Association of Government Relations Professionals (AGRP), http://grprofessionals.org.

CHAPTER

9

EXAMINING TOP CAREERS IN PUBLIC RELATIONS

Sports, Entertainment, and Travel & Tourism Public Relations

Reading 2.5: "Bringing Public Relations and Communication Studies to Sport" By Maria Hopwood, Paul Kitchin, and James Skinner

Our final chapter exploring top careers in public relations explores the world of enjoyment: from sports and entertainment to travel and tourism, promoting fun is at the heart of these jobs. These are also some of the fastest growing and most competitive career paths, so you really need to know how to promote people, organizations, and destinations.

As you will see in this chapter's reading by Hopwood, Kitchin, and Skinner (2010), sports public relations positions encompass everything from event marketing to athlete publicity to team media relations. Some are behind the scenes; others are out front representing the team or athlete. Crises are common in sports public relations as well: think about athletes' social media blunders or the recent National Football League (NFL) concussion scandal.

However, public relations professionals need to be mindful of the *cult of celebrity*, or the way audiences care too much about famous people. Those in entertainment public relations know their clients' lives are constantly followed and must be willing to keep people informed about their celebrity, find ways to get their client public appearances that build their brand image, and ease the blow to the client's reputation when bad news hits.

Those who do public relations for entertainment organizations are not immune. Think about the Sony Pictures Entertainment hack that ended up shutting down their computer systems worldwide and cancelling the release of *The Interview* starring James Franco and Seth Rogan (Alexander, Chase, and Chase 2016). Millions of dollars and brand reputations are often on the line when doing this type of public relations.

Finally, it takes more than simply loving to travel to be a travel and tourism public relations professional. Your skill set needs to include stimulating the public's desire to visit a place, staying abreast of travel industry trends, working with the media to get coverage of your area or attraction, and working with other travel agencies to cross-promote upcoming events. This includes making sure visitors are comfortable, well treated, safe, and entertained from the very beginning of their trips.

"BRINGING PUBLIC RELATIONS AND COMMUNICATION STUDIES TO SPORT"

By Maria Hopwood, Paul Kitchin, and James Skinner

In March 2009, the Sri Lankan cricket team toured Pakistan for a series of matches. On route to a match at the Gaddafi stadium in Lahore the team and their International Cricket Council (ICC) test match umpires were attacked by terrorists. The two buses carrying each group were targeted and eight playing staff of the Sri Lankan team were injured. Sadly a driver and six local police officers were killed in the attack, as well as nine policemen were seriously injured. Later that day match referee Chris Broad, one of the umpires in the second vehicle, addressed the media to respond to the growing pressure for details of the attack. Referee Broad was scathing in his criticism of the security arrangements provided to the umpires and the visiting team. As a key stakeholder of the ICC, Broad's comments added to the pressure on the event hosts (the Pakistan Cricket Board) and also on his organisation through his action. It is remarkable that a senior employee of an organisation, who could realistically be expected to be in a state of shock, was able to address the media without his statements being approved by the ICC public relations and communication officers. His comments started a public verbal confrontation with the Chairman of Pakistan Cricket, Ejaz Butt who did little to ease the situation. The situation exposed operational procedures concerning the safety and security of players and officials. However, it also exposed a serious flaw in the public relations and communication strategies of not only the ICC, but also some of its key stakeholders—the national cricket organisations that play in its tournaments.

Formula 1 racing has always been a cavalier sport where technology and passion meet in the desire to win. Unfortunately, in the recent past the sport has suffered from some cavalier management techniques. In 2007 the McLaren team was fined $100 million for spying on the rivals, Ferrari.

At the start of the 2009 season the same team was involved in an incident where race stewards were lied to about the use of less-than-legal tactics. However, an incident at the 2008 Singapore Grand Prix was described by sport writer Simon Barnes as "the worst single piece of cheating in the history of sport" (Barnes, 2009, *online*). In brief, Renault driver Nelson Piquet, Jr was part of a conspiracy with team principal Flavio Briatore and his number two Pat Symonds to crash his car on the Singapore circuit allowing his unknowing teammate to win the race (FIA, 2009). The crash brought out the yellow (caution) flags and allowed the teammate to effectively get his pit-stop strategy correct and therefore win. The public relations (PR) dilemma of this incident does not just affect the team involved in the incident but the entire sport, its fans, sponsors and partners and the governing authority of the sport itself (Fédération Internationale de l'Automobile—FIA). The sport is a network of organisations that creates one of the world's most watched sporting events. Despite the furore over the race-fixing a number of stakeholders took action to minimise the PR dilemma of the incident. First, Renault's major sponsor Dutch bank ING and partner Spanish insurer Mutua Madrilena withdrew their sponsorship immediately after FIA established wrong-doing to disassociate themselves from the team. However, this may have been premature as the corporation Renault ensured that the F1 team Renault responded immediately to the investigation by sacking Briatore and Symonds and ensuring that all staff cooperated with the government body's enquiry (Piquet had been released by the organisation in July). Also the governing body FIA released its findings to the press to ensure the justification for its decision, ultimately to keep the team in the competition on a suspended sentence, which would allay fears of a whitewash or cover up and maintain the sport's integrity. This decision was in no small part due to the management of relationships within the sport that can be enhanced by sound public relations and communication principles. Both the sport and the Renault team are tarred by this event, however, steps have been taken to repair these reputations.

It is clear from the above examples that there is a need for further development of public relations and communication strategies, knowledge and understanding of the management of sport. As seen in the above situations, even successful international sporting organisations have a need for well-honed practices. The coordinated implementation of sport public relations through sport communication methods can minimise the negative impacts on the organisation's publics occurring.

There is no doubt that sport has transformed over the last 30 years. At the elite end of the sport continuum it has become a complex commercial enterprise, while at the "participation" end it has become quite sophisticated in marketing its activities to local communities. As a consequence, sport marketing is now a recognised and rapidly developing sector with universities offering sport marketing degrees. However, the one area where sport marketing is underdeveloped is in public relations and communication strategies. For the most part, sport management students have been forced to go to the generic management literature to further their understanding. In many respects this has not been a bad thing, but it often means that some of the "nuances" and special features of sport are not given sufficient focus. This [chapter] customises its discussion of public relations and communications so that it is directly relevant to the sport management student. It provides a concise guide as to how public relations and communication strategies and principles can be applied to sport management and marketing issues and problems. In short, it demonstrates how the principles of public relations and communications can be successfully applied in practice within a sport context (Stewart, 2002).

The [chapter] is structured to address the wide and varied activities in sport organisations that public relations and communications can develop in order to achieve wider business objectives. Underpinning all of these themes is an acknowledgement that sport organisations rely on a network of partners and publics that constitutes stakeholders. [...] The reader is also directed towards suggested readings and supporting websites that assist in developing further the chapter content.

PUBLIC RELATIONS AND COMMUNICATION IN SPORT

This chapter serves to provide the theoretical basis for this publication. Maria Hopwood provides an overview of PR theory and practice that is encapsulated initially as organisations *doing the right things at the right time*. By establishing the basis of PR activity as a crucial management activity Hopwood provides a crucial distinction as to how the public perceptions of PR have been tainted by its past associations with propaganda and its current connotation with spin. Following a series of definitions on PR that covers the academic and practitioner environments, the author presents a critique of how well-managed PR can be used to convert negative situations into positive ones. The second part of the chapter examines the background to the two key areas … . Sport Public Relations and Sport Communications is all about relationships … . However, Hopwood here defines it as a separate form of sport communication as the former is the activities by which relationships are managed and the latter is the modes of media that are chosen. This distinction is highlighted through a case study on the England and Wales Cricket Board's development of Twenty20 cricket in 2003 and its subsequent success.

SPORT RELATIONSHIP MANAGEMENT

David Shilbury and Katherine Rowe address the importance of managing the relationship with the sport organisation's stakeholders and publics. … They stress that difficulties arise when organisations view their publics as static and assume that they will respond predictably to certain events and situations. Sport organisations should manage their publics through a strategic approach to relationship management that can minimise these eventualities. They then focus on Ledingham's (2003) work on organisation—public relationships and the importance of management consideration of strategic publics. The work required by organisations to develop relationships with these strategic publics may be time- and resource-consuming; however, these efforts can offer the sport organisations benefits over the long term. The case study highlights such a situation where the Canterbury Bulldogs RLF Club used SPRC to sustain its relationship with its key strategic publics; its fans. The case addresses how this was done through a five-step process that saw the club increase its attendances in light of its situation. They conclude with an overview of the importance of relationship management in the context of sport outlining some of the key authors in the area and providing a platform for further study and investigation.

SPORT MARKETING PUBLIC RELATIONS

The concept of sport marketing public relations (SMPR) and its place within the management and marketing of sporting organizations is then introduced. Hopwood serves up the SMPR Rugby Ball model which represents the environment and context for the collection of marketing communication-related activities and presents where SMPR is positioned within the organisation. This is highlighted in the case of Durham County Cricket Club which forms one of two … cases. Following this is the application of Harris' (1993) key areas where traditional marketing public relations (MPR) (sans Sport) is applied to the sport industry. Hopwood then concludes with an examination of one of the key issues within this text. That of how does sport public relations and communications differ from the practices of sport marketing.

SPORT SOCIAL RESPONSIBILITY

Despite the increasing commercialisation and professionalisation of sporting practices organisations need to consider their impact on their wider international, national and local communities. James Skinner discusses the importance of adhering to principles of corporate social responsibility (CSR) for organisations in wishing to examine their community impact. The author extends Carroll's (1979) model of CSR to the sporting industry to provide an overview of sport social responsibility and the resultant SPRC benefits that arise from such an approach. Through a discussion of economic, legal, ethical and discretionary responsibilities, Skinner addresses how sporting organisations across the globe are positioning their work for CSR goals. This is highlighted in two cases, the first on the National Football League (NFL) and their use of the Super Bowl to produce public relations benefits for the game as a whole and the second case demonstrates how English football has repositioned itself through its national governing association, the Football Association (FA), to engage with CSR activities.

COMMUNITY RELATIONS AND ENGAGEMENT

Throughout the local, national and international there are many examples of how sport organisations do good work in local and international communities. Paul Kitchin and Rob Lewis address the importance of using SPRC to highlight these community relations and engagement situations. The development of community programmes of sport organisations or the sport-related community programmes of non-sport organisations has led to increasing media clutter for good news stories. Many organisations are yet to use this work to reach its potential benefits through the strategic application of SPRC in order to break this clutter. The first case focuses on the challenges that exist for a small not-for-profit sport organisation implementing SPRC on minimal resources. The case highlights how an organisation of this size works with partners and agencies to provide sport activities that complement the work of partners and hence provide SPRC opportunities throughout these partnerships. Capitalising on community involvement organisations can look to develop cause-related marketing (cause-RM) initiatives that use sport and physical activities to achieve a number of organisational goals. Many of these initiatives have been developed due to the rise of socially conscious consumers (Webster, 1975), more recently known as the ethical consumers. The second case study ... focuses on two such programmes. Both programmes aimed to get young people active to increase long-term participation, however, the specifications of the programme highlighted how the SPRC benefits can vary. We conclude with a discussion of the management implications for cause-RM and other community programme partnerships.

SPORT VOLUNTEERISM

B. Christine Green and Lawrence Chalip examine how the SPRC function can be used to assist in the recruitment and retention of volunteers and how these volunteers can be used to achieve a range of benefits for the sport organisation. The authors' focus on how volunteer involvement can be beneficial not only for making volunteers feel more valued but also for heightening organisational profile and reputation. Additionally, by providing the local community with speakers to present a range of issues important to the sport organisation links can be developed with the local stakeholders. The first case focuses on how Special Olympics International uses it volunteers to fulfil key SPRC roles and increases awareness and understanding of the movement in the community. The second case focuses on the Purple Armband Games ... , which was established by supporter groups to highlight the plight of those caught up in violent and abusive situations. This volunteer programme was used by sport organisations to further develop links with stakeholders and create a proactive stance on these serious issues. The chapter concludes with a discussion on the benefits of using volunteers within the SPRC function itself. Although challenging, this can assist the organisation in achieving its objectives without requiring significant financial resources.

CRISIS COMMUNICATIONS AND SPORT PUBLIC RELATIONS

The importance of the SPRC function is instrumental when the sport organisation suffers a crisis situation. Allan Edwards and Wayne Usher focus on the need for crisis management practices. This is developed through considering the naturalist and positivist perspectives of crisis management. This ... develops into a discussion of crisis communication strategies in light of the case of the Brisbane Broncos RLFC. Edwards and Usher then draw attention to approaches used by sporting organisations in a number of contexts and focus on the Gonzalez-Herrero and Pratt (1996) model of crisis communications. Finally they focus on the professional sport leagues in the USA and the inability of two of their leagues to implement more proactive public relations in light of the incidents. Recommendations for practice are presented.

THE PUBLIC RELATIONS ROLE OF FANS AND SUPPORTERS' GROUPS

... We will be looking specifically at the role that fans and supporters play in sport public relations and communications. Referring to specific supporter groups such as the Barmy Army, Maria Hopwood highlights their intense public relations value to sport organisations and contends that those organisations need to use their fans and supporters' groups strategically for public relations purposes. Fans and supporters are the highly visible representation of sport public relations and communications as they are the living and breathing representation—the heart and soul—of sport. Fans and supporters are the lifeblood of any sport organisation. Without their support, the sport organisation would arguably cease to exist and function. For the astute sport organisation, fans and supporters are a key public relations tool. They only say good things about the sport organisation and they support it through thick and thin. Even more importantly, they are likely to pass on their passion for the sport organisation to their children and others. For this reason and others, fans and supporters' groups are extremely important brand ambassadors for any sport organisation and, consequentially, are an extremely powerful sport public relations and communication resource. Hopwood has included a case study based on the time she and her family spent with the Barmy Army at the 2004 test match series between England and the West Indies at Antigua when Brian Lara made his historic 400 not out.

CROSS-CULTURAL SPORT PUBLIC RELATIONS AND COMMUNICATION

Developing communication strategies that are designed to cross borders and cultures is a challenge for those involved in managing the SPRC function. Jacquie L'Etang discusses these challenges facing public relations in complex and increasingly international contexts. L'Etang takes a critical perspective to discuss the role and function of public relations in these environments. The importance of cultural analysis is considered in light of its implications for communication. This is applied through a brief analysis of mayoral justifications of four cities bidding for the 2012 Olympic Games. In this regard the reader is encouraged to compare and contrast bidding communications rhetoric. L'Etang then carries out a detailed discussion of factors that add complexity to the SPRC function with regard to cultures, borders and the forces of globalisation before presenting a critical review of its potential impact on sport business.

NEW COMMUNICATIONS MEDIA FOR SPORT

The rapid rise of telecommunication systems such as satellite television to the development of social networking sites has progressed beyond all early predictions. … Lewis and Kitchin address the evolution and role of new media and communications in developing SPRC strategies. The authors begin by presenting an overview of the PR uses of the Internet from 1996 to 2005. At this time sporting organisations were deemed to be reactionary towards SPRC opportunities but additionally faced with increased challenges presented by heightened stakeholder interest in these organisations. The first case addresses the Purple Armband Games … and how the movement was supported by a website that coordinated the group's advocacy work. The then consider the paradigm shift of Web 2.0 and its implications for SPRC. A number of Web 2.0 tools are developed in light of their potential benefit to SPRC. The second case examines MyColts.net, a social networking site developed for the Indianapolis Colts NFL team. They discuss social media and why it is important to sporting organisations looking to break through the communications clutter. The authors present a series of guidelines for developing a social media strategy for sporting organisations.

PUBLIC RELATIONS FOR PLAYERS

… Skinner draws predominately on the work of Summers and Morgan (2008) to explore the role of public relations in professional sport. In doing this, particular emphasis on how public relations and communication strategies can be used when dealing with potentially damaging situations for players, the sport organisation and the sport itself are discussed. A failure by sport public relations professionals to deal with a player's crisis can lead to unsavoury or bad press about players and has the potential to call into question a player's reputation and lead to poor public perception of the sport organisation and/or sport. This negative press has the potential to impact on future participation problems and a reduction in a range of revenue streams including sponsorships and player endorsements (Bruce and Tini, 2008). The author suggests that given the "market value" of a player's image and the reputation of the sport hinges on public perception, which is the domain of the sport public relations professional, it is vital for this professional to nurture and defend a player's image and a sport's reputation. It is argued that at its best public relations should be proactive in its efforts to create a positive player image and reputation; however, it is often forced to react to negative situations by using strategies to repair a tarnished player image or reputation in order to defuse a public perception crisis. The author concludes by highlighting that it is essential that sport public relations professionals need to focus on protecting and enhancing a positive player image and reputation through building and maintaining mutually beneficial relationships with key publics, in particular their fans (Hopwood, 2007).

INTERNATIONAL SPORT PUBLIC RELATIONS

… Skinner is joined by Kristine Toohey in examining the rise of international sport public relations. The authors first examine the rise in international public relations as a consequence of increasing international trade, communications and politics. Focusing on international SPRC the chapter examines previous use of the Olympic Games to provide non-sporting agendas to be broadcast across the globe. The first case examines the Olympic Torch Relay and the public relations difficulties the International Olympic Committee (IOC) and the Beijing 2008 organisers faced as it travelled from Greece to the Bird's Nest stadium in Beijing. Skinner and Toohey go on to focus on the role that International Non-Governmental Organisations (INGO—of which the IOC is one) can play in the development of society through sport. The public relations issues that these INGOs face in this work are discussed. Once again focusing on the IOC, and in this case on the Salt Lake City Bribery scandal, the authors highlight how the appointment of a well-known PR consultancy assisted in resolving stakeholder management issues.

RECOMMENDED WEBSITES

For coverage of the terrorist attack on the Sri Lankan cricket team readers can be directed to the BBC and Cricinfo websites at http://news.bbc.co.uk/1/hi/world/south_asia/7920677.stm and http://www.cricinfo.com/infocus/content/story/infocus.html?subject=38, respectively.

For coverage of the Singapore Grand Prix race-fixing scandal see the following: http://en.wikipedia.org/wiki/Renault_Formula_One_crash_controversy.

For journals relating to Sport Public Relations and Communication see:

International Journal of Sport Communication—http://hk.humankinetics.com/ijsc/journalAbout.cfm.

Journal of Sport Media—http://muse.jhu.edu/journals/journal_of_sport_ media/.

Additionally a special edition from Public Relations Review—https://enduser.elsevier.com/campaigntypes/specissue/index.cfm?campaign=public_relations_sport.

International Journal of Sport Marketing and Sponsorship—http://www. im-reports.com/SM/IJSM/?type=current.

For a general blog site on the area of Sport PR—http://sportprblog.com/blog/.

REFERENCES

Barnes, S., 2009. The worst act of cheating in the history of sport. Times Online. Retrieved on 17 September 2009 from: http://www.timesonline.co.uk/tol/sport/formula_1/article6837713.ece.

Bruce, T., Tini, T., 2008. Unique crisis response strategies in sport public relations: Rugby League and the case for diversion. *Public Relations Review 34*, 108–115.

Carroll, A.B., 1979. A three dimensional model of corporate performance. *Academy of Management Review 4* (4), 497–505.

Fédération Internationale de l'Automobile, 2009. Press release: World Motor Sport Council. FIA Online. Retrieved on 22 September 2009 from: http://www.fia.com/en-GB/mediacentre/pressreleases/wmsc/2009/Pages/wmsc_210909.aspx.

Gonzalez-Herrero, A., Pratt, C.B., 1996. An integrated model for crisis communication management. *Journal of Public Relations Research 8* (2), 79–105.

Harris, T.L., 1993. How MPR adds value to integrated marketing communications. *Public Relations Quarterly 38* (2), 13–19.

Hopwood, M.K., 2007. The sport integrated communications mix: sport public relations. In: Beech, J., Chadwick, S. (Eds.), The Marketing of Sport. Prentice Hall, Harlow, England, pp. 292–317.

Ledingham, J.A., 2003. Explicating relationship management as a general theory of public relations. *Journal of Public Relations Research 15* (2), 188–198.

Stewart, B., 2002. Foreword. In: Edwards, A., Gilbert, K., Skinner, J. Extending the Boundaries: Theoretical Frameworks for Research in Sport Management. Melbourne, Victoria, Common Ground Publications, p. XI.

Summers, J., Morgan, M.J., 2008. More than just the media: considering the role of public relations in the creation of sporting celebrity and the management of fan expectations. *Public Relations Review 34*, 176–182.

Webster Jr., F.E., 1975. Characteristics of the socially conscious consumer. *Journal of Consumer Research 2*, 188–196.

SECTION

BEST PRACTICES IN PUBLIC RELATIONS

The four chapters that comprise this section of our text cover some of the most critical areas in the practice of public relations.

Public relations practitioners have an extensive responsibility to grow, maintain, and restore the organization's reputation, so we'll begin this "best practices" review looking at the need to monitor the environment. After all, the best crisis is the one that never occurs, so understanding *risk* and *issues management* is imperative to that environmental monitoring. Brand and reputation exist together, so understanding the intersection and interactions of the two is critical. Chapter 10 ends with an extensive look at *crisis management* and *crisis communication*.

In order to be as effective and efficient as possible with our communication efforts, we need to understand the characteristics of our stakeholders to help us hone and deliver our messages. The goal of Chapter 11 is to help us understand how the values, concerns, motivations, pain points, behaviors, and goals of those groups who are affected by (or who affect) our organization can help us to craft messages that really resonate and to communicate with our stakeholders.

As public relations has grown more global, we need to expand this understanding of stakeholders to a global level. In Chapter 12, we explore how cultural attributes, political ideologies, and economic systems affect both the message and the interpretation of that message within our global stakeholder community.

We close this section in Chapter 13 with an in-depth tour de force of the common tactics utilized by public relations practitioners. Writing, broadcast, speech, and digital tools are discussed with an eye to helping you understand how they are best used as vehicles of both communications and understanding.

10 MONITORING THE ENVIRONMENT AND PREPARING FOR THREAT AND CRISES

Reading 3.1:
"Reputation
Management"
By John Doorley
and Helio F. Garcia

As we discovered in Chapter 4, one of the fastest ways to demonstrate the value of public relations and gain a seat at the table is to become the expert communicator in times of threat and crises. We'll begin drilling down into this important area of public relations with our reading on *reputation management*. According to coauthors John Doorley and Fred Garcia, reputation is the sum of all the images the various constituencies have of the organization, which are created through the organization's performance, behavior, and communication (Doorley and Garcia 2007, p. 3).

Reputation is the central responsibility of our communication efforts on behalf of the organization during threat and crisis. But to round out our understanding of this important responsibility, we'll also explore *risk management* and *issue management*. With regard to the latter, we'll look specifically at how governance impacts our ability to manage issues as well as the tools to do so, including issues teams, topic-specific task forces, issues-resource teams, threat assessment, and how we should prioritize issues. We'll finish with a holistic look at how to bring all these factors and tools to bear to ensure issues-management success.

An organization's brand cannot live separate from its reputation, and vice versa, so we'll discover and define the interaction of the two. Then we'll go into detail on the mechanics of *crisis management* and *crisis communication*, starting with the role of public relations in managing crises. Success in crisis communications is largely dependent on our ability to work with the media and understand the rules of engagement. Along the way, we'll look at the various types of crises you are likely to be confronted with in your career and how best to control or minimize rumors.

We'll build on a foundation of various theories and practices, including the contributions of various academic disciplines and media theories to our understanding of crisis communications. Public relations scholars and practitioners have also developed our own set of theories, including corporate apologia (Benoit 1995), image repair theory (Benoit 1997), situational crisis communication theory (Coombs 2007), and organizational renewal theory (Ulmer & Sellnow 2002). We will discuss how these fit within the three most important aspects of crisis communication: be quick, be accurate, and be consistent. Finishing on a high note, we'll discuss the emergence and advantages of a discourse of renewal.

"REPUTATION MANAGEMENT"

By John Doorley and Helio F. Garcia

In 1998 Abercrombie & Fitch published a back-to-school catalog with a section advocating that college students drink creatively, rather than just participate in the standard beer binge. The section, headed "Drinking 101," contained recipes for the Woo-Woo, the Beach Hemorrhage, and other potent mixtures. The organization Mothers Against Drunk Driving was irate. Within days, NBC's Today Show was set to interview MADD's president, but the clothing company refused to send a spokesperson (issuing just a brief statement). The question is: Should the company have sent a spokesperson?[1]

When that question is asked of communication or PR majors (this book's coauthor John Doorley has done this with many classes) most students say yes; often the teacher is the only dissenter. The reason for dissent: The company had not formulated any policy expressing embarrassment, let alone shame, and there was no commitment to mitigate the damage—for example, recall the catalog and help wage responsibility-in-drinking campaigns. Most college students are not of drinking age, and the company appeared to care little about the health of the people who wear their clothing. What could the spokesperson have said, in lieu of repudiation and correction, that would not have made the matter worse? For as Will Rogers was fond of saying: "When you find yourself in a hole, the first thing to do is stop digging."

Eventually, of course, the company had to issue statements and provide stickers for existing catalogs that advocated responsibility in drinking. MADD and most PR observers agreed it was too little too late.

It turns out that A & F has published catalogs for their young audiences with nude models, and been criticized for not featuring people of color. It seems that A & F is not concerned about their reputation with older audiences, believing perhaps that the younger audiences will not care about the social issues and may even want their clothing all the more. One has to hand it to the company: It is a bold marketing strategy, and a very risky reputation strategy, especially over the long term. Creating demand is one thing, but alienating the people who pay the bills, as well as groups that devote their lives to a cause, is another. (By the way, what is the name of that organization of mothers that almost single handedly forced the United States government into the nationwide drinking-age limit of 21?)

THIS CHAPTER COVERS

- Reputational capital
- Identity
- Can reputation be measured?
- Can reputation be managed?
- "Intangible asset"—the wrong perspective
- Comprehensive reputation management
- Confusing communication with performance and behavior
- Sidebar: It's all about the relationship
- The ten precepts of reputation management
- Reputation management: The best corporate communication strategy
- Sidebar: Systems theory
- Best practices
- Resources for further study
- Questions for further discussion

Shakespeare called it "the purest treasure mortal times afford." Men have fought duels and killed for it. Companies and other institutions have succeeded or failed because of it. Warren Buffett said: "If you lose dollars for the firm by bad decisions, I will be very understanding. If you lose reputation for the firm, I will be ruthless." It seems that Mr. Buffett was paraphrasing Othello: "He who steals my purse steals trash … but he that filches from me my good name … makes me poor indeed."[2]

The business scandals of the first years of the twenty-first century demonstrated how important it is to build, maintain, and defend reputation. The scandals spread to nonprofits, government, universities, and sports, and the public seemed to tire of the press reports. But fatigue did not convey immunity, so people demanded change: tougher laws, more governance, and greater accountability. At the same time, academic researchers and public relations professionals intensified efforts to quantify and manage reputation, heretofore thought of as an intangible asset.

Reputation scholar Charles Fombrun, professor emeritus, Stern School of Business, New York University, an editor-in-chief of the journal Corporate Reputation Review, defines reputation as the sum of the images the various constituencies have of an organization.[3]

John Doorley and Fred Garcia (this book's coauthors) accept that definition but also like their own—which leads us to:

Reputation = Sum of Images = (Performance and Behavior) + Communication

This definition helps make it clear that performance and behavior, as well as communication, are critical components of reputation.

REPUTATIONAL CAPITAL

Just as people develop social capital that helps them build relationships and careers, corporations and other organizations develop reputational capital that helps them build relationships and grow their organizations.

A good reputation has both intangible and tangible benefits. It is important for audiences, from customers to employees to consumer advocates, to feel good about an organization, and it is important to build a good reputation to sustain an organization through the tough times. But a reputation is worth much more than that. Companies with the better reputations attract more and better candidates for employment, pay less for supplies, gain essentially free press coverage that is worth as much if not more than advertising, and accrue other benefits that actually contribute to profits. Reputation adds value to the actual worth of a company—that is, market capitalization (the number of shares outstanding times the price per share) includes more than just the book value or liquidation value of assets. The reputation component of market capitalization, reputational capital, is a concept closely related to "goodwill," and it is worth many billions of dollars in many large corporations. It has a value in not-for-profits, government, and universities as well. For instance, a good reputation helps a university attract students and donors.

Although CEOs agree that reputation has a value—is an asset—few firms actually treat it as such. Few companies or nonprofits take a rigorous, quantifiable approach to reputation management—measuring, monitoring and managing reputation assets and liabilities—yet such an approach is intrinsic to the concept of asset management. Most organizations have no idea what their reputations are worth, yet reasonable measurements (absolute or relative) can be agreed upon and taken. Most companies do not have a system in place for regular, periodic accountability on variations in reputation, yet without such a system opportunities will be missed and problems will become magnified. Measurement, acknowledgment, and planning make possible proactive behaviors and communications to take advantage of reputational opportunities and minimize problems—thereby building reputational capital.

IDENTITY

To reputation scholars like Fombrun, "identity" is the raison d'etre of an organization. It is, simply, what the organization stands for above all else. To distinguish this concept from other uses of the term (such as corporate identity programs that try to position the company in a particular way through all its communications and graphic vehicles), Paul Verbinnen of Citigate Sard Verbinnen coined the term "intrinsic identity." (We use that term…)

Of course organizations, like individuals, have multiple identities. Research by George Cheney of the University of Colorado, in *Rhetoric in an Organizational Society: Managing Multiple Identities*, is consistent with the proposition that multiple identities need not pose any conflicts, as long as there is a clear, dominant identity.[4] Johnson & Johnson, for example, seeks not just to develop, make, and market quality health-care products for patients, it also seeks profits large enough to attract shareholders, reward employees, and stoke research. But the commitment to serving patients and the healthcare community, as expressed in the company's credo and demonstrated in the response to the Tylenol® tampering crises in 1982 and 1986, has clearly been the dominant identity over the years.

Other companies, such as the venerable General Electric and the relative upstart Starbucks, have each stayed true to a dominant identity: respectively developing and marketing consumer and technology products of the highest quality, and employing the best people to obtain, market, and sell quality coffee and collateral products in a warm and welcoming venue. Starbucks is not at all embarrassed to proclaim the ideals of mutually beneficial and profitable relationships with employees and communities. A Starbucks ad running in national media in 2005 stated: "It's about idealism, and community, and sustainability. It's about remembering how things should be, and striving to get there."[5]

Other organizations, sadly and notably, have recently failed to stay true to the dominant identities that made them successful:

The Catholic Church. The scandals over the sexual abuse of young children by some priests, which came to light starting in the Boston Diocese in 2002, were shocking and horrible enough. Catholics and non-Catholics recognized that evil could exist anywhere. But what drove many Catholics away from the church was the coverup by the church hierarchy, from bishops to cardinals. In numerous instances, they knowingly sent offending priests to other parishes without telling the legal authorities or the people in the new parish, leaving the priests free to commit the same crimes over and over. The average priest believes he exists to give spiritual and emotional guidance to the people in his parish, but many of the bishops and cardinals forgot that raison d'etre; instead, they believed they had to protect the church's image at all cost.

In his first public statement as Boston's new archbishop, Sean P. O'Malley made explicit reference to the need to return to the Church's intrinsic identity:

> We can only hope that the bitter medicine we have had to take to remedy our mismanagement of the problem of sexual abuse will prove beneficial, making all of us more aware of the dreadful consequences of this crime and more vigilant and effective in eradicating this evil from our midst. How we ultimately deal with the present crisis in our Church will do much to define us as Catholics of the future. If we do not flee from the cross of pain and humiliation, if we stand firm in who we are and what we stand for, if we work together, hierarchy, priests, religious and laity, to live our faith and fulfill our mission, then we will be a stronger and a holier Church.[6]

The New York Times. To its credit, *The New York Times* broke the story itself in a front-page exposé on May 11, 2003. Reporter Jayson Blair had plagiarized content from other newspapers, had fabricated whole stories, and had invented scenes for stories that appeared in the paper, including major front-page ones over a period of years. There were warning signs bold and numerous enough to have stopped him early on, but the top editors ignored them. Why did the people charged with seeing that the country's "newspaper of record," the one that exists to report "all the news that's fit to print," publish the unfit? An explanation that makes sense is that one of the paper's other identities—including its commitment to affirmative action (Blair is African American) and a desire not to rock the boat about a reporter thought to be a favorite of the executive editor—superseded, in this case, its commitment to quality. So while the paper can be proud of its various identities, it cannot be anything but humbled by its failure to live up to its commitment to quality journalism, above all else.

In the wake of the Blair scandal, *The Times* has reaffirmed its commitment to its intrinsic identity, and has established numerous structures, including a new public editor and a new standards editor, to try to assure that it is not distracted from its mission again.

It is important for employees to understand and be committed to the organization's dominant intrinsic identity. For example, if the CEO truly believes the organization is committed above all else to quality products, but the average sales person believes the dominant identity is the sales quota, there exists a prescription for disaster. For in difficult times, what the employees believe the organization stands for will determine what they will do, just as surely as it did with Blair and the church.

Another benefit of a clear identity is that it can drive behavior, performance, and communication, as it should. Then, internal and external constituencies will all understand what the organization is about.

CAN REPUTATION BE MEASURED?

Fombrun maintains that reputational capital is the difference, averaged over time, between market capitalization and the liquidation value of assets. Many chief financial officers disagree with that formula, believing that the difference overstates the value of reputational capital. But even those CFOs agree that much of that difference is reputational capital. The more common approach to measuring reputation is to take comparative measures against similar organizations. The annual *Fortune* magazine survey of America's Most Admired Companies is among the most widely known and respected by both industry leaders and academics. But it surveys only three constituencies: senior executives, (outside) board members, and securities analysts. A more comprehensive approach would include surveying all the major constituencies, including employees, customers, and the press.

Another is the Harris-Fombrun Reputation Quotient (by Harris Interactive in association with Charles Fombrun). It evaluates reputation among "multiple audiences," according to twenty attributes that are grouped into what are referred to as "dimensions of reputation": products and services; financial performance; workplace environment; social responsibility; vision and leadership; and emotional appeal. The results of that survey are widely covered by the press, including each year, Ronald Alsop of *The Wall Street Journal*, author of *The 18 Immutable Laws of Corporate Reputation*.

CAN REPUTATION BE MANAGED?

There are many organizations with "reputation management" in their names and their number has increased markedly since the Sarbanes-Oxley Act became law in the wake of U.S. corporate scandals. Yet most of them are actually reputation measurement organizations that offer little in the way of reputation management. There are many conferences on reputation management, yet they too focus on measurement or only on specific parts of reputation management, such as crisis communication. They do not produce a plan or a document that aims to manage reputation as other assets are managed—including the plusses and the negatives associated with any asset.

Some academics believe that reputation can be managed, while others believe it cannot be. While more research in the field of reputation management is needed, the pro-management body of academic literature is certainly as strong as the contrary studies, if not stronger. And one thing is certain, as recent business scandals have demonstrated in the sharpest relief: reputations can surely be mismanaged, and in many cases, not managed at all. There is a clear need for a new approach that will help companies and other organizations measure, monitor, and manage their reputations, and the factors that contribute to reputation, organization-wide, over the long term.

"INTANGIBLE ASSET"—THE WRONG PERSPECTIVE

The reason most organizations do not have formal programs to manage reputation is that they view it as something "soft"—intangible. Yet as nebulous as reputation can seem, it has real, tangible value (dollars, for example) that can be measured. So the historical view of reputation as an intangible asset is the wrong approach. Moreover, such a view is analogous to that of some parents who say they need not be that concerned about their young children's character, because "they will be influenced by their peers anyway when they become teenagers." Such laissez-faireism—whether in parenting children or organizations—is a prescription for disaster, as recent history has clearly demonstrated.

Like all other assets—a building or a product, for example—reputation has its liability side. So any reputation management plan has to measure, monitor, and establish a plan for managing both the reputation assets and vulnerabilities/liabilities. The important thing is to have a plan. If the following is not an ancient proverb, it should be: "If you don't know where you're going, any road will take you there."

So a major question for leaders of organizations is: Can reputation be managed? It follows that those who believe it can be managed—perhaps not totally, but which asset can be?—must establish a plan to do so, as they would for any other asset.

COMPREHENSIVE REPUTATION MANAGEMENT

"Comprehensive Reputation Management" (© *2003, John Doorley*) provides a formal framework for managing reputation. It is one way for an organization to get its arms around this asset, and a way to manage reputation problems, vulnerabilities, and opportunities. It has been vetted before the leadership of The Conference Board, many industry leaders and CEOs, numerous academic researchers, and heads of corporate communications at thirty major companies. Paul Verbinnen and Rich Coyle of Citigate Sard Verbinnen made significant contributions.

> Comprehensive Reputation Management =
> A long-term strategy for measuring, monitoring, and managing an organization's reputation as an asset. Comprehensive Reputation Management is to reputation what risk management is to other assets

This strategy results in the management of an organization's intrinsic identity (what it stands for) and external images, giving an organization a methodology for working to converge the two. The Comprehensive Reputation Management methodology is applied to the major areas of an organization—for example, finance, human resources, investor relations, manufacturing, marketing, and public affairs. Each area gets involved in a process that is a way of approaching total reputation management—(performance and behavior) + communication—and is distinct from brand management (the marketing value of a name) or corporate identity programs (which usually boil down to institutional advertising).

These are the six major components of Comprehensive Reputation Management:

1   *Customized Reputation Template.* The measurement tool begins with a basic template that is then customized for each organization. In some cases, the organization may simply want to improve its ranking in an established poll, such as *Fortune* magazine's, which is based on eight criteria or attributes: innovativeness, quality of management, employee talent, financial soundness, use of corporate assets, long-term investment value, social responsibility, and quality of products/services. Certain of the financial measures may be more important to some companies than to others, as might be environmental performance and community relations (under "social responsibility") and so on.

Reputation Criteria: Basic Template for Comprehensive Reputation Management program includes:

- Innovation
- Quality of Management
- Employee Talent
- Financial Performance
- Social Responsibility
- Product Quality

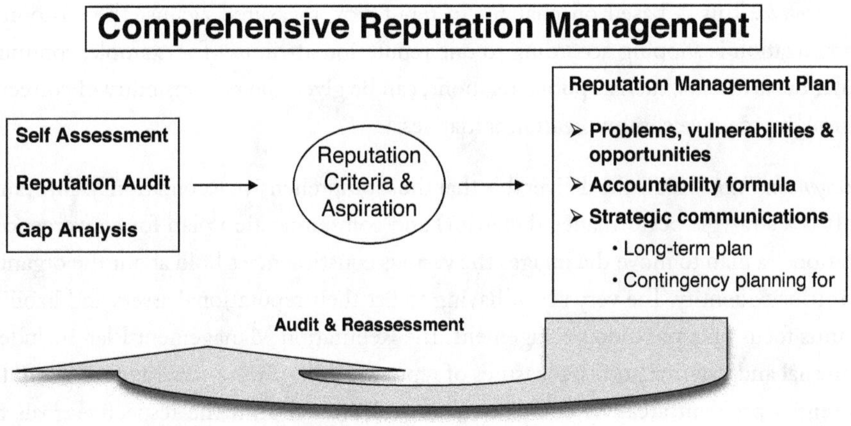

Comprehensive Reputation Management

FIGURE 10.1. Comprehensive Reputation Management

- Communicativeness (Transparency)
- Governance
- Integrity (Responsibility, Reliability, Credibility, Trustworthiness)

The first six are the time-tested *Fortune* criteria, with the three financial measures collapsed to one. Communicativeness is part of the template because there has now been more work done to demonstrate the link between an organization's transparency and its reputation. (See reference to *Corporate Reputation Review* paper in The Best Communication Strategy section, later in this chapter.) Governance is listed because it is now, especially post Sarbanes-Oxley, an important part of the reputation mix. Integrity is this model's way of encompassing the four character traits that research by Fombrun and others has shown to have a direct effect on reputation: responsibility, reliability, credibility, and trustworthiness.

The basic template can then be customized for the particular organization, and the resultant customized template becomes senior management's acknowledgment of which reputation factors are most important. The customized template becomes the tool for measuring changes in reputational capital. The template can also be customized by constituency, because different constituencies care more about different attributes.

2   *Reputation Audits of Internal and External Constituencies.* One audit assesses what employees believe to be the intrinsic identity (what the organization stands for) and compares that with what senior leadership believes the intrinsic identity to be. The gap between the two views is analyzed and a plan (part of the Reputation Management Plan) to converge them is created. A second audit measures how external constituencies view the organization, and the sum of those constituency images constitutes reputation. The gap between identity and reputation is analyzed, and a plan (part of the Reputation Management Plan) to converge the two is created.

3   *Reputational Capital Goals.* Goals are established for performance within an industry group, for example, or versus competitors. For example, a company might establish a goal of moving up into the top quartile of its industry sector. Progress toward that goal can then be measured, monitored, and managed.

4   *An Accountability Formula.* This is based on changes in reputation measured against the customized template. If the organization is slipping according to one reputation attribute (for example, communicativeness) particular departments, such as public relations, can be given the responsibility of correcting that impression through proactive communication initiatives.

5   *A Reputation Management Plan.* This is the deliverable that the Comprehensive Reputation Management process produces. It is a strategic performance (behavior) and communication plan for convergence of identity and reputation—a plan to move the images the various constituencies hold about the organization closer to the intrinsic identity. The very act of having to list their reputational assets and liabilities helps the various units focus on reputation management. The Reputation Management Plan includes: a summary of the internal and external audits; measures of reputational capital; a statement of reputation challenges and potential problem areas by company or organizational unit; the respective goals and opportunities; and corporate or organizational message strategies. With objectives, strategies, timelines, and so forth, the Reputation Management Plan becomes a strategic guide for units of the organization to follow, short—and—long term.

6   *Annual Follow-Up Audit and Assessment According to the Standards in the Reputation Management Plan.*

CONFUSING COMMUNICATION WITH PERFORMANCE AND BEHAVIOR

Pushmi-Pullyu. In Kurt Eichenwald's *Conspiracy of Fools*, Enron CEO Kenneth Lay proclaims to his public relations officer Mark Palmer, not long before the collapse of the company: "The reason we can't right the ship is we're not doing a good job in dealing with the press."[7] In other words, Lay saw a communication problem, not a performance or behavior problem. On the other hand, a major article about professional basketball in *The New York Times Magazine* of February 13, 2005, maintained that the National Basketball Association does not have a "drug problem or a thug problem (or a PR problem)." Instead, the players, despite their unprecedented athleticism, do not play with teamwork, the way the sport used to be played. "It has a basketball problem."

In the contest between the steak and the sizzle the steak will, inevitably, prove more important. Or, as in Enron's case, the sizzle will always evaporate. Wendy's television commercial from the 1980s, "Where's the beef?" said it best.

In *The Story of Doctor Doolittle*, by renowned children's author Hugh Lofting, the good doctor comes across a mythical, rare animal in Africa. It is a llamalike creature with one head at the front, where it would normally be, and one at the base of its spine, and it is called Pushmi-Pullyu. "Lord save us," cries the duck. "How does it make up its mind?"[8]

The Pushmi-Pullyu metaphor (devised by John Baruch, LittD, former CEO of Reed & Carnrick) is a fitting one to represent the problem that public relations and corporate communication practitioners face: the confusion of behavior or performance with communication—of the substantive issue with the communication about it. While the communication objectives and strategies should always be in synch with the business objectives and strategies, they are distinct. Communication cannot make a bad product good, at least over the long run. Of course it can make a good or fair product seem worse, as it did with the Exxon Valdez crisis in 1989. (Many observers agreed that Exxon did a pretty good job operationally in cleaning up the oil spill, but the communications were a disaster.) In 2006, the mishandling of communication regarding the hunting accident involving Vice President Dick Cheney clearly made the matter worse, and played right into the hands of the press and its insatiable appetite for sensationalism.

Pushmi-Pullyu is a syndrome that explains the generations-old lament of corporate and organizational communicators about their lack of a "seat at the table." The reason this has been a problem, of course, is that, too often, an organization develops an ill-advised product or position, or takes such an action, and then asks the communications group to justify it. The performance/behavior head is turning in one direction and saying one thing, and then it expects the communications head to turn and speak in a different direction.

Merck. When John Doorley was hired in 1987 to form Merck's first corporate communications department the company was not widely known outside of business and healthcare circles. But it was on fire with success—with important new medicines and excellent profits—under the leadership of P. Roy Vagelos, MD, whose own reputation as a scientist and businessman was impeccable. The ensuing public relations campaign, led by an aggressive media outreach initiative, produced quick results. For instance, an October 19, 1987, cover story in *Business Week* was headlined, simply, "The Miracle Company." The campaign continued through the nineties, fueled by an outstanding science and business story, and Merck landed on everyone's most admired list (including a record seven years as America's Most Admired Company in *Fortune*'s annual cover-story survey). It was all PR, essentially free, with virtually no corporate advertising.

Since 2000 the company has been hit by the perfect storm of dreadful events. Several late-stage investigational medicines failed in the clinic, and the company's pharmaceutical research, which had always been cyclical, hit a nadir. The profit picture began to look bleak and the company missed some of its own earnings projections. Then, in the fall of 2004, the company decided to recall the painkiller Vioxx, because of cardiovascular side effects in certain patients. Amidst what at this writing may turn out to be the largest wave of product liability suits ever, the company fights for its reputation against charges of side effect coverup.

In October 2004, presumably because of the ongoing litigation, the company chose not to aggressively discuss the matter with *The Wall Street Journal* reporters whose seminal front-page article exploring the allegation appeared on November 1, 2004. The company had provided an outside attorney as spokesperson and did not address questions about individual documents. Yet the *Journal* is one of the publications that could be most disposed to letting the company make its case, and Merck's failure to do so in the article predictably produced pack journalism reports on the major TV expose magazine shows. On May 30, 2005, after enormous reputation damage, the company launched a multimillion-dollar advertising campaign, which, the company said, had been in the works for a few years. If the campaign is to be successful, it will need to be matched by significantly improved research, financial performance, and an aggressive public relations program. The strategy of using controlled (paid) media makes sense, but only in conjunction with the more credible, albeit less controlled, communication initiatives that tell the story of performance.

Reframing the Problem. In 2002 this book's coauthor Fred Garcia was called into a company to consult on what the communications people called a "*Fortune* magazine problem." They said *Fortune* was working on a story about the company's chairman, a flamboyant, politically connected executive who had borrowed millions of dollars from the company to support a lavish lifestyle. The chairman's business and political enemies were pointing to the lifestyle, and to other personal foibles and business failures, and the company's stock was suffering. Investors and analysts were asking questions but getting no satisfactory answers. It seemed like the worst mix of Enron, Tyco, and WorldCom. Company leadership was also concerned that the weakening stock price could lead to a hostile takeover.

Fred asked the company leadership what would happen if *Fortune* magazine should be persuaded not to run a story: would the problem be solved? They acknowledged that they would still be as vulnerable to takeover and to critics' capitalizing on the company's weakness in other ways. "You don't have a *Fortune* magazine problem," Fred told them, "you have a governance problem." He met with the general counsel and several board members.

They discussed various scenarios under which they could remedy the company's weaknesses. Regardless of the scenario, one thing was consistent: success required the chairman to resign and to repay his loans to the company. The only meaningful question was timing: could he leave before the company suffered more harm, or would he resist, leading to calls by shareholders and others for his resignation, declines in the stock price, and eventually his ouster? Given the alternatives, the Board persuaded the chairman to leave quickly. He resigned within two weeks, and repaid his loan. The company's stock price rebounded. There was no takeover. And no *Fortune* article.

The solution to the struggle represented by the Pushmi-Pullyu metaphor—the solution to the push and pull of substance and communication—is to have the entire organization behave and communicate as one.

IT'S ALL ABOUT BUILDING THE RELATIONSHIP

By Kenneth P. Berkowitz, Esq.

A critical first step in reputation management, it seems to me, is the building and cultivation of relationships with key constituencies. Show me a successful PR practitioner or lobbyist, and I will show you someone who has developed strong individual relationships and cultivates them in a planned, concerted way on an ongoing basis. Building and maintaining relationships, as is true of reputation, should be viewed as a full-time effort.

The best way to establish a relationship is to understand that it must benefit both parties—in this case, the organization as well as other constituencies, the government including regulatory agencies, news media, customers, suppliers, employees, and other important constituencies. It should come as no surprise, therefore, that a critical first step is to identify the critical constituencies of the organization. Practitioners should then identify or, as necessary, conduct research to determine the constituency's needs and then use that information for the benefit of both parties, what the academics call the "two-way symmetrical" model. What often happens is that PR departments do the research and then try to exploit it for the organization's benefit alone ("two-way unsymmetrical"); this seldom proves a productive strategy over the long run. And once an established relationship "sours," it may prove to be unsalvageable.

Along those lines, relationships have to have a degree of unselfishness in order for the parties to be respectful of each other. It's a dot-connected world—Word gets around. And a PR practitioner or company lobbyist cannot afford to just disconnect from a relationship when it becomes unproductive: for example, when the reporter retires or a legislator loses an election, or when the constituency acts against the interest of the organization. Disagreement must be anticipated, as one can never expect both parties to be in agreement on all issues.

So that this aspect of relationship management is not viewed as "soft" and static or unmanageable, formal strategies and objectives should be established and monitored. The strategies and objectives should also force practitioners to go out and meet face-to-face on an ongoing basis with their constituencies, which is a hard thing even for some public relations people and lobbyists to initiate. You almost need to treat your constituencies as sales people would treat their customers. Here are five such strategies that I have encouraged my colleagues to implement over the years:

> (1) Target key areas that really matter to your organization. Public relations practitioners and lobbyists have to focus first on areas where the organization has business or other interests, particularly areas where they can make a difference. It does little good to try to meet with reporters at each of the one hundred top dailies, or to establish relationships with every congressional or state legislative staffer (and remember that staff can be as important

as the elected official). While you need to target the capitals (Brussels, Washington, and the state capitals, for example) absolutely do not forget the communities where the organization has a large business, factory, distribution facility, or employee base.

(2) Target the leaders but do not stop there. This can be a very difficult challenge unless you have sufficient resources at your disposal. Research can identify who the thought leaders are within particular constituencies and who or what influences their views on issues. Seek to cultivate relationships with as many of them and/or their staffs as possible. But do not stop here; instead, identify others (individuals or organizations) who may have important roles to play.

(3) Identify the emerging players. Who are the up-and-coming staffers and journalists, for example? A particularly good time to establish relationships is when a new official is elected or a staff member or reporter comes on board. PR practitioners who cultivate those people before they become major players can hope to establish strong relationships before anyone else even tries to. Once the staffer or journalist reaches the top, stand in line.

(4) Use the organizational resources. Work with key groups in your organization so that you have all the necessary data and facts at your disposal depending on the particular issues. Do not be fearful of bringing your experts to meet with constituencies. While preparation is critical, it is often the expert that reporters or governmental representatives would appreciate meeting with on an issue. It does not undermine your relationship, but should strengthen the other party's view of you and your organization. At the same time, make sure that you are always kept in the "loop."

(5) Always be the first to tell the "news" to your constituency—particularly if it is bad news. This is very important in maintaining strong relationships and credibility. Once a person has heard from others, it becomes extremely difficult to change views or opinions and could undermine existing relationships.

The U.S. healthcare industry, which I have always been proud to be a member of, is embroiled in controversy over pricing, access, and other significant issues. Never before has the industry faced such grave challenges. Yet few industries produce the societal benefits the health-care industry does. If the U.S. industry is to continue to lead the world in the discovery, development, and marketing of medicines and other healthcare products, we must rebuild our reputation. And if we are going to succeed we have to build stronger and more productive relationships with all our constituencies. One relationship at a time.

THE TEN PRECEPTS OF REPUTATION MANAGEMENT

These precepts are meant to help professionals who spend their workdays communicating on behalf of organizations. Because the precepts are intended to help with reputation management, they have as much to do with performance and behavior as with communication.

1 *Know and honor your organization's intrinsic identity.*

Jim Burke, the CEO of Johnson & Johnson during the Tylenol® tampering cases of 1982 and 1986, said he deserved little credit for the extensive product recalls, which were undertaken at much risk to the franchise and the finances of the company. He explained that the company credo—its intrinsic identity—puts the health of the patient first. That credo begins: "We believe that our first responsibility is to the doctors, nurses, and patients, to mothers and fathers, and all others who use our products and services."[9] When a company acts always in ways that reflect its first responsibility to the people who use its product, and people are dying after using its product, the decision to pull its product is an easy one.

The Johnson & Johnson case stands in stark contrast to the sexual abuse scandal in the Catholic Church, where bishops put what they perceived to be the interest of the organization above the emotional and spiritual well-being of the people they exist to help. Of course organizations have multiple identities (for example, quality products and competitive profitability), but as George Cheney and other researchers have demonstrated, the identities must be compatible, and one must be dominant. That dominant, or intrinsic, identity must be clear to the members of the organization. It is what the organization stands for, and it will often determine what the employees will do as a first resort, in good times and bad.

2   *Know and honor your constituents.*

The American Red Cross, among the most successful and highly regarded charities in U.S. history, had good intentions when it decided to withhold from the families of the victims of 9/11 some of the monies donated for them. The fund had generated an overwhelmingly generous response, and the leadership of the Red Cross reasoned that not all the monies were needed by the families, and that it would be prudent to save some to help when future disasters, man- and God-made, strike. Donors were outraged, and a major crisis ensued.

The moral: do not presume to know the will of your constituents, and do not presume that good intentions alone are sufficient to protect against criticism that the organization is acting against the interests of its key constituents.

3   *Build the safeguards strong and durable, for they are the infrastructure of a strong reputation.*

Former U.S. Federal Reserve Chairman Alan Greenspan maintains that greed was the root cause of most of the recent business scandals, but he acknowledges that weakened safeguards let the greed flourish. The misuse of company funds by the Rigas family at Adelphia Communications illustrates the point. According to the U.S. Securities and Exchange Commission, the scandal represents "one of the most extensive financial frauds ever to take place at a public company." Not only did the internal controls—from company lawyers to accountants to the board of directors—fail to function, the external ones—from auditors to bankers to regulators—did as well. The moral: strong, efficient safeguards, internal and external, are in an organization's best interests.

4   *Beware the conflict of interest, for it can mortally wound your organization.*

Few firms in history had better reputations than Arthur Andersen, and a statue of the company namesake and founder stood tall at the company's training facility as a reminder of what he stood for: the meticulous and rigorous auditing and reporting of a client's finances. Andersen's primary duty was to the shareholders of companies whose books it audited. But by 2001 Andersen's imperative to boost revenues and profits had eroded structures intended to assure the independence of auditors. Andersen allowed itself to act in its own short-term interest and against the interests of its clients' shareholders. The compromising of audit standards and auditor independence was discussed publicly within and outside the firm for years before the damage became apparent and severe.

After the Enron/Andersen scandal broke in late 2001 and early 2002, a committee of some of society's most respected leaders, including former U.S. Federal Reserve Chairman Paul Volker and former Merck CEO P. Roy Vagelos, was convened to save it. But by then the firm's intrinsic identity—meticulous, honest auditing—had already been so compromised that the core had been ruined; Andersen was convicted of a crime and soon closed its doors.

Paul Volker once said that it is only the people or organizations that have not accomplished very much who could be free of all potential conflicts. Nevertheless, when it comes to major conflicts or conflicts that threaten the viability of an organization, it's like U.S. Supreme Court Justice Potter Stewart said of pornography: it may be hard to define, but you know it when you see it.

5   *Beware of the "CEO Disease," because there is no treatment for it.*

It is the same malady the Greek gods said destroyed so many tragic figures, and it is called hubris. Chief executives command tremendous incomes, power, and prestige. Thousands of employees almost genuflect when they walk by, and powerful people from all sectors of society treat them with deference. It must be difficult not to fall into certain traps, such as wanting to be surrounded by employees who always agree with them. Ask anyone who has worked in corporate communications for a long time: There is a "CEO Disease" (and heads of governments, nonprofits, and universities are not immune).

One of the manifestations of hubris is an inability to see that a looming problem requires immediate attention. Many CEOs mishandle initial phases of a crisis out of either arrogance or willful blindness, caused by a misplaced sense of invincibility. The outcome is otherwise manageable crises that result, ultimately and after much hardship, in the CEO's ouster. The year 2004 saw more forced CEO turnover than any year since such statistics have been compiled. According to the consulting firm Booz Allen Hamilton's annual CEO succession survey, the "giant sucking sound heard in the business world during 2004 was the extraction of chief executives from seats of power … The first quarter of 2005 brought headline-generating forced successions at Disney, Hewlett-Packard, Boeing, and AIG, linked to shareholder dissatisfaction, scandal, or both."[10]

6   *Beware of organizational myopia, for it will obscure the long-term view.*

Especially during times of crisis, organizations tend to focus on the short term. It's part of the corporate and organization condition, and not falling into that trap is one of the lessons of crisis management. Sometimes organizations are given plenty of advance notice of issues looming large, but few heed the warning signs.

7   *Be slow to forgive an action or inaction that hurts reputation.*

Warren Buffett said it best to a group of Salomon Brothers managers after a 1991 trading scandal hit the bank in which he had an interest. The quote, at the beginning of this chapter, bears repeating: "If you lose dollars for the firm by bad decisions, I will be very understanding. If you lose reputation for the firm, I will be ruthless."

8   *Do not lie.*

People tell lies, most of which are small and harmless, and some of which may even be good things ("Honey, do I look heavy in this dress?"). Similarly, organizations are not always completely forthcoming with information and, indeed, that is sometimes a very good thing. But lying is of course a slippery slope, eventually dragging the organization into a deep hole from which there is no extrication. Organizations can often get away with lying for a while, but that's all. Sometimes, efforts to mislead have significant adverse consequences, a lesson learned by President Nixon with Watergate, President Clinton in the Monica Lewinsky scandal, and by Martha Stewart, who was prosecuted, convicted, and imprisoned for lying to law enforcement officers.

9   *Dance with the one that "brung" you.*

This aphorism, popular within sports teams, applies to organizations as well as individuals. By the fall of 2000, it was becoming clear that Firestone tires were leading to traffic accidents, and many of them were on the Ford Explorer. Bridgestone-Firestone blamed Ford and vice versa. A business and public relations crisis ensued, and in May 2001 the two companies severed their business relationship that had endured for almost one hundred years. Most analysts agreed that the crisis was compounded by the lack of cooperation, and although the relationship was later revived, the damage had been done. Likewise, it is not uncommon today for a firm that is downsizing to give pink slips to employees, and then have a security guard publicly usher them to the gate—even those employees with excellent, long-term records. Thankfully, however, many other companies take monumental initiatives to be loyal to their employees, customers, and other constituencies. Aaron Feurstein, owner of Malden Mills in Lawrence, Massachusetts, was able to retain all his employees after a fire destroyed his factory in 1995. He said he would simply not abandon his employees, and quoted from the Torah, or Jewish Law: "He is poor and needy, whether he be thy brethren or a stranger."[11]

10   *Reputation is an asset and must be managed like other assets.*

Reputation is intangible, but it has great, tangible value (worth many billions of dollars in large corporations, for instance). It is therefore an asset. Failure to acknowledge reputation as an asset can be self-fulfilling. By ignoring reputation and factors that harm or help it, companies often behave and communicate in ways that cause harm to the reputation. Successful stewardship of reputation not only protects against the downside, but can affirmatively enhance the enterprise value of an organization. Because the component parts of reputation (performance/behavior and communication) can be managed, one should devise a strategy and plan to measure, monitor, and manage it on an ongoing basis.

Reputation = Sum of Images =
(Performance and Behavior) + Communication

REPUTATION MANAGEMENT

THE BEST CORPORATE COMMUNICATION STRATEGY

The remaining discourse flows from a discussion of ethics, to a discussion of approaches to working with the various corporate communication constituencies, to ways of handling certain major responsibilities, to the challenges facing those who seek to build a career in corporate and organizational communication.

The premise ... —that reputation can be measured, monitored, and managed—begs for the adoption by corporate communications departments of a long-term strategy of reputation management, customized for the particular constituencies, and in synch with an intrinsic identity that the entire organization understands and believes in.

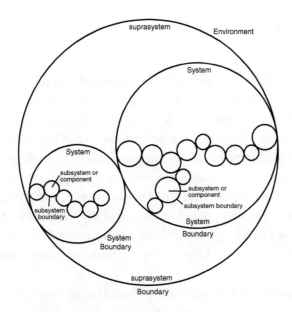

FIGURE 10.2.

A growing body of scholarship shows links between reputation and business performance, and the ability of public relations, particularly corporate communications, to impact reputation. Such studies include:

Journal of Public Relations Research, "Measuring the economic value of public relations," Yungwook Kim, 2001. "This study established a two-step model to measure the economic value of public relations by testing two relationships: the impact on reputation as a goal of public relations, and the economic impact of reputation on companies' bottom lines." The study showed a positive causal relationship between public relations and reputation, and a positive causal relationship between reputation and revenue.

Southern Economic Journal, "A latent structure approach to measuring reputation," Quagrainie et al., 2003. "The study provides estimates of reputation as a dynamic latent variable that is determined by price premiums and market data." It showed a positive effect between reputation and the prices a company can charge.

Corporate Communications, "Measuring corporate reputation," Bradford, Stewart Lewis, 2001. "This paper considers how corporate reputation is most influenced by the actions of an organization rather than a successful (or otherwise) PR campaign, and how a communication strategy can best influence reputation." The paper established that it is important to measure and manage reputation by constituency.

Corporate Reputation Review, "The concept and measurement of corporate reputation ... ," de la Fuente Sabate et al., Winter 2003. "This paper ... leads us to a new definition of corporate reputation, one that not only introduces the perceptions of how the firm behaves towards its stakeholders, but also takes into account the degree of transparency with which the firm develops relations with them." The paper established that information transparency (communicativeness) affects reputation and the ability to do business.

Positive reputations have a positive effect on a company's ability to do business.

Since reputation is the sum of performance/behavior and communication, an effective corporate communication strategy must be that inclusive. As with individuals, the relationships an organization has will succeed or fail based on performance/behavior and communication. In other words, relationships must be sound and aggressively fostered. Such a strategy can ensure that the organization moves forward, avoiding the Pushmi-Pullyu Syndrome and the reputation pitfalls.

SYSTEMS THEORY

Communication is the means by which an organization functions, and it is axiomatic that the better the communication the more productive the organization. That proposition is supported by communication theories, most notably in the case of corporate communication by General Systems Theory. It provides a communication framework which conceives of organizations as living things composed of interrelated components or parts. It provides a way of thinking of an organization not as an amalgam of distinct, seemingly unrelated disciplines, such as finance, customer service, or research, but rather as a whole that comprises components bound together by certain commonalities. As a system, the organization is part of a community that is part of other communities and they all interact, wittingly or unwittingly, in a planned or unplanned way. Systems theory can help communicators and leaders of organizations adopt a working philosophy that communication is the only way to unity and synergy within the organization, and to openness and harmony with systems (for instance, publics) in the environment outside the organization.

"One of the fundamental concepts of General Systems Theory can be traced to Aristotle," explains Rutgers University Communication Professor Brent Ruben, "who said in *Politics* that a state is composed of villages, which are in turn made up of households, which contain families.[12] Conceiving of entities in terms of wholes and interrelated parts is a basic concept in the general system framework of today."

The modern-day father of systems theory in organizational communication was Ludwig von Bertanffly, who conducted his research in the 1950s and 1960s. He was influenced by researchers who were working at the time to identify and express the generalities that tie the scientific disciplines together, so that biology and physics, for example, could be viewed in an interrelated way, rather than as separate, highly specialized fields. For example, cybernetics, which can produce a self-regulated machine that can perform functions greater than any part could, represents a specific application in the physical sciences; Gestalt psychology, which approaches psychotherapy from the perspective of the whole person, including the diverse systems of which he is a part, as opposed to an analytical approach, represents an application in psychotherapy.

Within the communication framework of systems theory, an organization can be pictured as a series of systems and subsystems within a supra system (see Figure 10.2). For example, a company could be pictured as a system, the departments as subsystems, and the particular industry as the supra system that functions within the environment of society. Of course, each supra system, system, and subsystem has a boundary and contains components (individuals). The boundaries are porous, opening subsystems to systems to supra systems to the environment. Subsystems and components are identified by the processes they perform. (Systems figure reproduced with the permission of Ruben, Gibson et al. of Rutgers University.)

Systems theory provides a framework for organizational communication based on the following properties and principles common to all systems. The properties and principles have implications for all communication enterprises, with employee communication, media relations, government relations, investor relations, and community relations being among the most obvious:

- Just as in a biological system where information flows from one cell to another, information in an organization flows across the borders in what theorists like Professor Ruben call the "metabolism of information." It follows that the more effective the communication, the more productive the organization.
- No part of a system, no person within an organization, can exist by himself or herself. This is the theoretical basis for tearing down the "silos," which became a theme throughout industry in the 1990s.
- Systems are dynamic. Feedback, from one component to another and with the environment, is essential. Implications for dialogue and engagement are clear in communication enterprises ranging from classroom learning to employee communication. The old communication model of sender-receiver may work for

thinking in terms of transferring information; it is not helpful for understanding more complex processes involved with attitudes and behavior.

- Participation in the system is mandatory. One cannot not communicate. (That is the phrase attributed to communication scholars Watzlawick, Beavin, and Jackson).[13] Engagement is essential.

- Human communication systems are "open systems." As opposed to closed, self- contained systems, which, for example, produce predictable chemical reactions in a test tube, the reactions of the things that go into an open system cannot be precisely calculated in advance; that is, the output cannot be calculated from the input. The open system has properties distinct from its parts; the total, therefore, is not equal to the sum of the parts.

- There are generalities that tie the parts together but one must be careful here. To say something meaningful about the whole—for example, the employee audience—is to omit specifics about the parts. "The key is to find the optimum degree of generality," Professor Ruben states. The implications for audience segmentation (internal or external audiences) are clear.

- The environments within and surrounding the supra system, systems, and subsystems shape those parts, and the reverse is true as well. Likewise, the environment shapes the individual's view of reality, and the individual actually shapes the environment. That is, the environments of a company (everything from the physical and cultural environments within and around the company to the country in which the company is based) shape the employees and vice versa. This point illustrates the great potential of communication.

"The systems approach," Professor Ruben states, "has been a particularly useful foundation for what may be thought of as the quality approach to organizations. The dominant metaphor for the Quality School is team, which relies on communication for success." Sports metaphors about teamwork may be clichéd, but they have solid foundation in theory as well as practice.

Professor Ruben: "Communication is the lifeblood of human systems. It is the means through which leadership functions, the mechanism by which parts relate to one another, the process by which systems relate and adapt to their environments. In organizations, quality and effective multidirectional communication go hand in hand."

BEST PRACTICES: REPUTATION MANAGEMENT

1   Understand and value the components of reputation, including integrity, governance, and communicativeness (transparency).

2   Establish a formal mechanism to periodically measure reputation.

3   Establish a formal mechanism—for example, a regularly scheduled meeting of senior officers, or a "Reputation Management Plan"—to manage reputation on an ongoing basis. The very act of establishing and adhering to a formal mechanism clearly expresses leadership's commitment to protecting the reputation asset.

4   A formal mechanism (for example, a Reputation Management Plan) can help your organization converge brand reputation and the broader corporate reputation with intrinsic identity (what the organization stands for).

RESOURCES FOR FURTHER STUDY

Ronald J. Alsop, *The 18 Immutable Laws of Corporate Reputation*, *A Wall Street Journal Book*, Free Press, New York, 2004.

Paul Argenti, *Corporate Communication*, Dartmouth University, The Amos Tuck School of Business Administration, McGraw-Hill, 1998.

The Corporate Communication Institute at Fairleigh Dickinson University.

The Corporate Reputation, an electronic newsletter by Peter Firestein, president of Global Strategic Communications Inc., at http://www.firesteinco.com/reputation.

Corporate Reputation Review: An International Journal, Henry Stewart Publications.

The Expressive Organization: Linking Identity, Reputation and the Corporate Brand, Majken Schultz, Mary Jo Hatch, and Mogens Holten, Eds., Larsen Oxford University Press, New York, 2000.

Charles J. Fombrun, *Reputation: Realizing Value from the Corporate Brand*, Harvard Business School Press, Boston, 1996.

The Institute of Public Relations, http://www.ipr.org.uk/reputation.

Measurement of "intangible assets." Refer to the work of Professor Baruch Lev of New York University, the Stern School, http://www.stern.nyu.edu/~blev/main.html - 9k.

Michael Morley, *How to Manage Your Global Reputation: A Guide to the Dynamics of International Public Relations*, New York University Press, 2002.

Leslie Gaines Ross, *CEO Capital: A Guide to Building CEO Reputation and Company Success*, John Wiley & Sons, New York, 2003.

NOTES

1   David W. Guth and Charles Marsh, *Public Relations, A Values-Driven Approach* (Needham Heights, MA: Pearson Education, Allyn and Bacon, 2000), 292–294.

2   Charles J. Fombrun, *Reputation: Realizing Value From The Corporate Brand* (Boston: Harvard Business School Press, 1996), 376.

3   Ibid., p. 9.

4   George Cheney, *Rhetoric in an Organizational Society* (Columbia, SC: University of South Carolina Press, 1991).

5   *The New York Times* advertisement, August 29, 2005.

6   Homily by Archbishop Sean P. O'Malley, July 30, 2003, at: Archdiocese of Boston Web site, http://www.rcab.org/News/homily030730.html.

7   Kurt Eichenwald, *Conspiracy of Fools: A True Story* (New York: Broadway Books, 2005), 590.

8   Hugh Lofting, *The Story of Doctor Doolitle* (A Yearling Book, May 1988), 76.

9   Johnson & Johnson Credo at: http://www.jnj.com/our_company/our_credo/index.htm.

10 "CEO Succession 2004: The World's Most Prominent Temp Workers," by Chuck Lucier, Rob Schuyt, and Edward Tse, *Strategy + Business*, at http://www. strategy-business.com/.

11 Guth and Marsh, *Public Relations: A Values-Driven Approach*, 164.

12 Brent D. Ruben, Linda Lederman, and David W. Gibson, Eds., *Communication Theory: A Casebook Approach* (Dubuque, IA: Kendall Hunt, 2000), 173–201.

13 Watzlawick, Beavin, and Jackson, *Pragmatics of Human Communication* (New York: Norton, 1967).

CHAPTER

11

UNDERSTANDING STAKEHOLDERS

In order for our communication efforts to be effective and efficient, we've got to understand our stakeholders, including their values, concerns, behaviors and information needs and preferences. The reading for this chapter helps us establish a baseline for this process by looking at how stakeholders organize around issues and constrain our communication efforts.

We will discuss the categories of public relations stakeholders including: limiters, customers, producers, and enablers. In addition, we will discuss understanding if they are apathetic, latent, aware, or active and what that means for our campaign efforts. In efforts to narrow down all our stakeholders to key publics for a campaign we will discuss segmenting and targeting. Along the way, we'll discover and define the three basic components of segmentation: demographics, sociographics, and psychographics.

Ethnography is the systematic study of people and cultures with an eye toward understanding the social life of humans. Ethnographies, through direct observation, can help us understand what people do and why they do it. This research methodology can add granularity to our understanding of stakeholders.

Marketers sometimes use personas to describe their target stakeholders. They will typically define one primary and two secondary groups and put this information into an attractive, easy-to-read format. Personas are a nice shorthand for describing stakeholders—particularly their goals, motivations, behaviors, and pain points.

We'll wrap up our discussion on understanding stakeholders by exploring age group differences as well as gender and lifestyle differences. All three have become increasingly important as we seek to communicate effectively and efficiently.

"BREAKING DOWN THE STAKEHOLDER ENVIRONMENT: EXPLICATING APPROACHES TO THE SEGMENTATION OF PUBLICS FOR PUBLIC RELATIONS RESEARCH"

By Jeong-Nam Kim, Lan Ni, and Bey-Ling Sha

This article reviews approaches to the segmentation of organizational stakeholders, recommending specifically that in the early (stakeholder) stage of strategic management, publics should be segmented using cross-situational approaches grounded in the notions of "consequences" and "resources". In the later (public and issue) stages, publics should be segmented using situational approaches, derived from notions of "problem" and "issue." The review and synthesis seeks to help scholars theorize more systematically about segmenting publics in public relations and to enable practitioners to more strategically segment and prioritize their organizational stakeholders.

Public relations practitioners work for organizations, and organizations operate within environments that include myriad stakeholders or publics. Thus, *strategic* public relations practice should start with formative research to segment or "enact"[1] the environment into "the most important components."[2]

Jeong-Nam Kim, Lan Ni, and Bey-Ling Sha, "Breaking Down the Stakeholder Environment: Explicating Approaches to the Segmentation of Public for Public Relations Research," *Journalism and Mass Communication Quarterly*, vol. 85, no. 4, pp. 751-768. Copyright © 2008 by Association for Education in Journalism and Mass Communication. Reprinted with permission. Provided by ProQuest LLC. All rights reserved.

Under resource constraints, organizations must selectively invest resources in building relationships with specific components of their environment.[3]

This article reviews one aspect of formative research—ways to segment organizational publics to facilitate the identification of strategic constituencies within the stakeholder environment. Such segmentation of publics has been recognized for decades as being critical to the success of public relations programs.[4] Yet most public relations efforts at stakeholder segmentation seem narrowly focused.[5] In contrast, this article argues for a more comprehensive approach that is both theoretically grounded and pragmatically effective.

Thus, this article will (1) provide researchers a review of segmentation approaches, framed by the theory of strategic public relations management;[6] (2) advance three propositions for future scholarly investigation based on this theoretical framework; and (3) provide practitioners a source to turn to as they prepare public relations programs.

STRATEGIC MANAGEMENT AND PUBLIC RELATIONS

According to the Excellence study,[7] public relations must be a part of the organization's strategic management process, and programs must be managed strategically. The strategic role of public relations lies in understanding and defining the organization's environment, which refers to the "sum total of all conditions and forces that affect the strategic options of a business but that are typically beyond its ability to control."[8] Within the macro-environment facing any organization, the strategic constituency refers to those who constrain or enhance an organization's ability to reach its goals.

Grunig and Repper suggested a three-stage model for strategic management of public relations: stakeholder, public, and issues.[9] In the *stakeholder stage*, public relations practitioners, through environmental scanning, need to identify those stakeholders whose behaviors will influence the organization and who will be influenced by organizational behaviors. In the *public stage*, groups find that they can use their stakes to influence the targeted organization or industry, and thus publics form to exercise their influence. Practitioners need to identify and segment publics to increase the possibility of achieving communication goals with these publics. Finally, in the *issue* and *crisis stage*, publics arise and then create and force issues that they believe need to be resolved in their interest. Practitioners should segment publics, use mass media and interpersonal communication, and engage in negotiation.[10]

The notion that the stages of strategic management of public relations are defined by the publics, rather than by the organization, reflects the reality that, although many public relations managers would like to enact the four-step process of strategic public relations planning,[11] their ability to do so often is constrained by the perspectives and activities of organizational stakeholders and publics. Thus, these stages of strategic management are used to determine the best approach to segmentation in public relations.

THEORIES OF SEGMENTATION BY STAGE OF STRATEGIC MANAGEMENT

"To segment" comes from the Latin "segmentum" and "secare," with the meaning of "cut."[12] To *cut*, one must draw a boundary that will result in one part being inside and one part being outside in the environment. In the segmentation process, components are judged to be "in" or "out" based on a conceptual criterion. Thus, this article reviews several kinds of theoretical criteria that may be used in segmenting publics.

In general, the segmentation of stakeholders is driven by two key concepts, *strategic threats* and *strategic opportunities*, which help distinguish successful organizations from unsuccessful ones. Successful organizations have adaptive systems as part of their management routine that can maximize strategic opportunities and minimize strategic threats.[13] These organizations tend to engage in co-adaptation and negotiation with their environments. In contrast, unsuccessful organizations devolve to maladaptive systems that tend to maximize strategic threats and minimize strategic opportunities. These organizations tend to use public relations to dominate their environments.[14]

These two key concepts—strategic threats and strategic opportunities—seem to be more balanced in the earlier stages of strategic management; but the emphasis moves toward managing strategic threats in later stages (i.e., issues or crisis). The following sections examine approaches to the segmentation of publics appropriate for each stage.

Stakeholder Stage. At this stage of strategic management, two major concepts that guide the segmentation of publics are *consequences* and *resources*. "Consequence" is a defining concept in public relations.[15] As an organization has some negative or positive consequences on publics and vice versa, there is a need for managing relationships between the two entities. Consequences from one entity's action and intention, thus, become a fundamental yardstick in breaking down the organization's stakeholder environment. Similar concepts include linkages, interconnectedness, interpenetration, relationships, and proximity.

The other core concept at the stakeholder stage is "resources," which refers to the necessary assets in operation toward achieving desired goals. Control of and access to resources become necessary conditions for organizational performance. Scarcity and value attached to resources generate "power" to those who possess more access or control, while it causes "powerlessness" for those who lack access or control.[16] Consequently, the degree of access and control over resources determines who could be strategic threats (e.g., competitors for the desired resources) and strategic opportunities (e.g., providers for the desired resources). In some situations, organizations try to minimize resource dependency on others, as this condition decreases their power and increases their strategic threats. Also, organizations attempt to prohibit competitors' resource access so as to decrease the latter's power and increase strategic threats against competitors. For that reason, organizations can enact their environment as they answer questions regarding who holds resources, who prohibits access to resources, and who contends for access to desired resources. In short, in the stakeholder stage, stakeholders can be segmented by examining how they relate to the organization's consequences and resources.

Public Stage. Organizations enter the public stage as the consequences that organizations and stakeholders have on each other become a problem; in other words, a public arises as it finds certain consequences to be problematic. In most cases, publics approach organizations hoping to gain organizational acknowledgement of their concerns and proactive corrections to the problem. Yet, should an organization fail to respond, publics may arise and turn to alternate sources of authority and resources for solutions. Thus, the key concept in the public stage is *problem*.[17] A problem, created from a consequence, is detected by publics and may disappear as it is resolved. Thus, "problems" are situational.

"Problem" is a necessary condition for a public to act on problem-solving tasks, but not a sufficient condition. Although a person may experience a severe consequence, he or she might not initiate any problem-solving efforts, if, for example, that person does not feel connected to the problem or feels severely constrained by time, resources, or knowledge in seeking solutions. These concepts of *involvement, constraint*, and *referent criterion*, combined with that of *problem*, are useful in the segmentation of stakeholders in the public stage. In fact, they are the independent variables[18] in the situational theory of publics: problem recognition, constraint recognition, level of involvement, and referent criterion.[19]

Issue and Crisis Stages. The issue stage is the third stage in the strategic management of public relations. Issues are created by publics out of problems that they consider to be serious. Publics arise and organize themselves to pressure organizations and other power- or resource-holders to solve the perceived problem. At this stage, it is easier for practitioners to determine which parts of the stakeholder environment to work on—the more vocal or communicatively active part. Yet, there is a tradeoff between the ease of segmentation and the difficulty of dealing with these publics. In addition, strategic opportunities in the environment are now outweighed by strategic threats. This is why the strategic management approach to public relations advocates for a proactive effort at the early stage.

One can see crisis as a final stage that requires management effort. During this stage, publics are key players in the environments, creating issues from the consequences affecting them and turning to governments, media, and other components that possess mobilizable resources and powers. Therefore, the core segmentation concepts from previous stages are all required at this final stage: consequences, resources, power, problems, and issues.

THEORIES OF SEGMENTATION

In addition to considering stages of the strategic management of public relations, this article offers approaches that vary depending on the stage of strategic public relations in which an organization may find itself. This section is divided into two basic approaches: cross-situational (more useful in the stakeholder stage) and situational (more useful in the public and issue/crisis stages).

Cross-situational approaches are those segmentation methods that use concepts based on enduring characteristics in the stakeholder environment. For example, one can break down stakeholders with *gross* and *static* notions such as formal membership in a group, demographics, or psychographics; once these characteristics arise, they tend to persist. In contrast, situational segmentation approaches focus on *non-enduring* or *dynamic* characteristics. For example, publics are born when a group of people finds a certain consequence to be problematic. They exist temporarily—arising as they find a problem and disappearing as the problem is resolved.

Static or Cross-Situational Approaches. In the static or cross-situational approach, the stakeholder environment is segmented by answering two major questions: First, who from the environment is likely to be interested in the organization? Second, who has the resources and power to help the organization in its operations? This approach hinges on a more stable notion of the stakeholder environment, and this article reviews three typical examples, grounded in marketing/sociological, business-management, and public relations perspectives.

Segmentation in Marketing/Sociology. Many public relations textbooks currently use marketing or sociological approaches to the segmentation of publics, which are easy to adopt but relatively low in utility. Furthermore, this reliance on the concept of "market" and marketing principles suggests a critical misassumption that "markets" and "publics" are the same kind of animal, when in fact they are not.[20]

Marketing deals with the organization's *economic* or *task environment*, such as consumers, competitors, and suppliers, whereas public relations deals with the *social* or *institutional environment* such as government, communities, and activist groups.[21] The relationship between an organization and its social or institutional environment is grounded in the notion of *consequences*, whereby the social environment determines the legitimacy of organizational mission and types of goals for organizations. In contrast, the relationship between an organization and its economic environment is grounded in the notion of *resources*, whereby the economic environment determines the scope of organizational operations and the amount of mobilizable resources.

In general, segmentation in marketing is primarily oriented for *cost effectiveness* in reaching current/potential markets. In contrast, segmentation in public relations is oriented not only for cost effectiveness in reaching current/potential publics but for *organization effectiveness* in obtaining stakeholders' and publics' support and resources to achieve organizational strategic goals. In other words, segmentation in marketing is used to reduce the high cost of promoting products or services; segmentation in public relations is used to reduce the high cost of problem-solving and relationship building. In this regard, the goal of market segmentation is *micro-level effectiveness*, while the goal for public segmentation is both micro-level and *macro-level effectiveness* for the organization.

The following paragraphs summarize several approaches that lean toward a marketing or sociological perspective. The most commonly used criteria are demographics and psychographics.[22] Cutlip, Center, and Broom also used six other methods of segmentation: geographies, covert power, position, reputation, membership, and role in decision process.[23] Sometimes publics are further segmented using these marketing or sociological perspectives within each category of stakeholders, such as employees, community, investors, and consumers.[24]

Segmentation in Business Management. This section examines stakeholder theory and resource-dependency theory, useful concepts drawn from the business-management literature. First, stakeholder theory examines which stakeholders take precedence over others, with stakeholders defined as "any group or individual who is affected by or can affect the achievement of an organization's objectives."[25]

When evaluating the relative importance of stakeholders, Mitchell, Agle, and Wood developed a three-dimensional model that included the attributes of power, legitimacy, and urgency.[26] Stakeholders have *power* when they can influence others to make decisions that they would not have otherwise made. *Legitimacy* is the extent to which the stakeholder has a legal, moral, or presumed claim. *Urgency* exists when a relationship or claim is of a time sensitive nature or when that relationship or claim is critical to the stakeholder.

These three dimensions are combined to segment stakeholders into different groups. *Latent* stakeholders possess only one attribute and are of low priority to organizations; they can be dormant, discretionary, or demanding. *Expectant* stakeholders possess two attributes, and include dominant, dependent, and dangerous stakeholders. Finally, *definitive* stakeholders have all three attributes and should receive the most attention from organizations.

Related to stakeholder theory, the stakeholder view (SHV) approach offers a more comprehensive view of stakeholder management as emphasizing the strategic importance of "relationships" in contributing to the organization's capacity to generate organizational wealth.[27] Going beyond other managerial views, such as a resource-based view (RBV, which only considers the most important components such as employees, investors, and customers) and an industry structure view (ISV, which considers joint venture partners or alliances, supply chain associates, and regulatory authorities), the SHV approach provides a more general classification tool because it also considers private organizations, local communities, citizens, and governments. Thus, the list of ten different stakeholders of SHV is a more comprehensive perspective using stakeholder concepts.[28]

Resource-dependency theory provides another perspective for segmenting stakeholders and can help answer our second question: Who has the resources, power, or leverage to solve this problem? In this approach, organizational success is defined as organizations maximizing their power.[29] This theory assumes that organizations are constrained by other organizations or institutions with power or resources.[30] One of the basic assumptions states that organizations are assumed to work toward two related objectives: (1) acquiring control over resources that minimize their dependence on other organizations and (2) acquiring control over resources that maximize the dependence of other organizations on themselves. The implications are that one can derive two types of stakeholder groups. The first group has resources needed by the organization, and thus the organization should be developing relationships with this group. The second group refers to the stakeholders that are dependent upon the organization and thus need to develop relationships with the organization.

Segmentation in Public Relations. Related to the idea of interdependence and resources, the concept of *linkages*[31] also is commonly used in segmentation. Linkages are based on interpenetrating systems that may upset an organization's equilibrium; these consist of political systems (e.g., Congress, political groups), social groups (e.g., interest groups, environmentalists), and economic contexts (e.g., stockholders, consumers).[32] Using the linkage approach in segmentation, public relations will (a) identify interpenetrating systems, (b) prioritize interpenetrating systems, and (c) plan communication programs with the systems most likely to upset organizational equilibrium.

Four major types of linkages are *enabling, functional, normative,* and *diffused.*[33] Enabling linkages provide the authority and control the resources that enable the organization to exist. Functional linkages provide inputs and take outputs. Input linkages include employees, unions, and suppliers, whereas output linkages include consumers and industrial purchasers. Normative linkages refer to those groups who face similar problems or share similar values, for example, associations. And diffused linkages are those that cannot clearly be identified by membership; but when the organization has done something that creates consequences, these linkages can organize to do something against the organization.[34]

Another useful segmentation theory in public relations is based on "inferred variables" rather than "objective variables," with the former available by questioning members of a population directly (e.g., perceptions, cognitions, or attitudes), while the latter are available from secondary sources (e.g., demographics or media use).[35] Grunig developed a nested model of segmentation, with inferred variables nested within objective variables.[36] This model includes seven layers: individual communication behaviors and effects; publics; communities; psychographics, lifestyles, cultures, and social relationships; geodemographics; demographics/social categories; and mass audience. This approach is also used in Heath and Coombs.[37]

Dynamic or Situational Approaches. Whereas static or cross-situational approaches divide the organizational stakeholder environment with its enduring notions of key players and institutions, dynamic or situational approaches rely on more ephemeral notions, such as problems or issues, whose characteristics may not endure through time. In analyzing cross-situational and situational approaches, it appears that ease of use tends to be inversely related to the value of use. While cross-situational approaches allow for easier identification of stakeholders via the use of enduring characteristics (e.g., a demographic variable such as gender, which does not change once identified), their utility is rather limited, especially when the organizational environment becomes turbulent.

In contrast, situational approaches, by relying for example on issues that may be created and eventually dissolved, are harder to implement but their utility is greater, especially in the public, issue, and crisis stages. The authors of this article classify the situational approaches into two typologies: across-problems/issues and within-a-problem/issue. The former is based on the *breadth of concern* one possesses across different related problems; the latter is based on the *depth* or *magnitude of concern* one possesses on a single problem.

Across-Problems/Issues Typology. The situational theory of publics asks stakeholders to reflect on multiple problems/ issues in a situation set. From his research, Grunig found four recurring types of publics: *all-issue publics* are active on all of the problems in the situation set; *apathetic publics* do not care about any problems/issues; *single-issue publics* care for only one or a small subset of the problems in the set; and *hot-issue publics* are active only on the issue/problem that already involves most of the population and receives heavy media coverage[38] (e.g., gasoline prices).

From this review of the literature, the situational theory seems to be the only method to segment publics across issues. Two of these four types of publics capture the *breadth* of the problems/issues of concern: the all-issue public (concern across all issues in the situation set) and the apathetic public (lack of concern across all issues in the situation set).

Within-a-Problem/Issue Typology. The hot-issue and single-issue publics are reflective of the within-a-problem/issue typology of segmenting stakeholders, which refers to those segmentation methods that subdivide stakeholders in a situation into different subgroups in terms of the extent of their concern or activeness regarding a specific issue. As is easily observable, different problems produce different types of publics. Hence, if practitioners anticipate which types of publics emerge with what types of behavioral characteristics (e.g., active information seeking), they will make a more strategic choice in dealing with that public (e.g., negotiation). The classic typology in this category is based on Dewey's concept of the public[39] and developed by Grunig and Hunt.[40] They labeled a group of people who face a similar problem but do not detect the problem a *latent public.* When group members subsequently recognize the problem, they become an *aware public.* If the public organizes to discuss and do something about the problem, they become an *active public*. Finally, those groups of people who do not meet any condition of Dewey's notion of publics are called *nonpublics*.

Hallahan modified these four types of publics using "knowledge" and "involvement." His four types of publics are "active (high knowledge and high involvement)," "aroused (high involvement and low knowledge)," "aware (high knowledge and low involvement)," and "inactive (low knowledge and low involvement)." The utility of his modification resides in the different strategies for different publics, with "negotiation" as the best strategy for active publics, "intervention" for aroused publics, "education" for aware publics, and "prevention" for inactive publics.[41]

Another notable within-a-problem/issue typology is derived from the diffusion of innovations theory.[42] Rogers' theory of how innovative ideas get dispersed in a population is rooted in the concept of *problem*. An innovation is in essence a *solution de novo* for a problem.[43] Hence, practitioners can easily extrapolate from Rogers' typology of groups (i.e., innovators, early adopters, early majority, late majority, and laggards) to the segmentation of stakeholders. For example, the innovator groups are those active publics who worked on a problem earlier and reached a solution *de novo*. The early majority and late majority groups are analogous to aware and latent publics.

Center and Jackson classified publics into three types: primary, intervening, and special publics.[44] The *primary public* refers to those who can or cannot do what the organization needs or wants to do. The *intervening public* is a "gatekeeper" who delivers messages to the primary publics and typically includes news media, politicians, activists, and opinion leaders. The *special public* refers to an organized group with formal rules and regular meetings, and includes both the *inward special public* that serves their own members' interests (e.g., a trade association) and the *outward special public* that serves people other than its own members (e.g., public-interest organizations).

More recently, Kim classified the active and aware publics in Grunig and Hunt's original typology into eight types of publics: *open-dormant passive public, closed-dormant passive public, open-situational active public, closed-situational active public, open-situational activist public, closed-situational activist public, open-chronic activist public*, and *closed-chronic activist public*.[45] These eight types of publics capture three major characteristics in the problem-solving process of publics: *openness to approaches* in problem solving, *extent of activeness* in problem solving, and *time* or *history* of the problem solving.[46]

These types distinguish conceptually among aware, active, and activist publics in terms of their information giving and selecting potential. In addition, the new typology allows practitioners to predict when the communication efforts would be more difficult (e.g., closed-chronic activist publics because of their strong selectivity), thus extending Grunig and Hunt's original four key types of publics.[47] One of the first empirical studies of the new typology was a qualitative exploration that identified seven of the eight new types of publics and illustrated their key communication features and their perceptions about problems.[48]

Synthetic Application of Cross-Situational and Situational Approaches. The present authors believe that the cross-situational and situational approaches need to be combined in their application to maximize the power of each approach. This article illustrates two ways of doing so. First, practitioners should anticipate any possible movement from the stakeholder stage to the public stage. Before a shift, practitioners will find that the business-management or linkage approaches are most useful because they provide a gross mapping of the environment, an initial segmentation that facilitates continuous monitoring with less cost. Then, as the organization enters the public stage, the combining of cross-situational methods with situational methods (e.g., demographics combined with the situational theory of publics) will be necessary. Such a shift requires a sequential *build-on* combination between two segmentation methods, e.g., from a linkage of shareowners to a concerned subgroup—active public—of shareowners for a new management policy.

A second way of integrating the two approaches is *combine-with* use. After an organization moves into the public or issue/crisis stages, a situational segmentation method holds greater value in practice. However, practitioners should continue to use some of the cross-situational methods. Although situational methods tell us what specific subgroups of a certain linkage/stakeholder component may arise as a public, they cannot tell us where to go to communicate with these groups (e.g., which media the given specific public would use for information seeking or processing).[49] Thus, in using the situational theory, practitioners should include some cross-situational questions, such as geodemographics, psychographics, and media use, so that they can learn where to go or how to communicate with the situationally active publics.

PROPOSITIONS FOR FUTURE SCHOLARLY INVESTIGATION

Based on the review and proposed framework above, three general propositions follow:

> **P1**: In the stakeholder stage, public relations is managed strategically and contributes most to the organization when (a) it identifies an organization's (public's) consequences, resources, power, linkages, interconnectedness, values, relationships and proximity in and around the organization and (b) it applies *build-on synthesis* of available segmentation options.

This proposition can be tested empirically. In fact, segmentation at the stakeholder stage is perhaps already the most commonly used because it is relatively easy compared to the other two stages. Many professional efforts, such as the Public Relations Society of America (PRSA) Silver Anvil award-winning entries, generally involved segmentation based on stakeholders only. Many studies in scholarly journals and publications also use publics in a broad sense that is similar to stakeholders.[50]

> **P2**: In the public stage, public relations is managed strategically and contributes most to the organization when (a) it identifies and monitors a public's perceptions of problems, involvement, constraints, and changes of referent criteria such as cognitions or attitudes and (b) it applies *combine-with synthesis* of available segmentation options.

This proposition already has been tested partially. For example, many studies using Grunig's situational theory of publics specifically have examined factors such as publics' perceptions of problems, involvement, and constraints. However, few studies have empirically investigated the changes of referent criteria among active publics over time. In addition, not many studies have linked these identified publics with organizational effectiveness.[51]

> **P3**: In the issue and crisis stages, public relations is managed strategically and contributes most to the organization when (a) it identifies and monitors issues created by publics, mapping consequences and resources in and around the organization, (b) it monitors the changes of problem perception among members of an active public, and (c) it applies *combine-with synthesis* of available segmentation options.

Research grounded in this proposition may occur in studies on activism, crisis management, and conflict resolution. So far, very few studies have tested this proposition empirically. Most crisis communication studies, for example, do not seem to include "segmentation of publics" as an integral step in the communication process. Rather, crisis responses have been tested on pseudo-publics (i.e., students).[52] One study explored a part of this proposition and found that many organizations that experienced an issue or crisis have not managed it in a strategic way; i.e., instead of focusing on the publics most affected in the issue or by the crisis (which thus should be the most active public), they chose to work with other publics with less strong ties (e.g., investors).[53]

DISCUSSION

Undifferentiated communication with a general population is costly and ineffective. This article has offered a theoretical review of methods to segment strategic constituencies in organizational environments, framing our efforts with the strategic management of public relations.[54] These stages—stakeholder, public, and issue/crisis-

TABLE 11.1   Summary of Strategic Management and Strategic Segmentation

	Theoretical Concepts in Segmentation	Available Segmentation Options	Types of Segmentation Approaches
Stakeholder Stage	Consequences, Resources, Power, Linkages, Interconnectedness, Values, Relationship, Proximity	**Sociological/Marketing Approaches:** Demographics, Geodemographies, Psychographies, Cultures, Relationships	**Static or Cross-Situational Segmentation Approach**
		Business-Management Approaches: Resource Dependency, Industry-based View, Stakeholder View	*Build-On* Synthesis
		Public Relations Approach (Social, Political, and Economic Contexts): External Linkages	
Public Stage	Problems, Involvement, Constraints (Referent Criterion)	**Across-problems/issues Typology:** Four Types of Publics: All-issue public, Apathetic, Single-issue, Hot-issue Public	**Dynamic or Situational Segmentation Approach**
		Within-a-problem/issue Typology: 1 Active Public, Aware Public, Latent Public, Nonpublic 2 Active, Aroused, Aware, Inactive Public 3 Diffusion of Innovation: Innovators, Early Adopters, Early Majority, Late Majority, and Laggards 4 Primary Public; Intervening Public, Special Public (Inward Special Public & Outward Special Public) 5 Open-dormant Passive Public, Closed-dormant Passive public, Open-situational Active Public, Closed-situational Active Public, Open-situational Activist Public, Closed-situational Activist Public, Open-chronic Activist Public, and Closed-chronic Activist Public	*Combine-With* Synthesis
Issues Stage/ Crisis Stage	Issues, Consequences, Resources, Power, Problems		**Dynamic or Situational Segmentation Approach** *Combine-With* Synthesis

require different segmentation approaches for organizations to maximize strategic opportunities and to minimize strategic threats.

Although it is not exhaustive, the review includes major segmentation methods available for public relations theory building and practice, delving into theoretical core concepts, such as "consequences" and "resources" (in the stakeholder stage), "problems" (in the public stage), and "issues" and other aforementioned concepts (in the issue/crisis stages). In the stakeholder stage, organizations are likely to benefit most from using cross-situational approaches, whereas in the later stages—public, issue, and crisis—organizations may more effectively employ situational approaches to segmentation.

The two different segmentation approaches—cross-situational and situational—should be integrated in most applications, regardless of the stage of strategic management. Furthermore, as organizational management fails to respond with the right strategy, the stakeholder environment may evolve from a more static to a more dynamic context, i.e., moving from the stakeholder stage to the crisis stage. In such an evolution—or devolution, some might argue—segmentation approaches should correspondingly be changed from the more static cross-situational approaches to the more dynamic situational approaches, in keeping with environmental characteristics. Table 11.1 summarizes the framework and offers an overview of the segmentation methods reviewed in this article.

For public relations scholars, the challenge is to continue the refinement of theories of segmentation in ways that are both conceptually rich and pragmatically useful. For the most part, the literature reviewed here suggests that public relations scholars are proactive and creative in the development of situational approaches; yet these are rarely useful to or used by practitioners because, pragmatically speaking, they are difficult to implement. Conversely, public relations textbooks, in instructing future practitioners on ways to segment publics, rely almost exclusively on cross-situational approaches, which often are insufficiently sophisticated for use in segmenting organizational stakeholders as the environment moves toward the later stages of the strategic management process. Thus, public relations scholars and practitioners need to build bridges across the situational and cross-situational approaches to the segmentation of publics. Only by synthesizing these approaches will the segmentation of organizational stakeholders become more theoretically useful and pragmatically effective.

NOTES

1   Karl E. Weick. *The Social Psychology of Organizing*, 2d ed. (Reading, MA: Addison-Wesley, 1979).

2   James E. Grunig and Fred C. Repper, "Strategic Management, Publics, and Issues," in *Excellence in Public Relations and Communication Management*, ed. James E. Grunig (Hillsdale, NJ: Lawrence Erlbaum, 1992), 31–64.

3   Grunig and Repper, "Strategic Management, Publics, and Issues."

4   For example, see Harold Mendelsohn, "Why Information Campaigns Can Succeed," *Public Opinion Quarterly* 37 (spring 1973): 50–61.

5   One notable exception is Brad L. Rawlins, *Prioritizing Stakeholders for Public Relations* (Gainesville, FL: Institute for Public Relations, 2006).

6   Grunig and Repper, "Strategic Management, Publics, and Issues."

7   David M. Dozier, Larissa A. Grunig, and James E. Grunig, *Manager's Guide to Excellence in Public Relations and Communication Management* (Mahwah, NJ: Lawrence Erlbaum, 1995); James E. Grunig, ed., *Excellence in Public Relations and Communication Management* (Mahwah, NJ: Lawrence Erlbaum, 1992); James E. Grunig, Larissa A.

Grunig, and David M. Dozier, *Excellent Public Relations and Effective Organizations: A Study of Communication Management in Three Countries* (Mahwah, NJ: Lawrence Erlbaum, 2002).

8   John A. Pearce II and Richard B. Robinson, Jr., *Strategic Management: Strategy Formulation and Implementation* (Homewood, IL: Irwin, 1982), 62.

9   Grunig and Repper, "Strategic Management, Publics, and Issues."

10 Should the issue become unmanageable, then the organization will enter the crisis stage. Much public relations research has been done on the crisis stage; for some examples, see W. Timothy Coombs, "The Development of the Situation Crisis Communication Theory," in *Public Relations: From Theory to Practice*, ed. Tricia Hanson-Hom and Bonita Dostal Neff (Boston: Allyn-Bacon, 2008), 262–77; or see Kathleen Fearn-Banks, *Crisis Communications: A Casebook Approach*, 3d ed. (Mahwah, NJ: Lawrence Erlbaum, 2007). This article cannot review all of these studies due to space limitations, so the issue and crisis stages are integrated in this manuscript.

11 See Scott M. Cutlip, Allen H. Center, and Glen M. Broom, *Effective Public Relations*, 9th ed. (Upper Saddle River, NJ: Prentice Hall, 2006).

12 Judy Pearsall and Bill Trumble, *The Oxford Encyclopedic English Dictionary*, 3d ed. (New York: Oxford University Press, 1996).

13 Jeong-Nam Kim, Jeff Hall, Jerry Swerling, and James E. Grunig, "From Strategic Public Relations to Corporate Strategic Management: Research, Empowerment, and Value of Public Relations" (paper presented at the annual meeting of the Academy of Management, Anaheim, CA, 2008).

14 Grunig, Grunig, and Dozier, *Excellent Public Relations and Effective Organizations: A Study of Communication Management in Three Countries*.

15 James E. Grunig and Todd Hunt, *Managing Public Relations* (NY: Holt, Rinehart and Winston, 1984).

16 Henry Mintzberg, *Power In and Around Organizations* (Englewood Cliffs, NJ: Prentice-Hall, 1983).

17 Kim and Grunig define a *problem* as a perceptual discrepancy between expected and experienced states in a given situation that produces an uncomfortable feeling of badness-of-fit. They define *problem solving* as one's effort to decrease this perceived discrepancy. In this vein, a member of a public is a problem solver who is looking for and/or bringing about a solution, not necessarily aware of or connecting with other problem solvers. For details, see Jeong-Nam Kim and James E. Grunig, *Situational Theory of Problem Solving: Communicative, Cognitive, and Perceptive Bases* (NY: Routledge, forthcoming).

18 Originally, the situational theory of publics also included a fourth independent variable, called referent criterion, which was "a solution carried from previous situations to a new situation"; see James E. Grunig, "A Situational Theory of Publics: Conceptual History, Recent Challenges and New Research," in *Public Relations Research: An International Perspective*, ed. Danny Moss, Toby MacManus, and Dejan Verčič (London: International Thomson Business, 1997), 11. Although dropped over the years because it seemed to have little impact on communication behavior, reference criterion may be coming back, as some scholarship suggests the presence of another independent or antecedent variable helps to better predict communication activity; for example, see Bey-Ling Sha, "Cultural Identity in the Segmentation of Publics: An Emerging Theory of Intercultural Public Relations," *Journal of Public Relations Research* 18 (2006): 45–65.

19 See Grunig, "A Situational Theory of Publics: Conceptual History, Recent Challenges and New Research."

20 Cutlip, Center, and Broom, *Effective Public Relations;* Dejan Verčič and James E. Grunig, "The Origins of Public Relations Theory in Economics and Strategic Management," in *Perspectives on Public Relations Research*, ed. Danny

Moss, Dejan Verčič, and Gary Warnaby (London: Routledge, 2000), 7–58. Markets can be created, whereas publics cannot be created. A public arises as its members find a problem. According to marketing scholars, a good market segmentation should meet three required conditions: *measurability*—the degree to which quantified information exists or is obtainable on a particular buyer characteristic, *accessibility*—the degree to which the firm can focus its marketing efforts on selected segments, and *substantiality*—the degree to which the segments are large enough to be worth considering for separate marketing. For details, see Philip Kotler and Kevin L. Keller, *Marketing Management*, 13th ed. (Upper Saddle River, NJ: Prentice Hall, 2008). This is another distinguishing feature between public relations and marketing. Although public segmentation should share the first two conditions in a good segmentation practice, unlike market segmentation, it cannot meet the third condition because *marketing problems* are qualitatively different from *public relations problems*. For details, see James E. Grunig and Larissa A. Grunig, "The Relationship Between Public Relations and Marketing in Excellent Organizations: Evidence from the IABC study," *Journal of Marketing Communications* 4 (1998): 141–62. Whereas marketing problems aim to create a market and increase sales through exploration of potential market—a group of individuals that market researchers create for the purpose of sales of their idea or products—public relations problems are most often created by a group of individuals who encounter a problematic state and who perceive the problems should or could be better dealt with organization(s) attentions and resources. Regardless of the size or substantiality of the group, thus, public relations should identify and interact with a public; see, for example, Mancur L. Olson, *The Logic of Collective Action: Public Goods and the Theory of Groups*, 2d ed. (Cambridge, MA: Harvard University Press, 1971). However, segmentation in public relations and marketing share the same feature, *systematic approach*, that grants communication planners power to identify and interact with most important segments in the given communication problem. They can then design better strategies and tactics and matching goals and objectives for the given communication problem.

21 James E. Grunig, "The Role of Public Relations in Strategic Management and its Contribution to Organizational and Societal Effectiveness" (speech presented to the Taiwanese Public Relations Society, Taipei, Taiwan, May 12, 2001).

22 For example, see Betty Attaway-Fink, "Market-driven Journalism: Creating Special Sections to Meet Reader Interests," *Journal of Communication Management* 9 (spring 2004): 145–55; Cutlip, Center, and Broom, *Effective Public Relations*; Dennis L. Wilcox and Glen T. Cameron, *Public Relations: Strategies and Tactics*, 8th ed. (Boston, MA: Allyn & Bacon, 2005).

23 See Cutlip, Center, and Broom, *Effective Public Relations*.

24 Richard Fletcher and T. C. Melewar, "The Complexities of Communicating to Customers in Emerging Markets," *Journal of Communication Management* 6 (winter 2001): 9–23; David W. Guth and Charles Marsh, *Adventures in Public Relations: Case Studies and Critical Thinking* (Boston: Allyn & Bacon, 2005).

25 R. Edward Freeman, *Strategic Management: A Stakeholder Approach* (Boston: Pitman, 1984), 46.

26 Ronald K. Mitchell, Bradley R. Agle, and Donna J. Wood, "Toward a Theory of Stakeholder Identification and Salience: Defining the Principle of Who or What Really Counts," *Academy of Management Review* 22 (autumn 1997): 853–86.

27 James E. Post, Lee E. Preston, and Sybille Sachs, *Redefining the Corporation: Stakeholder Management and Organizational Wealth* (Stanford, CA: Stanford University Press, 2002), 54.

28 Post, Preston, and Sachs' typology of stakeholders are elaborated with each stakeholder's contribution to the organizational wealth. For a more detailed description and the list of stakeholders, see Post, Preston, and Sachs, *Redefining the Corporation: Stakeholder Management and Organizational Wealth*, 47.

29 Jeffrey Pfeffer, *Power in Organizations* (Marshfield, MA: Pitman, 1981).

30 Jeffrey Pfeffer and Gerald Salancik, *The External Control of Organizations* (NY: Harper & Row, 1978).

31 M. J. Esman, "The Elements of Institution Building," in *Institution Building and Development*, ed. J. W. Eaton (Beverly Hills, CA: Sage, 1972), 19–40.

32 Grunig and Hunt, *Managing Public Relations*.

33 Grunig and Hunt, *Managing Public Relations*.

34 This concept of linkages was also used in Ronald D. Smith, *Strategic Planning for Public Relations* (Mahwah, NJ: Lawrence Erlbaum, 2004).

35 Grunig and Repper, "Strategic Management, Publics, and Issues," 131.

36 James E. Grunig, "Publics, Audiences, and Market Sgments: Segmentation Pinciples for Campaigns," in *Information Campaigns: Balancing Social Values and Social Change*, ed. Charles. T. Salmon (Newbury Park, CA: Sage, 1989), 199–228.

37 Robert L. Heath and W. Timothy Coombs, *Today's Public Relations: An Introduction* (Thousand Oaks, CA: Sage, 2005).

38 Grunig, "A Situational Theory of Publics: Conceptual History, Recent Challenges and New Research"; James E. Grunig, "Constructing Public Relations Theory and Practice," in *Communication: A Different Kind of Race Horse*, ed. Brenda Dervin and Steve Chaffee (Cresskill, NJ: Hampton Press, 2003), 85–115.

39 John Dewey, *The Public and its Problems* (Chicago: Swallow, 1927).

40 Grunig and Hunt, *Managing Public Relations*.

41 Kirk Hallahan, "The Dynamics of Issue Activation and Response: An Issues Processes Model," *Journal of Public Relations Research* 13 (2001): 27,43.

42 See Everett M. Rogers, *Diffusion of Innovations*, 4th ed. (NY: The Free Press, 1995).

43 Everett M. Rogers, *Diffusion of Innovations*, 5th ed. (NY: The Free Press, 2003).

44 Allen H. Center and Patrick Jackson, *Public Relations Practices: Managerial Case Studies and Problems* (NJ: Prentice Hall, 2002), 19.

45 Jeong-Nam Kim, "Communicant Activeness, Cognitive Entrepreneurship, and a Situational Theory of Problem Solving" (Ph.D. diss., University of Maryland, College Park, 2006); Lan Ni, Jeong-Nam Kim, and Eun-Ju Lee, "Classifying Publics: Communication Behaviors and Problem-Solving Characteristics in Controversial Issues" (paper presented at the annual meeting of the National Communication Association, San Diego, CA, 2008).

46 The new publics typology is linked closely to a new concept, *communicant activeness of problem solving* or CAPS; for details, see Jeong-Nam Kim and James E. Grunig, "Explicating and Validating Communicant Activeness in Problem Solving (CAPS)" (paper presented at the annual meeting of the International Communication Association, San Francisco, CA, 2007). In short, CAPS goes beyond considering only information acquisition (i.e., information seeking and processing), and introduces additional communicant characteristics: information selection (i.e., information forefending and permitting) and information transmission (information forwarding and sharing). Each dimension of problem-solving characteristics is conceptually corresponding to information behavioral characteristics: information acquisition with time or history of the problem solving; information selection with the openness to approaches in problem solving; and information transmission with the extent of activeness in problem solving. For details, see Kim and Grunig, "Explicating and Validating Communicant Activeness in Problem Solving (CAPS)"; Kim and Grunig, *Situational Theory of Problem Solving: Communicative, Cognitive, and Perceptive Bases*.

47 The combination of eight new types of publics with latent and non-publics gives ten types of publics. Such a combination enhances the theoretical and practical utility of the original four types of publics because the eight new

types of publics explain communicative distinctions between active and activist publics and the conditions when communication is ineffective.

48 See Ni, Kim, and Lee, "Classifying Publics: Communication Behaviors and Problem-Solving Characteristics in Controversial Issues."

49 Linda Aldoory and Bey-Ling Sha, "The Situational Theory of Publics: Practical Applications, Methodological Challenges, and Theoretical Horizons," in *The Future of Excellence in Public Relations and Communication Management: Challenges for the Next Generation,* ed. Elizabeth Toth (Mahwah, NJ: Lawrence Erlbaum, 2007), 339–55; Grunig, "Publics, Audiences, and Market Segments: Segmentation Pinciples for Cmpaigns."

50 For one example, see Linda M. Hagan, "For Reputation's Sake: Managing Crisis Communication," in *The Future of Excellence in Public Relations and Communication Management: Challenges for the Next Generation,* ed. Elizabeth Toth (Mahwah, NJ: Lawrence Erlbaum, 2007), 413–40.

51 For one exception, see Bey-Ling Sha and Pamela Pine, "Using The Situational Theory of Publics to Develop an Education Campaign Regarding Child Sexual Abuse" (paper presented at the annual meeting of the Interdisciplinary Public Relations Research Conference, Miami, Florida, 2004).

52 See, for example, W. Timothy Coombs, "Information and Compassion in Crisis Responses: A Test of their Effects," *Journal of Public Relations Research* 11 (1999): 125–42; W. Timothy Coombs and Sherry J. Holladay, "An Extended Examination of the Crisis Situations: A Fusion of the Relational Management and Symbolic Approaches," *Journal of Public Relations Research* 13 (2001): 321–40.

53 Lan Ni, "Exploring Relationship Management as an Integral Part of Strategic Management of Public Relations" (paper presented at the annual meeting of AEJMC, Chicago, IL, 2008).

54 See Grunig and Repper, "Strategic Management, Publics, and Issues."

"CULTURAL FOUNDATIONS IN COMMUNICATION: RELATIONSHIP-BUILDING IN THE CHINESE CONTEXT"

By Ming-Jer Chen and Kelly Thomas

Across industries, Chinese and Western managers say their main difficulty doing business with each other stems from poor communication. Both groups need to understand the cultural differences in business communication, etiquette, and how their actions may be interpreted. This note introduces readers to some of the most important cultural dissimilarities and suggests strategies for communicating effectively while respecting these differences.

THE CASE FOR IMPROVING CHINESE-WESTERN COMMUNICATIONS

With more than 1.3 billion people, the People's Republic of China (PRC) has nearly 20 percent of the world's population.[1] China attracts more foreign investment than any other country—$53 billion in 2002 alone—and the number of multinational corporations in China is increasing at a rapid rate.[2] While more than 400 companies in the Fortune 500 have operations in mainland China, Chinese business is by no means limited to the PRC.[3] Chinese émigrés have remained loyal to their homeland even while establishing substantial population centers in the United States, Australia, Canada, and throughout Southeast Asia. With assets estimated at $2 to $3 trillion, the Chinese diaspora constitutes the world's third-largest economy.[4] In light of these figures, a dramatic increase in business transactions between Chinese and Western corporations is likely to continue. Understanding the differences between the two business cultures is becoming indispensable to today's managers.

DIFFERENT ROLES, DIFFERENT CONTEXTS

Communication serves culturally determined, fundamentally different purposes in the East and the West. In Western culture, due in part to its history of formal contractual dealings, managers see business communications as an exchange of information that often ends when a deal is completed. The Chinese, on the other hand, regard communication as an integral aspect of building and maintaining long-term relationships.[5] In each, the role of communication is framed in a distinct cultural context. In Chinese (or "high-context") culture, verbal communication is most accurately interpreted in the context of nonverbal communication (such as gestures, stance, and tone), social hierarchy, and other background information. Social roles and a concern for respect and harmony inevitably have a bearing on communication. In fact, it is possible for the nonverbal aspects of communication to override what is being stated explicitly.

In contrast, in the United States and many other Western (or "low-context") cultures, the verbalized message is the principal source of information, rather than the context, delivery, or implications. Business interactions are expected to be direct and forthright—indirectness in communication may be considered devious or, in extreme cases, even deceitful. Given these fundamental differences in the role and context of communication, it is important for both Chinese and Westerners to understand the assumptions of the other culture.[6]

UNDERSTANDING *GUANXI*

To get a sense of the Chinese cultural context for relationships, consider the following phrase: "The meaning of person is *ren*." *Ren* can be translated as "humanity," also as "core," or "seed of a fruit." The Chinese character *ren* comprises the characters for "two" and "person." This etymology ("two people") suggests that in the Chinese context, no person exists except in relationship to another, and that in this relationship lies the birth of all possibility. *Ren*, in turn, leads to an understanding of *guanxi*, a type of connectedness achieved through relationships that are based upon trust, respect, reciprocity, and shared experiences.

For the Chinese, wealth is measured in terms of connectedness. In short, you are who you know. In this way, social networks are business resources and vice versa. Because the majority of Chinese businesses are family businesses, this interchangeability of social and business networks is especially noticeable. For example, when introductions are made, the Chinese want to know how a person fits into contexts that they recognize and to which they relate. Thus, the Chinese expect people to situate themselves immediately in a conversation, both professionally and socially. Westerners might try to find mutual acquaintances or ties through schools or professional organizations.

While providing some kind of reference for where one fits into the social structure is certainly not the same as having *guanxi*, it may offer the basis for pursuing the development of *guanxi* between parties.[7] *Guanxi* is usually strongest among family members, but it may also occur among people who have shared significant experiences. In general, the Chinese prefer to do business with friends and people they know, so they devote much energy to creating and nurturing relationships with people they see as having *guanxi* potential. These relationships are based on a notion of reciprocity in terms of gifts and favors that create a bond of mutual indebtedness over time. Westerners doing business in China have the greatest potential when they invest in the relationship as a long-term end in itself rather than a means to an end.

GROUP DYNAMICS

With the strong and lasting influence of Confucianism, Chinese culture greatly values group harmony. Accordingly, the Chinese style of communication aims to preserve harmony. Strong displays of emotion, especially negative feelings, are seen as disrupting the balance. Thus, the Chinese tend to rely on indirect comments and the larger context for communicating a message. In general, they seek to show respect toward everyone (including women) who holds the same social status as men in business culture, and they tend to speak in terms of "we" rather than "I," reflecting their fundamental value of the group as their primary social unit.

Moreover, because the Chinese do not want any individual to lose "face" in the eyes of others, they will not blatantly blame or call out another person for having committed an error. Rather, the group deals with the problem in a non-threatening, face-saving manner. Westerners should realize that face is a subtle concept, and it's possible for people to lose face with various degrees of severity. It might seem obvious that people could lose face if they failed to win a crucial negotiation, but they can also lose face if they are embarrassed or contradicted about even a minor issue in front of others. Loss of face can cause serious damage to relationships and business opportunities.[8]

Given this belief, the Chinese are also concerned about saving Westerners' face, whether or not Westerners are themselves concerned. Westerners may find this aspect of Chinese communication curious because they are accustomed to thinking in terms of the individual, rather than in terms of relationships or groups. It is important that Westerners realize that they lose respect in the eyes of their Chinese counterparts if they lose face in front of the group. In helping Westerners maintain face, then, the Chinese are keeping open the possibility of doing business by building a relationship based on mutual respect and reciprocity.

THE CHINESE "YESNO"

The emphases on building *guanxi*, promoting group harmony, and maintaining face converge also explains the reluctance of the Chinese to say no. The meaning and usage of the word "no" represents a fundamental difference between Chinese and Western communication practices. Westerners interpret and use *no* literally, as an indication that something will not happen, that a request will be denied, or that the issue should not be pursued further. From the Western point of view, no usually means no—end of story. This meaning presents certain challenges in the Chinese context. While the Western use of *no* in either business or cultural situations usually pertains to a separate transaction or demand, the Chinese have difficulty translating the Western nuance of the word's meaning into their own way of communicating because they do not readily split business or cultural exchanges into finite parts or disconnected concerns. The Chinese are much more interested in communication as a fluid element that supports the ongoing formation and refinement of a relationship. This means the Chinese are reluctant to use the word *no* at all because it signals that the overall relationship, rather than simply one request or dealing, may be in jeopardy.

The Chinese communicate *no* through a range of phrases and supporting facial expressions, gestures, silence, and deferral of the issue at hand. Essentially, the goal of a Chinese speaker is to remain polite and save face for everyone involved in the discussion. This means that, rather than saying *no* outright, a person may hesitate when responding to a specific request, may couch a reply using vague terms such as "perhaps," or change the subject altogether. The Chinese speaker expects his or her counterpart to pick up on these subtleties and react accordingly by neither engaging in confrontation nor pursuing the issue further. From the Western point of view, this indirectness can be interpreted, at worst, as indicative of secrecy or dishonesty, and, at best, as showing disinterest or incompetence. The simple word *no* carries the potential, therefore, for long, complicated, misunderstandings between Chinese and Western business associates (Exhibit 11.1).

EXHIBIT 11.1 CONTRASTING CHINESE AND WESTERN COMMUNICATIONS: CONCERNS AND PRACTICES*

	Chinese	Western
Concerns	saving face	frankness or "honesty"
	respect and politeness	assertiveness
	compromise and flexibility	self-assurance
	general feeling or "spirit"	specific terms
	social status	task at hand
	patience	time efficiency
Styles & Practices	reserved	extroverted
	tentative	firm
	personal	impersonal
	no body contact	hugging and back-slapping acceptable
	no pointing	index finger used to point

* Chen, 136

BASIC RULES OF BUSINESS ETIQUETTE

In order to understand the verbal and nonverbal exchanges that take place in Chinese business, one must first develop an awareness of the setting and social norms. The Chinese culture is based in large part on maintaining hierarchies while demonstrating mutual respect and avoiding conflict. This is especially true in business interactions, so it is best to be patient and polite at all times. Manners-based values provide the foundation for basic business etiquette in the following areas:

- *Introductions*: Beginning with the most senior person and working down the hierarchy, introductions tend to be formal and include handshakes as well as business card exchanges. As a sign of respect, cards are presented and received using both hands. The recipient should take a few seconds to examine the card. (Westerners need to be aware of the traditional Chinese naming convention that places the family name first and the given name second.) In general, the Chinese refrain from outward displays of emotion and do not embrace or kiss when greeting or saying good-bye. At the end of a visit, the Chinese often choose to demonstrate respect for a visitor by accompanying him or her to the outer door of the office.
- *Entertainment*: The Chinese typically entertain visitors with banquets consisting of several courses. Seating arrangements are expected to adhere to and reflect the social hierarchy. Numerous toasts are made throughout the meal, and everyone is expected to participate; it is acceptable to request a nonalcoholic drink for toasting. Smoking is common, and guests are usually offered cigarettes. Tipping is not customary, but both parties are expected to vie to pay the bill.
- *Gifts*: Gifts are important symbols used to cultivate relationships and demonstrate respect. Small gifts like company mementos are seen as signifying respect and consideration for the host. As with business cards, one should present and accept gifts with both hands as a show of respect. The Chinese do not usually accept a gift when it is first presented because accepting in haste is thought to be aggressive or greedy, whereas politely

refusing two or three times displays the more desirable characteristics of modesty and humility. Also, it is not expected that gift recipients will open presents in front of the giver unless they are encouraged to do so.

SOME STRATEGIES FOR EFFECTIVE COMMUNICATION

Due to the differing philosophies of relationship and communication, the possibility for misunderstanding between Chinese and Western business people is immense. Nonetheless, these differences can be bridged successfully if both parties make an effort to be attentive to the context of communication and—particularly in the case of Western business people—to be aware of the subtle nonverbal signals that may be used to indicate disagreement. All parties should be especially conscious of allowing speakers a way out of uncomfortable or potentially compromising situations. Above all, both parties should first cultivate self-awareness. Only after looking at our own culture with fresh eyes can we begin to see how others see us. Following are some suggestions from a group of Western expatriate managers working in Asia:[9]

- Use wording that is less directive and more suggestive. For example, "could be" instead of "should be" and "perhaps it could be seen in this way" rather than "I think."
- Structure exchanges so that they occur in a group context. Employees may be more willing to speak for the group than for themselves.
- Devote the time and energy to build and maintain personal, face-to-face communication. Perfunctory, infrequent visits will not be interpreted as an investment in the relationship.
- Refrain from showing anger.
- Give credit to others. The group will realize the context and see you as invested in the group.
- Handle criticism carefully so that individuals do not lose face in front of the group.
- Be aware that often there are other parties to whom you have not been introduced who may be involved in decisions.
- Make efforts to alleviate miscommunications as quickly and as earnestly as possible.

NOTES

1 The information contained in this note is adapted from Ming-Jer Chen's *Inside Chinese Business: A Guide for Managers Worldwide* (Boston: Harvard Business School Press, 2001), especially Chapter 7, "Never Say No: Communicating with the Chinese." Current statistics are from *World Almanac and Book of Facts, 2003.*

2 "Special Report: China's Economy," *Economist* (15 February 2003): 63–65.

3 "Pliant Middle Class Is Key for China," *CNN.COM*, 11 April 2002. Available at http://www.cnn.com/2002/BUSINESS/asia/04/11/china.middleclass/index.html.

4 Chen, 5–6.

5 Chen, 121.

6 Chen, 122–23. Also see Edward Twitchell Hall and Mildred Reed Hall, *Understanding Cultural Differences: Germans, French, and Americans* (Yarmouth, ME: Intercultural Press, 1989), 6.

7 Chen, 46–48.

8 Chen, 72–76.

9 Chen, 135.

CHAPTER

12 UNDERSTANDING THE GLOBAL AUDIENCE

Reading 3.4:
"The Impact of
Globalization
on Individual
Customers:
Implications for
Marketing"
By Sudhir Kale
and Sangita De

Public relations today is a global endeavor. Therefore, it's important for us to understand the various factors that make up our global audience. We'll begin our discovery with an interesting and informative article from the Darden School of Business on the importance of understanding cultural contexts in business communication, etiquette, and how differences may be perceived, specifically focusing on relationship building in the Chinese context.

Once we've defined culture, race, and ethnicity so we have a common understanding, we'll define and discuss a number of cultural attributes, including the differences between *high context cultures* versus *low-context cultures*. We'll go on to an in-depth look at the impact of the differing views of time; formality; the concept of individualism; rank and hierarchy; religion; colors; numbers and symbols; taste and diet; encoding and decoding; and gestures and clothing. We will take a look at why diversity matters to employees, customers, and publics. Along the way, we'll discuss assimilation and acculturation, techniques for communicating cross-culturally, and the dangers of ethnocentrism and stereotyping.

In order to understand how organizations operate in different parts of the world we will examine Systems Theory and Hofstede's (2001) understanding of the culture of an organization. Part of our inquiry will be based on exploring Marshall McLuhan's global village concept and global society theories. We'll look at how political ideologies and economic systems can impact our communication efforts and our public diplomacy. We'll finish up with how we can think globally but act locally.

"THE IMPACT OF GLOBALIZATION ON INDIVIDUAL CUSTOMERS: IMPLICATIONS FOR MARKETING"

By Sudhir Kale and Sangita De

One of the chief attributes of globalization is de-territorialization—the severance of social, political, and cultural practices from their native places. We explain how globalization creates de-territorialization and discuss the marketing implications of this phenomenon. Most research on globalization, particularly in the business discipline, has largely ignored the impact of globalization on the identity of those affected by it. Deterritorialization can have a destabilizing effect on people's identity, often prompting them to embrace beliefs and behaviours that will help them "re-territorialize" and thereby restore some sense of identity. This territorialization-deterritorialization dialectic has interesting implications for marketing researchers as well as practitioners. While limited research on the topic suggests that globalization often results in the divergence of cultural values across economically comparable societies, the precise mechanism of this divergence remains largely unexplained, and thus provides interesting research prospects. De-territorialization provides new opportunities for marketers to target re-territorializing consumers by offering ethnic products and services that would foster consumers' sense of identity.

Globalization has been an issue of much debate, controversy, and discussion among scholars and policy makers for over three decades. Often viewed—and sometimes equated—with other related topics such as internationalization, universalization, liberalization, westernization, and de-territorialization (Scholte 2000), the discourse and debate over globalization continues to generate considerable friction and intrigue. Of the various categorizations and depictions of globalization, the deterritorialization perspective has maximum bearing on consumer identity and view of the self. Identity and self image, in turn, significantly shape consumer behavior (Sirgy 1982). Consequently, one would expect the deterritorialization phenomenon to be of considerable interest to marketing scholars. Yet, discussion on deterritorialization and its impact on consumers' mindset and behaviors has been largely absent from marketing discourse except for a few exceptions (cf. Arnould and Price 2000; Kale 2004).

This paper is based on the premise that deterritorialization, a key outcome of globalization, in conjunction with advances in communication and information technology, has brought about massive and irrevocable changes in the way consumers view and deal with their identity. Deterritorialization entails the severance of social and cultural practices from their place of origin (territory). Up until about forty years ago, most social and cultural practices were fully embedded in an identifiable territory, mostly defined in terms of physical boundaries such as a town, neighborhood, state, or country. Territorial identification and anchoring of rituals and practices provided humans with a sense of stability and location, thus serving as important markers of their individual identity. Globalization has blurred the links between people, places, rituals, and events, thus making many people unsure of themselves and their place in the world.

Thanks to deterritorialization, people have been effectively deprived of their geographic isolation and territorial cohesion, thus creating a void in cultural and topical grounding. Furthermore, many cultural rituals are now severed from their physical origin. Consequently, the territorial markers of identity are fading away, forcing individuals to seek alternative measures to restore their identity. One approach to identity restoration is through selective consumption. Indeed, evidence continues to accumulate suggesting that the frequency of purchase and use of products providing the utility of reterritorialization is on the rise the world over (Arnould and Price, 2000; Kale 2004; Yazıcıoğlu, 2010).

Such evidence runs counter to the 'uniformity through globalization' hypothesis prophesized by scholars such as Ted Levitt (1983) and, more recently, Tomas Friedman (2006), both of whom have argued that globalization makes consumers the world over more alike in their beliefs, preferences, aspirations, and behaviors. Reality suggests that the power of homogenization accorded to globalization may be grossly overestimated or even misattributed. In the few locations where conversion of technology and narrowing of income differences between societies has occurred, supposedly due to globalization, differences in consumer preferences have not lessened. If anything, convergence of incomes has led to a higher manifestation of value differences (cf. de Mooij 2000; de Mooij and Hofstede 2002).

This paper integrates literature from a diversity of disciplines—psychology, economics, sociology, and marketing, to arrive at a better understanding of consumer behavior in the contemporary global environment. We will discuss the impact of contemporary globalization on individual identity and proceed to explain how the urge to reterritorialize manifests into specific product preferences and identity-fostering consumption. Research questions arising from this perspective will also be stated.

WHAT IS DETERRITORIALIZATION?

The notion of deterritorialization is indeed intricate and multifaceted. As Papastergiadis (2000, p.117) notes, "the cultural dynamic of deterritorialization has decoupled previous links between space, stability and reproduction; it has situated the notion of community in multiple locations; it has split loyalties and fractured the practices that secure understanding and knowledge within the family and social unit."

Wenjing (2005) notes that deterritorialization in the era of globalization calls the traditional notion of "community" into question. A national or regional culture can no longer be conceived as reflecting a coherent, distinct, and secure identity. Broadly conceptualized, deterritorialization involves the tearing apart of previously stable social structures, relationships, settings, and cultural representations. It involves the disembedding of humans and cultural symbols from their place of origin or belonging. The Globalization Website defines deterritorialization as, "Expansion of interaction and relationships not tied to or dependent on particular localities; reduced attachment to place or decreased identification with neighborhood or country resulting there from." Scholte (2000) views globalization as the spread of supraterritoriality and a reconfiguration of geography. According to him, globalization tends to obliterate the link between social space and physical territory thus rendering physical distances and territorial borders largely irrelevant.

Deterritorialization is thus a process of detachment of social and cultural practices from specific places, thereby blurring the age-old natural relationship between culture and geographic territories. A 'territory' is understood as the environment of a group (e.g., pack of wolves, a tribe, or a herd of elephants). It is constituted by the patterns of interaction through which the collective secures a certain stability and location (Kale 2004). The environment of a single person (the social environment, personal living space, and lifestyle) can also be seen as a territory in the psychological sense, from which the person acts and returns to. In times of modernity, territorialization involved a superior power (typically the state) excluding or including people within geographic boundaries, and controlling transboundary access and exchange. Such territorialization, though restricting trade and hampering internationalization, provided citizens of the state with stable identity, a feeling of being centered. The move away from modernity and toward contemporary globalization has weakened the salience of the nation state, and in so doing, has contributed to toppling the territorialization process physically and psychically.

A significant effect of globalization has thus been to deprive people of their isolation and territorial cohesion, thus causing them to question their identity or sense of being. The massive transnational flow of capital, media, and commodities in and out of previously sovereign territories means that culture and place become increasingly disconnected (Appadurai 1996, Hannerz 1989). Consequently, many people sense a void in cultural and topical grounding. The consequential rootlessness, for many, creates a threat to identity and an urgent, often frantic urge to reterritorialize. Attempts to reterritorialize in contemporary postmodern times are often symbolic wherein people want to hold on to vestiges of whatever they feel most defined their identity in the past. Such response to deterritorialization changes people's attitudes as well as behaviours, resulting in a culturescape that may be global and cosmopolitan in some aspects, but deeply tribal and territorial in others (Appadurai 2000). Thus, as globalization intensifies, it manifests deterritorialization, which causes alienation. Alienation, in turn, produces identity preserving responses by way of reterritorialization. Buchanan (2004) captures this phenomenon cogently when he writes, " … although most of us embrace the opportunities globalization affords us, we nonetheless continue to sense and long for a past none of us has actually known when the connections were local not global, when the food on our plate was the result of our own toil in the garden. This is the world, as imaginary as it obviously is, that we have been evicted from by our own success in transforming our habitat. The longing underpinning this feeling of exile manifests itself in the form of disorientation, we can't seem to get our bearings in this brave new world without borders. Disorientation brought about by the disembedding process requires in turn a compensating process of reembedding to accommodate us to the alienatingly 'faceless' world of modernity."

IMPACT ON CONSUMERS

New mobile communication technology, the Internet, massive migration, and the disappearance of the iron curtain have drastically increased the pace of globalization. This has been accompanied by massive deterritorialization and a reterritorialization in response. Appadurai (1996) was among the first to explore the cultural dimensions of globalization. In explaining how present-day globalization is different from earlier global eras, he observes that contemporary globalization has shrunk the distance between elites, shifted the dynamics of exchange between producers and consumers, broken many links between labor and family life, and most importantly, obscured the lines between temporary locales and imaginary national attachments.

Deterritorialization has resulted in enormous fragmentation in the constitution of people's demographics, tastes, preferences, and self-concept in any given geographic unit (city block, town, state or nation). Firat (1997, p.78) observes, "Fragmentation is reflected in the simultaneous presence of different and essentially incompatible patterns and modes of life represented by a variety of products, lifestyles, and experiences that do not fit with each other, instead representing different cultural identities and histories."

Contemporary consumption is increasingly undertaken to rediscover, preserve, or create one's sense of identity. Several scholars have discussed the relationship between various facets of globalization and identity. Baumeister (1996) explains how detraditionalization increases choice and, in so doing, problematizes identity formation. McDonald (1999) has argued that many young people feel marginalized by globalization and that their identities can no longer be constructed within the imagery and culture created by producers and employers. Touraine (1997) relates fragmentation and loss of identity to demodernization, and, likewise, Kayatekin and Riccio (1998) relate these problems to globalization.

Castells (1997, p.3) explains, "In a world of global flows of wealth, power, and images, the search for identity, collective or individual, ascribed or constructed, becomes the fundamental source of social meaning. This is not a new trend since identity, and particularly religious and ethnic identity, have been at the roots of meaning since the dawn of human society. Yet identity is becoming the main, and sometimes the only source of meaning in a historical period characterized by widespread destructuring of organizations, delegitimation of institutions, fading away of major social movements, and ephemeral cultural expressions. People increasingly organize their meaning not around what they do but on the basis of who they are."

Arnould and Price (2003) have observed that under globalization, key reference points for identity like community, nation, and people become fluid and contentious, thus rendering global culture "contextless" (Smith 1990). Similarly, Featherstone (1991) has argued that we are increasingly moving to a global society in which adoption of previously fixed and territory-bound lifestyles for specific groups has been surpassed.

The beseeching quest for identity in the throes of deterritorialization finds significance in consumer behavior. Increasingly, the act of consumption has been considered an important vehicle with which to shape one's self-image and define or rediscover one's identity. Arnould and Price (2003) explain that contemporary consumers, in the midst of multiple identities that globalization affords, and lacking authority and continuity formerly provided by tradition, actively hunger for a sense of continuity and integration. Consumers, through creative consumption, seek to create a foundation whereby their authentic selves and their connections to community could be reclaimed. In doing so, individuals rebuff the pressures of deterritorialization and engage in reterritorialization as a method of regaining lost identity. Appadurai (1996, p. 4) provided several examples of reterritorialization in the way diasporas engage in media consumption, "As Turkish guest workers in Germany watch Turkish films in their German flats, as Koreans in Philadelphia watch the 1988 Olympics in Seoul through satellite feeds from Korea, and as Pakistani cabdrivers in Chicago listen to cassettes of sermons recorded in mosques in Pakistan or Iran, we see moving images meet deterritorialized viewers."

We need to make it explicit that the reterritorialization motive is not simply confined to the consumption and media habits of diasporas. As Arnould and Price (2003) and Kale (2004) have argued, consumers everywhere are aspiring to reterritorialize; reclaiming their heritage wherever it could be found—in tribalism, nationalism, ancestry or religion. Consumption as reterritorialization helps explain the resurgent demand for local products from the former East Germany. Dornberg (1995/1996) reports that East German brands for wine, spirits, beer, cosmetics and detergents have all made a comeback thanks to renewed patronage from consumers in the east. Referring to the unification of Germany and the subsequent nostalgia (called 'ostalgie' in Germany), Alexander Mackat, an ad agency executive catering to Eastern consumers explains, "We were told our biography is horrible and has no meaning. We had to cocoon ourselves for self protection, and this was the beginning of ostalgie" (Fitzgerald 2003). This nostalgic feeling is not confined to those who grew up in the German Democratic Republic. Amazingly, it is also shared by their children, most of whom have only a vague memory, if any recollection at all, of the GDR.

The urge to reterritorialize has opened up new markets for ethnic products all over the globe. In so doing, it has transformed social and cultural practices across cultures and continents. Immigrant communities, for example, provide eager markets for Hindi and Greek films worldwide. Australia now hosts the much anticipated Greek-Australian Film Festival, and the development of Bhangra music in Britain has given new inflections to traditional forms, thus creating hybrid representations of cultural identity (Papastergiadis 2000). The 2010 Olympics Ice Skating Competitions featured a Chinese pair performing to a Bollywood theme, "Tanha Dil."

However, some forms of consumption for identity restoration may not be as benign. As Papastergiadis (2000, p. 116) observes in the case of migrants, "Diasporic communities have not always championed new and more inclusive modes of cultural understanding. They have also forged intense attachments to fundamentalist beliefs and offered financial backing to chauvinistic campaigns in their homelands. When identity is at the cusp of transformation there is also a tendency to retreat into, or even fabricate, hostile narratives which bolster boundaries and exclude any identification with the other." Indeed, managing deterritorialized identities has become a major challenge for policy makers and politicians worldwide.

CONCLUSIONS

There is an urgent need to better understand the relationship between identity and consumption in today's deterritorialized world. Several questions of monumental importance need to be addressed in the context of globalization and deterritorialization. Why do some people more readily reterritorialize using the channel of cosmopolitanism while others seek a more fanatical and often damaging option? Does the approach to reterritorialization vary by the ethnic culture of the person seeking to restore identity? What role does personality and education play in the choice of products identified for reterritorialization? To what extent should marketers play the "identity" card in trying to promote their products among diasporic communities? What role, if any, do spirituality and religion play in the reterritorialization process? Addressing these and other prescient issues will be of profound value to both macromarketers as well as public policy makers.

In underscoring the role of identity, Erikson remarks, "In the social jungle of human existence, there is no feeling of being alive without a sense of identity" (quoted in Gergen 1991, p. 38). In a similar vein, Kierkegaard's comments in his novel *The Sickness Unto Death* that, "The biggest danger, that of losing oneself, can pass off in the world quietly as if it were nothing; every other loss, an arm, a leg, five dollars, a wife, etc. is bound to be noticed" (pp. 62–63). Assessing the profound impact deterritorialization has had on human identity, Virilio observed almost three decades ago that identity is the major question for this century (Virilio and Lotringer 1983).

Previous markers of identity such as place and previous preservers of identity such as territorial isolation are being eroded amidst the ravages of deterritorialization. As of now, we are only beginning to understand how deterritorialization threatens previously secure identities and compels people to reterritorialize. Product consumption is but one albeit important paths toward reterritorialization.

REFERENCES

Appadurai, Arjun (1996). *Modernity at Large: Cultural Dimensions of Globalization*. Minneapolis, MN: University of Minnesota Press.

Appadurai, Arjun (2000). Disjuncture and Difference in the Global Cultural Economy," in *The Globalization Reader,* eds. Frank J. Lechner and John Boli, Malden, MA: Blackwell Publishers.

Arnould, Eric J. and Linda L. Price (2000), "Authenticating Acts and Authoritative Performances: Questing for Self and Community," in *The Why of Consumption: Contemporary Perspectives on Consumer Motives, Goals and Desires,* eds. S. Ratneshwar, David Glen Mick and Cynthia Huffman, London and New York: Routledge Press, 140–163.

Baumeister, RF. (1986). *Identity: Cultural Change and the Struggle for the Self.* New York: Oxford University Press.

Buchanan, Ian (2004), "Space in the Age of Non-Place," *Drain Magazine,* 3, available http://www.drainmag.com/issue03/html, accessed January 15, 2005.

Castells, Manuel (1997). *The Power of Identity.* Malden, MA: Blackwell Publishers.

de Mooij, Marieke (2000), "The Future is Predictable for International Marketers: Converging Incomes lead to Diverging Consumer Behavior," *International Marketing Review,* 17 (2), 103–113.

de Mooij, Marieke and Geert Hofstede (2002), "Convergence and Divergence in Consumer Behavior: Implications for International Retailing," *Journal of Retailing,* 78, 61–69.

Dornberg, J. (1995/1996), "Five Years After Reunification—Easterners Discover Themselves," *German Life.* Accessed December 29, 2004 from http://germanlife.com/Archives/1995/9512_01.html.

Erikson, Erik H. (1968). *Identity: Youth and Crisis.* New York: Norton.

Fitzgerald, N. (2003), "East Germans Hanker After Bygone Things," *International Herald Tribune,* March 12, 16.

Friedman, Thomas L. (2000). *Understanding Globalization: The Lexus and the Olive Tree.* New York: Random House.

Firat, A. Fuat (1997), "Globalization of Fragmentation—A Framework for Understanding Contemporary Global Markets," *Journal of International Marketing,* 5 (2), 77–86.

Gergen, K. J. (1991). *The Saturated Self: Dilemmas of Identity in Contemporary Life.* New York: Basic Books.

Hannerz, Ulf (1989), "Culture Between Center and Periphery: Towards a Macroanthropology," *Ethnos,* 54(3/4), 200–216.

Kale, Sudhir H. (2004), "Spirituality, Religion, and Globalization," *Journal of Macromarketing,* 24 (2), 92–107.

Kayatekin, Serap A. and David F. Ruccio (1998), "Global Fragments: Subjectivity and Class Politics in Discourses on Globalization," *Economy and Society,* 27 (1), 74–96.

Kierkegaard, S. (1989 [1849]). *The Sickness Unto Death,* trans. Hannay, A. London, UK: Penguin.

Levitt Theodore (1983), "The Globalization of Markets," *Harvard Business Review,* 61(3):92–102

McDonald, Kevin (1999). *Struggles for Subjectivity.* Cambridge, UK: Cambridge University Press.

Papastergiadis, Nikos (2000). *The Turbulence of Migration: Globalization, Deterritorialization, and Hybridity.* Cambridge, UK: Polity Press.

Scholte, Jan Aart (2000) *Globalization. A Critical Introduction,* London: Palgrave.

Sirgy, M. Joseph(1982), "Self Concept in Consumer Behavior: A Critical Review," *Journal of Consumer Research,* 9(3), 287–300.

Smith, Anthony D. (1990), "Towards a Global Culture?" *Theory, Culture and Society,* 7:171–91

Touraine, Alain (1997). *What is Democracy?* Boulder, CO: Westview Press

Wenjing, Xie (2005), "Virtual Space, Real identity: Exploring Cultural Identity of Chinese Diaspora in Virtual Community," *Telematics and Informatics,* 22 (2005) 395–404

Virilio, Paul and Sylvere Lotringer (1983) *Pure War.* New York: Semiotext(e).

Yazicioğlu, E. Taçli (2010), "Contesting the Global Consumption Ethos: Reterritorialization of Rock in Turkey," *Journal of Macromarketing,* 30(3), 238–253.

CHAPTER

13 KNOWING THE TOOLS OF THE TRADE

Reading 3.5:
"Media Relations
and Publicity"
By Youngjoon Lim

So far, we've taken a relatively strategic look at the practice of public relations. But there are tools of the trade with which we need to be familiar, so in this chapter, we'll explore the "things," otherwise known as *tactics*, produced by public relations professionals. This chapter's reading by Lim (2017) summarizes some of the tactics most often used by public relations professionals to get their messages to various publics.

Tactics can be categorized as advertising and promotion, interpersonal communication, news media, and organizational communication. Regardless of the tactic employed, writing is and probably always will be fundamental to success in public relations.

Advertising and promotion tactics include advertising and promotional items (e.g., clothing, accessories), electronic advertising, out-of-home (aka outdoor) advertising, and print advertising. By using advertising and promotion tactics, public relations professionals ensure control of their messaging. In other venues (e.g., news media and interpersonal), the public relations message can be edited, changed, or hijacked. Use of budgetary funds to purchase advertising and promotion tactics is sometimes the best way to get your organization's message out to publics.

Interpersonal communication tactics include information exchanges (e.g., meetings, speeches), personal involvement, and special events. In each of these instances, the public relations professional should make sure to carefully craft talking points for everyone representing the organization to use in messaging. Just as the crisis communication chapter spoke about the importance of "one voice," it is equally true in interpersonal communication situations.

News media tactics include direct news material, indirect news material, interactive news opportunities, and opinion material (e.g., letter to the editor, op-ed article, position statement). Direct news materials are items produced by public relations professionals in ready-to-publish format. For example, news releases and video news releases are created with the intent that they will go directly into a news package, while pitch letters, media advisories, and media kits are indirect news materials given to the press for journalists to be able to assemble their own articles. This chapter also discusses interactive news opportunities such as news conferences and interviews. *Media training* is an essential part of preparing your spokespeople for interactive news opportunities.

Finally, organizational communication tactics are those the public relations professional has the most control over. These include digital media (e.g., social media, email, website, blogs), direct mail, electronic media (e.g., podcasts, videos), and organizational publications (e.g., newsletters, annual reports). Digital media tactics are constantly evolving, with new platforms emerging every day. It is important for public relations professionals to understand which publics they are trying to talk to using digital media, what the tone and content of their messages should be, and how to handle public interactions on digital media before jumping to the newest platform.

"MEDIA RELATIONS AND PUBLICITY"

By Youngjoon Lim

Public relations cares about media relations. In a similar way, public relations relies on publicity, which refers to the notice or attention generated by the media. Public relations practitioners disseminating such information and messages rely on the media to reach out to target audiences and the public. They manufacture what the target audience and public need to hear and see in the form of publicity tools and techniques. These tools and techniques incorporate the information and messages into various forms customized for the media to use as news sources.

The most commonly used forms of publicity tools and techniques are:

- Publicity Tools
    - News releases
    - Guest editorials
    - Media advisories
    - Pitch letters
    - Video news releases (VNRs)
    - Audio news releases (ANRs)
    - Publicity photographs
    - Media Kits
- Publicity Techniques
    - Interviews
    - Media briefings
    - Media junkets
    - Media tours
    - News conferences
    - Publicity stunts
    - Talk-show appearances
    - Visits to an editorial board

These tools and techniques encompass what public relations practitioners use in light of delivering information and messages to the media in the hope that journalists publish them in the press or broadcast them on the air. When aiming to attract publicity, the practitioners need to customize such tools and techniques in favor of journalists; Journalists are more inclined to use them if they are formatted for the already-standardized practice in the media community. As public relations—unlike advertising—prays for free space and airtime in the media in exchange for saving money, practitioners generalize their public relations tools and techniques in response to the needs and requests of the media community. This is key to building good media relations, which involves coordination of the journalists who produce the news and the practitioners who feed information and messages to the journalists. Media relations is an important task that maximizes positive coverage in the media without paying for publicity through advertising. Excellent media relations saves money for the client or organization.

PUBLICITY TOOLS

There are commonly used formats and components for public relations practitioners to use when they send their material to journalists. Such tools are written or recorded through a strategic planning process, including the purpose of informing and persuading the target audience and the public. Popular tools that are mostly used for publicity are news releases, pitch letters, op-eds, and media kits.

TRADITIONAL NEWS RELEASES

A news release, also known as a press release, is the most popular and commonly used publicity tool in public relations. The news release is a short, compelling news story that a public relations practitioner sends to journalists or media outlets. It contains written information in one or two pages. The information should be written in the form of an inverted pyramid, which includes the most important information and facts in the first (or lead) paragraph. Journalists do not want to waste their time to select a newsworthy news release by reading every word of it. The first paragraph is enough for them to decide whether they want to use the release for their news story. Therefore, the first paragraph must look interesting and charming, as the climax of the release comes at the beginning to grab the journalist's attention. To make a news release interesting and charming, the practitioner should consider answering the following questions before crafting the news release:

Who?

The practitioner needs to define who the target audience is. The news release should contain information and messages that can benefit the specific audience that is likely to use the product or service. When the audience is defined and determined, the practitioner emphasizes why the product or service is great for them, and even the public, if necessary. If the target audience is a group of patients struggling with hair loss, the news release should be sent to journalists and media outlets that carry medical or health sections.

When?

Timing plays a significant role in getting the journalist's attention. If a news release offers information related to current social issues, the journalist will take more time to read it and choose to use it as a news source. For example, if the release introduces an organization's decision to increase its employees' wages more than 10 percent during a time of national wage debates, the release will have a higher possibility of being used in the media.

Where?

Depending on a news release's geographic angle, the practitioner needs to highlight the relevance of information and messages to the residents in the region in which the local or national media have great influence. If the release is about a fundraising event that will be held in a city to help the city's animal shelters, the release is going to be sent to local media. In contrast, if the release is about an outbreak of E. coli bacteria in several states, the release should be sent all national media.

What?

The practitioner should know what the objective and key message of a news release are. If the objective is to boost product sales of a new product, the release needs to contain messages about the benefits of using the new product. The messages should give the target audience the idea of newness and convenience in using the product. The message tells the audience about the merits and values of the product.

Why?

A news release needs to show why it is important to the journalist and the target audience. The practitioner places important and interesting information in the release that attracts the journalist's attention. The journalist checks if the release is considered newsworthy. For example, if the release says that new Ponzi schemes that are hurting thousands of citizens have been discovered, the release has more than enough newsworthiness to be used and published by the journalist.

How?

The practitioner needs to decide how a news release is structured and organized. The release should have a strong title, a clear dateline, a compelling first paragraph, proper spacing (single or double), a specific writing style (usually the Associated Press style), and a proper number of paragraphs. The release should include the practitioner's contact information. The "###" symbol must be placed at the bottom of the release, indicating that the release ends on that page.

Taking all these questions into consideration, the practitioner begins to craft a news release in the common format shown below.

After writing the news release, the practitioner sends it to journalists in various media such as newspapers, magazines, radio stations, and television stations, along with bloggers and professional news release distribution agencies. In particular, to craft and send more customized news releases, the practitioner needs to categorize the media into four sectors: (1) local media (the area in which the organization is based); (2) specialized media (the organization's industrial sector); (3) audience media (the target audience's favorite news outlets); and (4) national media (the organization's product and service for the public).

The *Los Angeles Times* offers some tips on how to increase the possibility of getting the release covered among hundreds of news releases the news outlet receives in a week. The paper recommends that practitioners:[1]

- Keep releases short.
- Double space.
- Write clearly, addressing who, what, where, why, and when in the first two paragraphs.
- Identify the organization or individual sending the release and include the name and daytime phone number (with area code) of someone we can contact if we have questions.
- Date the release and include whether the material is for immediate use or for release at a later date.

From a journalist's perspective, the contact information is important in case the journalist finds the release interesting and newsworthy. The journalist e-mails or calls the practitioner for more information about the release.

FOR IMMEDIATE RELEASE
Date

> Organization
> Logo

Contact Person
Company Name
Telephone Number
Fax Number
E-mail Address

Headline

City, State, Date — The lead paragraph

Remainder of body paragraphs, including detailed information and quotes from experts in the industry or authorities in society.

The last paragraph repeating key messages.

One additional paragraph about the organization's history.

#
(indicates this news release is finished)

ONLINE NEWS RELEASES

The basic format and principles of online news releases are the same as the traditional news release. Sending the release is easy via e-mail, but getting journalists' attention is even harder online. As journalists are inundated with news releases sent through e-mail, they have less time to open them. Capturing their attention in today's digital world has become a major factor in raising the possibility of releases being used and published. Malayna Evans Williams, managing partner of PWR New Media, reveals "three secrets to capturing journalists' attention with precisely targeted, visually stimulating multimedia releases:"[2]

1   Journalists are people too—they prefer to receive news releases with visually engaging content, rather than only word content. Today's digital climate conveniently offers simple ways of placing photos, graphics, and images in the release.
2   Journalists like great stories and engaging content, too—they want additional, usable material that is connected to the content of the release.
    • Illustrated videos
    • Embeddable slideshows
    • Behind-the-scenes images and/or audio
    • Tweetable quotes
    • Social media sharing links

- Infographics
- Downloadable recipe/craft/pairing ideas
- Pinnable graphs and charts

3 Journalists are just as addicted to their inboxes as you are to yours—they want to receive news releases via e-mail.

E-mail is journalists' favorite method for exchanging information and documents. When the practitioner e-mails a news release to the journalist, there are six principles that affect the likelihood that the journalist will open the e-mail and read the release:

- If the subject line is written as "PRESS RELEASE," the journalist will automatically delete it. Because the subject line is the headline in the email inbox, it should show the importance of the release. In fact, a valid subject line is essential.
- In the email, the practitioner attaches the release and offers additional information and material that the journalist finds handy and accessible. Video, photos, screenshots and promotion codes are appreciated.
- The journalist can remove the release with one click in no time if the email does not get to the point in two sentences. Email releases should be short and compelling, as the journalist reads tens of emailed news releases every day.
- Journalists don't like e-mailed releases that are full of extraneous adjectives and adverbs or hyperbole. Email releases tend to contain exaggerated descriptions in the digital climate.

Avoid Hyperbole

Overused hyperbole in a news releases diminishes the credibility of public relations practitioners. It is tempting to use extraneous adjectives and adverbs to demonstrate how the product or service is excellent and superior to other competitors' similar ones, but the abuse of such hyperbole has been seen as problematic by both public relations practitioners and journalists. Rob Burns, president and founder of prREACH.com, recommends ten words and phrases that practitioners should avoid when writing a news release: solutions, leading-edge, value-added, outside the box, industry leader, innovative, disruptive, world-class, synergy, and revolutionary.[3] Historically, news releases used cliché expressions such as "We are the best! We are the most innovative company out there with synergistic, disruptive technology! We are the true leader of the industry! Our product is revolutionary and innovative! Our service comes with cutting-edge solutions." Avoid this kind of language.

INTERNET NEWS RELEASES

As the competition to get news releases published in the media gets tougher, public relations practitioners have their own media outlets: their organizations' websites. Corporations, nonprofit organizations, and governments include the media or communication room on their websites. News releases are updated on a regular basis whenever the organization introduces new products or events. News releases on websites carry photos, video clips and hyperlinks, and they appear in the individual web addresses. Some public relations practitioners email the web addresses to journalists, asking them to visit the sites for news release information.

News releases are sent through social media such as Facebook, Digg, and Twitter. Social media releases are often embedded with blogs and online links that visitors can click to find news releases. Media rooms and social media are emerging trends in posting and publishing news releases, but online and social media releases have a limited or smaller number of visitors who read them. In other words, fewer people, like employees, future job candidates, or competitors are the main users seeking news releases about particular organizations on social media and online. However, social media news releases have a variety of advantages in sharing opinions and accelerating online conversations.

PITCH LETTERS

A pitch letter is used to request that journalists attend a particular event, organized by a public relations practitioner. It informs the journalist of the opportunity to cover a story. Unlike a news release, a pitch letter follows the regular business letter format, which doesn't require a particular writing style or compelling first paragraph. Rather, it is a teaser for possible media coverage that convinces the journalist to come to the event. The pitch letter, of course, should demonstrate the event is newsworthy.

Although a pitch letter is less formal than a news release, public relations practitioners have adopted a widely used style. A pitch letter is usually never longer than one page. It begins with the date and the receiver's name, job title, and the name of the media, including the media outlet's address on the top left corner of the page. The content begins with "Dear Mr. or Ms." and the journalist's last name. In the first paragraph, the practitioner needs to get to the point, offering the journalist valuable information about why the upcoming event is a great opportunity for the media to cover. In the next paragraph, the practitioner gives information on where and when the event will be held, who is going to attend, why this event is relevant to the journalist's audience, what messages will be produced, and how the journalist will be assisted at the event.

The following paragraphs should include a testimonial or quote from the host of the event or someone important in the community. The testimonial needs to demonstrate how the event is related to a good cause and benefits the audience in the community. In the next paragraph, the letter invites the journalist the opportunity to interview someone important. In the last paragraph, the practitioner places his or her contact information, assuring that the journalist will receive full support from the practitioner. A typical pitch letter looks like this:

Date

Journalist's name
The title
The media's name
Address

Dear Mr. XXXXX:

Write about the event
Give detailed information about the event
Place a testimonial or quote
Emphasize the newsworthiness
Assure all support the journalist will get
Place phone and e-mail information of the practitioner

Practitioner's name
Organization's Address

OP-EDS

An op-ed (opposite the editorial page) is a writing piece published by newspapers and magazines. Although there are some unconfirmed arguments about the origins of op-ed writing, the *New York Times* invigorated this publicity tool with its first inaugural op-ed page in 1970. Op-eds were created "to provide a forum for writers with no institutional connection" with the newspaper, and views different from those of the newspaper have been expressed in the form of op-eds.[4] Op-ed pieces cover subjects that "have not been articulated in the newspaper's editorial space." They also focus on disagreeing with the newspaper's view on particular subjects. A good op-ed piece makes a strong argument on a particular subject in the form of an essay. Indeed, the piece should contain the elements of "timeliness, ingenuity, strength of argument, freshness of opinion, clear writing, and newsworthiness."[5]

Op-eds are the highest level of writing in public relations, and they are designed to argue for or against government policies, pending legislation, and current social and international issues. The majority of people who read op-ed pieces are highly educated, wealthy, and influential in society. Many of them serve as opinion leaders and industry pioneers who want op-ed pieces to represent their causes and interests. In the same vein, contributors to op-ed pieces typically consist of politicians, corporate CEOs, celebrities, leaders of nonprofit organizations, and even presidents and kings. Famous and influential people—generally speaking—write op-ed pieces to argue about what should be done by the government, industries, or the public.

However, such powerful people are usually not able to write an entire op-ed piece without the help of their public relations practitioners. For example, if a car company's CEO writes an op-ed piece for the *New York Times*, the CEO, the company's public relations and marketing employees get together to produce a high-quality piece. The three parties are typically involved "in the ghostwriting process each have different motives, none of which are perfectly aligned."[6] If the piece is published in the newspaper under the name of the CEO, the public relations and marketing employees function as the byliners. This is one of the highest achievements for practitioners, as op-ed pieces are considered prestigious among powerful people.

When a public relations practitioner writes an op-ed piece for the CEO or head, he or she should include eight essentials:

1   **Have a clear editorial viewpoint:** pro or anti. There is no neutral attitude toward the subject.

2   **Don't slowly build to the point:** place the main point on top. In the first paragraph, the op-ed piece reveals the main argument.

3   **Concentrate on one main idea or a single point:** one themed argument with a fixed attitude is essential in making a strong point.

4   **Present facts and statistics to build credibility:** a strong argument is justified with scientific evidence and statistical data.

5   **Use short, firm, strong sentences and paragraphs:** a good op-ed piece relies mainly on simple declarative sentences. Break long paragraphs into two or more shorter ones.

6   **Acknowledge the other side's point of view:** write that the opponent's view can be right, but discredit the opposing argument by pointing out the superiority of the argument the practitioner's boss makes.

7   **Provide a recommendation:** the purpose of an op-ed piece is not to inform but to educate people with professional insights. The argument should lead to recommendations for the target audience or public.

8   **Conclude with repetition:** summarize the main argument in a final paragraph by repeating the ideas from the first paragraph.

Major US newspapers that publish op-ed pieces include the *New York Times*, the *Washington Post*, the *Wall Street Journal*, the *Los Angeles Times*, and *USA Today*. The commonly accepted length of a piece is between six hundred and 1,200 words. As space is limited for all the papers, the competition is extremely high; no op-ed piece is guaranteed publication.

MEDIA KITS

A media kit, also referred to as a press kit, is a total package of information in a folder. Public relations practitioners are in charge of placing information about clients or organizations in the folder. This can include photos, CDs, DVDs, brochures, samples, documents, and USB flash drives. The folder, or media kit, is sent to journalists who are encouraged to grow interested in the comprehensive information package. Today, it has become the trend to send media kits to journalists online instead of by mail. Not only does the online media kit save money on printing and mailing costs, but it also allows journalists to have easier access to the information. The online media kit, like offline media kits, features comprehensive information with photos, videos, graphics, and downloadable documents. Both online and offline media kits should include seven sections:

1   **A news release:** as a media kit is a package of comprehensive information, the news release(s) should be included in the folder or online media kit. The news release is supposed to contain the most recent information about the organization's special product or event.

2   **Organization overview sheets:** a brief historical overview of the organization's performance and its people, including the CEO or head, is placed in overview sheets. The sheets give a timeline of the organization's establishment, achievements, and major contributions to the society.

Copyright © Pascal Maramis (CC by 2.0) at https://www.flickr.com/photos/pascalmaramis/14442129321/.

3   **Biographies:** key players in the organization should be introduced. The key players are investors, founders, and executives of the organization.

4   **Media coverage:** if the media had reported any positive mentions or stories about the organization and its employees' performance, the stories should be included in the folder and online media kit. Reprints, clips, or screenshots of news coverage in a positive light impress journalists.

5   **Frequently asked questions:** questions that journalists ask repeatedly should be answered up front. This can save time and energy for both journalists and public relations practitioners.

6 **Visual content:** photos of the organization, its products, and key employees are offered. In addition, journalists look for videos, logos, and graphic images of the organization that can be used for reporting.

7 **Contact information:** clear information about how to contact public relations practitioners includes their names, email and mailing addresses, and office phone numbers. This section is placed in the back page of the media kit with the practitioner's business card.

Media kits of current organizations are mostly found online, which journalists and public relations practitioners find more convenient to share and cheaper to produce.

PUBLICITY TECHNIQUES IN PUBLIC RELATIONS

Whereas publicity tools are produced, controlled, and sent by public relations practitioners to journalists, publicity techniques provide journalists with more opportunities to be active in the newsgathering process. Practitioners employ publicity techniques to help journalists decide if they want to gather further information on media events the practitioners promote. Popular publicity techniques used to draw journalists to media events include interviews, news conferences, media tours, and talk-show appearances.

INTERVIEWS

A primary reason for journalists to contact public relations practitioners is to ask for a chance to interview CEOs or heads of organizations. When a request for an interview is delivered to the practitioner, the organization's CEO has to decide whether he or she will participate in the interview with the media. In particular, if the organization has a communication department, the department's staff will advise whether the interview is worth it for the CEO and organization. If the organization does not have communication staff, it hires a public relations firm to prepare for the interview. CEOs are commonly uncomfortable with interviews with the fact that journalists are inclined to ask tough, uncomfortable questions from an investigative perspective. When an interview occurs, the CEO and the journalist get together to talk. Although they are in the same environment, their goals are different. The journalist seeks a good story, while the CEO intends to promote his or her key messages and information through the media. The different goals often lead to conflict, and they may become less friendly to each other by the end of the interview.

There is no doubt that an interview is a great publicity opportunity for an organization. The practitioner needs to find a way of capitalizing on the opportunity by preparing the CEO for a smooth, productive interview. In fact, the practitioner trains and coaches the CEO before the interview, especially if it is for television. In a television interview, many CEOs not only appear anxious or frightened, but also stumble over their words. They assume that they know what they want to say as industry leaders, but appearing on television can be an incredibly daunting experience for anybody. They could end up just looking bad. If this happens, the organization just wasted a valuable publicity opportunity. The practitioner's main task is to coordinate the interview between the CEO and the journalist to meet their goals. Training the CEO with interview rehearsals is not an easy task, but it can be a promising opportunity for the organization.

Public relations practitioners and journalists agree that without the right preparation, "a media opportunity can quickly turn into a disaster, which can cause long-lasting reputational damage" to both the CEO and the organization.[7] Many media interview specialists follow ten dos and don'ts for a successful interview:

1   **Prepare for the interview**—Preparing for media appearances is essential. The practitioner reminds the CEO of key messages that the CEO has to remember and convey.

2   **Focus on the journalist asking the questions**—The CEO can be distracted by lights and cameras while being interviewed. The practitioner trains the CEO to focus on what the journalist says, how to answer the questions, and making eye contact.

3   **Wear something professional**—Television viewers pay attention to what the CEO wears and says. If the messages are heavy and serious, dark-colored outfits are recommended. If the messages are entertaining and fun, more casual outfits with some accessories are welcome.

4   **Look confident**—Appearing on television produces many butterflies in the stomach. The practitioner tells the CEO to lean forward when the CEO talks and to stay calm when the journalist asks questions. In order for the CEO to look confident, the practitioner recommends not using too many "ums" "you knows" and "ahs."

5   **Stick to the messages**—The practitioner emphasizes that the CEO's main goal is to relay the messages during the interview. Regardless of the journalist's tough and embarrassing questions, the practitioner trains the CEO to stick to the task of conveying the messages.

6   **Make it credible**—The CEO needs to convince the journalist that his answers are based on facts and credible sources. The practitioner supplies the CEO with facts, examples, and data that can support the credibility of the messages.

7   **Get ready for the worst**—The practitioner predicts worst-case-scenario questions from the journalist, and the CEO receives such questions in rehearsal. The CEO is trained not to look nervous under any circumstances.

8   **Don't say "No comment"**—In preparing for the possibility that the journalist will ask the CEO unrehearsed and unexpected questions, the practitioner tells the CEO to explain why the question is not answered instead of saying, "No comment," which makes it seem like the CEO is hiding something from the journalist.

9   **Don't try to be a know-it-all**—The CEO is pressured to appear professional and trustable, feeling that all questions should be answered without hesitation. The practitioner advises the CEO that giving and "I don't know" answer is better than coming up with improvised and bluffing answers during the interview.

10   **Don't ignore training**—Interview training is key to success. The practitioner plays the journalist in a simulated media setting, asking questions of the CEO. The training session is recorded and reviewed for improvement in terms of facial expression, body gestures, makeup, and outfits.

Interviews offer a great opportunity for the organization to achieve its goals. The practitioner uses various publicity tools to attract media coverage of the organization. In response to such tools, the journalist may ask for an interview with the practitioner or the CEO. When the interview is scheduled, the practitioner's number one priority is to train the CEO.

NEWS CONFERENCES

Copyright © Depositphotos/click60.

A news conference, or press conference, is a staged meeting that invites the media to the organization's location. In the meeting, journalists and public relations practitioners exchange messages and information related to the organization in a question-and-answer (Q&A) format. When there is a unique or newsworthy announcement from the organization, a news conference is arranged. The practitioner acknowledges that a news conference should not be abused as a publicity technique, because journalists expect a truly big news story at a conference. If they don't get one, they would probably never show up to any conference organized by the same organization.

A news conference should be held when the organization has real, important news and when the phone will not stop ringing. Frequent organizers of news conferences are corporations, government agencies, politicians, and sports teams.

Corporations:

When a new product that can change a market trend is produced, corporations hold a news conference by inviting as many journalists as possible. This type of news conference is also referred to as a promotional conference. The tech giant Apple has been an active user of such conferences since the birth of the iPhone. The founder of Apple, the late Steve Jobs, streamlined the trend of promotional conferences, introducing the corporation's new products in front of journalists by standing on a stage with big screens. The trend became the market standard as other smartphone corporations implemented the same style of news conferences. Public relations practitioners organize such public relations events, inviting a host of journalists.

Government Agencies:

The White House is one of the most enthusiastic organizers of news conferences. The press secretary of the White House holds news conferences whenever important social and international issues emerge. Emergency news conferences are held in the White House as disasters or provocative social unrest spreads across the nation. Holding a news conference at a government agency attracts more journalists to cover the event, as the media assign designated correspondents to the different agencies; by contrast, corporations normally invest a large amount of resources in asking the media to assign journalists to cover their news conferences.

Politicians:

When politicians announce bids for office, their public relations practitioners coordinate news conferences with the media and supporters. At the conference, the politician coveys the message of why he or she entered the race and how to make the country better. Political slogans and symbols are unveiled at the conference. Senator Barack Obama, in 2007, held a news conference to announce his candidacy for the White House, standing before the Old State Capital where Abraham Lincoln began his political career in Springfield, Illinois.

Sports Teams:

Before big sports events are held, athletes or team owners hold news conferences to announce how they will play the game. Boxing news conferences are often seen as pre-fight public relations stunts. When boxers pose for pictures, they usually "happen" to get into a heated conversation or bare-knuckle confrontation.

The success of news conferences is associated with the number of journalists who attend. Public relations practitioners strategize the means of increasing journalists' participation in the conference. There are five steps to convincing journalists to attend:

1   **Find a newsworthy story**—Every employee and product has a story to tell, but the practitioner should find the best newsworthy story to meet the journalist's expectations. The CEO's story sounds more charming than an employee's story.

2   **Find a time and location**—In the media business, meeting the deadline means everything. Morning hours give journalists more time to attend and write about the conference. As the conference requires physical attendance, the conference location should not be too far from the journalists.

3   **Send an invitation**—Addressed to individual journalists, the invitation e-mail or letter gives a brief explanation of the conference. As long as it's not an emergency conference, the invitation should be sent a week before the conference so the journalists can schedule to attend.

4   **Arrange the people**—The practitioner consults with the CEO about resource allocation for the conference. They need to decide who announces the messages, who is going to be interviewed, who escorts the journalists, who distributes the organization's samples, and what refreshments or gifts will be offered.

5   **Assist the journalists**—The practitioner stays at the conference until the journalists leave, answering all questions and offering additional information about the conference. The practitioner needs to respond to any requests from journalists at the conference. Media kits can be provided.

A news conference as a staged public relations event requires some work, yet it is an effective publicity technique for reaching many journalists. As a result, the organization's messages can reach larger audiences.

MEDIA TOURS

Public relations practitioners and journalists need each other to build mutually beneficial relationships at work. They become partners at best or enemies at worst. They, as humans, want to build rapport before, during, or after work. Media tours are a good publicity technique for the practitioners to build rapport and grab journalists' attention. Two types of media tours are commonly practiced: the junket and the newsroom tour.

- **The junket:** this is all-expenses-paid trip for the journalist. The practitioner invites the journalist to a place where an event is held. For example, if the organization releases a new product in a foreign country, the practitioner invites the journalist to the country by picking up the tab for the flight and accommodations. In return, the practitioner expects a favorable article or reporting toward the product.

The junket also applies to an organization's factory tour. Journalists are invited to travel with the organization's executives to its manufacturing facilities across the country, with all expenses paid by the organization. The practitioner focuses on showing the journalist good parts of the facilities in the hope that the journalist builds trust in the organization's products, which leads to positive coverage.

- **The newsroom tour:** the practitioner and CEO visit media outlets (in town or out of town) to build relationships with editors and journalists. As journalists work on tight, unpredictable schedules, the practitioner and CEO see these meetings as a good way of greeting journalists and expressing appreciation. They can have lunch or dinner together while talking about the organization's products or services, including upcoming events and conferences. Journalists may develop a story angle for the organization and schedule an interview.

Newsroom tours combine the tasks of promoting the organization's publicity and building relationships with journalists. Although some journalists refuse to participate in newsroom tours, public relations practitioners often successfully invite journalists to the places where the events are going to be held.

TALK-SHOW APPEARANCES

Some public relations firms tout their media relations networks. These firms specialize in connecting a client with the media. When the client wants to promote his or her product, such as a book, music, movie, or food, the firm finds opportunities for the client to appear on television shows. Television talk shows are considered the best publicity technique in terms of generating instant and broad impact for the client. There are three types of TV talk shows that public relations practitioners wish to use in promoting different products to different target audiences.

1 **Early morning shows**—ABC's "Good Morning America" and NBC's "Today Show" are popular, influential morning television shows. These shows provide top domestic and global news and weather reports. In addition, they conduct interviews with famous or rising figures, cover specific lifestyles of average people all around the world, and offer in-depth coverage on provocative social issues and touching humanitarian stories. In particular, specific segments of both shows are public relations practitioners' preferences. These segments include consumer issues, health, finance, cooking, and entertainment. During the shows, the hosts might participate in making fruit juice, following yoga poses, applying cosmetics, testing medicines, fixing quick breakfasts, wearing new clothes, learning new financial services, and watching clips from new movies. A wide range of new products and services can be introduced in the segments through the appearance of experts who are clients of the practitioners.

2 **Daytime talk shows**—CBS's "The Talk" and ABC's "The View" are popular daytime shows with panels of four or five female cohosts who discuss current issues and news items. They talk about hot social and political issues from the perspective of women. Both shows often highlight the themes of parenthood, health, and beauty, in addition to interviews with celebrities. These shows aim to represent stories of success and failure about working mothers, professional women, and female students. Controversial social issues such as gay marriage, racial discrimination, equal payment, and freedom of expression are discussed on the shows. Public relations practitioners' favorite parts of these shows come when the hosts compliment specific products. As both shows target female audiences, products and services related to motherhood, health, romance, and beauty earn a chance of being promoted on the shows.

3 **Nighttime talk shows**—Fierce competition has continued among nighttime talk shows throughout US television history. Unlike morning and daytime talk shows, a host of nighttime talk shows competes for high ratings. Popular shows are "Jimmy Kimmel Live!" on ABC, "The Late Show" on CBS, "The Tonight Show Starring Jimmy Fallon" on NBC, and "Conan" on TBS. These shows have almost identical traditional formats: (1) a male host gives an opening monologue; (2) the host has a brief conversation with the music players; (3) the host performs several skits; (4) the show invites a more famous celebrity as

its first guest; (5) the show invites a less famous celebrity as its second guest; and (6) a musical guest or comedy act ends the show. Nighttime talk shows are big fans of movie stars, who have the power to increase ratings. Movie stars also view the shows as a publicity technique for promoting their new movies (the same principle applies to musicians and authors). When a movie star appear on one of the shows, they disseminate the message of how entertaining their movie is. In response, the talk show host plays a short clip of the movie and informs the audience of the opening day of the movie, adding that this is a great movie to see. Movie stars serve as public relations practitioners for their movie studios.

Official White House Photo / Photograph by Pete Souza / Copyright in the Public Domain.

A talk-show appearance is a thoroughly organized publicity technique. It requires professional networking and assistance. Public relations firms and television companies orchestrate the appearance in hopes of promoting particular products or services and raising TV ratings.

EVOLVING PUBLICITY TOOLS AND TECHNIQUES

There are more tools and techniques for publicity. An audio news release (ANR) records the voice of an announcement, and the practitioner sends the recorded tape to radio stations. In a similar way, a video news release (VNR) is used to produce a videotaped news release. As it requires the specialized skills of shooting and editing, the practitioner normally hires a production company. A VNR is produced in a format that television stations use. The VNR is sent to the stations with B-roll footage that does not include sound. The footage allows the TV producers to insert voice or music to customize the VNR for its reporting. A satellite media tour (SMT), as a publicity technique, is a reserved interview with television programs. When a television journalist wants to interview a CEO or public spokesperson who is not physically able to appear on the program, the one-on-one interview is conducted via a satellite media tour.

Positive media coverage is a blessing for organizations and individuals. Free publicity is an even bigger blessing, although it takes a series of efforts and strategies. For better chances, public relations practitioners link their publicity tools and techniques to social media accounts which are connected to those of journalists. In general, the practitioner needs to develop social media skills to raise the chances of attracting media coverage.

CHAPTER SUMMARY AND REVIEW

1   Identify publicity tools
2   Identify publicity techniques
3   Study core elements of those tools and techniques

4   Understand how promotion is working between practitioners and journalists

5   Describe best ways of catching media attention

NOTES

1   *Los Angeles Times.* http://www.latimes.com/about/la-contactus-prguidelines-htmlstory.html.

2   *Communication World Magazine.* http://cw.iabc.com/2015/03/04/visual-storytelling-todays-news-releases/.

3   Blogworld. http://www.blogworld.com/2015/01/08/top-10-words-not-to-use-when-writing-a-press-release-2/.

4   *New York Times.* http://www.nytimes.com/2004/02/01/opinion/01SHIP.html?pagewanted=print.

5   Ibid.

6   *PR News.* http://www.prnewsonline.com/topics/internal-communication/2013/05/06/how-write-a-bylined-article-for-the-boss/.

7   *The Guardian.* http://www.theguardian.com/women-in-leadership/2013/jul/24/top-tips-media-training-interviews.

SECTION

THE FOUR-STEP PUBLIC RELATIONS PROCESS : RESEARCH, PLANNING, IMPLEMENTATION, EVALUATION (RPIE)

Part of the purpose of this text is to assist in preparing you to attain the PRSA Certificate in Principles of Public Relations, as well as to help you understand the cyclical nature of public relations campaigns. Each of the four chapters in this section covers one of the important steps in the four-step public relations process.

Research is always step 1 in campaign planning. Chapter 14 goes into depth on the different types and methodologies of research a practitioner undertakes to inform the elements of the plan and ensure the success of the campaign.

Chapter 15 addresses the second step in campaign development: planning. This moves the research from step 1 into an actionable plan that sets strategic goals, strategies, objectives, and tactics for completion during the third stage of the process: implementation.

Strategies are the statements of actions and communications that will be used to accomplish a specific objective of the campaign. Chapter 16 takes us through the array of strategies public relations practitioners have at their disposal, from action strategies such as alliances and coalitions, sponsorships, and special events to communication strategies, including transparency and newsworthy information. Message strategies are critical to the success of any campaign, so we will drill down into understanding how to craft messages that answer the question "What's in it for me?" We'll also discuss the critical aspects of verbal, nonverbal, and visual communication. We'll finish with a brief discussion of the steps, commonly called tactics, needed to accomplish each strategy.

Step 3 of the four-step process is implementation, and Chapter 16 will focus on scheduling and staffing as well as the critical function of budgets and how they enhance or constrain our implementation. Scheduling is an important part of implementation and we will focus on task scheduling as well as message scheduling with a look at reach versus frequency and the most common message scheduling patterns: continuous, flighting, and pulsing. Finally, we would be remiss if we didn't discuss creating the campaign plan book.

The last chapter in this section, Chapter 17, deals with the final step in the four-step process: evaluation. Evaluation actually occurs at all four stages, so we'll look at the criteria and tools used in ongoing evaluation. At the end of the campaign, we conduct summative evaluation to determine whether and/or to what extent we achieved our objectives. To that end, we'll explore various aspects of measurement, observation, feedback, and opinion formation as important parts of that summative evaluation. We'll finish with a look at the way people are affected by information, from exposure to awareness, developing an attitude, and on through to action.

14 RESEARCH

Reading 4.1:
"The Public
Relations
Process—RACE"
By Shannon Bowen

The first, and most important step in the public relations process is research. Author Dr. Shannon Bowen (2010) discusses the RACE (research, action planning, communication, evaluation) process. While PRSA (2017) currently endorses the RPIE model (research, planning, implementation, evaluation), it is important to understand there are other acronyms out there that represent the same steps. Examples include ROPE (research, objectives, programming, evaluation), STARE (scan, track, analyze, respond, evaluate), and ROSIE (research, objectives, strategies, implementation, evaluation) (Turney, 2011).

As noted by Dr. Bowen, research determines the goals, strategies, and tactics to be used in a campaign. This type of research is called *formative research* and involves examining the situation facing the organization, the organization itself, and the publics the organization interacts with.

Public relations professionals cannot just "go with their gut instincts." All of their campaign decisions should be based on primary or secondary research. *Primary research* is designed and carried out by the public relations professional and is specifically tailored to the organization's needs. *Secondary research* is carried out by other agencies. This research is usually collected in databases, online, or in specific government or commercial sources. Though the names sound different, secondary research should always be conducted first so you can see what research is already available to you. In both cases, the scientific method of asking a question, doing secondary research, constructing a hypothesis/research question, designing and carrying out the research method to examine the hypothesis/research questions, analyzing data and drawing conclusions, and communicating results should be used to gather the data.

Your findings from both primary and secondary research are usually collected in a SWOT (strengths, weaknesses, opportunities, threats) analysis. This allows you to look at things within the control of your organization—internal strengths and weaknesses—as well as those outside your organization's control—external opportunities and threats. Your SWOT should conclude with a problem statement that summarizes the need for and direction a campaign should take.

Research methods are *qualitative* (i.e., subjective, usually involving in-depth probes of why and how) or quantitative (i.e., objective, usually using forced-choice responses that have numbers assigned). They can also be formal (e.g., communication audit, benchmarking, polls) or informal (e.g., record keeping, advisory groups, field reports, contact lists, call logs). The primary qualitative research methods used by public relations professionals are interviews, focus groups, and case studies. The primary *quantitative* research methods used by public relations professionals are surveys and content analysis.

Formal systems also exist for observing trends and changes in public relations. As noted in our chapter on monitoring the environment and preparing for threat and crises, it is essential for public relations professionals to constantly research social, political, and technological environments that may influence their organization. Special techniques include PR audits, communication audits, social audits, image studies, publicity analysis, and usability research. With the increase in social media use, trend analytics are also used.

Research does not end when the campaign begins, however; it is an ongoing process. One of the most important steps that takes place during the campaign discussed in Dr. Bowen's (2010) chapter is *benchmarking*. This process allows organizations to understand their current situation and where they relate to their competitors, gain insight into media interest, and see the ongoing success of their campaign. Organizations' leadership also likes benchmarking because it allows organizations to examine public relations ROI (return on investment).

"THE PUBLIC RELATIONS PROCESS—RACE"

By Shannon Bowen

Public relations works best when it is a strategic management function. Strategic public relations is focused on achieving goals and objectives that contribute to the overall purpose and mission of an organization. To be strategic, public relations practitioners need accurate information about the situations they face, the audiences they communicate with, effectiveness of their communication efforts, and the overall impact the program has on building and maintaining relationships with critical stakeholders, without whom the organization could not fulfill its purpose. Public relations practitioners may be tempted to start with tactics—such as press releases, a blog, an event, and so on—but these first should be determined by research, to help inform the overall goals and strategies of the function, otherwise they may be wasted efforts.

CONSTRUCTING THE STRATEGIC PLAN FOR A PUBLIC RELATIONS CAMPAIGN

This process is primarily composed of four steps: using research to define the problem or situation, developing objectives and strategies that address the situation, implementing the strategies, and then measuring the results of the public relations efforts. Sometimes acronyms, such as John Marston's RACE (research, action planning, communication, evaluation) or Jerry Hendrix's ROPE (research, objectives, programming, evaluation) are used to describe the process.[1] You'll notice that that the process always starts with research and ends with evaluation.

Although it is easier to remember such acronyms, the four steps are essentially the following:

1   Use *research* to analyze the situation facing the organization and to accurately define the problem or opportunity in such a way that the public relations efforts can successfully address the cause of the issue and not just its symptoms.

2   Develop a *strategic action plan* that addresses the issue that was analyzed in the first step. This includes having an overall goal, measurable objectives, clearly identified publics, targeted strategies, and effective tactics.

3   Execute the plan with *communication* tools and tasks that contribute to reaching the objectives.

4   Measure whether you were successful in meeting the goals using *evaluation* tools.

STEP 1: FORMATIVE RESEARCH TO ANALYZE THE SITUATION

The first step in the process is analyzing the problem or opportunity. This involves research, either formal or informal, to gather information that best describes what is going on. Research used to understand the situation and help formulate strategies is called **formative** research.

For example, a natural gas company may be considering the route for a new pipeline. It must conduct research to understand what possible obstacles it might face. Are there any environmentally protected or sensitive regions in the area? Are there strongly organized neighborhood groups that might oppose the project? What is the overall public support for natural gas and transportation pipelines? Community relations professionals are very familiar with the NIMBY (Not In My Back Yard) sentiment. Additionally, are there acceptable alternatives to the pipeline construction? Alternative routes? Alternative drilling procedures? Alternative construction times? All of these questions should be considered before the first shovel breaks ground.

According to Cutlip, Center, and Broom, research "is the systematic gathering of information to describe and understand situations and check out assumptions about publics and public relations consequences."[2] Much of this information may already exist and may have been collected by other agencies. Research that has previously been conducted is called **secondary research**. For example, the Interstate Natural Gas Association of America has conducted surveys on public opinion and communication practices of pipeline companies. Research on NIMBY and other social behaviors is also available through a review of academic and professional literature. Secondary sources are the least expensive way to gain background knowledge.

However, you may need to conduct primary research or data you collect yourself for your purposes. You may need to conduct interviews or focus groups with neighborhood associations or environmental groups. You might consider surveys with homeowners and business that might be located near the pipeline. There are many different methods to collect the data that is needed to fully understand the situation. Analysis of previous news stories about pipelines in this region would give you a good idea about the way this story might be framed by media. Another analysis of blogs and other social media about pipelines also would be a good idea. Again the purpose for gathering the information is to help with understanding the situation.

Using a SWOT Analysis

A very popular tool for analyzing situations is the **SWOT** (strengths, weaknesses, opportunities, threats) analysis. This breaks down a situation by looking at the internal and external factors that might be

Internal Factors

Strengths	Weaknesses
Opportunities	Threats

External Factors

FIGURE 14.1. SWOT analysis.

contributing to the situation before developing strategies. The internal factors are the **Strengths** and **Weaknesses** of the organization. The external factors are the **Opportunities** and **Threats** existing in the organization's environment (see Figure 14.1).

The first step is to look *internally* at the strengths and weakness of the organization. For example, the energy company may find that it has very strong relationships with members of the media, has good employee morale, is financially sound, and has a culture that values innovation. It may also find that it has weak relationships with environmental groups and neighborhood associations, has a culture that promotes confidence in its decisions (perhaps even bordering on arrogance), and has dedicated few resources in the past toward community relations. This information helps inform the possible strategies it needs to take regarding the construction of a new pipeline.

The *external* factors, opportunities and threats, are usually the reasons the organization finds itself in the situation. In the case of the energy company, it sees an opportunity to drill into a new methane gas deposit and provide that energy to its clients. To the energy company, this appears to be a win-win situation because it can continue to provide energy to meet the demand of its consumers. However, it also needs to assess the possible threats, which include probable legal actions from opposition groups that could lead to court injunctions. Other threats might include negative coverage of the project by the media, leading to a damaged reputation and lower public support for the project.

After conducting the SWOT analysis, you can couple the internal factors with the external factors to suggest possible strategies.

- *SO* strategies focus on using organizational strengths to capitalize on the external opportunities.
- *ST* strategies also use organizational strengths to counter external threats.
- *WO* strategies address and improve organizational weaknesses to be better prepared to take advantage of external opportunities.
- *WT* strategies attempt to correct organizational weaknesses to defend against external threats.

Constructing a Situation Analysis

Once enough data and information has been collected so that you really do understand the core contributing factors and not just the surface conditions, then it is time to write a two-paragraph statement that summarizes the situation. The first paragraph should redefine the situation using the data collected by your research. Highlight the insights gained through formal and informal research. The second paragraph should identify the problems, difficulties, and potential barriers to resolving the issue. These also should have been identified in the research, and the research also should help you recommend solutions to these barriers. For example, the energy company would address the opportunity to provide a new energy source to its customers using innovation and technology for efficient and effective delivery of the natural gas, asking its employees to be ambassadors to the community, and working with the media to tell the positive story of the project. It would also need to identify that previous pipeline projects have been delayed, and in some cases halted, because of the effective opposition of environmental groups and neighborhood associations, and that it needs to improve its efforts with community relations before starting the project.

From the description paragraphs, a succinct one-sentence **problem/opportunity statement** is written that cuts to the core of the situation and identifies the consequences of not dealing with the problem or opportunity. For example, for the hypothetical utility pipeline situation, because environmental and neighborhood groups have been influential in stopping pipeline projects in the past and this pipeline route is planned to go through sensitive regions, the company needs to build better relationships with the community through communication and action that will eliminate or reduce obstacles to building the pipeline.

STEP 2: STRATEGIC ACTION PLANNING

The strategic plan should be focused on resolving or capitalizing on the situation identified in the problem/opportunity statement. It begins by flipping the problem/opportunity statement into a **goal.** In the case of the energy company, the goal might be the following: "To use communication and actions that improve relationships with key members of the community in order to successfully complete a pipeline that delivers newly found methane gas to customers." Notice that there is room for change with the pipeline plans in this goal statement. The end goal is to build a pipeline, and in order to achieve this the company may need to make adjustments to the routes or construction of the pipeline. Care should be taken not to write goals that suggest that the public will do something you want them to do. Because publics cannot actually be controlled, it might set up the organization for failure. Instead, focus should be on what can be done to achieve the goal, such as communicate and act in such a way that earns the consent or endorsement of these publics.

The goal provides the direction for the strategic plan and **objectives** provide the direction of specific and measurable outcomes necessary to meet the goal. A good objective meets the following criteria: it should be an end and not a means to the end; it should be measurable; it should have a time frame; and it should identify the public for the intended outcome.[3]

- **End and not means to an end.** An objective should be an outcome that contributes to the goal. There are three possible outcomes for these objectives: cognitive (awareness, understanding, remembering), attitudinal (create attitudes, reinforce positive attitudes, change negative attitudes), and behavior (create behaviors, reinforce positive behaviors, change negative behaviors). The opposite of these outcome objectives are what Lindenmann called "Output Objectives,"[4] which are the means to an end. They include the communication efforts to reach the objectives such as placement of messages in influential media. These are actually strategies and not objectives (more on this later).
- **Measureable.** Objectives also help hold public relations professionals accountable for their efforts. Public relations should engage only in strategies and tactics that actually contribute to larger organizational goals. Measurable objectives often require a comparative number, such as 65% awareness of a product or program. An objective cannot be set to increase awareness by 20% if the current level of awareness is unknown. This is why formative research is needed to establish benchmarks. If no such benchmark exists, then it is customary to establish a desired level, such as "increase awareness to 85%." The problem with this is that you do not know how close you are to that figure before the campaign. This might be an easy

objective to achieve (if your level of awareness is already at or above 85%) or a very difficult one (if your awareness level is around 20%).

- **Time frame.** When will the objective be met? If there is no time frame specified, then it cannot be accountable.
- **Identify the public.** It is a good idea to identify overall objectives before tying them to a public. This helps to think about *which* publics are connected to the objective. However, to make an objective truly measurable it must identify a public, because different publics will be at different levels of awareness, attitudes, and behaviors. For example, the objective may be to increase attendance at employee benefits meetings. Research may find that the messages are getting clogged at middle management, which has many people who have a negative attitude about the meetings and are not encouraging employees. One objective might focus on increasing the level of awareness of employees while creating another objective focused on increasing positive attitudes of middle management. Of course, this also means that you should look into your meetings and find out how to improve them.

The objectives should advance overall business goals such as increase sales, increase share values, retain employees, improve social responsibility, or reduce litigation. They should also be written within the parameters of possible public relations outcomes. For example, this might look like a good objective:

- Increase sales of product X by 20% over the next 6 months among younger consumers (ages 18–24).

However, there are many variables that contribute to increased sales of the product that are not under the control of public relations such as price, product quality, and availability. Unless the public relations effort can be isolated to show that it was the variable that moved the needle on sales (such as positive publicity in one market that showed increases to sales while all other elements in the marketing mix remained the same), you may be setting yourself up for failure. And, if sales do increase, you will not be able to take credit for the increase because of the other important variables. You would have to share credit with marketing, quality control, and sales representatives. Public relations can contribute to this larger goal through increased awareness, improved attitudes, and possible consumer trials of the product. Provided that the product is of high quality, reasonably priced, and available to consumers, these activities should contribute to increased sales. So the following might be the reworked objective:

- Increase awareness of product X among young consumers (18–24) by 20% within the next 6 months.

Generally there is a hierarchy to the different levels of objectives. Lindenmann identified three levels of objectives: outputs, outtakes, and outcomes.[5]

As mentioned previously, **output** objectives are focused on the effectiveness of meeting strategies such as the number of placed messages in the media, the size of the audience that received the message, the percentage of positive messages that were contained in the stories, and so forth. It is helpful to measure output objectives because they provide a good indicator of how well the strategy has been implemented. However, they are not considered objectives as defined in this section because they are not ends but means to an end. For example, an output objective might read, "Place 30 stories in prominent newspapers about the product in the next 3 months." This is a means to the end of increasing awareness and could be measured by the output of the message but not the impact of the message. Therefore, output objectives should be relegated to the strategies section.

Outtake objectives are focused on increasing awareness, understanding, and retention of the key message points. It is far more important to know that the audience received the message than whether it was sent out. For example, you may send out a message in an employee newsletter that reaches 10,000 employees. You need to be more concerned on the impact that message had than the number of people it reached.

Outcome objectives are perhaps the most important, but also the most difficult to achieve. For example, let's say the public relations program is for the state highway patrol to increase awareness of the importance of seatbelt usage and the objective is to decrease the number of fatalities caused by not using a seatbelt. There is a diffusion process that occurs with adoption of this behavior. First, drivers need to be aware and understand the safety advantages of seatbelts. Next, they need to have a positive attitude about wearing seatbelts. Finally, this positive attitude will hopefully translate to increased use of seatbelts. However, because people are not always the rational beings we would like them to be, there is a declining measure of success at each level. People who know what is good for them do not always like it. "But seatbelts are uncomfortable." "What if the seatbelt traps me in the car after an accident?" "Seatbelts wrinkle my clothes." Even if someone has a positive attitude toward an issue, they may still not behave congruently with the attitude. It could be out of habit, laziness, or dysfunction. So to increase behaviors by 30%, attitude needs to increase by a higher level (50%) and awareness by an even higher level (80%).

Once the goal of the public relations program and measurable objectives have been established, it is time to turn attention to **strategies**. Strategies provide the means by which objectives are reached. There are certain elements that should be included in this step. First, *identify* what is trying to be accomplished with each public (tie the strategy to an objective). Second, *segment audiences* based on common characteristics. Third, *create* communication strategies that are focused on the self-interests of the publics. And, fourth, identify how publics will be *reached* with messages or actions.

Tie Strategy to Objective

Too often public relations programs have been primarily tactical and have skipped the strategic step of creating objectives. Public relations professionals are doers and often want to get to the action first. However, too many tactics have been executed because of tradition ("We always send out press releases") than because of strategy. What makes public relations *strategic* is having the action tied to the real needs of the organization. If you come up with a really clever tactic but it does not help meet any objectives it should be seriously reconsidered. Far too many resources often are wasted on creative tactics and fall short of addressing the needs of the issue. At the same time, brainstorming on strategies may lead to a legitimate idea that was not considered during the objectives phase, and it may require reevaluating the objectives. But if a strategy cannot be tied to an essential outcome, then it should not be executed.

Segment Audiences

All groups within publics should be differentiated based on common characteristics such as demographics, geographics, or psychographics. Demographics include variables such as gender, income, level of education, and ethnicity. Females may be connected to the issue very differently than males. College graduates may have different attitudes than high school graduates. Geographics describe your public by their location. People living within a thousand feet of a pipeline may have different attitudes toward energy companies than those who live a mile or farther from those lines. Psychographics segment your audience based on their values and lifestyles. People who are single, adventurous, drive fast cars, and spend a lot of their income on entertainment may have very different opinions about seatbelts than people who have small children, drive minivans, and invest most of their money on securities. It is important to segment your key publics because it will help you identify their self-interests.

Create Communication Based on Self-Interests

People pay more attention to communications that are tied to their values, needs, and goals. You should ask yourself what your publics value and care about (based on research). Knowing the demographic, geographic, and/or psychographic differences of key publics, you can create a message that connects them to your program. For example, for young adventurous drivers you may want to show how seatbelts allow them to have more fun by showing how someone on a curvy road stays snug in the seat, whereas someone without a seatbelt is sliding around and has less control. Meanwhile, a soccer mom would be more interested in seat-belt safety messages geared toward children. Once the self-interests have been identified, a primary message can be created that will give direction to the communication efforts. These can become slogans if they are clever and effective enough. The "Click it or Ticket" campaign uses the threat of police monitoring to encourage compliance. For the young adventurous drivers it might be more effective to have a message from sports adventurists such as race car drivers or stunt drivers explain how they rely on seatbelts.

Choose Communication Channels

The last element in the strategy is identifying the channel or medium through which you can reach target publics. The channels can be mass media, such as newspapers or television or radio programming. They can be transmitted by other mediated channels such as e-mail, blogs, or Twitter. They can also be town hall meetings, mediated slide shows, and face-to-face (interpersonal) communication. Sometimes the channel is a group of people, usually opinion leaders, such as teachers, scientists, doctors, or other experts. For example, if we wanted to reach parents in our seatbelt campaign, information kits could be sent to teachers to use in classrooms with students. These materials could be designed to take home and complete with parents. The messages found in these kits could be supported with billboards and radio public service announcements, reaching parents while they are driving. Usually the target audience is reached through multiple points of contact to reinforce the message.

So the following could be one strategy for the seatbelt campaign: "Appeal to young parents' concern for family safety through educational materials that require interaction between parents and their children enrolled in elementary schools." Often, there are several strategies for each public and for each objective.

The most creative element in the strategic planning stage is the **tactic**. Tactics are the specific communication *tools* and *tasks* that are used to execute the strategy. In the case of the seatbelt campaign, the tactics would be the elements found in the educational kit, such as crossword puzzles, coloring books, or interactive games. They would also be the billboards, public service announcements, Internet Web sites, social media applications, and other materials. The challenge is to create tactics that cut through the clutter of all the messages competing for the audience's attention. A great deal of brainstorming takes place during this stage to develop the most creative and clever messages, designs, and activities. However, there is also the temptation to get carried away with the creativity and lose sight of the tactics' purposes. A cardinal rule is to always evaluate your tactics within established strategies and objectives.

STEP 3: COMMUNICATION IMPLEMENTATION

The best public relations programs include both communication *and* action. The old adage "actions speak louder than words" is as true for public relations as it is for other business disciplines. Sometimes an organization needs to act, or react, before it can communicate. For example, if employees are not attending training seminars it might not be enough to try more creative and persuasive messages. The seminars might need to be more relevant and interesting for the employees providing something to communicate that might change behaviors. Organizations should not only expect stakeholders to behave in ways that benefit the organization; sometimes the organization needs to change its actions and behaviors to improve these critical relationships.

Two additional components to the public relations process usually are developed during the communication and action stage: the **planning calendar** and the **budget**. Once the tactics have been determined it is best to plan

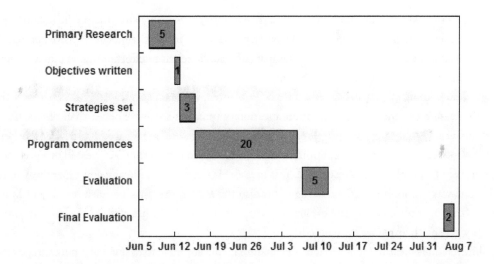

FIGURE 14.2. Sample Gantt chart (numbers within bars are days to accomplish task).

the development and execution of the tactics using a calendaring tool such as a Gantt chart (see Figure 14.2). A Gantt chart is a horizontal flow chart that provides a graphic illustration of when tasks should begin and end in comparison to all other tasks.

The costs for developing, distributing, and executing the tactics should also be determined. You might want to start with the wish list of all tactics and pare them down to those that will provide the greatest return on investment. Some tactics may fall by the wayside when you project their costs against their potential of meeting your objectives.

STEP 4: EVALUATION

According to Paine, four concerns should be addressed when evaluating the effectiveness of a public relations campaign:

- Define your benchmark.
- Select a measurement tool.
- Analyze data, draw actionable conclusions, and make recommendations.
- Make changes and measure again.[6]

If you have followed the steps in the public relations process then you have already identified your audiences and established objectives for each. If your objectives are measurable then you already have the criteria by which to evaluate the success of your program. If you set the objective of increasing awareness by 40% then a **benchmark has been set against which** to measure. *The benchmark compares your current situation to your past.* Paine also recommends comparing the data gathered to other organizations, such as key competitors. **Comparative analysis** makes the data much more relevant. Instead of knowing how much press coverage has been achieved; it can be compared to how much the competition is getting to determine what is called **share of voice**.

Based on this evaluation, the tools that will best help measure against stated criteria are selected. Generally, the same tools that helped establish the benchmark data are used. If primary research was used to establish benchmarks then the same methods are repeated to evaluate success. If you surveyed employees to establish awareness and attitude benchmarks, then a follow-up *survey* is the obvious measurement tool. If you used attendance at employee meetings to establish behavior benchmarks, then *counting attendance* after the public relations program is the appropriate measurement tool. As noted previously, primary research is the most expensive and requires the most expertise, but it is the best measure of the real impact of a public relations effort on stated outcome objectives, such as changes in awareness, attitudes, and behavior.

Probably the most popular evaluation tools used in public relations measure the output objectives. There are several ways to measure the effectiveness of communication output, but some are better than others. One of the earliest methods was **clip counting**. A clip is an article, broadcast story, or online message that mentions the company or product. You can either hire a clipping service or collect your own clips. At the end of a predetermined period, the number of clips obtained is examined. This measure is the most simple and convenient way to measure output and is one way to monitor media coverage. It is also the *least* informative because you do not know what the clips *mean* (they are only counted, not evaluated) except that, perhaps, it has stroked the egos of some senior management by getting their names in the media.

Many public relations measurement services will analyze media coverage to evaluate the **percentage of articles** that contain program key messages, the **prominence of the message** (for a press release, whether it was printed on page 1 versus page 16; in a broadcast, how much time was allocated to the story and where it appears in the program), the **tone of the message** (positive, neutral, negative), and how the media efforts compare with key competitors (**share of voice**). These organizations provide metrics that help establish benchmarks pertaining to program output objectives and strategies. However, to know if these communications actually affected people's awareness, understanding, attitudes, or behaviors, primary research such as surveys needs to be conducted.

Evaluation and measurement should not take place only at the end of your efforts. You should be monitoring the media constantly to determine whether your message is available for people to see (what advertisers call "reach," public relations professionals call "**opportunities-to-see**," or OTS). If the media strategy is not working, course corrections in the middle of the program are required, not after the program has been completed.

Although sophisticated measures of communication output have been developed over the years, it is still more critical to consider the outtake and outcomes of those messages. Getting the communication into various channels, be they traditional or new media, is only the means to the end of affecting attitudes, opinions, and behaviors. The outcomes need to be measured in order to tie back to organizational goals and purposes.

Cost comparisons between public relations and advertising messages are not generally used or encouraged as an evaluation tool because of the difficulty in measuring the actual impact of these messages. However, we do know that although public relations and advertising generate the same amount of product awareness, brand recall, and purchase intention, public relations content produces higher levels of product knowledge and positive product evaluation than advertising.[7]

To measure attitudes and opinions, the most popular tool remains the survey. Public opinion polls and attitude surveys can be conducted and compared to benchmarks to determine whether the messages and behaviors of an organization have had the intended effect. Intentions to behave and preferences for purchasing can also be measured through surveys, providing some figures on people's inclinations.

Behaviors can also be measured against benchmarks. Increases in employee retention, increased donations, and improved sales and investments could all be used to measure behaviors. Often the connection between communication strategy and behavioral changes could be due to other variables, so it is important to isolate and track the impact of the public relations efforts in order to evaluate whether they are the driving force in the change.

CHAPTER SUMMARY

This chapter reviewed the process by which strategic public relations efforts are accomplished. The process is very structured. It suggests that formal research be conducted for formative and evaluative purposes. It requires connecting communication efforts with goals, objectives, and strategies. This process works best with planned efforts such as public relations campaigns. You may wonder how it fits for everyday tasks such as responding to a reporter's inquiry or writing a speech for an employee meeting. Because these steps are required for strategic public relations, they fit everyday duties as well. Regardless of the situation, before acting or responding the public relations professional asks, "What do I know about this situation?" (situational analysis); "What do I want to accomplish with my messages?" (goals and objectives); "How will I accomplish this with my messages?" (strategy); and "What will I say?" (tactic). This process should be ingrained if the public relations professional is to become a strategic communicator.

NOTES

1　Marston (1979).

2　Cutlip, Center, and Broom (2006).

3　Anderson and Hadley (1999).

4　Lindenmann (2003).

5　Lindenmann (2003).

6　Paine (2007).

7　Stacks and Michaelson (2009), pp. 1–22.

REFERENCES

Anderson, F., & Hadley, L. (1999). *Guidelines for setting measurable public relations objectives*. Institute for Public Relations, retrieved February 6, 2010, from http://www.instituteforpr.org/ipr_info/measureable_public_objectives

Cutlip, S., Center, A., & Broom, G. (2006). *Effective Public Relations* (9th ed.). Upper Saddle, NJ: Pearson Prentice Hall.

Lindenmann, W. K. (2003). *Guidelines for measuring the effectiveness of PR programs and activities*. Institute for Public Relations. Retrieved February 6, 2010, from http://www.instituteforpr.org/research_single/measuring_activities

Marston, J. E. (1979). *Modern public relations*. New York: McGraw-Hill.

Paine, K. D. (2007). *Measuring public relationships: The data-driven communicator's guide to success*. Berlin, NH: KDPaine & Partners.

Stacks, D. W., & Michaelson, D. (2009). Exploring the comparative communications effectiveness of advertising and public relations: A replication and extension of prior experiments. *Public Relations Journal, 3*, 1–22.

15 PLANNING

Reading 4.2:
"Establishing
Goals and
Objectives"
By Ronald D.
Smith, APR

The planning process is often referred to by the acronym GOST, which stands for goals, objectives, strategies, and tactics. In this stage, we move from the general goals of the organization to the specific tactics used in the campaign. Before we do that, however, we need to understand the positioning of the organization. How do we want people to think about us? What position do we seek with our publics? These questions should be written into a positioning statement that helps distinguish us from our competition.

As you will see from this week's readings by Ronald D. Smith, APR (2012), goals should then help provide the direction from where the organization is to where the positioning statement says we should be. Organizations usually write 1–3 goal statements that highlight what the organization wants to accomplish in regard to *reputation* (the identity and perception of the organization), *relationship* (the organization's connection to its publics), or *task* (getting certain things accomplished, like social change, favorable attitudes, public support).

Once organizational goals are in place, it's time to set campaign objectives. These are specific, measurable indicators of whether the goals that deal with intended campaign outcomes have been met. These should be SMART objectives, which means that, when writing them, we should make sure they are specific, measurable, attainable, results-oriented, and time-bound. There are three types of objectives, and they are listed here in order of difficulty in accomplishing: 1) *awareness* (exposure to information), 2) *acceptance* (comprehension and attention to information provided), and 3) *action* (hoped-for responses to information provided).

The next step is creating campaign strategies, which fall into two categories: proactive (set up when creating campaign) or reactive (occur when a situation/issue happens independent of campaign). In either instance, public relations professionals can respond with action (activism, alliances and coalitions, audience engagement, organizational performance, special events, sponsorships, strategic philanthropy) or communication (what you will say, to whom and through what media category you will say it). Communication strategies usually center around a theme or big idea, a spokesperson, a message (structure, content, creative elements, nonverbal and visual elements), and media channels.

Media channels are categorized as advertising and promotional media (e.g., print advertising, electronic advertising, out-of-home advertising, promotional items), interpersonal communication (e.g., tours and open houses, door-to-door canvassing, exhibits and demonstrations, speeches, special events), news media (e.g., press releases, video news releases, letters to the editor, news conferences), and organizational media (e.g., newsletters, direct mail, websites, social media). Each of these comes with its own strengths and weaknesses. While advertising and promotional media can reach a vast audience, they are less persuasive. On the opposite end of the spectrum, interpersonal communication can have a large persuasive impact but reach a much smaller audience.

Each strategy will have several tactics that help deliver campaign messages to various publics. These publics can be *internal* (e.g., employees, stockholders, board members) or *external* (e.g., customers, donors, media). Each of these publics is considered to be in a different stage regarding knowledge of the organization. *Apathetic publics* do not perceive the issue facing the organization as important or interesting. *Latent publics* are not yet aware of the issue facing the organization. *Aware publics* recognize the issue facing the organization but are not organized to act yet. Finally, active publics are those that are already preparing or are prepared to act on the issue facing the organization. Chapter 13, "Knowing the Tools of the Trade," discusses many of the tactics available to public relations professionals.

"ESTABLISHING GOALS AND OBJECTIVES"

By Ronald D. Smith, APR

This step is about looking inward and deciding what you want to achieve. To better understand this step, you need to understand the twin concepts of goals and objectives. It should be noted that public relations and marketing strategists generally make the distinction that goals are general and global while objectives are specific. However, some advertisers and other specialists rooted in business disciplines either reverse the meanings of the terms or use them interchangeably. In your actual practice, you may find people applying different definitions to these terms, so make sure you understand what the words mean and how colleagues use them. ... We use the terms as they are outlined below.

Here are short definitions of key concepts used in this step. They will be fleshed out in the subsequent pages.

- A positioning statement is a general expression of how an organization wants its publics to distinguish it vis-à-vis its competition.
- A goal is a global indication of how an issue should be resolved.
- An objective is a statement of specific outcomes expected for a public, indicating a way to more precisely conceptualize the goal.

POSITIONING

As you set out to articulate the desired interaction you can have with your publics, first focus on positioning. Having previously identified the relevant public relations situation in Step 1, ask yourself these simple questions: What do we want people to think about us? What position do we seek with our publics?

A successful approach to strategic communication in a competitive environment is to position the organization according to its own particular niche.

Positioning is the process of managing how an organization distinguishes itself with a unique meaning in the mind of its publics—that is, how it wants to be seen and known by its publics, especially as distinct from its competitors. A **position statement** is the articulation of how an organization wants to be seen and known, especially vis-à-vis its competition.

The concept of distinctiveness is an important one for all organizations: large and small businesses, educational and charitable organizations, political and human service groups, hospitals, churches and sports teams.

In most settings, organizations are known more by their distinctiveness than by their similarities. For example, in the field of higher education, a dozen or more schools might be located in a particular metropolitan area. Each is likely to be identified by its unique characteristics: the large public university, the small church-affiliated college, the high-priced two-year private school, the community college with an open admissions policy, the midsized public institution that used to be a teachers' college, and so on. Problems can occur when the niche is not unique. For example, if your school is one of two small church-affiliated colleges in the area, you will emphasize what distinguishes it from the other, such as lower costs, a suburban campus, graduate degrees, evening/weekend programs or the particular denomination or religious community that sponsors the college.

Organizations have found that the concept of positioning is fluid, and some organizations have made successful attempts to reposition themselves to keep pace with a changing environment. Consider the "This is not your father's Oldsmobile" campaign, which tried to reposition Oldsmobile from a line of cars popular with middle-aged and senior drivers to one fashionable for a younger generation. The campaign had a lot going for it: a catchy slogan, upbeat music, a sporty new design for its new models. And it achieved high levels of awareness. Unfortunately, sales declined, and in terms of average age, the typical Olds owners became … well, older. So much for the value of awareness alone.

How does an organization position itself? First it conducts and analyzes research to determine just how the organization is perceived by various publics. It also considers the position held by its major competitors. The organization then identifies the position it would like to hold, seeking to capitalize on its uniqueness and to distinguish itself from its competition. Having done all this, the organization develops a strategy to modify its current position or perhaps simply to maintain the niche it already holds.

EXAMPLES OF POSITIONING STATEMENTS

Here are some examples of how various organizations might try to position themselves. Note how each statement highlights a desired attribute of the organization by implying a distinction from competitors:

- the leader that sets industry standards;
- the best value, reflecting low cost and high quality;
- the most economical;
- the most expensive and most prestigious;
- the hospital preferred by women;
- the family-friendly restaurant;
- the "green" brand.

Make sure that your desired position is realistic. Who wouldn't want to be known as "the industry leader" or "the first name in (whatever)"? But there can be only one leader, one first name. A good strategic planner will be wary of pretense and of stretching beyond possibility. At best, it would be an exercise in futility. At worst, chasing an impossible dream wastes valuable organizational resources, invites ridicule and exposes the organization to risk.

Don't confuse the public relations concept of positioning with its use in marketing, where the term refers to the competitive approach for a persuasive message (that is, positioning according to features such as customer focus, competitive advantage, social responsibility, lifestyle or product attribute).

When we talk about positioning in public relations, we refer less to the presentation of the products or services and the messages about these, and more to perception—how we want our organization to be seen by our publics. As Al Ries and Jack Trout explain in *Positioning: The Battle for Your Mind*, "Positioning is not what you do to a product. Positioning is what you do to the mind of the prospect" (2001, p. 2).

POSITIONING ETHICS

Carefully think through the ethical implications in creating a positioning statement for your organization.

Don't state your desired position merely to brag, particularly if the bragging is based on an inflated view of reality. Wanting to be the first, biggest, cleanest or fastest is not the same as actually being the first, fastest or whatever. Your publics will easily see through boasting and swaggering.

More important, don't use the positioning statement as a putdown for another organization. For example, a candidate for political office might seek to position herself as "a soccer mom who cares about her community." There could be a lot of potential to such an appeal. But it raises an ethical question if she were to aim at being seen as "a better parent than the other candidate." While that might be true, it's far better for individual voters to conclude this rather than for the candidate's political organization to explicitly state such a positioning theme.

GOAL

With the positioning statement hinting of what we want people to think about us, we turn our attention to a more direct assertion of what we want to accomplish. This is called the **goal**. It is a short, simple statement rooted in the organization's mission or vision. Using everyday language, a goal acknowledges the issue and sketches out how the organization hopes to see it settled. A goal is stated in general terms and lacks measures; these will come later, as objectives.

In their classic book *Public Relations Management by Objectives*, Norman Nager and T. Harrell Allen (1984) use the analogy of transportation: Goals provide the direction while objectives pinpoint the destination.

Various explanations have been given for how to understand public relations objectives. This textbook presents a concept of three types of goals, an explanation that has been adopted by many public relations strategists, as well as by textbooks such as Patricia Swann's *Cases in Public Relations Management*. The concept presented here is that communication goals are of three types. These can be categorized as relating to a trinity of public relations situations that are part of the management function within every organization.

- **Reputation management goals** deal with the identity and perception of the organization.
- **Relationship management goals** focus on how the organization connects with its publics.
- **Task management goals** are concerned with getting certain things done.

The three types of goals together offer a way of laying out the various aims associated with public relations and integrated communication campaigns. It is unnecessary, even unlikely, that every campaign will have each type of goal. Planners mix and match these as they consider appropriate to their specific campaign.

Who sets an organization's communication goals? Generally, public relations managers do, usually as an implementation of the organization's strategic plans, which ideally the public relations people have had a hand in developing.

There are two sources for these overall organizational plans that give rise to goals. They may be global documents such as a strategic business plan. Or they may be embedded in implementation guidelines such as an annual strategic plan or a statement of priorities or directions.

Either way, public relations goals should map out a vision of success for achievements and consequences that are important to the organization as a whole. In doing so, strategic communication planners should note how the organization defines what it means to be successful and then develop goals that grow out of this understanding.

EXAMPLES OF PUBLIC RELATIONS GOALS

Here are several examples for each of the three different types of public relations goals.

Reputation Management Goals
- Improve the company's reputation within the industry.
- Enhance the hospital's prestige as the leading center for sports medicine.
- Reinforce the organization's image with potential donors or investors.
- Strengthen the agency's standing within the environmental movement.

Relationship Management Goals
- Promote better appreciation of the firm among potential clients.
- Enhance the relationship between the company and its customers.
- Maintain a favorable relationship amid social or organizational changes.

Task Management Goals
- Increase public support for organizational goals.
- Advance social change on a particular issue.
- Impact public behavior on matters associated with the organization's mission.
- Create a favorable climate for our client among regulatory agencies.
- Attract a sell-out crowd to a fundraising concert.

CASE IN POINT BYU in Israel

Sometimes public relations goals are stated in negative terms: to reduce opposition or minimize hostility, perhaps even to prevent a situation from developing into a public issue. Such was the goal when Brigham Young University attempted to build a student center in Jerusalem. Initial opposition emerged from conservative Jewish organizations, fearful that the American-based Mormon university would use the proposed student center to try to convert Jews to its brand of Christianity.

Gitam, an Israeli public relations and advertising agency, signed on for a campaign aimed at reducing opposition. The agency focused on key publics such as conservative Jewish organizations, liberal secular groups and lawmakers who ultimately would decide the case. Research identified causes of public opposition and the potential basis for public support; it also identified opinion leaders on both sides of the issue.

Campaign messages focused on Israel's self-identity as a Jewish state that valued freedom for all religious organizations, on efforts to show Mormons as ordinary people doing ordinary things in Israel, and on portraying Mormons as threatened underdogs by publicizing curses and threats received by BYU's office in Jerusalem from hostile opponents. The campaign also sought to allay fears that Mormons would try to convert Jews. To this end, it featured a testimonial by the chief rabbi of Salt Lake City, home of the Mormon religion, pointing out that more Mormons converted to Judaism than Jews to Mormonism.

The result was permission for the student center, along with assurances that BYU would not enroll Jews and would require students and faculty to sign a non-proselytizing pledge.

CASE IN POINT Toyota's Reputation

Toyota has shown the importance of reputation goals, which are particularly significant in crisis situations.

With auto recalls in 2009 and 2010, Toyota endured what was initially called the worst-handled auto recall in history, with predictions that the reputation of the Toyota brand would be damaged for years.

Faulty accelerators were linked to 19 deaths, and reports in both established and emerging social media whipped consumer anxiety to near-panic levels. The company that had built its reputation on quality and safety recalled 9 million vehicles worldwide to fix floor mats and faulty gas pedals that caused unintended acceleration.

Toyota's own confidence in its reputation may have caused the company to fumble its public relations in the early stage of the recall crisis. Perceiving a bigger transgression than faulty technology, some critics accused the company of corporate arrogance: withholding internal test reports; hiding the problem from unsuspecting customers; paying off lawsuits behind closed doors without remedying the problems.

The allegations sparked congressional hearings in Washington, though some accused the government of over-reaching, perhaps a political response to the simultaneous bailout of Toyota's U.S. competitors, General Motors and Chrysler. But there is no question that the incidents that surrounded the recalls increased customer fears and caused the company's stock prices to fall by 15 percent. Kelley Blue Book lowered the resale value of the recalled Toyotas by 3.5 percent (about $300 for a Corolla).

Toyota supporters countered that the company acted as quickly as it could on the information. It took full-page ads in major U.S. Sunday newspapers alerting consumers of the recall, and it temporarily halted sales and shut down production until the problem could be corrected. American and Japanese officials gave television interviews and the company presented messages of reassurance.

Within a year, Toyota stock prices were even higher than before the recall and the Toyota reputation was once again an asset to the international corporation.

Toyota customers by-and-large stayed with the company, maintaining trust that the technical problems were correctable and negligible. Toyota continued as the No. 1 automaker in the world, with its Camry the best-selling car in America. Toyota held that position until it slipped to third place behind General Motors and Volkswagen, not because of the recall but after supply problems following the earthquake and tsunami in Japan.

Edmunds.com reported that, even after the recall, Toyota ranked 17 among the top 20 carmakers for customer complaints, with fewer complaints than American and most other imported automakers—another testimony to the importance of keeping reputation as a top goal of any organization.

A Rasmussen poll reported that 81 percent of Americans viewed Toyota favorably or very favorably. Another poll indicated that a quarter of Americans thought the government had criticized Toyota mainly to help General Motors after the bailout.

To an unknown extent, the manner of media coverage appeared to have made the crisis appear worse than it was. For example, most media reports failed to note other contributing factors in the accelerator-related accidents: reckless driving, texting or cell-phone use while driving, DUI. One driver was indicted for vehicular manslaughter and DUI for marijuana.

Analyses published in *Car and Driver* magazine said the risk of an unintended acceleration was 1 in 10,000 for the Toyota vehicles, compared with a more-frequent 1 in 8,000 for American-made cars.

Was there a silver lining to the recall? Perhaps. In the aftermath of the crisis, Toyota set a renewed priority on customer responsiveness.

OBJECTIVE

A public relations **objective** is a statement consistent with an organization's positioning and emerging from the organization's goals.

An objective is a clear and measurable statement, written to point the way toward particular levels of awareness, acceptance or action. Objectives often are established by communication managers responding to broader organizational goals. Like goals, objectives deal with intended outcomes rather than procedures for reaching them.

A single goal may be the basis for several objectives. In fact, every goal should generate at least three objectives, focusing specifically on awareness, acceptance and action.

Management by objectives is the process by which effective and efficient organizations plan their activities. While the acronym **MBO** has somewhat gone out of favor, the approach remains useful. From this perspective, organizations don't merely do something because they can; rather, they act because managers have determined that doing this particular something will further the work of the organization in some strategic and measurable way.

For instance, a reactive and nonstrategic public relations or marketing communication department may decide that because the company has just purchased new publishing software, a scanner and a color printer, the department should prepare new promotional brochures and fliers. But a proactive and strategic department would first determine what needs to be done, say, to promote more understanding among potential customers. Then it might conclude that it should produce new brochures and buy the equipment with which to do so, or not. This is managing by objectives, not by whim.

As you can see by this example, objectives help direct the organization to act in ways that make sense.

Objectives also serve another purpose: They give the planner a reference point for evaluation. When you measure the effectiveness of your strategic communication program in Step 9, you will look back to your objectives and determine whether your messages and actions have had the effect you wanted. You will then scrutinize each objective to determine if you have been successful.

ELEMENTS OF OBJECTIVES

An objective is a three-fold subset of a goal, an articulation of the various elements that are necessary to achieve the goal. Eleven specific elements can be identified for public relations objectives. These will become the elements of effective and practical objectives.

Goal Rooted

Objectives grow from the organization's goal statements, which themselves emerge from the mission or vision that the organization has defined for itself. Thus, objectives are responsive to a particular issue that the organization has recognized as important to its effectiveness. Public relations objectives often reflect organizational strategic plans and they may parallel financial projections, marketing ambitions, advertising or promotional expectations and objectives associated with other aspects of the organization.

Public Focused

Objectives are linked firmly to a particular public. They are based on the wants, interests and needs of that public. Objectives for one public may be similar to those for another public, but each must be distinct.

Impact Oriented

Objectives are oriented toward the impact they can achieve. They define the effect you hope to make on your public, focusing not on the tools but on intended accomplishments. In writing objectives, avoid statements about writing and disseminating news releases, producing brochures, holding open houses and other activities that belong with an eventual tactical response to the objectives. Such nonobjective language is dangerous. It confuses activity with achievement, and it can lull you into a false belief that because you are doing something you are also accomplishing something.

Research Based

Objectives are linked to the research that you gathered in Phase One of the planning process. Good objectives aren't just pulled out of the air; they are tied to research. For example, if research shows that 40 percent of your key public is familiar with your organization's products or services, your objective might be to increase that to 55 percent—not because 55 percent is a magic number, but because it represents a reasonable ambition based on the current situation, as revealed through research.

Explicit

Objectives are specific and precise. There is no room for varying interpretations; everyone involved in the public relations activity must share a common understanding of where the objective is leading. Don't use ambiguous verbs such as "educate", "inform", "promote" or "encourage". Instead, use strong action verbs to state your objective specifically. For example, instead of saying you want "to enhance knowledge of recycling," say your objective is "to increase residents' understanding of the benefits of recycling."

Measurable

Objectives are defined and quantifiable, with clear measures that state the degree of change being sought. These *key performance indicators* (KPIs) are known more commonly as *metrics*. Simply stated, metrics are performance indicators that can be quantified and compared to other data. Avoid adjectives such as "appropriate" or "reasonable." Instead, for example, state that you want "to effect a 20 percent increase in recycling of paper products." Metrics for public relations objectives can be milestones achieved, or they can be data showing how the performance compares with a benchmarked standard or with baseline performance.

Time Definite

Objectives are time definite. Objectives include a clear indication of a time frame—"by December 31," "within six months," "during the spring semester," and so on. Avoid ambiguous phrases such as "in the near future" or "as soon as possible." Some objectives may indicate a graduated or multistage approach to the time frame. For example, you might indicate that a certain effect is expected in two stages: a 50 percent increase within six months, a 75 percent increase after the first year.

Singular

Objectives focus on one desired response from one public. Don't state in an objective that you want "to increase awareness and generate positive attitudes." You may be successful in the first effort but unsuccessful in the latter, making it difficult to evaluate your effectiveness. Most strategic communication programs will have multiple objectives, but each objective should be stated separately.

Challenging

Objectives are challenging. They should stretch the organization a bit and inspire people to action. Don't aim at too safe a level of achievement or you might find that you haven't really achieved anything worthwhile. Instead, set your sights high.

Attainable

Though challenging, objectives need to be attainable and doable according to the organization's needs and resources, so don't set your sights too high. Seldom is it realistic to aim for 100 percent of anything, whether you are trying to expand your customer base or reduce opposition. Don't create a recipe for failure by setting objectives that are unattainable.

Acceptable

Objectives enjoy the understanding and support of the entire organizational team: public relations or communication staff, managers, right up to the CEO. The value of objectives is not that they are written but that they are used. They need the strength of consensus if they are to be useful to both your organization's planners and its decision makers.

EXAMPLES OF PUBLIC RELATIONS OBJECTIVES

Here are two examples of well-written objectives in each category.

Awareness Objectives
- To have an effect on the *awareness* of senior citizens in Lake County; specifically *to increase their understanding* of the advantages that Upstate Health Program offers senior patients (60 percent of senior residents within six months).
- To have an effect on the *awareness* of legislators from the Southern Tier; specifically to *increase their understanding* of the environmental impact that House Bill 311 will have on their constituents (all 15 Republican and seven Democratic members of the House Committee on Environmental Affairs within two months).

Acceptance Objectives
- To have an effect on the *acceptance* of senior citizens in Lake County; specifically to *increase their positive attitudes* toward membership in Upstate Health Program (30 percent within six months).
- To have an effect on the *acceptance* of legislators from the Southern Tier; specifically *to gain their interest* in the environmental issues addressed by House Bill 311 (10 of the 15 Republican members and six of the seven Democratic members of the House committee within two months).

Action Objectives
- To have an effect on the *action* of senior citizens in Lake County; specifically *to obtain an increase in their membership* in the Upstate Health Program (10 percent within six months, and an additional 10 percent within a year).
- To have an effect on the *action* of legislators from the Southern Tier; specifically for them *to vote in favor* of House Bill 311 (six of the 15 Republican members of the House and six of the seven Democratic members of the House committee when the bill comes to a vote next spring).

HIERARCHY OF OBJECTIVES

An ordered hierarchy exists among communication objectives, growing out of a logical progression through three stages of persuasion: awareness, acceptance and action.

- Awareness begins the process, increasing gradually. This aspect of persuasion is based on what we want people to know about our organization.
- Interest then builds in stages and attitudes bloom into an acceptable choice. This acceptance stage of the persuasion process deals with what we want our publics to think or feel about what they know.
- Verbal and physical actions are modified in steps. This culmination of the persuasion process focuses on how we want our publics to act, based on what they think or feel about what they know.

Note how this model parallels the AIDA pattern (attention, interest, desire and action), the hierarchy of effects associated with advertising since the 1920s (Lipstein, 1985). It also echoes the standard communication effects of cognitive, affective and conative changes (Ray, 1973). Similarly, Philip Kotler, Ned Roberto and Nancy Lee (2007) focused on objectives for social-marketing campaigns, identifying these as knowledge objectives (information or facts), belief objectives (values or attitudes) and behavior objectives (specific actions).

Whatever formula you use, remember: In your enthusiasm to resolve the issue, don't let your expectations get ahead of themselves. Develop a plan that will take your communication with each of your publics through each of the necessary steps. Make sure your message first will reach your target publics, who will then agree with this message and finally will act on it. Here's a closer look at the three levels of objectives:

Awareness objectives deal with information and knowledge.

- attention
- comprehension
- retention.

Acceptance objectives focus on how people react to information.

- interest
- attitude.

Action objectives address a hoped-for response to information and feelings.

- opinion
- behavior.

Awareness Objective

The first level of objectives, **awareness objectives**, focuses on information, providing the **cognitive** (or thinking) **component** of the message. These objectives specify what information you want your publics first to be exposed to and then to know, understand and remember. Awareness objectives particularly deal with dissemination and message exposure, comprehension and retention.

When would you use awareness objectives? They are appropriate for transmitting purely functional information, for communicating on noncontroversial issues and for the early stages of any communication campaign. Awareness objectives also are particularly useful for publicity and public information models of public relations. In general, awareness objectives impact on what people know about an organization and its products, services and ideas.

Acceptance Objective

The next level, **acceptance objectives**, deals with the **affective**, or feeling, **component** of the message—how people respond emotionally to information they have received. These objectives indicate the level of interest or the kind of attitude an organization hopes to generate among its publics. Acceptance objectives are useful in several situations: forming interests and attitudes where none existed before, reinforcing existing interests and attitudes, and changing existing positive or negative attitudes.

Acceptance objectives are particularly important amid controversy and in persuasive situations using the advocacy (or asymmetrical) model of public relations. They impact on *how* people feel about the organization and its products, services and ideas. Notice how the examples of acceptance objectives above differ from the earlier examples of awareness objectives.

Acceptance is the key to effective public relations, and its importance has been obvious since 1947 when one of the accepted "fathers" of public relations, Edward Bernays, wrote about "the engineering of consent." This implies more than merely disseminating information. It involves connecting with people's inner desires. We must take time to foster the public's acceptance of both our organization and its messages, through means that are both practical and ethical. For example, in a political campaign, news releases and debates may be useful tools for achieving awareness. But awareness doesn't guarantee acceptance, and through the release or the debate voters may actually learn that they disagree with the candidate on important issues. Thus, successful awareness efforts could actually hinder acceptance of your client—just one of life's little ironies.

Sometimes this affective element is the most direct way to realize a goal. Take, for example, Fitness First for Women. This women-owned, women-focused network of 13 gyms in the United Kingdom had a goal of increasing membership. Its objectives and subsequent strategy were focused on the emotional issue of how women feel about themselves and their bodies.

The campaign identified a theme of "sexy weight." This was described as an alternative to the often unrealistic and frequently unhealthy weight-loss target that some women set for themselves, usually based on what they thought would please their romantic partners (present or potential). Instead, the campaign set about to help women reimagine themselves, with an attitude that curves could be desirable. The specific task was to help women set an achievable weight goal at which they would feel more energized, their clothes would fit better and they would begin to feel good about themselves. Hence, their "sexy weight" (a term that became a registered trademark of the company).

The concept was researched through a nationwide survey. Psychologists were engaged both as advisers and as spokespersons. Eventually the campaign achieved measurable results, not only in attitude change associated with the presentation strategy, but also in actual numbers of new members for the fitness centers.

Action Objective

The final level of objectives, **action objectives**, takes aim at expression and conduct, providing the **conative**, or behavioral, **component** of the message. These objectives offer two types of action: opinion (verbal action) and behavior (physical action). Action objectives may attempt to create new behaviors or change existing ones, positively or negatively. They should be focused on the organization's bottom line, such as customer buying, student enrollment, donor giving, fan attendance, and so on.

Action objectives can serve not only as persuasive objectives that encourage audiences to act according to the wishes of the organization but also as objectives for building consensus and enhancing the relationship between the organization and its publics.

DEVELOPING OBJECTIVES

Just as most issues will have more than one goal, so too will each goal have a full set of objectives—at least one in each of the above categories for each of the identified publics. Too often, efforts in public relations and marketing communication fail because they pursue the awareness objectives and then jump quickly to action, forgetting the important bridge step of generating acceptance.

Note how the action objectives shown in the example box differ from the earlier examples of awareness and acceptance objectives. As this hierarchy moves along the awareness–acceptance–action path from least important to most important objectives, the impact on the public will inevitably decrease. You might achieve an 80 percent awareness level among the public, for example, but perhaps only 40 percent will accept the message favorably, and only 15 percent or 20 percent may act on it.

Students often ask, "Where do you get the numbers from?" Good question. Here's an example that might shed some light, based on a real campaign being developed by a student group for a local Alzheimer's association. The goal was task-oriented: increasing volunteers for the local chapter. At first, the students were all over the place, setting unrealistic objectives. They were trying to create awareness in 40 percent of college students, acceptance in 20 percent and action in those same 20 percent. This meant that everyone who might want to volunteer actually would have done so. Unlikely. It also means that if the objectives were to be met, there would be 10,000 new volunteers, an impossible number for the chapter to deal with.

Here's how we talked things out in class. First we worked backwards, focusing on just how many volunteers the organization realistically could use. The number: about 200. Then we considered how many college and university students there were in the region: about 50,000. Then we discussed some realistic expectations. How many of those 50,000 could the campaign reach? The 40 percent (20,000) seemed realistic, given the fact that students are reachable through a relatively narrow channel of communication vehicles such as campus media, social networking, and perhaps direct mail with fraternities and sororities.

Then came the questions about acceptance and action. How many of those 20,000 students who hear about the organization would think it was a good idea? The planners estimated perhaps one in 10, or 2,000 students; that is, 4 percent of the original population. And how many of that 2,000 would be likely to volunteer? Perhaps another one in 10, or 200 student volunteers; 0.2 percent of the original total. Sounds like a small percentage, but that's just what the Alzheimer's association needed.

Adding some complexity to the process, the planners were aware that most of the current volunteers for the chapter were women and the organization needed some male volunteers. So a mix of 70 to 30 for women and men volunteers was factored in. Here are the resulting objectives:

- To create awareness of Alzheimer volunteer opportunities among college students, specifically 40 percent, or 20,000 of the 50,000 students in area colleges and universities within six months.
- To create acceptance among college students, specifically generating interest among 4 percent of the student population, or 2,000 students within six months (of these, 70 percent or 1,400 women; 30 percent or 600 men).
- To generate action among college specifically, specifically to achieve a 0.4 percent action rate with 200 new volunteers (70 percent or 140 women; 30 percent or 60 men).

WRITING OBJECTIVES

In writing public relations objectives, keep your language simple and brief. Avoid jargon. Use everyday language and strong action verbs. As part of the planning for a strategic communication campaign, objectives are not meant to be presented publicly, so don't worry if they begin to sound repetitious and formulaic. The guidelines that follow can help you deal with each important element of a well-stated objective.

WRITING PUBLIC RELATIONS OBJECTIVES

Public	Objective for	_____			
Category	To have an effect on	☐ Awareness			
		☐ Acceptance			
		☐ Action			
Direction	Specifically, to	☐ Create, Generate			
		☐ Increase, Maximize			
		☐ Maintain, Reinforce			
		☐ Decrease, Minimize			
Effect	(w/awareness category)	☐ Attention	or	☐ Comprehension	
	(w/acceptance category)	☐ Interest	or	☐ Attitude	
	(w/action category)	☐ Opinion	or	☐ Behavior	
Focus	About	_____			
Performance Measure		_____			
Time Period		_____			

Public

Indicate the public to whom the objective is addressed.

Category

Indicate simply the category of the objective: awareness, acceptance or action.

Direction

Indicate the direction of movement you are seeking. Here are your choices: to *create* or *generate* something new that did not exist before; to *increase* or *maximize* a condition; to *maintain* effects or *reinforce* current conditions; or to *decrease* or *minimize* something. Notice that *elimination* is not an option because a public relations undertaking is seldom able to completely remove an unwanted effect; the best we can hope to do is minimize it. Another observation: public relations and other strategic communication programs too often don't pay enough attention to maintaining current support. While generating new support is important, don't overlook those who currently help you and agree with you.

Specific Effect

Indicate the specific effect that you will address. If you are writing an awareness objective, the specific effect should deal with receiving the message, remembering it and understanding it. If you are focusing on the acceptance level, deal with generating interest, reducing apathy or fostering attitudes (usually positive attitudes, such as support for wearing a helmet while bicycling; sometimes negative attitudes, such as a sentiment against drinking alcohol during pregnancy). For action objectives, focus on evoking a particular opinion or drawing out a desired action.

Focus

Indicate the focus of the specific effect you hope to achieve. Provide some detail about what you are seeking. However, don't move away from objectives by providing information about either strategy or tactics. That will come later in the planning process. Stick to articulating what impact you hope to make on your public. If you get into how to make the impact or what tools you will use to communicate, you've gone too far for this step.

Performance Measure

Indicate the desired level of achievement in measurement terms. Raw numbers or percentages usually do this well. The number itself should reflect baseline research and/or desired outcomes. For example, a university library might calculate that 35 percent of students use the library facility in any two-week period. However, guidelines from the Association of College and Research Libraries might suggest that 50 percent is the desired usage pattern, including both in-person use and Internet connections. Therefore the campus library's public relations campaign might aim for a performance increase to 50 percent of the students. Stated other ways, the objective might specify a 30 percent increase over the present usage or an increase from the present 2,800 students to 4,000 out of a total student population of 8,000. Each variant aims for the same level of usage.

Time Period

Indicate the desired time frame, either within a single period or in multiple stages. Here again, you can be specific (a May 15 deadline) or relative (within six weeks, by the end of the fall semester).

POORLY WORDED OBJECTIVES

Here are three examples of poorly worded objectives. Note how each can be improved.

Poorly Worded Objective 1
- To interest more people in recycling as soon as possible.

Critique: No public is indicated, merely a vague reference to "people." "Interest" is a nonspecific term. Recycling is a very broad concept. The focus is on communication activity rather than impact in the public. Measurement is nonexistent. The time frame is imprecise.

Restatement: To have an effect on the *action* of Allen County residents; specifically *to generate telephone inquiries* to the CLEAN-UP help line (100 telephone calls during the first two months of the campaign; 400 telephone calls within six months).

Poorly Worded Objective 2
- To prepare a new brochure about recycling.

Critique: No public is indicated. The focus is on communication activity rather than impacting the public. Measurement and time frame are not included.

Restatement: To have an effect on the *awareness* of residents of the Oxford Apartments; specifically *to increase the understanding* of students about the benefits of recycling (45 percent during the fall semester).

Poorly Worded Objective 3
- To become more student focused.

Critique: This is a strategic choice more appropriate for the next step, but it doesn't indicate a desired outcome.

Restatement: To have an effect on the *acceptance* of students at St. Martin's College; specifically *to increase positive attitudes* toward the student-centeredness of the Career Counseling Center (50 percent increase within two years).

WHAT'S NEXT?

This concludes Step 4 in the strategic planning step. With this step behind you, you should have a clear indication of what you hope to achieve through your plan. This includes the positioning you hope to nurture, as well as the goals and associated measurable objectives that the plan aims to achieve.

PLANNING EXAMPLE 4 Establishing Goals and Objectives

Here is the first part of strategic planning for Upstate College.

Position
Upstate College wants to be known for its quality education and for its accessibility in terms of both cost and admission standards.

Goals
1 Re-create the college's image into that of a four-year institution (reputational goal).
2 Recruit more students (task goal).
3 Generate new donor support (task goal).

Objectives
Re: Goal 2 for High School Students in a Three-County Area [selected examples]

2.1 To have an effect on *awareness* of high school students; specifically *to increase their knowledge* that Upstate College is expanding into a four-year college (75 percent of students during their junior year)

2.2 To have an effect on *acceptance*; specifically *to generate interest* in attending a growing institution (25 percent of high school students during their junior and senior years)

2.3 To have an effect on *action*; specifically *to obtain inquiries* from an average of 15 percent of high school students in the college's primary three-county area during their junior or senior years

2.4 To have an effect on *action*; specifically *to obtain applications* from an average of 5 percent of all high school graduates in the college's primary three-county area during their senior year.

[Note: You also will have objectives for each of your other key publics for every goal.]

Here is the first part of strategic planning for Tiny Tykes Toys.

Position
Tiny Tykes wants to be known as the company that cares about babies more than about its own profitability.

Goals
1 Regain customer confidence (reputational goal).
2 Recapture the company's previous sales rates (task goal).

Objectives
Re: Goals 1 and 2 for Parents [Selected examples]

- To have an effect on *awareness*; specifically *to create knowledge* among 75 percent of parent-customers about the redesign of the baby toy within six weeks.
- To have an effect on *awareness*; specifically *to create understanding* by 65 percent of the parents about the sacrifices and commitment that the company has made by recalling and redesigning the toys.
- To have an effect on *acceptance*; specifically *to regain trust* among 40 percent of these parents that the company has acted responsibly in redesigning the toy.
- To have an effect on *acceptance*; specifically *to create interest* among 30 percent of the parents in buying toys from the company within the next two years.
- To have an effect on *action*; specifically *to foster sales* to 25 percent of the parents from the company within the next two years.

[Note 1: You will have objectives for each of your other key publics for every goal.]
[Note 2: Each of these examples uses a different format for presenting the outline of goals and objectives. Use whatever style works best for your presentation.]
[Note 3: Numbering goals and objectives makes it easier to reference them within the planning team and when meeting with clients.]

CHECKLIST 4 GOALS AND OBJECTIVES

BASIC QUESTIONS

1 What position do you seek?
2 What are the goals?
3 What are the specific objectives (awareness, acceptance and action for each public)?

EXPANDED QUESTIONS

A. POSITION
1 What is a key public for this product/service/concept?
2 What position do you seek for your product/service/concept for this public?
3 Is this desired position appropriate? If no, reconsider the position.
4 What is your current position?
5 What change do you need to make to achieve the desired position?
6 What is the competition?
7 What is its position?

[Note: Replicate the above position questions for each public.]

B. GOALS

1 What are the organization's reputation goals on this issue?

2 What are the organization's relationship goals on this issue?

3 What are the organization's task goals on this issue?

4 Do any of these goals contradict another goal? If yes, which goal(s) will you eliminate?

5 What is the relative priority among the viable goals?

6 Does the organization have resources (time, personnel, money, etc.) to achieve these goals? If no, can resources be obtained? From where?

7 Does the organization have willingness to work toward these goals? If no, how can willingness be generated?

8 Are there any ethical problems with these goals? If yes, how can you modify the goals to eliminate the problems?

C. OBJECTIVES

1 Write at least one awareness objective for each key public, such as "To have an effect on awareness; specifically …"

2 Write at least one acceptance objective for each key public, such as "To have an effect on acceptance; specifically …"

3 Write at least one action objective for each key public, such as "To have an effect on action; specifically …"

4 Answer the following questions for each individual objective:

- Is this objective linked to the organization's mission or vision statement?
- Is this objective responsive to the issue/problem/opportunity/goal?
- Is this objective focused on a particular public?
- Is this objective clearly measurable?
- Does this objective indicate a time frame?
- Is this objective challenging to the organization?
- Is this objective realistically attainable?

CONSENSUS CHECK

Does agreement exist within your organization and your planning team about the recommended positioning, goals and objectives?

☐ Yes. Proceed to Step 5, Formulating Action and Response Strategies.

☐ No. Consider the value and/or possibility of achieving consensus before proceeding.

16

IMPLEMENTATION

Reading 4.3:
"Implementing the
Strategic Plan"
By Ronald D.
Smith, APR

The previous chapter discussed planning the overall campaign messages, the channels to put those messages in, and the tactics used to get messages to various publics. In this chapter, we will examine how the campaign comes to fruition. This step is called implementation and involves scheduling, budgeting, and creating a plan book for everyone in the organization to work from.

As noted in this week's reading by Ronald D. Smith, APR (2012), the first step in implementation is deciding how to package the tactics you are using in your campaign. Perhaps the easiest way is to package according to the objective you are trying to achieve. This allows you to directly see the desired end result, the action and communication strategies envisioned, and the tactics that follow. It is also possible to package based on media category (advertising and promotion, interpersonal, news, organizational), public, goal, or department.

You may be tempted to begin creating tactics immediately after this stage; however, we suggest finalizing your campaign budget before doing so. You don't want to waste time on tactics you might not have the money to implement. You also don't want to build them into your schedule (the next step) for the same reason.

Smith introduces several different approaches to determining an overall campaign budget. The one used most often is the objective-based budgeting method. Regardless of the method you choose, your budget should contain amounts needed for administration, donated items, equipment and facilities, materials, media, personnel, program, and production, and it should have a 5–10% contingency fund for unforeseen items. The budget should be used to monitor spending by each category as well as to ensure you have the funds to carry out each tactic.

Once you determine all the tactics and establish you have enough in the budget to complete them, it's time to schedule them. The schedule should include the planning, approvals, creation, drafting, finalizing, production, and delivery/distribution dates of all tactics in your campaign. For tactics that occur over a period of time or frequently, you should specify how many times (*frequency*), when, and where (*reach*). The schedule should also include what type of evaluation will be used and when it should occur. Different types of schedules you can use are discussed in depth by Smith. The most common is the timeline of tasks. The key to the schedule is to be very detailed so successful segments of your campaign can be replicated.

Finally, the campaign plan book puts together everything you've done in the RPIE process.

"IMPLEMENTING THE STRATEGIC PLAN"

By Ronald D. Smith, APR

Now that you have put together a full plate of ways to present your message, turn your attention to implementing these tactics. In this step, you will consider two aspects of implementation: turning your inventory of tactics into a logical and cohesive program, and then dealing with the specifics of scheduling and budgeting.

PACKAGING COMMUNICATION TACTICS

The various communication tactics have been likened to items on a menu, so let's take the analogy a step further. Menu items can be grouped into categories: appetizers, salads, main courses, desserts, beverages, and the like. When you order a meal, you'll probably cover the whole range of menu categories.

Additionally, when you review the restaurant menu, you often make your selections based on a particular culinary focus—Japanese, Tex-Mex, Southern, Italian, and so on. You don't order every item, and you don't order haphazardly.

It's unlikely you would start with tuna sashimi as an appetizer, add a dollop of cole slaw on a bed of lettuce, feature jalapeño chili relleno as main course, add sides of grits and ravioli, and end with a flaming cherries jubilee for dessert—served with ouzo and Pepsi Max. Rather, you'd probably develop a culinary theme. You would creatively package your choices to concoct a special dining experience appropriate to the occasion and suitable to your resources, needs, and interests.

The same is true with strategic planning for communication. In Step 7, you considered items in each of the menu categories. You discarded some possibilities and sketched out ways to do others.

Now you need to package them into an effective set of tactics to help you achieve your objectives. This should be much more than a "to do" list. Consider how various tactics can be woven together. Group some around the themes associated with your strategic planning from Steps 5 and 6.

Remember: You don't need to be tied into a chronological implementation scheme just because you selected interpersonal items before those in the other categories. Let the natural relationship among tactics determine how they fit into your plan.

Consider what you learned in Phase Two, Strategy. For example, the diffusion of innovations theory tells us that information presented through the news media can pave the way for personal interaction between opinion leaders and the ultimate public. … There is precedence for implementing a publicity program before an advertising schedule, thus allowing for a smaller advertising budget with higher-than-usual results.

THINKING CREATIVELY

What's the best way to present your plan? You decide. Look for the simplest and most logical way to present the tactics that grow out of your planning. Later on we'll look at some suggestions to help you get started. First let's consider the importance of creative thinking. As you decide how to package your tactics, try to leap ahead of the crowd with an innovative approach to the problem or opportunity you are dealing with.

For example, if you have a new organizational logo to unveil, consider making it a real unveiling. How about a ceremonial removal of a sequined cloth covering the logo? Or maybe you could have the logo painted large on the outside of the company's building, temporarily draped. One nonprofit organization introduced a new logo by involving five local political and media celebrities who each gave a short testimonial about the organization and then, one by one, placed together cut-out pieces of a giant jigsaw puzzle to create the new logo.

Consider another scenario. Your organization has an announcement to make—usually a routine matter. But you want to have it stand out. One corporation engineered an interactive announcement in two cities at different ends of New York State, with a teleconference hookup. The president of the corporation was in one city, a congressman who actively supported the organization in the other. The two together announced a significant multimillion-dollar project that the corporation was developing. Just in case the technology failed, the public relations planner had prepared a script and a videotape that could be used at each location.

An Indiana group used a symbolic protest as part of its announcement strategy. Hogs Opposed to Government Waste and Silly Highways (HOGWASH) sent Arnold the Pig to deliver a ham to the governor's press secretary, announcing its opposition to the extension of a highway in southern Indiana. The protesters said the road project was an example of pork-barrel politics, so it was only fitting for Arnold to be their spokespig.

Some organizations have specially designed vehicles used for promotion and other public relations objectives. For example, Rural/Metro Ambulance Service has a three-foot high talking, winking, lighted ambulance called Amby that paramedics take into classrooms during safety presentations. United Parcel Service has a miniature delivery truck that it uses in athletic arenas to deliver a coin for the ceremonial coin toss, such as at the start of football games. Notice that each of these vehicles relates to the primary mission of the organization.

Some award-winning campaigns have found their success through creativity, such as the "man sled" race by Snausages … .

"Organ donor" is a negative reference to motorcycle riders. But the nonprofit Lifeline of Ohio creatively embraced the term as a double entendre, changing it from an insult to a positive. The campaign registered 3,000 new organ donors among motorcyclists in Central and Southeastern Ohio, with thousands more expected over the four-year cycle for renewing riders' licenses.

Likewise, AMResorts and its public relations agency got creative to combat health worries. The company's Mexican resort hotels were only half-full in 2009 because of fears of H1N1 swine flu. The company issued a "flu-free guarantee," promising that any guest who contracted swine flu at one of its resorts would get free return visits over each of the next three years. Bookings shot up 140 percent. Several other resort chains imitated the guarantee, and the Mexican government praised AMResorts for helping get Mexico's economy back to recovery.

Another example comes from a public relations agency in England trying to raise brand awareness of an auto-insurance company. Goals included driving traffic to its website, increasing visibility and generating requests for insurance quotes.

Company statistics on insurance claims were researched to identify the most accident-prone street in the United Kingdom: Somerville Road in Worcester. Then eight people worked 12 hours to bubble wrap the entire street. Nearly 1,800 square yards (1,500 square meters) of bubble wrap covered cars and trucks, houses, bicycles, dog houses, swing sets, trees and shrubs, even garden gnomes. The light-hearted publicity event carried a serious message about the dangers of winter driving, raising it well above the level of a mere publicity stunt devoid of news value. Rather, it was a means of attracting media attention to a serious issue of public safety.

The public relations team contacted established news media, including major national newspapers, as well as emerging social media by posting photos on Twitter, Flickr and Facebook. The combined buzz attracted more than 125 million viewers to blogs and articles, and the story was picked up by international news media in Australia and the US. The company's website saw a 20 percent increase in visitors on the first day of the publicity event, which passed its objective of generating an additional 4,000 requests for insurance quotes.

In a final burst of publicity, the bubble wrap was donated to Oxfam, the international food-aid program, that used it to package aid to earthquake victims in Haiti.

PUTTING THE PROGRAM TOGETHER

When the time comes to begin putting your public relations or marketing communication program together, first review the information gathered during the research phase of the program (Steps 1, 2 and 3). Reconsider the issue and review pertinent information about the organization, its environment and perceptions about it. Next examine the various publics and your analysis of them.

Following this review, consider several different ways to package the tactics you have chosen. No particular format is best for every issue, so let common sense be your guide. Consider the most distinctive element of your program. Your purpose is to select the format that most readily allows you to present your analysis and recommendations to your colleagues, boss or client.

Among the various ways of packaging your tactics is by tactical media category, public, goal, objective and department. Look at each of these with an open mind. Perhaps you'll be able to devise a more effective way to package the tactical recommendations in your program.

Packaging by Media Category

Using this approach, you move from the research phase to an overview of the goals, objectives and strategy associated with Steps 4, 5 and 6. Next, list each tactic according to the outline of media categories provided in the Step 7 inventory. That is, list each tactic in order of interpersonal communication, organizational media, news media and advertising media. With each tactic, indicate the relevant publics and objectives.

This presentation by media type can guide you to draw tactics from each category, though the presentation can appear a bit disjointed because it may overlook a more logical grouping of tactics. Nevertheless, it may be a good starting point, at least an effective preliminary checklist before using one of the following presentation formats. The presentation by tactics is followed by evaluation methods (Step 9), ...

Packaging by Public

The research phase moves to an outline of each key public and, for each, an overview of the relevant goals and objectives (Step 4). Then the strategy phase focuses on interacting and communicating with each public (Steps 5 and 6). This approach to packaging should include tactics associated with each strategy (Step 7) and evaluation methods (Step 9).

Use this format if the internal cohesion of your plan centers on the differences among several publics. For example, if you are planning a program that identifies three categories of publics—customers, employees and community—you may decide that you can present your analysis and ideas best by focusing separately on each public.

Packaging by Goal

Using this approach, the plan begins with the common research phase and provides an overview of goals associated with the issue. It then identifies a series of initiatives based on each goal and focuses the rest of the plan serially on each initiative.

In your presentation of each initiative, identify relevant research and background information, key publics (Step 3), objectives (Step 4), strategy with key messages (Steps 5 and 6) tactics (Step 7), and evaluation methods (Step 9).

Use this format when goals are sufficiently distinct to allow you to treat each one independently. For example, a public relations and marketing communication program for a university might identify several goal-based initiatives. These might include enhancing the university's reputation among students in high school and community colleges; increasing support from the business and civic community; recruiting more students to professional development programs; and enhancing knowledge and pride among students, faculty, staff and alumni. Campaign tactics could be associated with each of the four goals, a kind of sub-campaign for each component.

Packaging by Objective

Presentation by objective begins, like the previous approach, with the common research phase of Steps 1, 2 and 3. It then provides an overview of the goals and objectives from Step 4. Then it selects each objective as the focus for the remainder of the presentation, identifying key publics (Step 3), strategy with key messages (Steps 5 and 6), tactics (Step 7) and evaluation methods (Step 9) for each objective.

Use this approach when the objectives rather than the goals or publics are the most significant distinction within the plan. For example, a plan that has only a single goal might be presented according to the objectives associated with awareness, acceptance and action.

Packaging by Department

Similar to presentation by goals or objectives, presentation by department acknowledges that the distinctive segments of the strategic communication plan parallel existing organizational structures, such as departments, divisions and programs within the organization.

Use this approach when the structure of the client's organization coincides with program areas in your strategic plan.

PLANNING EXAMPLE 16A Packaging the Communication Tactics

The following initiative is packaged according to one of the four task goals identified in Planning Example 4: Establishing Goals and Objectives.

Initiative on Transfer Students
(Transcribe research, goal, key public, objectives and strategy information.)

- *Interpersonal Communication Tactics:* Upstate College will sponsor the "Celebration! UC" *weekend* (Friday evening, Saturday afternoon and evening, and Sunday afternoon), celebrating the expansion of UC to a four-year institution. Entertainment during this event will include a *picnic* with two *bands*, a formal *banquet* and strolling *entertainers.* The event will include a *rededication ceremony* with public officials, leaders of neighboring colleges and universities, and UC students, faculty and alumni; a *fall festival* for current students and alumni; and *an open house* for prospective transfer students
- *Organizational Media Tactics:* Support materials for the festival will include a revision of the college *viewbook*, a new transfer *brochure* and a *poster*, as well as production of a *video*. A special page will be added to the UC *website* home page. Students who applied to UC within the last two years and were accepted but did not attend will be sent a letter inviting them to the festival events, along with a fact sheet about Upstate College.
- *News Media Tactics:* More generally, the festival will be promoted with media fact sheets and *news releases*, a *photo* with caption and a *cable TV crawl*. Students attending the event will be given an Upstate College *T-shirt* designed by UC art students. A *media advisory* will be sent to the news media, inviting them to cover the event, and *news interviews* will be offered with the UC president, provost and student government president. Additionally, the media relations office will seek out an *editorial conference* with the local newspaper to elicit editorial support for the expansion. Failing that, a *letter to the editor* will be sent by a UC official noting the benefits of the program expansion for the community.
- *Advertising and Promotional Media Tactics:* The festival also will be promoted with a *newspaper advertisement* in campus newspapers at other colleges and with radio *commercials*. Additionally, a *display ad* in the local newspaper will be aimed at parents as well as community leaders, alumni and donors.

(Note that each of the other goals would be developed in a similar manner.)

The following initiative is packaged according to the four key publics identified in Planning Example 3A: Identifying Publics.

Public Relations Program for Tiny Tykes Employees
(Transcribe research, goal, objectives and strategy information.)

- *Internal Tactics:* The internal component of a training program for employees will include *workshops* on customer satisfaction as well as a *training session* on product safety and quality; *brochures* and *e-mail notices* about safety and quality issues will be available. Several *work-group meetings* will be held, at least one involving a *motivational speech* by the CEO. Similar motivational themes will be presented in *newsletter articles* and in the online employee *bulletin*.

- *External Tactics*: The program will have an external component to provide employee support. Elements of this component will *include letters to families* of employees, *letters to the editors* of local newspapers about employee dedication to customer safety, and print *advertisements* in trade magazines and in the local newspaper. A *news release* will announce the new safety and quality initiatives, and a *story idea memo* will be given to reporters about employee dedication to customer safety.

(Note that each of the other publics would be developed in a similar manner.)

CHECKLIST 16A Packaging Communication Tactics

BASIC QUESTIONS

1 What specific initiatives or sections make up this plan?
2 What tactics are associated with this plan?
3 What public and objective does each tactic serve?

EXPANDED QUESTIONS

A. SELECTING THE APPROACH
1 From the following categories, indicate which one offers the greatest likelihood of a package of program tactics that is cohesive and logical: by public, by goal, by objective, by department or by tactic.
2 List specific initiatives or sections in your plan.

B. STRATEGIC IMPLICATIONS
1 Will this approach help the organization to interact with the appropriate public?
2 What is the main advantage to this approach?
3 What advantages does this approach offer that other approaches do not?
4 Are there any disadvantages to this approach?

CAMPAIGN PLAN BOOK

The **campaign plan book**—or, more simply, the book—is the formal written presentation of your research findings and program recommendations for strategy, tactics and evaluation. This report should be concise in writing, professional in style and confident in tone. Here are some of the elements the plan book should include:

- *Title Page.* List a program name as well as the names of the client organization, consultant or team members, and date.
- *Executive Summary.* Prepare a one- or two-page synopsis of the plan written as an overview for busy executives and for readers who are not directly involved in the program.
- *Table of Contents.* Outline the major segments of the program.
- *Statement of Principles* (optional). Lay out the planner's approach to strategic communication campaigns (particularly whether it is rooted in public relations, marketing communication or integrated communication). Also included are definitions of key concepts used in the book.
- *Situation Analysis.* Outline your research and synthesis of the issue (Step 1), organization (Step 2) and publics (Step 3). Some program plans present the research data and summaries on paper of a different color from the rest of the report.
- *Strategic Approach.* Present your strategic recommendations such as spokesperson, theme, key message, etc.
- *Tactical Program.* Present your tactical recommendations in whatever format you think works best (such as by public, by goal, by objective, by program or by tactic) to show your plans and to address the issue.
- *Schedule.* Outline the time and calendar considerations for implementing the various tactics.
- *Budget.* Outline resources needed for the program. Include in this figure the cost of personnel time, money and equipment, as well as any income to be generated.
- *Evaluation Plan.* Provide information on the methods to be used to measure the program's effectiveness.
- *Consultant Credentials & Resources* (optional). Indicate the resources the consultant or agency can offer. This element of the plan is especially useful in competitive situations in which more than one consultant or agency prepares program recommendations. …

Sometimes you may decide not to use a particular tactic, perhaps passing up even a particular category of communication tactics. For example, an employee relations project may not lend itself to involving the news media, or an investor relations project may not include advertising. It is appropriate to note the absence of a tactic and the reason behind your choice for not using it.

When you choose not to use what might seem to be an obvious tactic, it is particularly important to offer your reasoning in your plan. Especially if you are developing a proposal on competitive-bid basis, let the potential client know why you recommend against using what others might suggest.

Regardless of the way you package your tactics, it is important to show the internal logic within your planning program. Make it clear to your client or boss how the various elements work together for a common purpose.

A good way to show this internal harmony is to note for each tactic the specific public, goal and objective to which it is linked. In this way, planners can make sure that each public is adequately served by the various tactics. Likewise, planners can be certain that each goal and objective is played out through a variety of tactics.

EXAMPLE: TACTICS FOR OPEN HOUSE

Consider the following example outlining one tactic, an open house as part of a campaign proposal for a new graduate program at a university in a mid-sized city. This tactic shows the internal linkage between a single tactic, previously identified publics, already determined objectives and strategy, administrative details such as budgeting, and subsequent evaluation methods.

- *Public*: Professional architects (specifically, approximately 145 practicing architects within a three-county area).
- *Objective*: To increase the understanding of professional architects about the new program (50 percent of the professional community prior to beginning the academic program).
- *Strategy*: Attract attention of the professional community and create a core of opinion leaders; give specific attention to leading architects, particularly those who have received recognition from the Midstate Association of Professional Architects.
- *Tactical Elements*:

  1 Promotional materials including news release, e-mail invitations, Facebook note and outreach to appropriate blogs ($100).
  2 Information materials including an eight-minute video ($15,000 value; $1,000 cost in-house by broadcasting students).
  3 Information packet for visitors, with parallel information at website ($200).
  4 Logistical support including reserved space, parking arrangements, snacks and beverages ($100).

- *Budget*: $14,500 value. Actual cost $1,500.
- *Evaluation Methods*: Attendance figures; follow-up minisurvey conducted as part of a telephone thank-you for attending.
- *Oversight*: Assistant Director of Community Relations

In a complete proposal, each tactic would receive similar treatment. Even individual tactics might have multiple components. For example, the open house noted earlier might have additional publics, perhaps donors or potential students. Each of these would require its own statement of objectives and strategies, though the budget and evaluation methods may remain constant.

CAMPAIGN SCHEDULE

You already addressed one aspect of scheduling when you built into your objectives in Step 4 an indication of when you planned to achieve each. This provided the deadline upon which you will measure your effectiveness in reaching the objectives.

Now that Step 7 has generated an outline of tactics, you can establish specific time requirements. This involves two considerations: (1) the pattern and frequency of your communication tactics and (2) the actual timeline of tasks to be accomplished as the tactics are implemented.

FREQUENCY OF TACTICS

As noted in Step 6, the average person is exposed to thousands of public relations and marketing messages each day, yet most fall on deaf ears. Clearly, mere exposure to a message is insufficient to move someone to action. However, the frequency of exposure is an important factor in whether the message takes root in a person's consciousness.

Repetition increases awareness and leads to greater acceptance. Research has been done both on **message frequency** (the number and pattern of messages presented to a particular public in a given period of time) and on **message reach** (the number of different people who are exposed to a single message).

Most of this research has been focused either on advertising or on the learning process. However, it is possible to generalize a bit about applications for public relations. It is known, for example, that one exposure to a message has little or no effect unless the audience is unusually attentive. Three exposures are needed to make an impact.

This concept has enjoyed general support within the advertising trade since it was articulated by ad manager and theoretician Herbert Krugman (1972). Subsequent researchers have noted that studies in laboratory settings confirmed Krugman's three-exposure formula. However, in natural settings in which consumers are distracted by competing messages, three presentations of the message may not be enough to generate three mindful exposures to the intended audience.

What do we learn from such research? Here are a few of the important lessons and observations for the public relations manager.

Multiple Presentations

Don't rely on just one presentation of your message to key publics. Don't think that even three exposures guarantee success. Find ways to repeat and reinforce your message, especially through various media. This will not only increase retention among your key publics but also add to the credibility of the message because it will have the third-party endorsement of several different media gatekeepers.

Repetition Over Time

Another lesson gleaned from research is the value of repetition over a period of time. Most audiences remember a message they have seen daily for several days more than one presented several times in a single day. Too-frequent presentation of the message seems unnecessarily redundant and can lead to wear-out—which, by the way, comes faster with a humorous message than with a neutral or serious one.

Audience Confusion

A message presented may not be a message heard, and there is no specific number for how many repetitions are best. Sometimes, even your best efforts won't gain complete success, especially with audiences who are not particularly interested in the issue. This is an unavoidable result of the information overload that all audiences encounter every day. They are aware of a message, but not particularly mindful of its content.

For example, for several years one of the most consistent television advertising campaigns featured a pink rabbit beating the drum for a battery company. Yet 40 percent of viewers in a national survey identified the wrong company as the sponsor of the ad, despite the company's best effort to promote the Energizer Bunny.

Key Public

Bruce Vanden Bergh and Helen Katz (1999) point out that most organizations with limited budgets must find a balance between reach and frequency. A basic guideline for advertising seems to hold true for other aspects of marketing communication and public relations: Focus on key publics. Rather than trying to reach a greater number of people, try instead to reach a targeted number of strategically important people more frequently.

TIMELINE OF TASKS

At this point in your planning, you know three things about your tactics: (1) which ones you want to use; (2) how you will package them; and (3) how often to run them. Now turn your attention to carefully considering

PATTERNS OF MESSAGE REPETITION

An insight drawn from advertising is that the pattern of communication can be of crucial importance for public relations and marketing communications. If you know that a one-time message is not likely to be effective, the questions are about when and how you should plan for repetition of the message. Consider four concepts: continuity, flighting, pulsing and massing.

- **Continuity** is an approach to scheduling that presents a message at a consistent level throughout a particular period of time. Use this approach if you need to maintain a consistent presence over a given period of time. But realize that it is expensive to use a continuous approach with enough intensity to generate an effective reach and frequency.
- **Flighting** (also called **bursting**) refers to the presentation of messages in waves, with periods of intense communication interspersed with dark periods of communication inactivity. A variety of media can be used during the peak communication periods. This approach is useful when organizational activity falls into predictable and discrete periods.
- **Pulsing** is a combination of the two approaches, with a continuous base augmented by intermittent bursts of communication activity.
- **Massing** is the bunching of various presentations of a message into a short period of time.

These techniques are associated with advertising and most commonly involve different ways of timing a single advertising message. However, the concept of timing can be used to plan and schedule various complimentary public relations and marketing communication tactics. These could involve not only advertising messages but also meetings and special events, posters and brochures, blogs and e-mail, postings on the online newsroom, and so on.

each significant task needed for these tactics. One of the easiest ways to schedule tasks is to work backward from the final tactic date. For example, if you want a brochure to be received in the readers' homes by May 15, work backward to develop the following hypothetical schedule:

May 12	Deliver to the post office.
May 11	Attach address labels.
May 10	Receive from printer.
May 5	Deliver to printer.
April 29	Finalize copy and design, and obtain approvals.
April 21	Complete draft, including copy, artwork and layout.
April 14	Begin writing, develop artwork.
April 8	Assign writer and designer.
April 6	Obtain approval for objectives, determine budget.
April 2	Begin planning for brochure.

Total time required: **45 days**.

This plan is your **timeline** or implementation schedule. Timelines are essential when you are dealing with a variety of tactics and managing different programs at the same time. Having a written plan makes it easier to train others and delegate responsibilities. Similarly, having a written timeline makes it easier to keep work records that may be needed for billing purposes.

A good way to manage the scheduling process is to chart out each of the tasks you have identified. You could use a large calendar or a timetable narrative with sections for time periods and bulleted task items to be accomplished during each time period.

However, flow charts are particularly helpful in tracking public relations tactics because they provide a visual representation of the tasks to be completed. Two commonly used types of flow charts at the Gantt chart and the PERT chart.

Gantt Chart

One frequently used type of flow chart is the **Gantt chart**. This was developed by engineer Henry Gantt during World War I to track shipbuilding projects. The Gantt chart lists each tactic and the various associated tasks, then indicates the time needed for each task. Times can be indicated in days, weeks or months, depending on the type of project.

The advantage of the Gantt chart is that it provides a map of the work that needs to be done. These charts can be kept on computer, written on paper charts or displayed as wall charts. Several free templates for Gantt charts are available for download from online sites that can be found with a search engine. Some software or online sites allow for interactive Gantt charts so multiple users can work on comprehensive projects.

Exhibit 16.1 shows a Gantt chart for an activity for which implementation is just beginning. X indicates planned tasks. When these tasks are completed, replace the Xs with solid dashes.

	April															May						
	2	4	6	8	10	12	14	16	18	20	22	24	26	28	30	2	4	6	8	10	12	14
Brochure																						
Planning (myself)	xxxxxxx																					
Objectives (supervisor)		x																				
Assign writer (myself)		x																				
Writing (freelancer)						xxxxxxxxx																
Complete draft (freelancer)										x												
Final copy (myself)												xxxxxx										
To printer (myself)																x						
From printer (printer)																	x					
Labels (staff)																		x				
To Post Office (staff)																		x				
Deliver (Post Office)																				xxx		

EXHIBIT 16.1 Gantt Chart for Brochure

EXHIBIT 16.2 PERT Chart

Because the Gantt chart shows every task associated with the various tactics, planners can spread out activity according to a convenient schedule. For example, under normal conditions preparation of a brochure may take about six weeks. But the Gantt chart may show that several other important and time-consuming activities will be taking place within the same six-week period. Thus you may need to begin work on the brochure earlier.

Pert Chart

Another commonly used flow chart is the **PERT chart**, a process first developed for the Polaris missile system in the 1950s. PERT (Program Evaluation and Review Technique) charts generally include dates and assignment to particular individuals, though they lack the calendaring aspect of the Gantt chart. This chart, shown in Exhibit 16.2, lists tasks within circles or boxes, with arrows indicating how one task flows into another.

An effective implementation schedule of public relations tactics generally includes more than dates. Include the name of the person or group responsible for the task. In addition to the deadline date, some charts indicate the latest date by which the tactic can be implemented and still remain useful.

CAMPAIGN BUDGET

The development of resources needed to achieve objectives, **budget**, is a topic that has been "on the table" since the beginning of this planning process.

In Step 1, you considered the importance of the issue and its potential impact on the bottom line of the organization. In Step 2, you analyzed the organization itself, with some consideration going to the level of resources available to address various aspects of public relations and marketing communications. These resources included personnel, equipment, time and budgeted money.

Throughout the strategic development in Steps 4, 5 and 6, you were advised to be realistic in setting forth on a course of action appropriate to the organization. One measure of propriety is based on the organization's resources. At every turn in a planning process, you must be practical. Consider budget constraints and limitations—no organization is free of these—so your recommendations will be realistic, practical and doable.

BUDGET ITEMS

Remember that budgeting is about more than money. It deals with all the needed resources to implement a tactic. Thus budgets for public relations and marketing communications should consider five categories of items to be budgeted: personnel, material, media costs, equipment and facilities, and administrative costs.

Personnel

Personnel items in a budget include the number of people and the amount of time needed to achieve the results expected of the tactic. This may include both organizational personnel and outside people, such as consultants, agency staff, subcontracted specialists and freelance workers. Personnel costs may be associated with research, analysis, planning, writing, editing, design, photography, events management, and the like.

Personnel costs can be expressed either in terms of time (hours or days) needed to complete the task or in labor dollars. In some billing situations, public relations agencies present personnel items in the form of billable hours. Some agencies have a general and average hourly rate. Others make distinctions among strategic planning, research, account management, and administrative and support activities.

Remember to account for the time of salaried public relations staff within an organization. Increasingly, many corporations and nonprofit organizations have structured their public relations department to serve as in-house agencies. These often charge back the cost of their public relations activities on behalf of other departments, at least on paper. This chargeback allows the organization to more accurately see the role of public relations in its various programs and projects.

Material

Material items in a budget include the "things" associated with the tactics: paper for brochures, banners for an open house, media kits for a news conference, software for an online newsroom, uniforms for the company-sponsored softball team, and so on. Additionally, material items may be associated with research activities, such as the cost of questionnaires or materials for focus groups. This category also includes the time associated with activities such as developing websites and overseeing MySpace sites.

Each of these tasks and items carries a price tag, and it is very important to know exactly the cost of each recommended tactic. If you simply guess or work from old figures, you may find that you cannot implement the tactic for the amount that has been budgeted. By budgeting for each item separately, you are able to make adjustments if, for example, you need to decrease the overall budget or channel more money toward a particular tactic.

Media Cost

Money generally is needed for outside communication activities, particularly the purchase of time and space associated with advertising tactics. Budgets often identify commissionable media, which is advertising in newspapers and magazines, or commercials on radio and television.

When working with an advertising agency, you may find that a commission or agency fee of about 15 percent has been added as a surcharge to the cost of the final art, production charges for audio and video, and talent or model fees, as well as the cost of buying advertising time or space. Public relations agencies sometimes bill all out-of-pocket expenses (perhaps with the exception of travel expenses) at cost plus 15 percent. In the face of growing competition among agencies, however, commissions increasingly are being replaced with flat fees.

FEE STRUCTURES FOR PUBLIC RELATIONS AGENCIES

Several different approaches to billing are common with public relations consultants and agencies, as well as with the growing number of public relations departments that are being reorganized using the in-house agency model.

- **Hourly** or ***per diem*** **rates plus expenses** are based on the actual amount of time spent on a project, plus the amount of money spent on materials, production costs and media purchases.

Some agencies lower the hourly rate as the actual number of hours increases. Examples of hourly rates are $45 an hour for copyediting, $150 an hour for research analysis, or $200 an hour for account supervision.

- **Project fees** or **fixed fees** are flat charges for projects, such as $250 for a news release or $1,000 for preparing a brochure for printing.
- **Retainer fees** are fixed monthly base charges paid in advance for a predetermined level of agency availability. The benefit to the agency is that a minimum income is guaranteed. The client benefit is that the retaining charge is calculated lower than regular hourly rates and gives the client access to a guaranteed minimum amount of public relations services.
- **Performance fees** are a new and somewhat controversial way of obtaining compensation from a client. Under this system, the agency bills based on its success in achieving stated objectives, such as placement of news releases, generation of telephone calls or web hits, and so on. This is controversial because public relations practitioners deserve to be paid for their work, which cannot always be guaranteed to have the desired effect. For example, a practitioner can research, write and distribute a news release, but he or she cannot guarantee that the new media will print it. If the client is charged only for releases that actually are published, the agency must be prepared to absorb the cost of work done on behalf of the client that does not generate the hoped-for use.

Equipment and Facilities

This category includes the capital cost of equipment that must be purchased to implement a tactic. Examples of this would include computers, scanners, printers or software needed to publish a newsletter or support a blog. Also included here are the capital costs of obtaining a needed facility, such as modifying a storage area into an in-house television studio.

Note that items in this category generally are one-time expenditures. Thus the cost might be calculated separately from the project for which the resources are purchased, under the notion that they may be used for other projects in the future. However, a forward-looking budget process would amortize such expenses over the expected life of the equipment or facility and would be prepared for the time when replacements will be needed.

Administrative Items

A budget also should include the cost of telephone charges, delivery costs, photocopying and other office activities, as well as travel costs associated with the project. Some organizations assess a surcharge, often 15 percent, to offset the cost of overhead expenses such as rent, maintenance, utilities, taxes, and so on. Items such as software licenses and maintenance contracts also are included in this category.

APPROACHES TO BUDGETING

A recurring problem with budgeting is that public relations sometimes is seen not as strategic management but rather as the mere production and distribution of messages. Public relations may be thought to deal with hard-to-measure intangibles such as goodwill or visibility.

Because of this mindset, public relations budgets sometimes are set according to a formula based on last year's budget, or worse, as an arbitrary percentage of the wider administration or marketing program of an organization.

If you have followed the guidelines in *Strategic Planning for Public Relations*, you should find that you can overcome these difficulties. You have learned to conduct public relations and marketing communication as a management activity, and you have learned to work with precise objectives that bring an element of measurement to concepts such as goodwill and support.

Still, the question often comes up: How much should an organization spend on public relations and marketing communications?

People asking this are often looking for a simple, accepted formula. But there is no simple answer to that question, because so much depends on variables: the nature of the issue being addressed, the objectives sought, the tactics employed, and so on.

Some nonprofit organizations can operate impressive and successful campaigns for only a few hundred dollars. On the other hand, some corporations may spend literally millions on public relations and marketing communications tactics. For example, some major motion pictures, which easily run into the hundreds of millions of dollars to produce, may spend even more on promotions, most of that for paid advertising. National political campaigns raise millions of dollars for advertising and other promotional activities.

Every organization and every issue is different. Each requires careful attention and insightful management.

Establishing an appropriate budget can be a difficult task. Often you will find that a client simply has no notion what the appropriate budget should be. Every organization wants to prevent unnecessary spending, but most also are willing to spend the necessary amount to get the job done.

Let's consider some of the many different ways to approach budgeting: competitive parity, same-as-before, percentage-of-sales, unit-of-sales, all-you-can-afford, cost-benefit analysis, what-if-not-funded, stage-of-life-cycle, zero-based and objectives-based methods.

Competitive Parity

The **competitive parity** approach bases an organization's budget for various activities on the level of similar activity by major competitors. For example, University A may base its budget for recruiting new students on the apparent budget of University B, its biggest competitor.

A drawback of this approach is that University A will have to guess what University B is spending, and much of that may not be apparent. Additionally, the two universities may have significantly different situations, such as the amount of informal recruiting being done by alumni, the reputation of the two institutions, and their financial resources.

Same-as-Before Budgeting

A budget developed on the **same-as-before** approach looks at how much the organization spent on a similar recent project and allows the same budget for this project. But such an approach presumes that two projects are sufficiently similar that one can serve as a benchmark for the other. It also presumes that the first project was successful and deserves to be imitated.

A related approach is *same-as-before-but-more* budgeting, which adds an inflationary increase to a same-as-before budget.

Percentage-of-Sales Budgeting

The **percentage-of-sales** approach to budgeting is drawn from the field of marketing, where some companies base their advertising budget on the previous year's profits. This approach may give a generous marketing budget following a good year but only a meager budget after a lean year—perhaps just the opposite of what is needed to overcome a sales slump.

In the university recruiting scenario above, the budget for public relations might be based on the amount of money obtained through tuition fees. For example, 2 percent of each tuition payment may be earmarked for the recruiting public relations program. However, because much public relations activity is difficult to quantify on a short-term basis, the percentage-of-sales method generally is a weak approach in this field.

Unit-of-Sales Budgeting

Similar to percentage-of-sales budgeting, the **unit-of-sales** approach is based not on dollars but on prior outcomes.

In the university recruiting situation, the budget might be pegged to the number of people who register as full-time students. For example, for every student recruited, the university might earmark $100 for the public relations program. This approach has a similar drawback to the percentage-of-sales approach in that it pegs future budgets on past prosperity rather than current needs.

All-You-Can-Afford Budgeting

The **all-you-can-afford** approach to budgeting works better in good times than in bad. It provides for public relations funding when the organization's financial condition is sound, but limits funding during lean times. While this is not a good approach, in reality it is the way too many organizations approach public relations, as an optional luxury that can be dispensed with when money is tight. Actually, the hard times are when even more public relations activity may be needed.

Cost-Benefit Analysis

A budget based on the **cost-benefit analysis** approach identifies the cost of implementing a tactic, then compares this cost to the estimated value of the expected results. Ideally, the cost will be significantly less than the probable benefit.

For example, the cost of holding an open house for a day-care center for seniors with Alzheimer's disease might be $1,500, while the benefit of this tactic, if the projected registration goal is met, might be $10,000 from new donors to the program. Based on this formula, the open house would be considered a tactic worthy of being implemented.

What-If-Not-Funded Analysis

The consequence of inaction and the effect on the organization's mission is the concept underlying the **what-if-not-funded budget**. This approach forces a planner to consider expected outcomes. It is tied to objectives that previously have been accepted by the organization.

For example, the what-if-not-funded scenario for the tactic of producing a video would have you indicate the expenses necessary to achieve the objective without the video. This might mean more workshops involving additional time from the CEO, or perhaps more brochures with fewer benefits than with the video. Implicitly or explicitly, the recommended tactic is compared with the alternatives. Some organizations pair the WINF scenario with a cost-benefit analysis to keep the advantages in view while comparing alternatives.

Stage-of Life-Cycle Budgeting

The **stage-of-life-cycle** approach to budgeting looks closely at the phase of development of the issue, knowing that start-up programs generally require more financial resources than maintenance programs.

Consider, for example, the needs of a university communication department in transition. Let's say the university is well known for its "academic" approach to communication, with a focus on research, theory and critical analysis. Let's further presume that the university decides to extend itself into more applied communication areas such as public relations, advertising and electronic journalism. Because of the change in emphasis, the financial resources needed to recruit students for the new program will be greater than what is simply needed to maintain applications to the current program focus.

Zero-Based Budgeting

A technique known as **zero-based budgeting** is rooted in current needs rather than past expenditures. It is commonly used with ongoing organizational budgets, such as those associated with annual community relations or investor relations programs. However, the zero-based approach can work with one-time campaigns as well.

In this approach, various tactics are ranked according to their importance. The cumulative cost of each tactic is then calculated. The cut-off line of the predetermined budget indicates in effect when the client has run out of money and therefore must reject the remaining tactics.

This is not really an effective method for public relations planning, because it allows a financial formula and a calculator to determine what tactics will be implemented. It can, however, serve as a useful first look at tactical planning, but this initial ranking needs to be re-evaluated with a cost-benefit analysis and a what-if-not-funded approach.

Objective-Based Budgeting

A more enlightened approach is *objective-based budgeting*. By focusing on objectives, this approach deals with already identified needs and goals. It aligns with decisions already made by the organization or client.

The underlying premise of objective-based budgeting is that the organization will provide the resources necessary to achieve its objectives, which already have been approved by organizational decision makers. The consensus check that concludes Step 4 is perhaps the most important part of this approach to budgeting. It is at that point that agreement is reached on what must be accomplished. The tactics simply provide ways to achieve what already has been adopted as the objective.

Usually, this means that the organization will assign the needed resources to carry out tactics that are integral to reaching the set objectives. Occasionally, however, it means that the organization will scale back objectives to limit some of the tactics originally recommended.

Either way, objective-based budgeting puts the responsibility on the organization or client to establish objectives that it will support with appropriate tactics.

Even with the objective-based approach to budgeting, financial reality and common sense must rule. The wise strategic planner will develop tactics that are within the reach of the organization. The ability to create effective programs suitable to almost any budget is one of the real advantages of an integrated approach to public relations and marketing communication.

BUDGET MANAGEMENT

In Step 8, you are developing the actual budget for your public relations program. The best way to do this is to list each of the tactics you recommended in Step 7, then indicate the various costs associated with each tactic.

For example, if you have recommended the creation of a brochure, indicate the various costs associated with this tactic. Include one-time costs such as copywriting, artwork and design. Include costs based on the number of brochures needed, such as paper, printing, folding and mailing. Add in the value of personnel time, such as hourly

$125	for administrative cost for public relations director (in house)
	• 7 hours @ $17.85/hour, based on annual salary of $37,000
$1,500	for creative costs
	• $800 copywriting (8 hours @ $100/hour)
	• $500 artwork (4 hours @ $150/hour)
	• $200 design (4 hours @ $50/hour)
$775	for production costs @ 2,500 copies
	• $125 paper
	• $600 printing (two-color @ $0.24)
	• $50 folding
$500	for distribution cost
$2,900	TOTAL

EXHIBIT 16.3 Sample Fixed Budget for Brochure

figures based on annual salaries of organizational employees or the hourly fees for outside consultants, agency personnel or freelance workers. Then total these various costs to obtain a full cost for the brochure tactic. Exhibit 16.3 shows how this budget item might look as a fixed amount (that is, for a specified number of brochures produced).

By breaking down each of the various costs associated with the tactic, you are able to more precisely predict the total cost associated with the program. Additionally, this breakdown allows you to adjust the total budget more easily. Say, for example, that all of your recommended tactics add up to $12,500, but your overall budget is supposed to be only $11,000. You need to shave $1,500 from your recommendations.

One way would be to find a tactic that costs $1,500 and eliminate it, but this probably would leave a hole in your plan. After all, the tactic was recommended to achieve a particular objective.

However, by knowing the cost of each aspect of every tactic, you can make minor revisions in several areas. Perhaps you could use spot color rather than four-color printing and save a few hundred dollars on the brochure, or perhaps mail fewer brochures and find an alternative distribution method that would cost less. By modifying enough tactics without eliminating any of them, you can keep your original plan intact and still meet the budget.

How closely should you stick with the overall budget that your boss or client originally indicated? That probably depends on the boss or client, and how you read the budget projection. If you think the budget was meant merely as a guideline, then going a bit over probably won't hurt. If you know the boss to be the type of manager who routinely cuts a percentage of every budget request, then you may be tempted to pad your budget request a bit, knowing that it will be cut back to the point where you really want it to be. But if you sense that the budget figure was firm, you should make sure your recommendations fall within the projected budget.

When a budget doesn't seem to stretch quite far enough for your ideas, one solution is to offer the client a range of costs—low-end and high-end tactics, perhaps with a preferred or optimal level of funding. Take another look at the brochure budget. The $2,900 total cost is based on printing with spot color as an accent. But the final

$125	for administrative cost for public relations director (in house)
	• 7 hours @ $17.85/hour, based on annual salary of $37,000
$1,500	for creative costs
	• $800 copywriting (8 hours @ $100/hour)
	• $500 artwork (4 hours @ $150/hour)
	• $200 design (4 hours @ $50/hour)
$550–$1,375	for production costs @ 2,500 copies
	• $125 paper
	• $275–$1,200 printing (one-color @ $0.15; two-color @ $0.24, four-color @ $0.48)
	• $50 folding
$100–$500	for distribution cost
	• $100 non-mail/bulk-mail distribution
	• $0–$500 mail distribution
$2,275–$3,500	TOTAL

EXHIBIT 16.4 Sample Variable Budget for Brochure

cost actually could range from a low of $2,275 by printing in one color only and not using the mail for distribution, to a high of $3,500 for four-color printing and mail distribution. Exhibit 16.4 presents such a variable budget.

Still another way to stretch a budget is to provide a basic set of recommendations that fits within the projected budget, then offer an add-on list of optional tactics that the client may wish to fund because of the added expected benefit.

Budgets also have a way of inching upward. Perhaps a supplier charges a bit more than when you first called for an estimate. Or some of your expense items were based on a similar project six months ago, but those items now have increased in price. Most organizations are aware that budget creep can occur, and agencies or consultants often build into their contracts provisions for such changes. A common technique is to assure the client that, for any increase of more than 10 percent, the cost overrun will be submitted for the client's prior approval.

Once the budget has been approved, it should be used as a tool to help manage the implementation of the project. The budget can offer guidance in scheduling tasks, monitoring their progress and assessing their results.

The budget should be treated as part of a living document. The strategic plan is not set in stone once it is approved. Rather, it must have the flexibility to respond to a changing environment and differing organizational needs.

FULL-COST BUDGETING

In presenting the budget to your boss or client, include the full cost of all the tactics in the program (**full-cost budget**). Some tactics may not have a specific price tag, but if they are of value to the organization they should be noted, along with equivalent costs if the tactics were to be purchased.

$0 cost for administrative cost for public relations director; *actual value $125 for administrative costs*

     (in house; 7 hours; $17.85/hour, based on annual salary of $37,000)

$600   for creative cost; *actual value $1,500*

- $0 photography donated; actual value $500 (4 hours @ $150/hour)

- $400 copywriting discounted; *actual value $800* (8 hours @ 50/hour; discounted from $100/hour)

- $200 design (4 hours @ $50/hour)

$775   for production costs @ 2,500 copies

- $125 paper

- $600 printing (two-color @ $0.24)

- $50 folding

$500 for distribution cost

$1,875   TOTAL *$2,900 actual value*

EXHIBIT 16.5 Sample Full-Cost Budget

Note the value of donated or contributed services. In particular, include the value of volunteer time as you calculate the full cost of the budget items. For example, a human service agency might get help from a college public relations class in developing a brochure for new clients. The students may not charge for their services, but the project budget should include a dollar estimate of what those services would cost if the agency had to hire professionals such as a freelance copywriter or a design firm.

Communication plans usually don't include many income items, but don't overlook implicit revenues. Corporate sponsorship may have a specific dollar value, which should be presented in the budget as an offset to expenses. It also is appropriate to include projected revenues if you have built a fundraising tactic into your program recommendations.

Likewise, it may be appropriate to include both the actual expense and real value of that expense item. For example, the full value of discounted consulting fees or free airtime for a public service advertisement can be listed to show the difference between the total value and the actual cost to the organization. A word of caution: Don't be tempted to set a dollar value on publicity by calculating how much the same space would cost for advertising. This is discussed in more detail in Step 9; for now let's just agree that publicity should not be confused with advertising.

By including all of this information, you are presenting a full view of the real value of the campaign, even though the organization's actual cost may be considerably less.

Exhibit 16.5 presents an example of a hypothetical budget for a brochure project for a nonprofit organization, a community dance troupe. Let's say that a friend of the artistic director for the troupe is a professional photographer whose daughter dances with the troupe. He is volunteering to take photos for the brochure and an accompanying website. Let's also say that a woman with a decade of public relations experience is relocating to this community and wants to network and become known as she sets up a freelance business. She has done similar work with artistic groups in other cities is offering to cut her copywriting fees by 50 percent as she introduces herself to this community. Exhibit 16.5 shows how the budget for this project might look.

HOW MUCH SUCCESS IS NECESSARY?

It sometimes is important to ask the question: How much success is necessary? Or put another way: What level of achievement is needed simply to cover the cost of the program?

Calculate the **break-even point** (BEP) in three steps:

1   Identify the total project cost (c).
2   Determine the outcome value (v), the dollar value for each unit of the desired outcome, especially those associated with the action objectives.
3   Divide the total project cost by the value of the desired outcome.

Thus the formula is:

$$\text{BEP} = c/v \text{ (cost divided by value)}.$$

Let's say a private college will spend $160,000 of its recruiting budget this year to develop brochures and booklets, produce and distribute an informational video, and place paid radio commercials and billboards. Let's add $100,000 in salaries associated with this particular project. Add another $20,000 for expenses such as postage, travel and phone calls. That's $280,000 for c, the total project cost.

Now let's presume that tuition at this private college is $35,000. Apply the formula: cost $280,000 ($c$) divided by outcome value $35,000 ($v$) equals 8 (BEP). That's the break-even point. Eight additional students must be recruited through these brochures, videos and commercials before the communication program has paid for itself. (Note that this is an oversimplified example that doesn't take into account that the real cost of education is borne not only by tuition but also by donations, endowments and state aid.)

Another useful budgetary calculation is the **per-capita cost**, the cost associated with the number of people needed to cover the cost. Calculate the per-capita cost (PCC) by dividing the total project cost (c) by the number of people (p) who perform the desired outcome. The formula is:

$$\text{PCC} = v/p.$$

Returning to the college scenario, divide the cost by the number of new recruits (let's say that's 1,800). Apply the formula: $280,000 divided by 1,800, which equals $156. This is how much the college is spending to recruit each new student through these new tactics of the brochures, videos and commercials. In percentage terms, this is about 0.0056% of tuition income, or less than half a penny for every dollar of the $35,000 tuition.

Break-even points and per-capita costs also can be calculated for other public relations objectives, as long as the objectives themselves have been stated in precise and measurable terms.

WHAT'S NEXT?

By completing this step, you have brought your campaign to the point of implementation. Practically, you can say you have completed your strategic planning.

But there is one more element, which is the evaluation that will take place after the plan has been implemented. Even though you won't do the evaluation until later, you plan for it now. That's the focus of Step 9.

PLANNING EXAMPLE 16B Implementing the Strategic Plan

The following schedule shows one of several events within the four initiatives of the plan to publicize Upstate College's expanding program. It shows the event and its component tactics, along with a cost, an assigned manager, and a start date for each tactic (as the number of weeks prior to the event).

Event: Rededication Ceremony

Tactic 1: Print and mail 1,000 invitations

Cost: $800   Manager: Publications Office   Begin Work: 12 weeks prior

Tactic 2: Print 500 programs

Cost: $0   Manager: Publications Office   Begin Work: 10 weeks prior

Tactic 3: Keynote speaker honorarium

Cost: $1,000   Manager: President's Office   Begin Work: 12 weeks prior

Tactic 4: Musicians

Cost: $800   Manager: Music Dept. Chair   Begin Work: 6 weeks prior

Tactic 5: Academic processional/ritual

Cost: $200   Manager: Provost   Begin Work: 6 weeks prior

Tactic 6: Video about UC expansion

Cost: $4,000   Manager: Video Task Force   Begin work: 20 weeks prior

Tactic 7: Viewing equipment

Cost $300   Manager: Facilities Office   Begin work: 4 weeks prior

Tactic 8: Plaque engraving

Cost: $400   Manager: Facilities Office   Begin work: 4 weeks prior

The following schedule shows one of the several events outlined for the employee publics of the strategic communication plan focusing on consumer confidence.

Tactic: Newsletter articles in employee publication about safety, quality and customer satisfaction.

Implementation Schedule: With publication slated for the first Wednesday of each month, relevant articles will be written for each publication date, according to the following schedule:

Safety Issues
- *January*: Industry-wide safety standards and government safety regulations;
- *April*: Product safety record of Tiny Tykes Toys for the last 15 years;
- *July*: External—marketing consequences of product safety;
- *October*: Internal—employee consequences of product safety.

Quality Issues
- *February*: Industry-wide quality issues in the toy industry;
- *May*: Quality comparison between Tiny Tykes Toys and major competitors;
- *August*: Quality-control and quality-goal programs at Tiny Tykes Toys;
- *November*: Involvement of employees in quality issues at Tiny Tykes Toys.

Customer Satisfaction Issues
- *March*: Industry-wide importance of customer satisfaction to company's bottom line;
- *June*: Importance of customer satisfaction to Tiny Tykes Toys' reputation;
- *September*: Empowering employees to achieve customer satisfaction;
- *December*: Employee training/motivation for customer satisfaction.

Staffing: The communication director in the public relations office will notify appropriate interviewees two months prior to publication date. A communication specialist will arrange interviews three to four weeks prior to publication and will give completed article to the communication director two weeks prior to publication date.

Budget: There is no significant operating cost to research or write articles. Staff time is already provided, but approximately five hours will be allocated for each article for preparation, research, interviewing and writing.

CHECKLIST 16B Implementing the Strategic Plan

BASIC QUESTIONS

1. What is the schedule for this project?
2. What is the budget for this project?
3. Who is responsible for this project?

EXPANDED QUESTIONS

A. SCHEDULING

1. What is the message repetition?
2. What is the message frequency?
3. What is the scheduling pattern (optional): continuous, flighting, pulsing or massing?
4. What is the timeline for each tactic?
5. Who is the assigned manager for each tactic?

A. BUDGET

1. Identify the following budget line items:
   - personnel
   - materials
   - media costs
   - equipment and facilities
   - miscellaneous expenses.
2. What is the full-cost budget?
3. What administrative cost items are associated with this tactic?
4. What is the break-even point?
5. What is the per-capita cost?

CONSENSUS CHECK

Does agreement exist within your organization and your planning team about the selection and analysis of these key publics?

☐ Yes. Proceed to Step 9, Evaluating the Strategic Plan.
☐ No. Consider the value and/or possibility of achieving consensus before proceeding.

CHAPTER

17

EVALUATION

Reading 4.4:
"Evaluating the
Strategic Plan"
By Ronald D.
Smith, APR

Though it is the last letter of all the public relations process acronyms, evaluation research is both ongoing and summative. This means you will be responsible for evaluating the effectiveness of communication tactics throughout a campaign and for evaluating the overall success of the campaign at the end.

As noted in this week's reading by Ronald D. Smith, APR (2012), during evaluation we examine public relations *outputs* (attention to or awareness of what you made, examined by total number of stories, articles, impressions, or placements), *out-takes* (acceptance of and opinion formation about the messages you distributed, examined by information understood and retained by audiences), and *outcomes* (quantifiable changes in attitude and behavior due to your campaign).

When it comes to social media, measurement expert K. D. Paine (2011) suggests looking at five different levels of engagement with your organization: 1) lurkers, measured by click-throughs, likes, and unique visitors; 2) casual observers, measured by comments, followers, and repeat visitors; 3) active users, measured by repeat comments, reposts, retweets, shares, and use of hashtags and @messages; 4) committed users, measured by positive sentiment/attitudes and site registration; and 5) loyalists, measured by advocacy, purchase, trial, donations, and volunteering.

Important questions to ask when creating your evaluation strategies are: Who is your audience? What do you want the audience members to do? When do you want them to do it? Where will you measure these changes (markets, channels, spaces)? Why are you measuring (i.e., What will you do with the data)? How will you measure? (Burke 2010).

It is important to note that, even though evaluation corresponds to the last letter of our RPIE acronym, evaluation strategies are created after you set your campaign goals and before you implement your tactics. Public relations outputs align directly with awareness objectives, out-takes align with acceptance objectives, and outcomes align with action objectives. They are built into your implementation (i.e., campaign schedule) and carried out throughout your campaign.

"EVALUATING THE STRATEGIC PLAN"

By Ronald D. Smith, APR

Program evaluation is the systematic measurement of the outcomes of a project, program or campaign based on the extent to which stated objectives are achieved. As part of the strategic planning process, establishing appropriate and practical evaluation methods wraps up all the previous plans, ideas and recommendations.

In this section, we will look at various aspects of evaluative research: what, when, and—most important—how to evaluate.

WHAT TO EVALUATE

You've heard the phrase "starting off on the right foot." In precision marching, the first step is the most important, because it sets up the pattern for the rest of the cadence. The same is true in putting together an effective research program. Starting on the right foot means setting out to answer the appropriate questions.

Katie Delahaye Paine, an authority on evaluation research, notes that "the future of public relations lies in the development of relationships, and the future of measurement lies in the accurate analysis of those relationships" (2011, p 217).

The key to creating any program evaluation is to establish appropriate criteria for judging what is effective. This research plan considers several issues: the criteria that should be used to gauge success, timing of the evaluation and specific ways to measure each of the levels of objectives (awareness, acceptance and action). It may prescribe the various evaluation tools, and it also should indicate how the evaluation would be used.

Note that this planning happens before any tactics are implemented. Although the design of evaluative research focuses on the results of the program, it is developed as part of the initial planning. It points to how evaluation will be conducted at the appropriate times.

DESIGN QUESTIONS

As you design an effective program for evaluation research, ask yourself the following questions:

- On what criteria should the program be judged?
- What information is needed to make the assessment?
- What standards of accuracy and reliability are needed for this assessment?

Next, focus some attention on the source of the information needed:

- Who has this information?
- How can this information be obtained from them?

Finally, consider how the information will be used:

- Who will receive the final evaluation and what will be done with the information? How willing and able are decision makers to receive less-than-fully-positive evaluations?
- Besides decision makers, who else would have an interest in the evaluation?

Remember that research design is always a trade-off between the perfect and the practical. Strategic planners must make choices about the importance of the program, the accuracy and reliability of the information to be received, and the needed resources (time, personnel, financial, and so on).

EVALUATION CRITERIA

Before you develop specific evaluation techniques, consider first the criteria on which you will judge something to be effective. These criteria are called *metrics*, the standards of measurement to assess the outcome of a program or project. Each metric needs to be appropriate for the objective it is measuring. In essence, a metric is the yardstick against which an objective is measured.

What metrics should you use? The appropriate standards vary with the objectives and the tactics, but here are a few general guidelines. Evaluation criteria should be (1) useful to the organization by being clearly linked with the established objectives; (2) realistic, feasible and appropriate as to cost, time and other resources; (3) ethical and socially responsible; (4) credible because it is supported by accurate data; and (5) presented in a timely manner.

Consider various criteria that might be evaluated in a public relations campaign. The best structure for this is to draw on the earlier-stated objectives. Here are some categories of appropriate evaluation metrics for each of the three types of objectives:

- *To evaluate awareness objectives*:
    - Metric: media coverage and calculation of media impressions;
    - Metric: post-campaign awareness survey.

- *To evaluate acceptance objectives*:

    - Metric: tabulation of requests for information;
    - Metric: post-campaign attitude/opinion survey;
    - Metric: tabulation of letters, e-mails and phone calls expressing interest or support;
    - Metric: post-event audience evaluation.

- *To evaluate action objectives*:

    - Metric: measures of results (ticket sales, attendance, memberships, donations and so on);
    - Metric: measures of improvement;
    - Metric: organizational or environmental change.

Additionally, be prepared to identify and evaluate unplanned results of a campaign. Sometimes a campaign generates reaction beyond what was anticipated. This reaction may be positive or negative in the eyes of the organization, but it is worth considering unplanned results and unintended consequences, if for no other reason than they might be built into subsequent similar campaigns.

Here is an example of how one organization established criteria to judge the effectiveness of its website:

- ability to navigate easily throughout the site (a measure of awareness objectives);
- breadth of content (awareness objectives);
- ability to convey key messages (awareness objectives);
- stats tracking the number of web visitors (awareness objectives);
- number and tenor of questions and comments by site visitors (acceptance objectives);
- number of visitor names that are captured for organizational response or follow-up (action objectives);
- number of web visitors who take online surveys or respond to online offers (awareness or action objectives).

Notice that measures of message production and exposure are not included as significant. For example, what matters is not so much the number of hits but rather the number and content of comments by visitors to the site and the number of retrievable names so the organization can engage the visitor in two-way communication. With appropriate evaluation metrics in mind, the public relations strategist can turn to the task of developing evaluation measures that can rate the website on those criteria.

Notice, too, that all of the criteria should be developed before any implementation of the website, because the particular criteria you identify as necessary will determine some of what you do in putting the website together.

It is interesting to note that public relations practitioners generally value positive media stories more highly than CEOs value such publicity. It's not hard to understand this disparity. Public relations people operate in a world in which awareness generated through media is an intrinsic value. CEOs live in a show-me world where the value of results needs to be documented. But the question is worth asking: Just what should we be measuring? Or more pointedly: Why should we continue to focus on awareness when our bosses and clients want to see how we influenced action?

Ken Gofton (1999) has noted the difference between advertising and public relations measurement. He observes that advertising often focuses evaluative research on audience exposure. Public relations evaluation, on the other hand, goes beyond exposure metrics toward techniques such as profiling audiences, tracking attitude change and assessing impact in terms of behavioral outcomes.

Walter Lindenmann, the guru of public relations research, observed that CEOs and organizational executives are increasingly more demanding of public relations practitioners. They expect practitioners to justify their existence, be accountable for their programs and document their contributions to the bottom line.

TWELVE REMINDERS ABOUT EVALUATIVE RESEARCH

Here are a dozen suggestions for an effective evaluative research program. Most of these tips are based on common-sense principles that you probably already know. But reminders are meant to be remembered, so review these tips as you prepare your evaluation program.

1   *Don't wait for the program's completion before you evaluate.* Evaluation begins with the planning process, before you actually "do" anything. Effective planning means you determine in advance what you will evaluate and how you will measure.

2   *Guesses aren't good enough.* Evaluation must rely on facts, not estimates. Hunches and gut feelings can point the way, but hard facts are needed to accurately assess impact.

3   *Friends may be telling you what they think you want to hear.* Get beyond the limitations of information volunteered by people who already look kindly on your organization. Be cautious of relying too heavily on information solicited from friends and other supporters in situations that don't encourage candor.

4   *Employees have a stake in the program's success.* Realize that they may be seeing what they want to see, for the programs they evaluate affect their own job security and economic future, as well as their day-to-day social relationships on the job.

5   *Samples must reflect the population.* Formal evaluative research draws on a sample that represents the publics addressed in the public relations activity. This kind of research is likely to generate information that is accurate.

6   *Hard work and cost aren't measures of effectiveness.* Be careful not to equate activity with achievement. Your campaign may have claimed many resources in time, energy and budgets, but these are not the measure of program effectiveness.

7   *Creativity is not a gauge of effectiveness.* "Everybody thinks it's a neat idea" may indicate innovation and a professional award may attest to your ingenuity. But neither is the mark of a successful program.

8   *Dissemination doesn't equal communication.* A mainstay principle of public relations is that distribution of a message does not guarantee that real communication is achieved. Every piece of unopened junk mail, every commercial zapped or TiVo'd, and every half-time show missed by spectators heading for the rest room is an example of failed communication.

9   *Knowledge doesn't always lead to acceptance.* Well-informed publics are supportive ones, says the common wisdom. Not necessarily. Knowledge is important on the road to support, but this road has an off-ramp as well. Sometimes the more people know about an organization or the issues it faces, the less supportive they may be.

10 *Behavior is the ultimate measure.* Awareness and acceptance objectives are important, and many public relations activities seek to increase knowledge, generate favorable attitudes or foster supportive opinions. But knowledge that doesn't lead to action is pretty weak, and attitudes or opinions that don't have an outcome in behavior are like books sitting unread on the shelf. Missed opportunities. Unrealized potential.

11 *Evaluation doesn't have to be expensive or time-consuming.* Like other aspects of strategic planning, evaluation research is linked to the organization's resources. Proper evaluation requires insight and creative thinking, not necessarily a lot of time or money.

12 *Evaluative research enables action.* It allows organizations to modify programs, analyze and justify the current program, or make decisions about similar future programs.

A study of evaluation research for the Institute for Public Relations (Lindenmann, 2006) suggests that any credible evaluation program requires four major components: setting measurable goals and objectives, measuring outputs, measuring out-takes and outcomes, and measuring institutional outcomes.

WHEN TO EVALUATE

There are three stages in the process of program evaluation related to timing: implementation reports, progress reports and final evaluation. Each is different; each is important.

IMPLEMENTATION REPORT

The first potential point for evaluation is in tracking the implementation of each tactic, making sure that it is proceeding according to plan. This **implementation report** documents how the program tactics were carried out. In it, include a schedule of progress to date toward implementing each tactic, as well as any work remaining. Identify any gaps, defects or potential delays that could hurt the plan. Note any difficulties encountered and how they were (or might be) resolved. Discuss the efficiency with which the tactics were set in motion.

Additionally, note the name of the person or group responsible for each tactic, as well as other personnel resources such as staff, freelancers, consultants, and so on. It might also be useful to include budgetary information, such as how much money has been spent or committed thus far.

PROGRESS REPORT

It is important to monitor progress at various key points as the tactics are being implemented. **Progress reports** are preliminary evaluations on which planners can make strategic modifications as they further implement the program. Such midcourse corrections can keep the project functioning at peak efficiency. In this way, the plan is used as a written guideline rather than a rigid rulebook.

Consider this analogy of an interactive computer travel map for a cross-country road trip. This mapping program receives hourly weather updates and daily progress reports on highway construction projects. It also monitors traffic jams around congested urban areas and newspaper reports of tourism-related events. Before you leave on the road trip, you map out a tentative plan, indicating your goal (travelling cross country) and your objectives (stopping at various points of interest along the way to the destination). A rigid use of your plan would be to follow the map with no deviation—after all, you've planned this trip for a long time and you shouldn't be distracted by unscheduled changes. However, a more effective use of the map would allow the computerized mapping program to alert you to an interesting community festival only a few miles off the scheduled route or to travel delays resulting from snow buildup on a mountain pass.

The mapping program demonstrates the value of feedback: You can use information gathered during the course of the project to update strategy, modify objectives and adjust tactics. This type of in-process evaluation is important for both public relations and marketing communication programs. After a pilot project and following each significant phase within a program, evaluate whether the program is unfolding as it was planned to do. Ask questions: Are the messages being disseminated as expected? Are they being understood? Are people responding as expected? If the answers turn out to be "no," there is still time to make adjustments before the rest of the program is implemented.

This kind of evaluation allows a public relations plan to be a living document that enhances the atmosphere of open communication. It allows the planning organization to be impacted by its environment and by its publics.

FINAL REPORT

Final reports, sometimes called **summative reports**, review the whole of the program. They measure impact and outcome for the various tactics. The final evaluation gauges how well the tactics achieved what they set out to achieve—namely, the various objectives.

RESEARCH DESIGN

The question of when to evaluate leads to a related aspect of **research design**: how to structure the evaluation in relation to the measurement standards. There are several possibilities, the most common being after-only studies and various approaches to before-and-after models.

After-Only Study

The simplest research design is the **after-only study**, which is common in public relations precisely because of its simplicity. Implement a tactic, measure its impact, and presume that the tactic caused the impact. This approach can be appropriate for action objectives that measure audience response, such as attendance, contributions, purchase and other easily measured reactions. For example, a political candidate running for office may need no preliminary baseline. She simply would be interested in the numbers of votes received in the election.

However, the after-only approach is not appropriate for every situation. Its weakness is its very simplicity, because this design presumes a cause-and-effect relationship that may not be accurate. The after-only approach does not prove that the tactic caused the observed level of awareness or acceptance, only that the result occurred after the tactic. Perhaps the levels were there all along but simply not noticed.

Before-and-After Study

Another format for evaluation research is the **before-and-after study**, also called a **pretest/post-test study**. This model involves an observation before any public relations programming is implemented. The initial observation provides a benchmark or baseline for comparing studies that will be conducted later.

For example, if the candidate noted above wanted to gauge the effectiveness of a new campaign message, she would need to measure her support before the message was presented and measure it again following the presentation. The difference would indicate the change—positive or negative—created by the new campaign message. In another example, a public transit system might compare ridership figures before and after a promotional campaign. Note that a before-and-after study is integrated into both the formative research and evaluative research phases of the planning process.

The simplest before-and-after study involves three stages: (1) observe and measure a public; (2) expose the public to a public relations tactic; and (3) measure the public again. Any change in the public's awareness, acceptance or action can likely be attributed to the tactic.

Remember, however, that public relations activities generally don't take place in a vacuum or in a pure environment. Be aware of extraneous factors. Not every change in your key public may appropriately be linked, cause-and-effect fashion, to your programming. One of the challenges for evaluative research is to sort out the effective public relations tactics from unrelated outside forces.

Controlled Before-and-After Study

A more sophisticated type of evaluative research takes into account those unrelated outside forces. A **controlled before-and-after study** involves two sample groups drawn from the same key public. One sample is the group to receive the message; the other is a control group that does not receive the message.

This process has four elements: (1) observe and measure each group; (2) expose one group to a tactic, but do not expose the control group; (3) measure each group again; and (4) compare the results of each group.

The control group is likely to have remained unchanged, while any change noted in the exposed group presumably can be linked to exposure to the public relations tactic—the key difference between the two groups. For example, the transit system noted above might also compare before-and-after ridership figures with those of a transit system in a similar city in another state (the control group), where riders were not exposed to the promotional campaign.

Remember that research design is always a trade-off. Strategic planners must make choices that consider the importance of the program, the accuracy and reliability of the information to be received, and the needed resources (time, personnel, financial and the like). They also should look at the whole picture, focusing not on each tactic in isolation but on how the various tactics together have achieved their objectives.

Also be aware of extraneous factors that can mask your evaluation efforts. Not every change in a public's awareness, acceptance or action may be caused by your public relations programming. Try to account for other activities and influences that the publics have been exposed to.

Let's return to the example of the transit system. If, a few days after the ridership campaign begins, an international political crisis sends oil prices up 30 percent, you probably would notice a lot more riders on the trains and buses. But you shouldn't attribute this to your public relations campaign. It's more likely that motorists are reacting to the higher cost of gasoline at the pumps, and your research report must note this.

CYBERNETICS AND PUBLIC RELATIONS

Norbert Wiener's cybernetic model of communication (1954) was noted in Step 6, Developing the Message Strategy.

Cybernetics deals with the feedback mechanisms of goal-seeking systems, in which goals are established, action and **output** is monitored, and feedback mechanisms implement corrective action to keep the system on the target of its goal. Furnace thermostats, heat-seeking missiles and cruise-control devices on cars are examples of cybernetics.

In public relations and marketing communication, examples of cybernetics include crisis planning and issues management that feature a radar-like early warning system of monitoring the environment in which the organization operates. An example is the kind of in-process evaluative research being presented in this book.

Cybernetics in public relations operates most effectively in an open-systems approach. In this approach, public relations functions as the liaison between the organization and its publics, with responsibilities to each and to the mutual benefits of both.

Two-way communication between the organization and the environment keeps the organization moving toward its goal, with this approach continuously adjusted through the feedback provided by the publics.

A benefit of most evaluative research is that it is a form of **unobtrusive research**—the subjects in the study do not know they are being observed, at least not until after the fact, when their awareness of being observed can't affect what they have already done.

An exception to this is the before-and-after study. When conducting a before-and-after study, be aware of the **Hawthorne effect**, also called the **placebo effect**.

In the 1930s, researchers at Hawthorne Works, an electric power company near Chicago, were trying to find out how the intensity of lighting affected factory workers. The researchers increased the lighting, and productivity increased, then slowly settled back to the earlier level. Then they decreased the lighting and productivity increased again. At first, the researchers believed the changes were the result of teamwork among the employees. Similar studies manipulated other aspects of the work environment: pay incentives, shorter hours, longer hours, more breaks, fewer breaks. In each case, productivity increased for a short time.

In 1955, Henry Landsberger reanalyzed the older studies. He concluded that the boost in productivity was not caused at all by the amount of lighting but simply because the subjects knew they were being observed and knew that the company was concerned about worker productivity. Landsberger coined the term "Hawthorne effect," which since has been broadened to explain any impact, usually short-term, through which employees are made to feel important or are aware that they are being observed.

HOW TO EVALUATE

A question was posed at the beginning of Step 9: What information is needed in order to evaluate a program's effectiveness? Answer this question wisely, and you'll have a strong final phase to your strategic planning. Answer blindly, and you could end up measuring the wrong thing. Consider five levels of evaluation: judgmental assessments, evaluation of communication outputs, awareness, acceptance and action.

JUDGMENTAL ASSESSMENT

An evaluation made on hunches and experience is called a **judgmental assessment**. This type of informal feedback, sometimes called **seat-of-the-pants evaluation**, is not uncommon in public relations and marketing communication. It is the kind of research that everybody seems to do sometimes, because it comes naturally.

Judgmental assessment relies on personal and subjective observations such as the following: "The boss liked it," "The client asked us to continue the project," "Everybody said this was a success," "The customers seem happy" and "Hey, we won an award for this project."

This approach is based on personal observation, which can be both a strength and a limitation. Some judgmental evaluations, though informal, can be helpful to an organization. For example, assessment by outside experts, perhaps public relations colleagues in another organization, might offer an excellent analysis of the program.

So too with judgmental assessments based on a formal review of an organization's program by a panel of outside experts. An example is the review teams fielded by the Accrediting Council on Education in Journalism and Mass Communications that assess various aspects of a college or university communication program seeking professional accreditation. Another example is an evaluation based on a program that received an award through a competition sponsored by a professional organization, such as the Silver Anvil sponsored by the Public Relations Society of America or the Gold Quill Award of the International Association of Business Communicators.

Additionally, senior practitioners often draw on their experience to make informal judgments about program effectiveness.

Such informal research has its limitations, however. For one thing, informal assessments often are made by program managers, who are never disinterested and seldom impartial. For another, their personal observations are often imprecise and arbitrary, sometimes downright fickle. Granted, the anecdotes on which this feedback is based can provide much insight into the success or failure of a program, but because informal research and gut feelings don't involve representative samples and standard measures they can't confirm the effectiveness of public relations activity.

Another problem with judgmental assessment is that it often gives undue emphasis to apparent creativity and to the expenditure of energy and resources. Throughout this entire planning process you have put in a great deal of effort and energy. In doing so, you have articulated a strategy and produced a range of tactics. These, of course, are important, but they are not what you should be measuring. Rather, the evaluation phase should focus on your objectives at each of their three levels: awareness, acceptance and action. Just like objectives, evaluation research should deal with the impact your program has made on your various publics.

METHODS OF EVALUATIVE RESEARCH

Like formative research, evaluative research involves techniques that can be either quantitative or qualitative.

- **Quantitative research** methods used frequently for evaluation include surveys, content analyses, cost-effectiveness studies, readership studies, head counts and tracking of feedback, as well as direct observation and monitoring of specific results.
- **Qualitative research** techniques commonly used for evaluation include interviews, focus groups and case studies.

Don't let the availability of so many different research methods hide the fact that direct observation of outcomes can be the simplest way to evaluate the effectiveness of public relations programs. ...

Judgmental assessment also can lull you into taking for granted what you should be analyzing. Consider tax-free shopping weeks. Increasingly, state lawmakers are periodically waiving sales tax to encourage spending and help consumers save money. One popular time is the back-to-school shopping time in late August. It's oh-so-obvious that consumers win; they save money when buying clothing and school supplies. Politicians benefit from the gratitude of their constituents. And merchants like it because buyers flock into their stores. On the surface, tax-free shopping weeks are both popular and successful.

Yet is popularity a valid standard? Some stores that used to discount merchandise 15 or 20 percent no longer have sales because they know the consumers will flock in to save—what? 8.5 percent (the average sales tax across the country)? Meanwhile, states lose important tax revenues, threatening services or leading to increases in other kinds of taxes and fees to make up the difference. So customer satisfaction, if it is based on whim rather than fact, isn't a useful measure.

The lesson is this: Effective evaluation requires careful analysis. Don't rely only on the obvious—because what obviously seems true sometimes isn't. Let's look at a complementary approach to evaluation, this one based on the results of communication tactics.

COMMUNICATION OUTPUTS

Measuring communication products and their distribution is the focus of **outputs evaluation**, a method that concentrates on the development and presentation of a message. As an evaluation method it is not particularly effective.

Outputs may be necessary tasks to do, but they really are not effective measurement tools. Yet current researchers report that many practitioners still rely primarily on output measures (Rice and Atkin, 2002; Xavier et al., 2005). Various methods of measuring **communication outputs** include message production, message dissemination, message cost, publicity value and advertising equivalency. Let's look at each.

Message Production

Several techniques of evaluation research deal simply with whether the message is produced. For example, count the number of news releases written, brochures printed or pages formatted for a website. Or note the creation of special message vehicles, such as a company float for the Fourth of July parade. Measurement of **message production** quantifies the work output of a public relations office, but not much more. While it may be useful for a measure of individual job performance, don't be deluded into thinking that it is a measure of program effectiveness.

Message Distribution

Another approach to awareness evaluation focuses not merely on the production of messages but also on their **distribution**. In this category, the evaluator focuses on media contacts and asks how many news releases were mailed, faxed, tweeted, posted on the blog or uploaded to the website. Measuring message dissemination tells what an organization did to spread the message, but it doesn't measure the message's effectiveness or its impact.

Message Cost

Another type of measurement deals with **message cost**. This approach analyzes how much money an organization spends to present its message. For paid media, such as brochures or advertisements, the organization simply divides the cost of the communication vehicle by the number of times the message has been reproduced. For example, if it costs $150 to produce 2,500 copies of a flier, then each piece costs 6 cents.

When dealing with electronic media, the common standard is **cost per thousand**, identified as **CPM** (from the Latin word *mille*, meaning "thousand"). For example, if a radio station with 75,000 listeners during a particular time period charges $150 for a 30-second commercial, it would cost $2 for each thousand listeners—a mere one-fifth of a penny per listener. Cost per thousand is an effective way to compare costs among various media, even print vehicles. Consider the following:

- A national magazine with a regional edition circulating 17,000 copies charges $9,000 for a full-page color ad; CPM = $529 (nearly 53 cents per each local subscriber).
- A city newspaper with a circulation of 338,000 charges $22,000 for a full-page ad; CPM = $65 (about 6½ cents per reader).
- A local radio station with an estimated 10,000 listeners charges $35 for a 30-second commercial; CPM = $3.50.

- A transit system of bus and light rail service in a metropolitan area charges $290 for each transit poster, with 40 needed to saturate coverage in what is called "100 showing" (100 percent of the audience, 3 million people likely to see the poster within a 30-day period). The cost for 40 posters is $11,600; CPM = $3.87.
- A cable advertising service charges $150 for a 30-second commercial on a cable network providing 25 channels to 520,000 subscriber households (average per-channel subscriber base of 20,800); CPM = $7.21 (less than a penny per subscriber).

When comparing media costs, however, remember that the elements you are comparing may not be similar. The impact of various media and the amount of repeat presentation for messages to have an impact must be considered, as well as how closely a particular media audience coincides with an organization's key public.

Consider this example of a newspaper ad and a direct-mail letter. A 50,000-circulation newspaper charges $5,500 for a half-page ad; CPM = $110. A printer charges $600 for 10,000 copies of a direct-mail letter; CPM = $60. Additionally, it will cost $1,900 to distribute the letters; now the CPM cost to the organization is $250 for the direct-mail letter.

Purely based on production and distribution costs, the newspaper ad is a better deal. But most newspaper readers skip over the ads because they are not particularly interested in the topic. Chances are you don't need to communicate with 50,000 newspaper readers because most of them are not even in the key public you identified in your planning. Meanwhile, people who receive letters are often more likely to read them, especially if the organization did a good job identifying its public and designed the letter to be of obvious interest to the readers. So the $2,500 letter could well be the more cost-effective way to communicate with members of the key publics. It costs less and, more important, results in more effective message delivery. On the other hand, if your public is widespread and difficult to reach individually, then the newspaper cost would be the better way to communicate with them.

Publicity Value

The measurement committee of the Canadian Public Relations Society has developed a point system now used by most Canadian public relations agencies. Called **media relations rating points** (MRP), it is a standard for evaluating and reporting editorial media coverage for public relations initiatives. MRP is intended to help both practitioners and clients understand the relative value of various public relations tactics.

The principle is simple: The practice of public relations is enhanced by having a consistent and systematic way to calculate the relative value of various communication tactics.

While the principle is simple, the process of MRP is sophisticated. Using proprietary software, MRP yields a percentage point based on a calculation that includes the total number of articles or reports, reach or total impressions, budget and tone. It also takes into account company/brand and product mentions, quotes by spokespersons, use of photos, call-to-action, key messages and the length of the broadcast/print/online report.

Advertising Value Equivalency

A common but highly inappropriate evaluation technique is related to the message cost. **Advertising value equivalency** (called AVE for short) means trying to place a dollar value on publicity. The technique treats a nonadvertising item as if it were an ad. Specifically, AVE tries to measure the supposed value of news coverage, equating the amount of publication space or broadcast time to the cost of purchasing that same amount as advertising.

For example, a news report about your organization is published in a local newspaper, involving a space totaling 21 column inches including headline, story and photo. How can you evaluate this report? Using the advertising equivalency method, you would look up the advertising cost for a 21-inch ad in that newspaper. At $165 per column inch, for example, that story would have cost $3,465 if it were an advertisement. So the publicity is said to be worth exactly $3,465.

That's a neat way to put a dollar figure on a news story, costing it out as if it were an ad. But that "as if" causes a big problem. A news story isn't an advertisement, so the dollar figure is meaningless. Why? Audiences know the difference between news and advertising, and they treat the two information vehicles differently. Generally news stories are far more credible than are advertisements. So how much extra should you add for credibility?

On the other hand, many news stories don't necessarily have only positive information about an organization. Maybe you should you deduct some amount because the news report wasn't glowingly positive. But wait. People read news stories more than they do ads. Perhaps you should add value because of higher audience attention. Then again, what's the value of no coverage when the organization's public relations practitioners have been trying to keep a story out of the papers?

Back and forth it goes, and in the end any dollar value you give to the news story is simply a fiction, and bad fiction at that. It is worse than worthless because it gives a false impression that a meaningful assessment has been made.

Despite the obvious misconception that underlies advertising equivalency, it's a myth that doesn't want to go away. Some public relations or marketing agencies even have devised formulas to impress their clients, taking AVE to the next absurd level. They apply a **multiplier**, calculating that if A represents the cost of advertising time or space in the media, as publicity it must be worth A x B. For example, they calculate the value of publicity as being four times the cost of advertising. Or ten times. They can calculate it however they want. It's still just an arbitrary weighting scheme that is all smoke and mirrors.

The Institute for Public Relations points to two major shortcomings with AVE:

- Editorial matter is not "free advertising."
- Dollar cost does not equal dollar value.

Why has AVE survived in the practice?

For one thing, it's simple, it looks good and it appeals to a client or boss without savvy. But the overwhelming argument to shove AVE off the research palette is that it's a work of fiction. Advertising is not public relations, and thus any attempt to give a dollar value to public relations tactics as if they were advertising simply doesn't make sense. Advertising value equivalency simply isn't equivalent.

The Institute for Public Relations says "AVEs, random use of multipliers, and other silly metrics and practices diminish the integrity of the profession …" and adds that AVEs are "rejected as a concept to value public relations."

Organizations have an obvious desire to track their return on their investment, so it's not unreasonable to look for a way to do this. The following sections outline several more valid alternatives that do have a place in the public relations game plan.

AWARENESS OBJECTIVES

The methods associated with outputs evaluation focus on documenting communication activity. Perhaps that's a worthwhile exercise, but it doesn't give a solid basis for measuring effectiveness. Rather, it is more important to demonstrate the value that communication tactics offer an organization, specifically their effectiveness in achieving awareness, attitude and action objectives that already have been established.

The first level of public relations objectives—awareness—provides an important category of evaluation research.

Awareness evaluation focuses on the content of the message. It considers how many people were exposed to the message, how easy the message is to understand, and how much of the message is remembered. Some of the common measures for awareness evaluation include message exposure, message content, readability measures and message recall.

OUTPUTS, OUT-TAKES AND OUTCOMES

Public relations evaluation includes some related concepts: output, out-take and outcome. It is important to make a clear distinction among these terms.

James Bissland (1990) identifies a communication output as the work done in a public relations activity. He likens this work to the who-says-what-in-which-channel part of Harold Lasswell's classic verbal formula for communication. Walter K. Lindenmann (2006) has described outputs as short-term, immediate results of a public relations program.

Outputs are the "things" produced by public relations practitioners: news releases, tweets, blog posts, special events, and so on. They often involve numbers: How many speaking engagements? How often is a company official quoted? How many people attend a special event? How many web pages are viewed? How many placements appear in the media?

Being things that people see and hear, outcomes are relatively easy to measure. Often this is done by observing audience participation or by measuring program results.

An **out-take** is the thing that publics take away, such as their understanding of a news report or their initial emotional response to a speech. Out-takes might be considered short-term results. Often they are measured through benchmarking and monitoring of the social environment.

A **communication outcome** is far more important. Bissland calls outcomes "terminal goals," but often they are more like what this book calls objectives because they are measurable and time-specific. Examples of outcomes are the number of new recruits, the amount of money raised or the passage of desired legislation.

Writing for the Institute for Public Relations Research, Lindenmann focused on the communication process. Outcomes "measure whether target audience groups actually received the messages directed at them, paid attention to them, understood the messages, and retained the messages in any shape or form. They also measure whether the communications materials and messages which were disseminated have resulted in any opinion, attitude and/or behavior change on the part of those targeted audiences to whom the messages were directed" (Lindenmann, 2006, p. 14).

Measuring outcomes often calls for more sophisticated research techniques.

What do we learn from this glossary of evaluation terms? Measure outputs if you wish. They can provide useful assessment of what has been done and how you have used your resources. But don't stop there. Measure out-takes every time you engage your publics. Even more importantly, measure program outcomes, specifically as they relate to your objectives.

Message Exposure

Measurement of **message exposure**, which focuses on the number of people in key publics who were exposed to the message, is a bit more sophisticated than the previous evaluation methodologies. That's because these objectives-based measures look more closely at communication tactics, evaluating not only distribution but also audience attention.

For example, the evaluator may use metrics for media exposure that ask how many hits were registered at a website or the actual number of people in the audience who heard a speech or saw a performance. Instead of counting the number of news releases distributed, the evaluator would ask how many newspaper stories or broadcast reports resulted from the release or, more important, how many people actually read those newspaper stories, heard the broadcast reports or read the online posting of the news release.

This can be a difficult number to obtain. Some public relations offices track this on their own. Others may hire a **clipping service**, a company that tracks publications and/or broadcasts on a regional, national or even international basis. A variety of services and software exists to track traffic at an organization's website, which might include a media room where reporters can download releases and other visitors can read releases. The software can measure not only the number of visitors but where they came from, how long they stay at the site, what pages they visit, what they download, and so on.

Some measures of message exposure count actual audiences, such as the number of people who attend an open house or some other public relations event. Unfortunately, some other measures deal with inferred or potential audiences, weakening the value of this measure by linking it to mere estimates.

Some concepts associated with message exposure are drawn from advertising. Audiences could have been exposed to the message presented in various media, from interpersonal settings, to viewers of a television newscast, to motorists who pass by a billboard. Sometimes these calculations can be quite impressive, even seductive. Consider, for example, the 1.1 billion impressions counted by MasterCard for its sponsorship of the World Cup Soccer Championship through public relations tactics such as news conferences, news releases, interviews and bylined columns. Or the Epilepsy Foundation, which recorded 140 million impressions through a public service radio advertisement and a news release.

The Interactive Advertising Bureau has some guidelines on how to measure advertising impressions among new and emerging media.

Remember, however, that **media impressions** and other counts of message exposure may simply estimate audience size. Even if the count is an actual one, such measures indicate only how many people saw or heard the message. They don't measure the extent to which the audience overlaps with key publics. And they don't indicate whether the audiences understood it, accepted it or acted on it in any way.

Message Content

An important type of evaluation focuses on the content of the message. Was it positive or did it provide erroneous data? Unwarranted conclusions? Outdated information? It is far more important to analyze the content of a message than merely to count the number of newspaper clippings. … For now, don't forget to include this method of research prominently in your evaluation program.

Readability Measures

Another way to evaluate awareness deals with comprehension—how easy a message is to understand. One of the first steps in developing a public relations plan is to identify and analyze the publics to be addressed. Part of that analysis involves an assessment of their reading level, usually translated into the level of education achieved by members of the public.

For example, most newspapers are written at about a ninth-grade reading level so everybody with that level of education or more—the majority of readers—should be able to understand the articles, columns and editorials. They may not necessarily agree with them or even be interested in them, but they are able to understand the writing. If you are preparing a news release or guest editorial for such a publication, plan on writing for readers with a ninth-grade reading ability. On the other hand, if you are writing a fundraising letter aimed at health care professionals, it would be safe to presume that all your readers will have completed some level of higher education. Whatever you estimate to be the appropriate reading level, test your writing against that estimate.

Robert Gunning's **Fog Index**, which measures reading ease or difficulty, is one of the easiest readability measures to use; review the directions in the discussion of verbal communication in Phase Two, Strategy. Some other commonly used readability instruments include Rudolf Flesch's Readability Score, which is more complicated than the Fog Index but which measures human interest; the associated Flesch-Kincaid readability grade level; Edward Fry's readability graph, which relies on a chart to calculate reading ease; the Dale-Chall formula, based on sentence length and the number of infrequently used words; the Cloze Procedure, which measures comprehension of spoken and visual messages; and Irving Fang's Easy Listening Formula, which provides a comparable way to calculate the comprehension of broadcast copy.

Many computer word-processing programs feature one or more of these readership aids in the program's tools section. For example, Microsoft Word counts 17.2 words per sentence in this chapter and calculates a 12.3 grade-level readability score, based on the Flesch-Kincaid score.

Message Recall

Message recall involves techniques drawn from advertising research, where day-after recall studies are commonplace. Using this method, participants in interviews, surveys or focus groups are exposed to a news story, television program or the like. Then they are interviewed to determine what they remember from the message. A staple of research drawn from advertising is the Starch Readership Reports (starchresearch.com/services.html). These indicate three levels of reader study: "noted" readers who remember having previously seen an advertisement; "associated" readers who can link the advertisement with a particular brand or advertiser; and "read most" readers who are able to describe most of the written material in the ad.

Consider this awareness objective: to increase clients' understanding of changes in insurance policy coverage. Possible evaluation metrics include noting exposure patterns, doing content analysis to gauge how consistent the messages are with the facts, and asking a focus group to discuss message recall.

Here's another awareness objective: to increase awareness of a new consumer product being manufactured by a client. Three ways to evaluate this might include tracking dissemination of messages and noting the size of the potential audience, analyzing the message content with attention to its accuracy and the use of the client's telephone number and/or website address, and surveying customers in the company data base regarding message recall.

ACCEPTANCE OBJECTIVES

A major shortcoming of all the message-based evaluation techniques noted earlier is that they do not address the consequence of the public relations tactics. Instead, they simply gauge the existence of the tactics. At best, message-based evaluation techniques can deal with the level of awareness surrounding a public relations message.

However, a more effective area of evaluation is based on levels of acceptance and action. Objectives in Phase Two, Strategy, note the desired impact on interest and attitudes (acceptance) and on opinion and behavior (action). Take steps now to evaluate how well each of those objectives has been achieved.

Two common approaches to measuring acceptance objectives are audience feedback and benchmark studies.

Audience Feedback

Some evaluation measures count and analyze the voluntary reaction of the audience, such as the number of hits on a webpage, the number of telephone calls and letters, or the number of requests for additional information. Such **audience feedback**, an acceptance evaluation based on the voluntary reaction of an audience, can be an effective measure of the level of the audience's information and interest.

WHAT SHOULD BE MEASURED?

Knowing what to measure often is the key to effective evaluation research. The answer for what metrics to use generally can be found in the objectives. But sometimes the objectives themselves are in conflict, with one of them measuring positively and another barely moving the dial.

That was the case with the Got Milk? campaign by the National Fluid Milk Processor Promotion Board, which presumably sought—as a range of objectives—awareness, acceptance and action.

The advertising series, which began in 1993, features celebrity photographer Annie Leibovitz's popular photos of celebrities with milk mustaches. Visibility is high, and everybody seems to be familiar with the campaign and the ads. The Promotion Board claims a 90 percent awareness rate.

Acceptance also runs high. The Promotion Board's research shows that attitudes toward milk have improved. The ads themselves have become collector items and have earned praise from creative designers. They found appeal with a diverse audience largely because of their use of many different celebrities and characters: Batman, David Beckham, Jackie Chan, Cirque du Soleil, Tony Hawk, Kermit the Frog, Marilyn Manson, Nelly, Conan O'Brien, Rihanna, Pete Sampras, Usher, Bart and Lisa Simpson—the list goes on and on.

There's just one problem: It costs $110 million a year, and there's no evidence that the campaign has increased milk consumption beyond California, where it was modestly successful the first couple of years. The U.S. Department of Agriculture's inspector general reported that milk usage was up 0.85 percent one year, down 0.42 percent the next.

Overall milk sales have, in fact, dropped. Oops! Milk usage continues on an overall downward spiral, as Americans consume only about half the amount of milk recommended by the government's dietary guidelines.

So the question is posed: How effective is a campaign that generates high awareness, measurable acceptance and even improved attitudes but doesn't effect action?

Benchmark Study

Another type of research is a **benchmark study** (also called **baseline study**), which provides a basis for comparing program outcomes against a standard. Actually, benchmark studies can be based on any of several different standards: the starting levels of interest or positive attitudes, outcomes of similar programs by other organizations, outcomes of the same program during a previous year or cycle, outcomes of industry or professional models, or the hypothetical outcomes of an "ideal" program.

Consider this acceptance objective: to enhance favorable employee attitudes toward a client's company. Here are four possible evaluation metrics: (1) Compare retention figures from before and after the tactic was implemented; (2) record oral and written comments given to the human resource department of the company; (3) solicit anecdotal input from managers and supervisors; and (4) survey employees about their attitudes and try to learn what they have been telling family and friends about working for the company.

Here's another acceptance objective: to increase employee affirmation of the company's need to change employee benefits. Possible evaluation techniques include recording immediate anecdotal feedback after the announcement is made, conducting a survey within two days of the announcement and after two weeks inviting employee feedback through response cards provided in pay envelopes.

REAL-WORLD RESEARCH PRACTICES

Broadcast Mainland, a British public relations agency, reported on its 2010 study of how senior in-house public relations and marketing professionals evaluate their communication activities. Here are some highlights:

51% do not measure broadcast coverage;

50% measure social media coverage based on gut reaction;

50% not satisfied with tools they use to measure social media;

40% expected to demonstrate value of public relations to senior executives;

48% use advertising equivalency to demonstrate such value;

34% realize that advertising equivalency is misleading.

Interestingly, this study shows a greater reliance on advertising equivalency when compared with an earlier study by Ketchum Public Relations (Corder, Deasy and Thompson, 1999). Here are some highlights from that study:

61% increase in sales volume;

59% number of news releases, direct mail and other tactics distributed;

53% number of impressions generated;

45% content analysis of key messages in reported stories;

37% advertising equivalency;

33% opinion change based on before-and-after surveys.

ACTION OBJECTIVES

The ultimate objectives for most public relations activities should focus on bottom-line issues for an organization, primarily the action sought from the key publics. In this evaluation phase of the planning process, careful consideration should be given to ways to measure these action objectives. Three approaches to action-focused evaluation research involve audience participation, direct observation and relative media effectiveness.

Audience Participation

Figures on the number of people who actively responded to the message generally are easy to obtain. Attendance figures are effective measures when attendance itself is the desired objective, as may be the case with concerts and exhibitions, athletic competitions, benefit fundraising events, and the like. Implicit in these attendance figures also is a measure of the effectiveness of publicity and promotion that preceded the events.

However, attendance figures can be misused if the presumption is made that attendance at some information-sharing session necessarily equates with action impact. For example, attendance at an event in which a political candidate gives a major speech can't be used as a reliable indicator of either audience acceptance or eventual action in the voting booth. People heard the speech and the message was presented, but desired action is not guaranteed. Therefore, be careful how attendance figures are interpreted and what value is placed on them.

Direct Observation

Sometimes the simplest way to measure the effectiveness of action objectives is to look around. It's called **direct observation**. Let's say the objective sought an outcome of enough voter support to win an election. If your candidate won, your objective was achieved. If you sought financial contributions of $2.2 million, count the total of donations and pledges; anything above the target amount means you were that much more successful than planned. Some other easy-to-quantify objectives deal with capacity attendance for sporting and artistic events, sales figures, academic scores and membership expectations.

In some instances, the action objective deals with the general outcome rather than with any quantification. For example, passage (or defeat) of a particular piece of legislation may fully satisfy an action objective. Some evaluation research calls for strategic and creative thinking.

Individual behavior that may not be easily observable is more difficult to measure than the preceding examples. Here is an example of how to deal with a difficult-to-evaluate action objective: to increase the use of seat belts. One possible way to evaluate this objective would be to place observers in highway tollbooths and have them record the number of drivers and driver-side passengers wearing seat belts as they pass through the booths.

Or consider this objective: to have elementary, secondary and college teachers become more active in lobbying state government for increased support of education. An evaluation plan might include a tactic that encourages the sending of e-mail letters to state officials, with instructions for sending a copy to your organization. A simple count of the number of copies received would yield data to evaluate this objective. To take it to a higher level of sophistication, an organization might work with several sympathetic state legislators and compare the number of e-mail messages sent to their office with the number of copies the organization received. From the difference, the organization could extrapolate the number of messages sent by teachers to all legislators.

Some of the benchmark techniques for evaluating acceptance objectives, noted earlier, can be equally useful for evaluating action objectives.

HOW TO MEASURE PUBLICITY EFFECTS

Measuring the effects of media relations takes a bit of creativity, but it's not impossible. Consider the following possibilities:

1 *Set clear objectives* in advance and establish the criteria that will form the basis for success.
2 *Do a pretest* such as an awareness survey to identify the beginning point.
3 *Do a post-test* to measure changes in awareness in comparison with results of the pretest.
4 *Use a focus group* to probe the relationships among awareness, acceptance and action.
5 *Track media placement* with clippings and logs. Evaluate these not only in terms of distribution, use and other measures of audience exposure but also conduct some form of content analysis to evaluate the effectiveness of the message itself.
6 *Measure action* in some way, such as by noting changes in attendance, traffic, purchase or other behaviors associated with the campaign.

Relative Media Effectiveness

A final method of evaluating action objectives deals with the behavior generated by a particular medium compared to others. For example, did people vote for a candidate because of television coverage of a live debate or because of the candidate's Internet advertising? Often it is difficult to sort out the impact of a specific medium or tactic. But here's an example of how one organization managed to make the comparison.

In 2007, SeaWorld San Antonio introduced a new roller-coaster ride, Journey to Atlantis. The theme park invited members of the media to try out the new ride. The park's public relations–marketing team decided to include social media in the mix. Twenty-two blogs and media forums were identified for their focus on roller coasters and invited to write about the new ride. Eventually 12 did so. The result was that SeaWorld San Antonio received 50 links from coaster-oriented websites. Media posted on YouTube, Flickr and other social media sites generated hundreds of thousands of downloads, along with many positive comments.

Over two weekends two months later, a standard exit interview for SeaWorld visitors asked a typical question: Where did you hear about Journey to Atlantis? Forty-seven percent of respondents indicated social media as a source of their information. The research team looked at the various media used to promote the new ride (television commercial, newspaper ad, social media, radio spot, billboard, and so on) and concluded that the cost per impression for social media was 22 cents, compared with $1 for each television impression.

DATA ANALYSIS AND REPORTS

Having gathered the data through a variety of means, it is now time to analyze it carefully. Match the observed and reported results with the expectations outlined in your statement of objectives. If the program failed to meet its objectives, do some further analysis. Try to learn if the shortfall was because of a flawed strategy that undergirded the program or because the tactics were not implemented as effectively as they might have been. Consider also if there might be a flaw in the evaluation techniques used to gather the data.

If evaluation of the program is particularly important, ask an outside auditor to review the data. For some formal presentations of research findings, in order to enhance credibility, an organization may ask an outside expert or a panel of stakeholders to attest to the validity of the tools used in the evaluation research.

After the evaluation is completed and the information gathered and analyzed, make sure it is presented in a form that is understandable and accessible to decision makers within the organization. They usually are busy executives and managers with global but not necessarily specific understandings of the issue. They may not have a high level of insight or information about the program, so be careful not to obscure evaluation findings in the final report. Instead, be very clear, draw obvious conclusions, and highlight the most important data.

If the decision makers have been involved in establishing the objectives of the program, they probably will be disposed to using the evaluation findings. Another way to increase the likelihood that the evaluation will be used is to concentrate on elements that can be changed in subsequent programs.

There is much variety within evaluation reports, which can be of several types. These may be presented separately or merged into a single report. The report itself can take the form of a formal document, an oral presentation or a meeting agenda item. Whether written or verbal, evaluation reports should be carefully crafted to clearly link the expectations outlined in the objectives with the outcomes.

When writing a report, note how the outcomes were measured, discuss the degree to which they achieved the objectives, and note the significance of this achievement (or lack of it). Finally, make clear recommendations closely linked with the data. For reports of major significance, visual elements such as photographs, tables and charts can enhance the under standing of readers and listeners.

MEASURING THE IMPACT OF SOCIAL MEDIA

As public relations practitioners increasingly use social media as part of their media mix, the question eventually turns to matters of methodology and metrics: How can we evaluate the impact of social media? It isn't easy, but it is necessary to measure its effectiveness. One approach focuses on the engagement that web users display.

At her blog The Measurement Standard and her website (measuresofsuccess.com), Katie Delahaye Paine suggests that *engagement* is a synonym for *relationship*. It's something public relations practitioners are continually trying to nurture, though less often attempting to measure.

Likewise, blogging expert Robert Scoble suggests that engagement is an appropriate measurement of the effectiveness of blogging. To what extent does the reader become engaged in the piece? To what extent is dialogue taking place among readers who add comments? For example, Scoble suggests that people engaged in a corporate blog are likely eventually to buy the product (Scoble, 2006). For more information, see his blog, scobelizer.com and @Scobelizer on Twitter.

Meanwhile, Eric Peterson defines engagement as "an estimate of the degree and depth of visitor interaction on the site against a clearly defined set of goals" (2007). He has developed a matrix for calculating visitor engagement at websites, which he outlines at his blog WebAnalyticsDemystified. com. His approach uses concepts such as click-depth, recency, duration, brand, feedback, interaction, loyalty and subscription. The matrix counts, for example, the percentage of visitors who give their e-mail addresses, the number of sessions that include visits to more than five pages, the number of visitors who return more than five times, and so on.

Here are several no-cost or low-cost steps that an organization can take to measure the effectiveness of its website and other social media:

- Use Google Analytics or another visitor-tracking device.
- Have visitors register for full access to the site.
- Connect a blog through your website and collect the names and e-mail contact of those who leave comments.
- Post a poll at your website and see how many readers respond.
- Review the ratings and comments of your posts on sites such as YouTube and or Flickr.
- Write an e-book, report or other information source and make it available for free upon request.
- See how many people have joined sites such as Facebook. Post a question there and count replies.

Evaluation reports sometimes become the basis of a news release or even a news conference if the topic under review is one that is particularly newsworthy. For example, the final evaluation of public relations programs on popular and highly visible social issues such as campaigns to reduce drug abuse or bullying may warrant a news report.

Any evaluation report longer than five pages should be preceded by an **executive summary** that provides an overview of the findings and a simplified set of recommendations. An executive summary serves the needs of those decision makers—sometimes the most important ones—who may not have the time to digest the longer document.

ULTIMATE EVALUATION: VALUE-ADDED PUBLIC RELATIONS

Most evaluation of public relations and other strategic communication programs focus on objectives and tactics: What did we do? What did we accomplish by doing it? How effectively did this achieve what we set out to do? These questions are very important. But there is another equally important question to be answered: What did public relations do for the organization as a whole?

Once again, a reminder: The premise underlying *Strategic Planning for Public Relations* is that strategic communication is about more than mere tactics and activities.

Rather, it deals with the overall planned program of both proactive and reactive communication that enhances the relationship between an organization and its various publics, a relationship that needs to be linked to the bottom-line concerns of the organization. You might call it value-added public relations, the notion that public relations offers value and benefit to the organization as a whole.

Sometimes public relations practitioners are challenged to calculate the **return on investment** (ROI) for their client or boss as a way to justify the cost of public relations activities. ROI is the ratio of money gained or lost relative to the cost of a program or product. In some ways, this is an unfair expectation, because ROI is a financial metric measuring dollars spent vis-à-vis dollars saved or earned or offset by other revenue. Rather than return on investment, public relations practitioners prefer to deal in value that their activities add to an organization.

Based on qualitative interview research with both public relations practitioners and their CEOs, Linda Childers Hon (1997) has reported six such values that effective public relations bring to organizations or to the clients of a consultant or agency. Keep these in mind as you complete your evaluation and present it to your client or organization:

1   Effective public relations helps organizations *survive* by reversing negative opinions, by promoting awareness of organizational benefits to the community and by effecting balanced media coverage.
2   Effective public relations helps organizations *make money* by generating publicity about products and services as well as the organization's plans and accomplishments; by attracting new customers, volunteers, donors and stockholders; and by improving employee performance and productivity.
3   Effective public relations helps other organizational functions *make money* by creating an environment of understanding and goodwill, by influencing supportive legislation, and by enhancing fundraising efforts.
4   Effective public relations helps organizations *save money* by inducing favorable legislation, by retaining members and by minimizing negative publicity during crisis incidents.
5   Effective public relations helps organizations *weaken opposition* by generating favorable public opinion and by obtaining cooperation from governmental and other organizations.
6   Effective public relations helps organizations *save lives* through social goals such as advancing highway safety, medical care and research, and the like.

PUBLIC RELATIONS METRICS

We noted earlier in this chapter that metrics are standards of measurement used to quantify performance outcomes and to measure the level to which objectives are met. Don Bartholomew of Ketchum Public Relations has introduced a hierarchy for public relations metrics:

- **exposure metric**: how publics have been exposed to a message;
- **engagement metric**: how publics interact with the organization and with each other vis-à-vis the message;

- **influence metric**: the degree to which message exposure and engagement impact on the publics' perceptions and attitudes;
- **action metric**: how the public acts on the message.

Bartholomew believes his model applies to both traditional and emerging media, though he developed it mainly with social media in mind. (For more information, see Bartholomew's MetricsMan blog at wordpress.com.)

Applied to social media, metrics for exposure might include the number of hits to a website, the number of unique visitors, search-engine ranking, and objective analysis of online comments or discussion. Engagement metrics could be repeat visitors, likes and recommendations, message recall measures, and RSS subscriptions. Examples of metrics for the influence category include measured change in awareness or attitudes, brand association and purchase considerations. Action metrics might be store visits, event attendance or the logical close-the-loop action such as purchases, votes, memberships, and so on.

GAME CHANGER FOR PUBLIC RELATIONS EVALUATION

Public relations practitioners from around the world met in Spain in 2010. Their mission was to articulate standards and common approaches for measuring and evaluating public relations. The Barcelona Declaration of Measurement Principles emerging from these discussions includes seven principles. For a download, search "barcelona" at instituteforpr.org.

Goals

It is important to set and manage goal setting and measurement in a process that is quantitative and holistic.

Quantity and Quality

Rather than measuring media placement, evaluation should consider the quality of media coverage including tone, credibility, relevance, message delivery, spokespersons and prominence in the medium.

Advertising Equivalency

This approach measures the cost of media space and is rejected as a concept to place a value on public relations. Likewise, multipliers intended to present a formula for media cost as a factor of public relations value should not be applied.

Social Media

There is no single metric for measuring social media, but an evaluation program should be developed for organizational use of social media.

Outcomes

It is more important to measure the effect on outcomes (including awareness, comprehension, attitude and behavior) rather than outputs. Measurement requires quantity and quality.

Results

Measurement should be focused on business/organizational results and the impact of public relations activity on the bottom line.

Reliability

Measurement methods should be both transparent and repeatable.

Some observers are calling the Barcelona Declaration a game changer for public relations. They predict that the new principles will sound a death knell to AVEs and multipliers that try to fix a dollar value on public relations by falsely comparing it to advertising. They are excited to envision the use of well-planned evaluation programs in every strategic communication plan.

CASE IN POINT Southwest Airlines

Southwest Airlines engaged in a series of evaluation tools as part of its media relations strategy, specifically its plan to link public relations with sales (Watson and Noble, 2007). Here's the company's five-point program:

1 Southwest conducted keyword research to learn how people search online. For example, research into 1.3 million searches during one month revealed 1.3 million searches for "Southwest Airlines" but only 400,000 for "Southwest."

2 With this information, the company edited its news releases to include the full "Southwest Airlines" search term, making it more likely that online readers would find the company's postings.

3 Because research also showed that many online news readers do not scroll to the bottom of the release for links to additional information, Southwest imbedded links within its online news releases. Thus a release about a particular offer included a link to a web page where the visitor could purchase it and where the company could track it.

4 Southwest distributed its new releases through wire services that are "crawled" by Google, Yahoo and AOL News, increasing the likelihood that online searchers would find the company information.

5 The airline evaluated three news releases to link publicity with sales. It found evidence that one release about a new route resulted in $80,000 in ticket sales, a Spanish-language online release led to $38,000 in sales, and the third release with a hyperlink in the first paragraph resulted in more than $1 million in ticket sales.

Additionally, the supporters expect organizational executives and CEOs to embrace these principles, especially as they lead to more accountability for public relations and more integration with the organization's bottom line.

WHAT'S NEXT?

This ends the nine steps of strategic planning. In that sense, nothing is left to do. You've learned all the elements that go into an effective and efficient campaign for public relations or marketing communication.

In a very real sense, though, you've only just begun. Take the knowledge you've gained from this text and the practical experiences you have in working through the various activities you have encountered and run with them.

PLANNING EXAMPLE 17 EVALUATING THE STRATEGIC PLAN

Upstate College will evaluate its Initiative on Transfer Students according to the following five-part plan:

1 placement report tracking distribution and media use of news releases and other materials disseminated by its public relations department;

2 telephone survey among people who applied to UC two, three and four years ago but did not attend; the purpose of this survey will be to assess awareness about the expansion and attitudes toward it;

3 focus group of new applicants to UC, discussing the source of their information about the expansion and their reasons for applying;

4 content analysis of newspaper articles, radio and television news reports, and newspaper letters to the editor and editorials, studying the positive/negative nature of the reports about UC's expansion;

5 brief survey as part of the application process, asking applicants the source of their information about the UC expansion.

The evaluation report will be provided to the college president and provost, who prefer a well-documented and candid report. This report will become the basis for future recruitment and development activities.

(Note: You will develop similar evaluation plans for the other initiatives.)

Tiny Tykes Toys will evaluate the employee-oriented phase of its public relations program according to the following plan:

- *Before-and-After Survey.* Develop surveys of both employees and employees' family members, dealing with employee morale, job satisfaction, pride in company, and knowledge of recall, safety and quality issues. The results of these surveys will be compared to ascertain any change in knowledge, attitudes and behavior associated with the public relations program.

- *Employee-Initiated Feedback.* Review copies of comments and suggestions in the suggestion box, notes to company managers, letters to the editor of the company newsletter or other publications, and other print and/or e-mail messages regarding the reintroduction program. These messages will be summarized and analyzed.

- *Analysis of Media Coverage.* Track placement, measure employee awareness of coverage, and do a simply content analysis on articles and news reports as to their positive or negative reflection of Tiny Tykes employees.

A written final evaluation will be presented to company managers and then will be shared with employees.

CHECKLIST 17 Evaluation Plan

BASIC QUESTIONS

1 How will you measure awareness objectives?
2 How will you measure acceptance objectives?
3 How will you measure action objectives?

EXPANDED QUESTIONS

A. METHODOLOGY

1 How and when can this information be obtained: via after-only study or before-and-after study?
2 Which research methodologies would be most effective?

- Judgmental assessment: personal experience or outside experts.
- Interviews with key people. Which people?
- Focus groups with representative publics. Which publics?
- Survey of representative publics. Which publics? Control group?
- Content analysis of representative artifacts. Which artifacts?
- Readership study
- Media tracking

B. EVALUATION CATEGORIES

1 Indicate how each of the methodologies below might be used to evaluate each individual tactic.
2 What standards of accuracy and reliability are needed for the evaluation?
3 Who can provide information for evaluation?

Evaluation of Outputs
- Message production
- Message dissemination
- Message cost analysis
- Advertising equivalency

Evaluation of Awareness Objectives
- Message exposure
- Message content analysis
- Readability measures
- Message recall

Evaluation of Acceptance Objectives
- Audience feedback
- Benchmark (baseline) study

Evaluation of Action Objectives
- Audience participation
- Direct observation of results

C. AUDIENCE

1　Who will receive the final evaluation?
2　How will it be used?
3　What level of candor are decision makers willing to receive?

D. EVALUATION SCHEDULE

1　Timeline for implementation report.
2　Timeline for progress report.
3　Timeline for final evaluation.

E. EVALUATION PROGRAM CHECKLIST

For this evaluation program:
- Is it useful to the organization?
- Is it clearly linked to established objectives?
- Is it appropriate as to cost?
- Is it appropriate as to time?
- Is it appropriate as to other resources?
- Is it ethical and socially responsible?
- Is it credible, with accurate data?
- Is it doable?

REFERENCES

Alexander, Meredith, Ashley Chase, and Kelly Chase. 2016. "Sony Pictures Entertainment Inc.: A Cybersecurity Attack from North Korea." Case study, Arthur W. Page Society 2016 Case Study Competition, winner, second place, business school category. http://www.awpagesociety.com/attachments/fa4bc642c80c9c1f39e 1f5a6a7e2413906b131fa/store/eadb7324c8431d8d90d4e19b408cffe387e0afc9df0479f1e4994e67bd1a/ Sony+Cybersecurity+Attack+%28A%29.pdf.

Benoit, William L. 1995. *Accounts, excuses and apologies. A theory of image restorations strategies.* Alban NY: State University of New York Press.

Benoit, William L. 1997. Image repair discourse and crisis communication. *Public Relations Review* 23(2): 177–186,

Bloomfield, Victor A., and Esam E. El-Fakahany. 2008. *The Chicago Guide to Your Career in Science: A Toolkit for Students and Postdocs.* Chicago: University of Chicago Press.

Bowen, Shannon A. 2010. *An Overview of the Public Relations Function.* New York: Business Expert Press.

Burke, Shonali. 2010. "Measurement in the Age of Now." Slide presentation presented at the International Conference of the Public Relations Society of America, Washington, DC, October 18, 2010.

Chen, Ming-Jer, and Kelly L. Thomas. 2003. "Cultural Foundations in Communication: Relationship Building in the Chinese Context." Case study, 1–7. Charlottesville, VA: Darden Business Publishing.

Coombs, W.T. (2007). Protecting organization reputations during a crisis: The development and application of situational crisis communication theory. *Corporate Reputation Review,* 10(3), 163–176.

Doorley, John, and Helio Fred Garcia. 2007. *Reputation Management: The Key to Successful Public Relations and Corporate Communications.* Florence, KY: Taylor & Francis.

Finkelstein, Sydney. 1992. "Power in Top Management Teams: Dimensions, Measurement, and Validation." *Academy of Management Journal* 35(3): 505–538.

Harasta, Joseph. 2016. *The Fundamentals of Public Relations: What It Is and How to Do It Well.* San Diego: Cognella Academic Publishing.

Hofstede, Geert (2001). *Culture's Consequences: comparing values, behaviors, institutions, and organizations across nations* (2nd ed.). Thousand Oaks, CA: SAGE Publications.

Hopwood, Maria, Paul Kitchin, and James Skinner. 2010. "Bringing Public Relations and Communication Studies to Sport." In *Sport Public Relations and Communication,* 1–11. Boston, MA: Butterworth-Heinemann/ Elsevier.

Kale, Sudhir H., and Sangita De. 2013. "The Impact of Globalization on Individual Customers: Implications for Marketing." *International Journal of Management,* vol. 30(4): 286–293.

Kim, Jeong-Nam, Lan Ni, and Bey-Ling Sha. 2008. "Breaking Down the Stakeholder Environment: Explicating Approaches to the Segmentation of Public for Public Relations." *Journalism and Mass Communication Quarterly* 85(4): 751–768.

Lim, Youngjoon. 2017. *Public Relations: A Guide to Strategic Communication.* San Diego, CA: Cognella Academic Publishing.

Martin, Dick and Donald K. Wright. 2015. *Public Relations Ethics: How to Practice PR Without Losing Your Soul.* New York: Business Expert Press.

McLuhan, Marshall. 1962. *The Gutenberg Galaxy: The Making of Typographic Man,* 31. Toronto, Canada: University of Toronto Press.

———. 1964a. *Understanding Media: The Extensions of Man*, 8. New York: Mentor.

Paine, Katie Delahaye. 2011. *Measure What Matters: Online Tools for Understanding Customers, Social Media, Engagement, and Key Relationships*. Hoboken, NJ.: John Wiley & Sons, Inc.

Plank Center. 2016. "Betsy Plank." http://plankcenter.ua.edu/about/betsy-plank/.

Porter, Michael E. 1979. "How Competitive Forces Shape Strategy." *Harvard Business Review* (March 1979). https://hbr.org/1979/03/how-competitive-forces-shape-strategy.

PRSA. 2016. "The Four-Step Process: RPIE Readiness for the Examination for Accreditation in Public Relations." http://www.prsa.org/Learning/Calendar/display/5520/The_Four_Step_Process#.WBoXMOErKuo.

Smith, Ronald D. 2012. *Strategic Planning for Public Relations*. Florence, KY: Routledge, Taylor & Francis Group LLC.

Springston, Jeffrey, and Ruth A. Lariscy. 2003. "Health as Profit: Public Relations in Health Communication." In *Handbook of Health Communication*, edited by Teresa L. Thompson, Alicia M. Dorsey, Katherine I. Miller, and Roxanne Parrott, 1–20. New York: Lawrence Erlbaum Associates.

Stewart, Bill. 2000. "Marshall McLuhan Foresees the Global Village." *Living Internet*. http://www.livinginternet.com/i/ii_mcluhan.htm.

Turney, Michael. 2011. "Acronyms for the Public Relations Process." *From: PR Class To: Practicing Public Relations*. http://www.nku.edu/~turney/prclass/readings/process_acronyms.html

Ulmer, R.R., & Sellnow, T.L. (2002). Crisis management and the discourse of renewal: understanding the potential for positive outcomes of crisis. *Public Relations Review* 28, 361–365.

Walsch, Daniel. 2013. *Communication Wars: Our Internal Perpetual Conflict*. San Diego: Cognella Academic Publishing.

Printed in the USA
CPSIA information can be obtained
at www.ICGtesting.com
LVHW081923250823
756276LV00016B/1256